Vance Packard, one of the most astute observers of the contemporary scene, here turns his skills at social analysis to the most fascinating subject of all: men and women—why they are behaving the way they do today.

"Packard tells it the way it is. He takes no definite positions, but permits the reader to do what he will with the evidence and conclusions of the many authorities, at home and abroad....This is good. Packard has written a book which adolescents as well as adults will find both informative and helpful—although adults stand more in need of it than adolescents. It is an adult book. Packard has done an immense amount of work and given a great deal of thought to the making of this book. It deserves the widest possible audience."

—Ashley Montagu

THE SEXUAL WILDERNESS
was originally published by
David McKay Company, Inc.

Other books by Vance Packard

The Hidden Persuaders
The Naked Society
The Status Seekers
The Waste Makers

Published by Pocket Books

VANCE PACKARD

The
Sexual Wilderness

The Contemporary Upheaval in
Male-Female Relationships

PUBLISHED BY POCKET BOOKS NEW YORK

THE SEXUAL WILDERNESS

David McKay edition published July, 1968
Pocket Book edition published August, 1970

This *Pocket Book* edition includes every word
contained in the original, higher-priced edition. It is printed
from brand-new plates made from completely reset, clear, easy-to-read
type. *Pocket Book* editions are published by Pocket Books, a division
of Simon & Schuster, Inc., 630 Fifth Avenue, New York, N.Y. 10020.
Trademarks registered in the United States and other countries.

Standard Book Number: 671-78010-7.
Library of Congress Catalog Card Number: 68-29632.
Copyright, ©, 1968, by Vance Packard. All rights reserved.
This **Pocket Book** edition is published by arrangement with
David McKay Company, Inc.

Printed in the U.S.A.

To Clarice and Irving Chaykin

WHENEVER THE OLDER GENERATION HAS LOST ITS
BEARINGS, THE YOUNGER GENERATION IS LOST
WITH IT.

> —Bruno Bettelheim, professor of psychiatry,
> University of Chicago

Contents

PART II

ASSESSMENTS AND POSSIBLE DIRECTIONS

IV. On Improving the Prospects for Sound Marriages

The
Sexual Wilderness

Introduction: About This Exploration

This is a report on a pleasant but quite strenuous inquiry that took me a great deal longer to complete than I had expected. In the years that I grappled with the subject of this book my daughter moved from being a high-school sophomore to completing her sophomore year in college.

I found myself trying to understand a situation where many of the old certitudes were crumbling and where there were a host of conflicting reports and opinions. Meanwhile the whirlwind of social change was opening up fascinating ramifications of male-female relationships that had barely been explored.

In all my efforts at inquiry in the past dozen or so years I have sought to explore the impact of recent social changes upon the individual. The possible impact of the social changes of the past quarter-century upon the individual's relationships with members of the other sex seemed a tempting and timely subject to explore.

For one thing, it was clear that the facts of demography were about to produce an explosion of mating and career-launching in the United States and in several other Western societies. All those post-World War II infants were growing up. The forecasts were that in the late 1960s more than 20,000,000 young U.S. men and women would be in their 18-to-22-year-old phase. Most of these persons of both sexes would be making life plans and making decisions about physical intimacy, courtship, or marriage. An examination of the forces that would influence their decisions might serve the public interest.

Another reason I was attracted to this subject was that a number of factors affecting our personal lives seem to intersect at the male-female relationship. Changes in the male-female relationship, for example, seem clearly related to

1

changes in politics, marketing, education, religion, the entertainment media, home building, business employment practices, the location of plants and offices—and national ideology.

In comparison with the past, furthermore, our personal interests are centering less on such hard questions as livelihood and more on how—in a radically new kind of environment—we should behave with other people. This applies particularly to how we behave today as males and females. Questions of life roles, sexual identity, inter-generational differences, morality, and new patterns in marriage are all involved in these questions about appropriate behavior.

Erik H. Erikson, lecturer in psychiatry at Harvard University, suggests in fact that changes being produced in our environment by scientific and other innovations necessitate "a redefinition of the identity of the sexes within a new image of man."

Throughout this investigation I have tried to direct my inquiry to the four questions that seem central:

1. What changes, if any, are in fact occurring in the male-female relationship that deserve public scrutiny?

2. What are causing the changes that are occurring?

3. Where do the changes seem to be taking us?

4. And, wistfully, what kind of male-female relationships should we strive for in the future to promote for males and females both personal fulfillment and a strong society?

I have come out of the research with a number of fairly firm convictions, but the research experience has been sufficiently sobering to impel me to examine the evidence that lies ahead in a mood that is more curious than contentious.

One could search for answers to these questions in a number of ways. I will here describe briefly my own highly personal method of search. It obviously has its shortcomings, but by its nature may provide some fresh perspectives and impressions.

I talked with or corresponded with about 400 persons in the United States who are recognized as authorities on some aspect of male-female relationships or who had a specific reason to be knowledgeable in some aspect of male-female relationships that interested me.

I traveled to 10 countries in search of insights and comparative information. In Sweden I talked with 32 persons recommended as being especially knowledgeable. Perhaps I should add that I also corresponded with persons in 14 countries that I did not visit. (At one point or another in the total research, I called upon 12 translators for help.)

During the 4 years while I was actively engaged in this research I visited approximately 130 college campuses and on most was able to talk with students or faculty members about some area of my interest where they could be helpful. At several colleges I participated in classroom discussions on male-female relationships or took part in seminars with psychologists, theologians, etc. (I also participated in a discussion of Life and Love with the male and female residents of a communal pad of hippies in the Haight-Ashbury section of San Francisco.)

As another aspect of my research I attended 7 national conferences dealing with some aspect of male-female relationships and received transcripts of 8 other conferences. (At one conference in the Midwest dealing with the intimate behavior of husbands and wives, there were uniformed guards at the door at each session to keep out the morbidly curious.)

My reading included several hundred reports of research projects and many thousands of smaller reports containing some corroborative or tantalizing detail. The published material that I pondered would easily, if put in one stack, rise 30 feet in the air.

In exploring the problems of modern women I participated in a national seminar of women executives and, among other things, spent an evening with 35 women who were being briefed by my local auto service manager on the mysteries of carburetors, generators, spark plugs, and mufflers (which in our society only men are supposed to understand).

I conducted a number of surveys of varying complexity on intriguing questions where I could find no adequate information. One whimsical inquiry, conducted in 13 different U.S. towns and cities and in 2 European locations, was aimed simply at assessing the proportion of women who now wear pants instead of dresses, and under what conditions.

A questionnaire was used at two colleges to gain some understanding of the extent to which coeds were using contraceptive pills, and what they thought about them. At two men's colleges that permit students to entertain female guests in their bedrooms, I sought, through a questionnaire, to explore the forms this entertainment takes.

And I became involved in one survey that, in terms of effort at least, might be characterized as massive, since it required quite a few thousand hours of effort on the part of the people involved. This as it turned out was a cooperative venture between a working group I had developed and a group at the University of Connecticut. Briefly, here is the story.

After I had concluded two years of research, I found that there were many questions about attitudes and behavior of young adult males and females that still puzzled me. To seek illumination I constructed an informal checklist of several dozen items. I first arranged a distribution of it to junior and senior students at several colleges in the Northeast.

The questions—all on male-female relationships—dealt with such subjects as the attitudes of women toward careers, attitudes of both sexes toward coeducation, attitudes toward marriage while still undergraduates, and attitudes and individual experiences regarding physical intimacy.

The rate of returns from the first few schools, approximately 80 percent, elated me to the point that I expanded and expanded, to try to get schools in every major region of the country and to seek a variety of types of colleges, including a Catholic and a Protestant university. Altogether the U.S. sample included 21 colleges and universities. The overall rate of return was about 67 percent. Then arrangements were made to sample universities in other countries. Several hundred checklists were distributed at a broadly based university in each nation. These distributions posed a number of obvious added difficulties; but the returns from Germany, Norway, England, and Canada were within the same range as the returns from U.S. schools and averaged more than 60 percent. (Also, we received a small but interesting return—one-third—from Italian university girls sampled.)

With every checklist there was a special sheet where respondents could if they wished make amplifying comments. The comments received ran to about 110,000 words.

As we began crossing regional and national boundaries in the search for samples I became a bit dismayed as I pondered how to tabulate, correlate, and analyze all the checklists I hoped would be coming in.

Informal as the procedures had been up to this point the survey drew interest from a number of researchers and counselors concerned with the study of male-female relationships because of the scope it had developed and its element of uniqueness. (There had never been, for example, a sampling that would permit a comparison of male and female responses in the United States and its various regions with those in a variety of countries outside the United States.)

The head of a national organization concerned with male-female relationships suggested I take the problem of coping with the tabulation and analysis to psychologist Eleanore Braun Luckey, a highly respected methodologist in the field of family study. Not only was she nearby at the University of Connecticut as head of the Department of Child Development and Family Relations, but she has served on the executive committee of the National Council on Family Relations, on the board of the American Association of Marriage Counselors, and as an Associate Editor of *The Journal of Marriage and the Family*.

The data that were starting to come in won her interest, despite my somewhat unsophisticated research approach (and the casual wording—from a scientific standpoint—of a few of the questions). She believed the total response would deserve a careful examination. Ultimately, after a review of the survey procedures and several conferences, she set up the procedures for the tabulation and the analysis.

One of her colleagues in the department, sociologist Gilbert D. Nass, supervised the data processing, which was executed primarily by a graduate student, John Jennewein. (Dr. Nass, incidentally, had just finished a fascinating study of his own on the role of conflicting motivations in courtship behavior.) Later Dr. Nass, in consultation with Dr. Luckey, drew up a comprehensive report for the department setting forth the principal survey results. A copy of the report was supplied to me, and I have been guided by its tables in presenting the responses to survey questions in this book.

Dr. Luckey and Dr. Nass summarized their findings regarding international comparisons in a paper presented at a seminar of the 34th annual Groves Conference on Marriage and the Family, meeting in Boston, April 22–24, 1968. The seminar was on "Cross National Family Research." Their paper was entitled "A Comparison of Sexual Attitudes and Behavior in an International Sample."

I will take up the results of the survey at a variety of points where they may help illuminate questions being explored. Survey results will be reported in 14 different chapters (and comments offered by students who responded will appear in perhaps 20 chapters). A description of the survey procedures is offered in Chapter 10 and in the Appendixes to that chapter.

I am deeply indebted to the Department of Child Development and Family Relations at the University of Connecticut, to the university's computer center, and especially to Eleanore Luckey and Gilbert Nass for their collaboration in making the analysis of the survey data.

There are four other persons to whom I feel a very special debt of gratitude because they not only provided me with helpful information but, more importantly, guided me at crucial points by directing me to others who could be helpful. These are David R. and Vera C. Mace, who were, during most of the period of my research, the Executive Directors of the American Association of Marriage Counselors; Birgitta Linnér who assisted me greatly in my visit to Sweden; and Robert Boudet, the General Secretary of the International Union of Family Organizations, which has its headquarters in Paris.

I also wish to express my appreciation to a number of other highly knowledgeable people who took time from busy schedules to talk with me or correspond with me regarding my research. Among such people in the United States I would like especially to single out the following, who are mostly educators, counselors, researchers, psychiatrists and other physicians, lawyers, government officials, business consultants, and authors.

Louise Bates Ames, Robert R. Bell, Jessie Bernard, Irving Bieber, Graham B. Blaine, Jr., Mary S. Calderone, Harold T. Christensen, Lester Dearborn, Nina vas Dias, Evelyn M. Duvall, Max Eastman, Albert Ellis, Dana L. Farnsworth, James K. Feibleman, Keith Fischer, Elizabeth Force, Mervin B. Freedman, Harrop A. Freeman, Wallace C. Fulton, John H. Gagnon, Frederick J. Gaudet, William J. Goode, B. Y. Glassberg, Henry M. Graham, Robert E. Grinder, Robert D. Grove, Richard N. Hey, Elsie Hill, Reuben L. Hill, Evelyn Hooker, Ruth H. Jewson, Richard L. Judd, John Keats.

Lester A. Kirkendall, Lawrence Lader, Judson T. Landis, Harold I. Lief, Frank R. Locke, Donald S. Longworth, Jean

Walker Macfarlane, Charles M. McLane, James Mills, George E. Moore, O. Hobart Mowrer, Emily H. Mudd, George P. Murdock, Bernard I. Murstein, Grace Naismith, Ethel M. Nash, Gerhard Neubeck, F. Ivan Nye, Harriet F. Pilpel, the late Gregory Pincus, Wardell B. Pomeroy, John R. Rague, Lee Rainwater, Ira L. Reiss, Susan F. Roberts, Alice S. Rossi, Isadore Rubin, Nevitt Sanford, William M. Smith, Oscar Sternbach, Murray A. Straus, Clark E. Vincent, John Weber, Aubrey Wendling, Robert F. Winch.

Among those outside the United States I wish particularly to express my gratitude to:

In Argentina, Lida Bianchi, Carlos Alberto Floria, Torcuato S. DiTella, Jorge Rizzi.

In Denmark, the late Kirsten Auken.

In France, Philippe Cahen, Paul-Henry Chombart de Lauwe and Mme. M. J. Chombart de Lauwe, Mme. M. Harari, Lolay M. Mann, Rose Vincent.

In Germany, Helene Edom, Hans Giese, R. v. Hunoltstein, Hans Luxenburger, H. Schelsky, Gunter Schmidt.

In Great Britain, Mrs. M. F. Bligh, Eustace Chesser, Alex Comfort, Dorothy Cook, J. R. Napier, Griselda Rowntree, Gerald Sanctuary, Arnold J. Toynbee.

In Japan, Hiroshi Minami, Jiro Tokuyama.

In Norway, Harriet Holter and her associates at a round-table discussion at the Institute for Social Research, Oslo.

In Sweden, Gunilla Ahlborg, Annika Baude, Kai Blomquist, Gunnar Boalt, Carin Colliander, Per Holmberg, Joachim Israel, Georg Karlsson, K. F. Karlsson, Eva Moberg, Alva Myrdal, Gösta Rodhe, Thorsten Sjövall, Jan Trost.

In Switzerland, Eva Maria Borer, Selma Lerch.

I cannot identify the dozens of university and college students who assisted by serving as distributors of our College Checklist since doing so would identify their schools. They have my gratitude. And I wish to thank the following students encountered at colleges and universities in the U.S.A. and abroad who were especially helpful in providing me with insights or case material:

Constance Albright Sprong, Gerald Allen, Erik Bergensen, Janet Cady McCoy, John Foote, Geoffrey Fuller, Edward Glusman, Jr., Bjorn Humberset, Marion Jordan, Lois Lichtenstein, Stephen Roos, Pam Rush, Timothy Ryan, Tom Snell, Thomas Steiner, Douglas Werner, Margaret Zug.

I might add that while certain of the material in this book may raise some scary questions, for some, about where the so-called Younger Generation is headed, I was deeply impressed by the fidelity and good sense of virtually all the young people who contributed to my research.

As usual I imposed on numerous friends for counsel at various points. These include particularly Elizabeth and Clarence Barnes, Audrey and Lester Cooper, Mitty Darrow, Jane Eager, Peggy and Robert Johnson, Audrey and William Roos, Nancy and Charles Saxon, Joan Stern, Kay and John Tebbel.

I am indebted to Marion Fuller and Ann Bridgman for preparing checklists for distribution, for assisting with the various drafts of this manuscript, for the analysis of certain research materials, and many other valued forms of assistance.

My son Randall, age 23, and daughter Cynthia, age 20, each spent several hundred hours previewing or processing research materials for me. My son Vance and his wife Jane, though now living some hundreds of miles away, were able at several points to offer badly needed help. As usual I gained an abundance of data, insights and stiff criticism from Virginia Packard, to whom I have been happily, if tempestuously, married for some decades.

And finally, at my publishers, I am particularly indebted to Eleanor and Kennett Rawson, who not only supplied guidance, insight, and criticism at many points, but who were unfailingly patient—and encouraging—when I had to tell them in three different years that I hoped finally to get down to writing this book "maybe next year."

Vance Packard
New Canaan, Connecticut

Part I

CHANGES AND NEW PROBLEMS

CHAPTER I

The Wilderness—and Six Forces in the Background That Are Shaping It

---

"Everything dat's fastened down is comin' loose. . . ." de Lawd to Noah, in Marc Connelly's *The Green Pastures.*

The male-female relationship has never been an easy one. Males and females in many societies have been raised to view each other as dangerous or ridiculous creatures. And even when males and females have fallen in love, it has usually been easier for them to adore each other than to like each other.

In the past there have almost always been rules, standards, and sharply defined roles for each sex within which their maneuverings took place. Today the rules, standards, and assigned roles are in disarray.

The confusion affects most importantly how males and females conceive their roles in life. The social changes of the past quarter-century have had their greatest or more obvious impact on the lives of women. This may explain why there have been at least four times as many symposiums in recent years devoted to the problems of the New Woman as there have been symposiums devoted to the problems of the New Man.

But you cannot overhaul the status of one sex without also altering the status of the other in the process. Consider the matter of relative power. If the woman gains in power, the man quite obviously must give up some, and make the best of it, or fight back. The primary drama of recent decades is that women have been acting, and men have been reacting.

11

In all the shifting we are seeing not only some transfer of power, but also some impressive evidence that each sex is taking on some of the characteristics of the other. A journal of the American Medical Association, as an example, carried a psychiatrist's report in 1967 flatly alleging that sexual roles were "being reversed." He related that many women who came to him did not know how to act like a woman and the men were equally confused about how to be men. At the same time, millions of young rebels have by their dress and mode of address to each other been scorning traditional secondary sex characteristics.

The confusion about roles spills over into marriage. Harold T. Christensen, Purdue University sociologist, points out that marriage roles that were formerly assigned by society now increasingly must be worked out by the persons involved. "There is more confusion today," he explained, "and new husbands and wives frequently face a period of maneuvering for a role advantage or at least role clarification. There are more role tensions and conflicts between the spouses since the situation is more confused."

The confusion about appropriate sex roles and behavior includes questions about transition to maturity in both sexes. Increasingly the young have to wait longer and longer to have any feeling that they have achieved adult status. We offer them no rites of passage (except perhaps for the males a draft classification of eligibility for combat). They are left to grope, and to evolve ways to prove themselves.

Many young rebels, such as those in the hippie movement that peaked in 1967, have added to the confusion by questioning just about everything assumed about appropriate male-female roles and relations. A quite lovely but tormented 23-year-old ex-upper-middle-class hippie in San Francisco, dressed only in sandals and a tattered Moroccan robe, rejected the whole bit about love-marriage-motherhood. She told me that despite her current hardships she had no intention of becoming "a baby factory in the suburbs." Her contempt for the way of life of her mother and father in New Jersey was profound.

June Bingham, writer on psychiatry, has suggested that the greatest contribution to modern thought the young rebels such as the hippies may be making is their "set-breaking," or shaking us up in our assumptions. They have, at least among the young, been exploding "old mental associations, such as 'love leads to marriage, marriage leads to children.' Why? What if they don't?" She added that in many well-publicized hippie pads, sex has been broken out from "the old privacy, the old heterosexual one-to-one, the old erogenous zones."

Despite their sophisticated manner, there is considerable confusion among the majority of young people about the status of rules regulating physical intimacy between the sexes. In earlier times there were indeed violations of the rules. Today there are few rules that could command a majority vote if the voting were done by both adults and adolescents. It is not the violations, but the normlessness, that makes the contemporary problem a historically significant one. The Provost of Columbia University, David Truman, summed the situation up by stating, "The present problem seems to be less one of rebelling against an established and known code than one of floundering in a situation with almost unknown limits." Some of the new moralists are arguing that we don't need boundaries or norms, that in today's world the best approach is to let each individual decide what is best for himself.

Historian Max Lerner has suggested that we are living in a moral interregnum. The king is dead, but there is no king to replace him. The old standards are gone, but there are not yet new standards to take their place. There are new operative standards, yes, but these are the result of patterned evasion.

Many who quite seriously would like to live moral lives are left to wonder how they can behave so that they will not be left feeling out of step. Anthropologist Margaret Mead compares today's lovers to two ballet dancers who no longer have traditional lines to follow but must improvise, with each wondering what the next steps will be.

At a conference of late adolescents in Oregon one boy complained, "We are told so many different things by so many different people." Among the students responding to our College Survey many suggested that uncertainty was a major problem. A girl at a women's college known for its liberal rules observed, "I am continually struck by the lack of fulfillment that sex experiences seem to give girls here. They have no idea of what context to put sex into, what to expect from it, or what to give it."

The confusion found in the younger generation obviously derives in large part from the uncertainty of the older generation and the mixed signals being communicated between generations. A report on college students by the Group for the Advancement of Psychiatry took note of this by stating, "In the matter of managing sexual drive, the late adolescent's problems are compounded by the fact that the adult world itself has no clear standards of behavior."

At the secondary-school level an official of the National Association of Independent Schools seemed to be having some trouble controlling his anxiety as he acknowledged that students were stumbling into new attitudes because of the lack of any moral code. The president of the association, Cary Potter, confessed that in the private schools everybody was "substantially bewildered" about what could be done to help students formulate sexual values and responsibilities.

Many parents have responded to the confusion by exhibiting what West Coast theologian Robert E. Fitch has called "an orgy of open-mindedness." Most, however, are not just permissive. They are baffled.

In reckoning the confusion we must also note the contrasting counsel and opinions from a number of scientists whose special training qualifies them to speak authoritatively. Consider the contrasting viewpoints of some sociologists. One noted sociologist, Ira L. Reiss of the University of Iowa, has stated that we are seeing a "sexual renaissance" (in the sense of a rebirth of a more open attitude toward sexuality). On the other hand, the renowned Harvard University sociologist, Pitrim A. Sorokin, argued moralistically some years ago, "Our sex freedom is beginning to expand beyond the limits of safety. It is beginning to degenerate into anarchy."

What is the state of marriage in North America? At a conference of U.S. and Canadian family specialists in Toronto in 1965 one principal speaker said the family had never been stronger, and another principal speaker said the family was far from healthy and indeed showing symptoms of pathology.

Or what about the new role of women? At a symposium on women in 1966 the director of the Women's Bureau in Washington said women were at the threshold of a golden era of achievement. Other presumably competent observers have contended that movements to give equality to women have usually turned out to be disorganizing to society. Sociologist Jacques Ellul of France, in speculating about the new technological society, has tended to equate working women with retrogression rather than with progress. In Argentina behavioral scientists report there is substantial argument there whether the family can survive the growing independence of women.

David Mace, one of the most respected marriage counselors in the U.S.A., takes a wait-and-see attitude. He points out that in looking at all the confusion about the identity of the roles of men and women in our contemporary culture it can from one angle "look like a pretty sorry mess. Yet fundamentally it represents something we've never had before, a real opportunity to find out what are the true roles of men and women in human society. And this I consider to be a great gain."

There have been suggestions that we are in the midst of a "sexual revolution." What in fact is occurring seems too chaotic and varied to describe yet as a revolution. A revolution implies a clear movement in an understood and generally supported direction. As I have examined my evidence the phrase that kept springing to mind as more appropriately descriptive of the state of male-female relationships in the late 1960s is "sexual wilderness." This "sexual wilderness" describes pretty much the whole range of areas where males and females find themselves in confrontation.

The word "sexual" has specific meanings involving intimacy, but it also is the best word in the English language, as far as I can find, to describe the many ways that males and females relate to each other. One definition of "sexuality" is that offered by Mary S. Calderone, Executive Director of the Sex Information and Education Council of the United States (SIECUS). In her view, sexuality is "everything in each of us that has to do with being a man or a woman." She points out that sex education has moved well beyond the former emphasis upon details of reproduction into the dynamics of male-female roles and relationships. The broad goal of education for sexuality, she feels, "should be the exploration of the whole realm of evolving and unanswered questions on the sexual nature and behavior of human beings and of the changing roles and relationships of men and women today." While sex may be an *act,* sexuality is a *being.*

Our interest in this exploration will be on all the major problems that males and females after the age of 12 encounter today as they confront each other in life and seek to work out agreeable accommodations.

THE SIX FORCES IN THE BACKGROUND

The bewilderment and normlessness characterizing so much of male-female relationships today are in large part caused by the dislocation in our way of life produced by rapid social change.

Many societies in the past have had to hold onto their hats during periods of rapid social change. But few societies in recorded history have been propelled into a brand-new environment as abruptly as the Western world has in the past quarter-century. Wilbert E. Moore, authority on social change at the Russell Sage Foundation, states, "By any crude measurement, the contemporary world appears to be changing more rapidly than at any time in human history. . . ." And he added that the rate of change seems to be accelerating.[1]

What is new in our changed world the past quarter-century that might reasonably be having an impact on male-female relationships?

We will in this book often note environmental conditions that seem clearly related to the way males and females are acting today. But behind all the new conditions in environment loom six background forces that have been particularly potent in creating this new environment.

Before we start examining the changes occurring in male-female relationships in the past quarter-century—and what they imply—it might aid our perspective to look briefly at these six background forces.

Changes produced by the life-modifying sciences

Human beings have been searching for ways to remove the likelihood of pregnancy from the act of coitus for at least 2500 years. Aristotle suggested cedar oil as a contraceptive. And there has been a long search to isolate "safe" periods.

A major improvement in contraceptive aids came in the 19th century with the vulcanization of rubber. Undoubtedly what will stand as the most historic breakthrough came in 1954 when two doctors working together, Gregory Pincus of the Worcester Foundation for Experimental Biology and John Rock, of the Reproductive Study Center in Brookline, Mass., discovered a drug that when taken in pill form by a woman could interrupt the process of ovulation and thus in effect prevent a union of female egg and male sperm.

Contraceptive pills were accepted by women at a rate unprecedented in the history of medical innovations. By 1967 at least 6,000,000 American women were taking some form of The Pill. The popularity of The Pill might be explained by figures cited by Dr. Pincus of the failure rates of various approaches to contraception at a clinic in Slough, England. The reported failure rate where condoms were used was nearly 50 percent, for example, whereas the failure rate where oral contraceptives were used was less than 1 percent.[2]

Meanwhile another sensational improvement, the intrauterine device—almost as effective as The Pill—gained popularity. It apparently creates a commotion that prevents the fertilized egg from finding any secure anchor.

For the first time in human history, men and women now have an assured way to separate the recreational from the procreative function of coitus. The British demographer Richard Titmuss has suggested that birth control has done more to emancipate women than their gaining the right to vote. Some of the restless young unmarrieds are asking whether, in our enshrinement of chastity before the advent of effective contraceptives, we had been simply making a virtue of necessity.

One significant effect of the newer contraceptives, in terms of our interest, is that they shift the responsibility for birth control from the male to the female. Another significant effect is that such contraceptives, by providing peace of mind, enable many women to find considerably greater enjoyment from their sexual encounters. Males usually never have had a problem enjoying their encounters. (The greatly increased use of hormone preparations also was contributing to the enhanced interest married women were showing in physical intimacy.)

Meanwhile about two million American married couples have quietly arranged surgical birth control. It has no effect upon physical capacity for intercourse. In fact, it appears in most cases to improve the enjoyment. The male operation, vasectomy, is usually preferred because it is simpler. Considerable progress has been achieved in making the operation reversible so that the couple still have the option of impregnation if they later decide they want a baby (or another baby).

In Eastern Europe, where doctors have been freer to experiment with abortion than in the West, excellent results are reported from a simple new suction technique that eliminates the hazard inherent in the conventional surgical scraping.

Equally dramatic in modifying our lives has been the achievement—largely credited to science (and improved nutrition)—in lengthening the span of vigorous life.

Marriages launched today will usually continue, if successful, well into the 21st century. A girl who sees herself in a race to marry by the age of 20 or 22 is taking on a commitment that will ordinarily last more than half a century. Today's teenagers, certainly the female ones, will live on average to be close to 90 years old.

In just the 20 years between 1940 and 1960, males managed to increase their life span by 5½ years while females of the U.S.A. were increasing their life span by 7½ years.

Even given the state of medicine today, the male born in 1962 has a life expectancy of about 67 years and the female an expectancy of close to 74 years in the U.S.A. Males and females in England, France, and Sweden have even longer life expectancies than U.S. citizens. (One travel agent in Kansas reported that three-fourths of his clients were widows, often traveling on insurance money.)

Since U.S. women are also completing their childbearing phase earlier, the mother now finds on average that her last child has gone off to school by the time she is 32 years old.

Because of the prolonged years of good health and vitality, and because of improved cosmetics, women need no longer fear that their beauty will fade in their twenties. Many women today described in the press as beautiful are in their forties and fifties. In theory at least, this should take the pressure off girls to marry early. Young women can also assume they will be sexually responsive for several decades. This prolonged beauty and vigor poses a novel challenge of adjustment for humanity. In all previous eras, parents were expected in effect to recreate physical attractiveness and sexual vitality in their children as their own attractiveness and vitality faded. Today we hear of instances of divorced mothers double-dating with their daughters.

The life-modifying sciences (and improved nutrition) have

helped create two other changes worth noting in the female's life. Women now stop menstruating in their early fifties, or about 4 years later than they did a century ago. At the other end of the procreative circle, girls start menstruating about 3½ years earlier than they did a century ago, or usually while they are 13.

Social changes produced by technological innovation

Yale psychologist Kenneth Keniston has stated, correctly I believe, that "central to American society is the unquestioned primacy of technology in virtually every area of our collective existence. Technology provides the motor for the continual social change to which we must somehow adapt. . . ."

Technology has taken most of the danger, dirt, and requirement for muscle out of work and thus has opened up opportunities for women in many areas of the economy. At the same time technological innovation has created rapid job obsolescence. An expensively learned technical skill such as chemical engineering is likely to have a half-life of 10 years (i.e., half of what the person learned at technical schools becomes obsolete within 10 years). This rapid obsolescence can undermine the self-assurance of a male breadwinner. Also it tends to weaken the ties between generations, because the father is often no longer competent to transmit valued vocational skills to a son.

A part of the social change produced by exploding technology is that it seems to encourage the growth of large business organizations, with far-flung operations and with highly mobile employees. Also it encourages the growth of metropolitan areas. These factors in combination have a number of impacts that might reasonably affect profoundly male-female relations. There is the growing sense of anonymity, the reduction of adult scrutiny over the behavior of the young, an increased separation from kinfolk, a weakened sense of significant citizenship, a separation of job from the area of the home. (The rather desperate effort of those most alienated of sane young Americans—the hippies—to establish "tribes," farm "communities," and even communal pads might be viewed as an outspoken symptom of a more widespread yearning for "community.")

Eli Ginzberg, specialist in manpower mobility at Columbia

University, suggests, "Pretty soon we are all going to be metropolitan-type people in this country without ties or commitments to longtime friends and neighbors." *The Wall Street Journal* carried a report on "corporate gypsies" and cited the case of a manager of Montgomery Ward who, with his wife, had moved 28 times during the 26 years of their marriage.

The Atlas Van Lines estimates that the average corporate manager in engineering or marketing moves about every 2½ years. In my own hometown in Connecticut, which has more than its share of these corporate gypsies, the turnover in home occupancy between 1955 and 1960 was approximately 54 percent. Over all, the average family in the United States now moves 14 times in its lifetime, according to the Family Service Association of America. Clark E. Vincent, family specialist at the Bowman Gray School of Medicine, Winston-Salem, N.C., argues that a highly adaptable "nuclear" family with few close kinship ties is becoming a necessary social unit for our kind of industrial society. (A nuclear family is one stripped down to parents and kids, with no grandparents, uncles, cousins, or in-laws in the living area.)

As for the home itself, it has shifted from being a production center to being a service station. With available electrical appliances, prepackaged foods, laundry services, many homemakers are hard put to consider themselves fully employed unless they follow the models in the television ads and keep their floors and glassware gleaming, or unless they get heavily involved in chauffeuring children.

The Ladies' Home Journal found in a survey of women that a substantial majority of the respondents did no sewing. And the same journal in reporting the life of a remarkable mother of two children in Grapevine, Texas, stated that despite her large house with five bedrooms and three baths and no maid, she completed her housework in one hour, by 8:30 a.m. when her youngest went off to school. She explained, "I am free to play bridge, attend club meetings or stay home and read, listen to Beethoven, and just plain loaf" until the family returns.

As we will see, a great many of these wives and mothers rather suddenly are interested in jobs, and plenty of jobs are available thanks to the growth in demand for service employees, office employees, and many other growing job categories where women are welcome in a technologically advanced society. Robert O. Blood, Jr., sociologist at the

University of Michigan, believes that the increase in the number of married women—and mothers in particular—who work outside the home "is one of the most startling social changes in American history."

Two specific technological innovations that by general usage in recent decades have modified male-female relationships in an interesting way are (1) the automobile and (2) the baby bottle.

With most non-slum families having at least one automobile, and with millions of youngsters owning their own, courtship activity is more likely to take place in an automobile than in the family parlor.

As for the baby bottle, the first U.S. patent for an artificial feeding device was obtained in 1841, for a deerskin pseudo-breast filled with sponge that was strapped to the mother's chest to deceive the tyke into believing it was getting real human milk. The difficulties in getting widespread use of artificial feeders centered not so much on the feeder as in developing a formula for milk that was nutritious and did not create severe reactions in babies. It was only in the past quarter-century that bottle feeding got general medical and public acceptance. In terms of the male-female relationship the significant contribution of the baby bottle was that it has enabled the mother to delegate some of the feeding and burping of babies to the father.

Changes in the age distribution of the population

All during the early 1960s the number of U.S. inhabitants under the age of 18 was growing four times as fast as the rest of the population. It is estimated that after 1968 each succeeding year's crop of 19-year-olds will be bigger than the one before and the figure will reach at least 4,000,000 by 1974.[3]

Thus one aspect of the so-called generational gulf can be stated in sheer numbers. Approximately half the population already is under the age of 27. The proportion of the U.S. population that is teen-age is the greatest in many decades. In some suburban communities where teenagers alone constitute more than 40 percent of the total population fearful adults have been setting up special citizens' groups to watch for rampaging adolescents.

All these tens of millions of adolescents, born after World

War II and now surging up toward adulthood, create mixed feelings among adults preoccupied with the direction of the economy. Some union leaders tend to want to keep young people off the labor market as long as possible; and the marketing people tend to want the young people to become major consumers through "family-formation" or otherwise as quickly as possible (so they will become prospects for such big-ticket items as beds and refrigerators). On the other hand, if the young get jobs and remain single—especially as "swinging singles"—they are more attractive to certain marketers than married young people, since they are better prospects for high-priced sports cars, travel abroad, champagne, expensive hi-fi sets, and other amenities.

One advertising man advised me that if our economy is to flourish, young people will have "to become more active consumers at a fairly early age," long before marriage. Apparently this wish has become a reality. Edward Bond, as president of the Young & Rubicam advertising agency, stated of the young generation in 1965, "They are strongly consumption oriented —in fact the consumption of goods and services appears to be life's goal."

The younger generation has been setting the mass-buying trends for a great many products (such as automobiles, filtered cigarettes and canned beer) that are eventually taken up by adults, which is certainly a new kind of tyranny. Lester Rand of the Youth Research Institute contends that the greater affluence of teenagers in the past 10 years has enabled them to be more independent in their attitudes toward adults (even though much of their affluence comes from their allowances!).

Changes created by the expansion of higher education

In 1937 about 12 percent of young Americans of college age actually went to college. Thirty years later, in 1967, the proportion had risen to more than 40 percent. U.S. Office of Education figures indicate that between 1940 and 1965 the proportion of high-school graduates who went on to college rose from 35 percent to 55 percent. And a rapidly increasing proportion go on to graduate school.

Why has there been this great increase in college enrollment? First, of course, is the real or imagined need of industry for managers who have the proper ticket of admission, the college diploma. Affluence has increased the number of parents who feel they can send their children to college. The alternative of military service has certainly inspired a considerable interest in higher learning. Then there is the seldom acknowledged economic gain of holding down unemployment by delaying entry of the young onto the job market. Also colleges increasingly are meeting the need of a highly mobile society for an acceptable meeting ground for marriage-minded males and (especially) females of similar background.

And finally there is the considerable new interest among young women in the idea of preparing for interesting careers. An ever higher proportion of collegians are females. The proportion of students enrolled in institutions of higher learning who were female increased from 31 percent in 1952 to 39 percent in 1965. In India there is a saying: "Educate a woman and you put a knife in the hands of a monkey!" Few American males would dare to venture that opinion today.

As some of the universities have grown to have 10,000 . . . 20,000 . . . 30,000 . . . 40,000 students, many of these students feel lonely and on their own—in need of human companionship—and often seek out the warmth of sexual involvement. A student sign at Harvard University said, "It's the two of us against the world—and the world is winning."

The most noteworthy fact about the growth of college-goers, in terms of our inquiry, is that we are delaying for ever more young people the time when they become self-supporting and capable of establishing self-supporting marriages. Millions of young adults who are biologically mature are not becoming independent in any real sense. While we give young people more freedom, we keep them in de facto dependence upon adults much longer. Mrs. Alva Myrdal, noted authority on modern women's role and recently a Swedish cabinet member, suggests that "the discrepancy between biological and social maturity may be one of the most fundamental causes of the so-called 'youth problem' besetting so many countries just now."

When young people feel dependent, they seem to have to prove to themselves their independence fairly constantly. Students at publicly supported institutions, incidentally, have a much better chance of approaching independence through self-support and institutional loans than students at private schools, where annual costs may run close to $4,000.

Changes in ideals, beliefs, and national mood

Such changes can profoundly affect male-female relationships.

Changes in religious emphasis are perhaps easiest to identify. In the U.S. the proportion of the population formally affiliated with churches has shown no serious drop-off. But many clergymen have felt it necessary to strain to appear modern in order to hold the interest of churchgoers, especially the younger ones. Examples are the staging of rock-and-roll dances at church services . . . the fondness for extreme modernity in church architecture, a tendency that has been described as an edifice complex . . . and the brightening up of the titles posted for sermons. A church in Dayton, Ohio, advertised this sermon: "To Put God On A Pedestal Is A Monumental Error."

The discoveries of astronomers, geologists, and space explorers have undermined the faith of all but the most devout that there is a physical Heaven or Hell. And among believers, God is more likely to be seen as a force or spirit than as an all-seeing watcher over human behavior above.

A Gallup Poll revealed in 1965 that in the preceding 7 years the percentage of Americans who saw religion losing its influence has more than tripled. In several countries of northern Europe the drop in religious influence is considerably more noticeable. A survey in England among more than a thousand teenagers produced the conclusion that "Most of the young people we interviewed were not interested in Christianity."[4]

The decline of religious belief as a vital source of guidance in everyday life will be pertinent to our inquiry at a number of points because the major religions of the Western world have always shown a considerable interest in the male-female relationship. Not only has there been concern about what constitutes moral behavior in various aspects of male-female encounters, but most of the major religions have provided strong support for the concept of male dominance.

Early Christians saw woman as the primary cause of sexual sin. St. Paul especially glorified austerity in sexual matters, even in marriage, apparently as a part of purifying rites in preparation for the Second Coming of Jesus. St. Paul stated, "It is good for man not to touch a woman. . . . But if they do not have self control let them marry, for it is better to marry than to burn."

The Dean of Students at Hope College suggested that "our society is giving up the Judaic-Christian tradition as a basis for law and morality without replacing it with any consistent rationale for morality."

Meanwhile a number of forces in Western life have been encouraging a mood of hedonism. Industries have a vested interest in promoting instant gratification. Living for the moment is also encouraged by the new affluence in most Western societies and by social security systems that offer protection against personal adversity.

In the mid-1960s one of the fastest-growing major magazines, *Playboy*, dedicated itself to extolling the hedonistic, sensual way of life. A professor of philosophy at a college in North Carolina told me, "I teach philosophy from Socrates to Hefner." (Hugh M. Hefner, the publisher of *Playboy*, has written a couple of dozen essays amplifying his magazine's philosophy.) The professor said that *Playboy* was then the most widely read publication on campus and added, "I read it because the students do." *Playboy*, he explained, believes in the pleasure of the body, while Socrates believed in a split between body and mind, and de-emphasized the mere body.

In recent years we have also been seeing a gradual movement throughout most of the Western world toward a real acceptance of the equalitarian ideal. The acceptance has developed in part from ideals proclaimed during the revolutionary wars from 1776 to the mid-19th century and in part from the continuing trends toward political liberalism in most of the West. It is difficult for a person who honors logic to glorify the equalitarian ideal and at the same time keep woman in the subordinate role expected of her in patriarchal societies.

The decline in arranged marriages and the growth of the concept of romantic love also have been factors in strengthening the hand of woman vis-à-vis the male. A man who claims to be in love with a woman will concede more power to her.

Along with equalitarianism there has been the glorying of individual rights. Perhaps the more the individual feels hemmed in and threatened by the pressures of large organizations and prolonged dependency, the more he reacts by asserting that only the individual counts. Carried to its logical

extreme, this enthronement of the individual tends to undermine group norms and even implies a kind of anarchy as an
ideal. A coed at a Midwestern university in a metropolitan
area wrote to us on her comment sheet in the College Survey,
"Standards for behavior are hard to find on the college
campus. Individualism might be said to be the norm. I can
tell you what I believe, yet I find it hard to prescribe for
society." That same thought in a variety of phrasings came to
us in many dozens of student comments.

This question of the ideal of individualism (and impinge-
ments upon the rights of the individual by modern society),
which your author has examined in several contexts in the
past dozen years, seems to raise more perplexing questions in
the male-female relationship than in any other area explored.
Is it possible that at some point the pursuit of individualism in
male-female relations becomes simply irresponsible and socially dangerous privitism [self-absorption]? Most of us now
are wary when free-wheeling, hard-driving private entrepreneurs advance under the banner of rugged individualism. But
what about amatory adventurers who argue that anything goes
as long as the sexual partner does not get "hurt"? What constitutes "hurt"? And can society too be hurt? We will come
back to these questions at several points.

Beliefs about what is appropriate in behavior between the
sexes have also been influenced among most young Western
people by the fact that they are far more exposed to people
outside their home community than ever before in history.
They read more, travel more beyond their home states and
home country.

Changes in individual life produced by wars and international tensions

The male, of course, has long been fascinated with combat
as a way of proving his prowess, but in recent major wars the
male has usually discovered that while he was away at war
the woman back home had been gaining independence from
him. Women, who have traditionally opposed wars, have
gained the most from recent ones. The wars have given them
a chance to prove their talent in the new technological society.

During World War I, women were urged to enter into many
previously male roles, and it is probably no coincidence that

they won the right to vote in the United States during the turmoil of the war and the months immediately following it. During World War II, women by the millions took on jobs traditionally held by males.

The upheaval of war also has had the effect of churning the population, separating loved ones, and in general creating an environment for a freer expression of sexual intimacy. And the tensions of hot and cold wars and living in a period when the Bomb or a draft call may strike all tend to contribute to the mood of living for the moment.

Henry David Aiken, Brandeis University philosopher, suggests that "the bomb has created the most extreme of all the predicaments that have ever confronted man" in its constant potential for instant extinction of the human race. This possibility makes it tempting to be unconcerned about tomorrow and to strive today for intensity of experience.

Most of these background forces that have helped create a sexual wilderness in the U.S.A. are at work in many of the world's societies in addition to those of North America and Western Europe. In many parts of the Near East the more worldly prosperous males are likely to join their unveiled monogamously mated wives for strolls. In the urban parts of Greece the arranged marriage is disappearing for all but the quiet rich. Young men and women can be seen in public holding hands, which would have been unthinkable 20 years ago. Some of the bolder Greeks are even appearing on beaches, along with the tourists, in Western-style brief bathing suits. In much of rural Greece it is still considered disgusting for either male or female to expose any flesh beyond hands and face.

Thirty years ago Japan was perhaps the most patriarchal of all societies, and the Japanese head of a family was one of the more awe-inspiring human figures conceivable. He expected and got considerable deference from his family. The most explosive force unleashed in postwar Japan was the Japanese woman, and Americans were at least partly responsible for the unleashing. General Douglas MacArthur, in pressing the adoption of the postwar constitution with its liberating provisions for women, launched a battle of the sexes that is still shaking the nation and causing many husbands to come home later and later at night. Women who were long considered to be little more than chattels by the men gained not only the right to vote but the right to have equal educations and even the right to get divorces. All of this has given them a far greater say about what goes on in the house. They began firmly requesting washing machines, prettier, less inhibiting clothes, and a chance to see more of the world.

Jiro Tokuyama, head of the Nomura Research Institute, advised me that today 80 percent of young Japanese husbands in urban communities turn over their pay envelopes, unopened, to their wives!

There is of course no clear one-to-one relationship between social changes produced by these six background forces and specific new patterns in male-female relationships. The forces that have been cited, furthermore, come to bear at a variety of points in the male-female relationship. The Pill, for example, may affect not only premarital coitus but the power relationships between husband and wife.

At any rate, an awareness of the possible reverberating effect of these six forces may add to our understanding as we now take up the specific changes in male-female relationships that have been occurring during the past quarter-century.

In this Part I of the book I will describe what seems to be happening in the area of male-female relationships and try to keep personal commentary to a minimum. In Part II, devoted to assessing the trends and exploring possible new directions, my personal impressions and convictions will undoubtedly intrude at a number of points.

I. The New Environment for Sexual Awakening and Maturing

CHAPTER 2

The Crumbling of Traditional Controls

"We actually place our young people in a virtually intolerable situation, giving them the entire setting for behavior for which we then punish them whenever it occurs." Margaret Mead, New York anthropologist.[1]

According to news accounts, an apprehensive Sicilian father recently succeeded in obtaining an insurance policy on his daughter's chastity. The apprehension of adults about the behavior of their young is not a new phenomenon. At least 4,000 years ago an Egyptian scribe wrote of the disrespect, lack of control, and generally appalling behavior of the young people of that day.

The gulf between the generations of today, however, has been matched few times in recorded history. This younger-older gulf based on age now offers a greater separation in mood and style of life in most technologically advanced countries than differences between social classes. The adolescents and young adults who may seem so defiant of traditional restraints have, as noted, new strength in their sheer numbers.

Our generational gulf is clearly related to the extraordinary rapidity with which social innovations are occurring. In any era of social change, Columbia University sociologist William J. Goode points out, "parent-youth conflict will be intense, since the values and attitudes of the adult were acquired in a situation which the younger generation no longer experiences."[2] Even middle-aged social scientists are complaining that they can't keep up with the special vocabulary of their younger colleagues today.

Our large organizations, including our multiversities, have

tended to promote this apartness of the generations. In 1967 the American Psychiatric Association heard a report from the director of psychiatry at the University of Wisconsin that a student can spend months on a large campus without having a conversation with a person over 30.

The increased difficulty parents are having in feeling they are relevant models or teachers for their children was described neatly by columnist Art Buchwald when he talked about his own difficulties in coping with the New Math. He suggested that the reason Johnny can't add today is that his parents can't help him with his homework.

In a well-ordered society there is at least a recognized pattern for introducing young people into the adult world and conveying what society has learned and expects of them. The accumulated wisdom of several generations on what is appropriate behavior is passed on to the new generation. Today we have the paradox that young people, because of prolonged education, are dependent upon adult financial aid for more years than ever before and yet with increasing vehemence are indicating they do not consider their elders to be appropriate guides in matters of behavior, values, or taste.

An example of the gulf regarding taste presents itself in Jamestown, N.Y., where there are two radio stations. One plays rock-and-roll music virtually all week long. The other features "memory music." In the New York metropolitan area one major radio station features what it calls "the grown-up sound" and another calls itself "the station with the young sound."

The generational gulf is one symptom of the drastically changed environment in which sexual awakening and maturing now takes place. We will examine here several ways in which the traditional controls for guiding the awakening process have been crumbling. Most of these were external controls. (Later we will examine the prospects for some new modes of control to replace them.)

I. The decline in parental control over the awakening process

Mothers and their adolescent daughters have quite dramatically different attitudes today on what is appropriate in premarital sexual behavior.[3] Some of this difference may be due to the daughters' wish to seem daring; but what is quite new is the decline in what mothers (and adults generally) do to implement their expectations of appropriate behavior in their children. Chaperonage of daughters has virtually disappeared in the U.S.A. and in northern Europe. It is even declining sharply in societies where scrutiny of daughters has traditionally been most vigilant, as in a number of Latin American countries, especially near the Caribbean Sea. In Argentina today, at the far south of Latin America, chaperonage is scorned as old-fashioned, and marriages by family management have virtually disappeared.

In the United States less than one suitor in fifty now makes a gesture of consulting the parents of his beloved before the couple announce their engagement.[4] The attitude of a good many parents seems to be that of the early 20th-century dowager who resignedly explained, "I don't care what people do, just so long as they don't do it in the streets and scare the horses."

Actually, parents today are not that indifferent. In their groping they are often at a loss to take positions that are credible even to themselves. Aubrey Wendling, sociologist at San Diego State College, was trying to explain to me the considerable evidence of youthful promiscuity in that area and said, "The main problem is the lack of any real guidance here. The parents always want to do the right thing, but end up doing nothing, so the young turn to their peer group for guidance on behavior."

Partly because of uncertain parental guidance and partly because of their greatly increased numbers in the population, the young now have their own well-publicized subculture. This is described by an authority on adolescents, James S. Coleman, in these terms: "Society is confronted no longer with a set of individuals to be trained toward adulthood, but with distinct social systems, which offer a united front to the overtures made by adult society."

Such a subculture may, as some suggest, serve the positive function of resolving generational discontinuities, but on the other hand it stresses boldness, living for the moment, and scorn for the adult world. In a few localities the subcultures have even set up their own teen-age churches.

Unquestionably the mass media have played a substantial role in encouraging the generational gulf. TV critic Richard L. Doan after some years of close observation has concluded,

"The drift is toward total command of our entertainment media by a stratum of adolescents that cannot articulate much beyond a yeah-yeah, yet is mysteriously able to cow its elders into deferring to its shabby tastes in music, comedy and sex."

Teen-age idols delight their followers by demonstrating their tyranny over adults. One wealthy young singer built a $100,000 home filled with electronic gadgets for "Mom and Dad" and reported with indulgent pleasure how much fun his wide-eyed parents were having in exploring this marvelous playhouse awarded to them. And the press agents of the young actress Tuesday Weld kept her running battle with her mother in the headlines with such items as "Tuesday Weld and her mother are speaking again, but not living together."[5]

The continued enormous appeal of abrasive rock-and-roll to the young generation for more than a decade suggests that one source of its appeal is that it symbolizes defiance of adult control. Also, of course, the carefully cultivated sloven appearance in vogue among the young has the well-known merit of being offensive to adults.

The generational gulf probably can be found in its purest form in southern California, where many stretches of beach are age-segregated and even towns are known as young go-go towns or "old" towns. In describing "the new life out there" writer-social observer Tom Wolfe told of the lean, tan kids who dominated a stretch of beach near La Jolla. They scoffed at anyone over 25 who came onto their sandy preserve as "black feet" people, meaning, for example, "a woman's pair of black street shoes out of which stick a pair of veiny white ankles." Wolfe added that all up and down the coast from Los Angeles to Baja, teenagers can take off from home and get to the beach, and if they need a place to stay, "well, somebody rents a garage for $20 a month and everybody moves in—girls and boys." He added, "All right, Mother gets worried about all this, but it is a limited worry . . . the thing is, everybody, practically everybody, comes from a good family. Everyone . . . has been reared well, as they say . . . it's just that this is the new order."

The mother of a stunningly shaped 14-year-old girl in Ohio told us that when she tried to moderate her daughter's frenetic dating habits, the girl flung a jacket in her face and exclaimed, "Mother, for goodness sakes, you don't know *anything* about love!"

Perhaps the best recent evidence that there is a predictable relationship between parent-offspring rapport and sexual behavior can be found in a large, careful study made in England under the supervision of Michael Schofield on the sexual behavior of young people. His group interviewed 1783 teenagers.

Schofield sought to assess whether there was any clear association between sex experience of the youths and the degree of family influence in their lives.[6] It was found that those who are most influenced by their families were the least experienced sexually. Schofield reported that sexually experienced boys were more often away from the home and when they were at home they more often had the place all to themselves. He observed, "Experienced boys are more likely to support the teen-age mythology . . . and are more likely to be against adult standards and outsiders of any kind."

As for the sexually experienced girls, he said they more often reported poor relations with both parents. These girls, he said, "did not tell parents where they were going, did not have to be in at a definite time, spent more time outside the home and more often entertained their friends at home when their parents were out." They were also more likely to go around in a mixed group, to spend more time on commercial premises. Like the experienced boys, they went to bars more often, got drunk more often, and smoked more cigarettes.

Many of the mass-buying trends, as indicated, start with teenagers and move upward to the adults. This ranges from styles in dress such as blue jeans to styles in automobiles. The sales manager of Dodge explained, "The market is teen-oriented." The teenagers usually do not have the money to buy the cars themselves, but they set the styles.

Quite possibly this confusion about generational leadership is ominous. Plato in discussing the decline of democracy in Greece in his *Republic* said, "The parent falls into the habit of behaving like a child, and the child like the parent. . . ." He added that the young "will not do as they are told; and the old, anxious not to be thought disagreeable tyrants, imitate the young."

But perhaps the gulf is not as wide as it sometimes might appear. One study of adolescents' choice when they are faced with a puzzling decision indicates that an adolescent's peer group is more influential in decisions that involve his status in the peer society, but that the parents' judgment is most respected in questions that concern society at large.[7] Evelyn M. Duvall, the noted counselor to adolescents, who now lives in North Carolina, reports in a recent book on today's teen-agers that on projective tests teenagers rate their parents higher than themselves on things of consequence.

2. The decrease in general community scrutiny of young people during the period of sexual awakening

In Biblical times if a new husband had reason to suspect that his bride was not a virgin at the time of marriage, and if she failed to pass an inspection, "the men of her city shall stone her with stones that she die."[8]

There has been a generally agreed procedure in most civilized societies where community scrutiny has functioned effectively for assuring that the community's well-brought-up maidens remain virgins until marriage—or (as in some of the more liberal rural areas of Scandinavia) until the girls are safely betrothed. Many of the same societies have accepted the idea that boys will be boys.

In stable communities it has been fairly easy for citizens to maintain scrutiny over the behavior of girls. Everybody knew everybody and was quick to gossip. It was exceptional for the girl to travel more than a few miles from home, and she would almost always settle down eventually with one of the community's eligible males.

The changes of recent decades have pretty well undercut the possibility of such effective scrutiny in advanced societies. In the larger city citizens often do not know a fifth of the people living on their own block. A girl can come and go in an apartment building with little notice of her or her visitors. If she is living with her parents, it is likely that they will be moving every few years.

When we add to this the velocity with which modern youth can escape the scrutiny of neighbors in an automobile, we can perceive the difficulty of community scrutiny. A survey of teen-age attitudes reveals that 67 percent of them now consider a car "essential" for dating. One 17-year-old girl said, "I wouldn't go on a walking date." And a 19-year-old lad said, "If a guy doesn't have a car he doesn't have a girl."[9]

Testimony before a Senate committee indicated that a high percentage of young males in the correctional institution at Chillicothe, Ohio, were there for stealing a car to take a girl on a date.

The cramped seat of a four-wheeled vehicle is hardly ideal as a place for sexual awakening. But it is the place where, it is reported, a majority of U.S. illegitimate children are conceived.[10]

3. The wavering role of religious doctrine in controlling specifically the process of sexual awakening

Until the very recent past, any close approach to premarital intercourse would assuredly arouse, at least in the female, extreme feelings of anxiety because of religious beliefs about what constitutes sin. Studies made in the 1940s and early 1950s indicated a quite clear relationship between abstinence from premarital coitus and religious devoutness or regularity of church attendance.[11] Our own College Survey of sex behavior indicates that both male and female students at the two institutions with specific religious affiliations tended to be substantially more conservative in their reported behavior and attitudes than American students in general. This was especially evident with students at the Catholic university.

As the number of people deeply influenced in their everyday personal behavior by religious belief has decreased, religious leaders have shown some signs of wavering on the issue of premarital intimacy. A writer in the *Christian Century* said intercourse before marriage was the aspect of morality where "the traditional armour seems to be crumbling fastest." And clergymen have been arguing the pros and cons of *Playboy*'s highly permissive and hedonistic philosophy in, of all places, the pages of that journal. An Episcopal minister in Raleigh, N.C., wrote that *Playboy*'s philosophy "has opened many doors for me and has caused some deep and exciting thoughts as well as discussion."

O. Hobart Mowrer, psychologist at the University of Illinois, has been much interested in the erosion of traditional values regarding moral behavior. In discussing the changing role of the churches he states, "By and large, religion has become sophisticated and soft. Good theology, taking its cue from psychiatry and clinical psychology, is supposed to be *accepting* rather than in any way 'judgmental.' Hell has conveniently been liquidated, and that leaves only Heaven, where *everyone* is presumably 'accepted.' Preachers are told that if they say anything about 'sin' it will only make people feel guilty; and everyone knows that guilt feelings are the specific foci of neurotic suffering. So, if you don't want to make people sick, don't talk to them about being good or bad."[12] He sees all this as the churches' effort to accommodate themselves to what they take to be scientific and modern.

4. Until recently one of the more effective controls over young people in their sexual awakening was the very real fear of premarital pregnancy

The fear has declined (but not the incidence). The fear was effective not only because of the general awkwardness of unmarried pregnancy, but because of the social stigma that was attached.

For those youths intelligent and prudent enough to make use of them, assured protections are available, as indicated, against the hazard of premarital pregnancy. And at the same time, because of the growing anonymity and mobility of society, the condemnation of society is less severely felt by the pregnant unmarried girl, even though society still frowns on premarital pregnancy.

(And lest we forget, fear of contracting a venereal infection was more of a deterrent before the development of penicillin, since the drug offered the promise that if a disease was contracted, it could more readily be cured.)

The premarital pregnancies that still occur are usually due to carelessness or ignorance, or because some girls who are unmarried secretly yearn for pregnancy either for reasons of emotional satisfaction . . . or to spite their parents . . . or to nudge a wavering male into marriage.

Schofield found in his English study of teenagers that the girls having sexual intercourse usually left any effort at contraception to the boy; and less than half the boys regularly used contraceptives. A quarter of them never used them. In the United States one authority on sex behavior, Lester A.

Kirkendall, marriage and family specialist of Oregon State University, learned in his study of college males with coital experience that less than half of those having casual pickup-type liaisons with girls bothered to use any kind of technique to prevent conception.

There is some argument among experts whether the availability of assured birth-control methods is or is not producing an increase in premarital intimacy. The evidence of carelessness on the part of the male in non-serious affairs led Kirkendall to doubt that the improved availability of effective contraception necessarily would lead to more premarital coitus. On the other hand a widely respected New York doctor, active in the birth-control movement, Alan F. Guttmacher, has been quoted as suggesting that while giving contraceptive information to young people might bring about an increase in sexual relations, any disadvantages would be more than offset by a decrease in unwanted pregnancies.[13]

There seems as yet to be no substantial evidence about impact one way or another. But perhaps in any case the quality of premarital encounters may be due for a change. Jessie Bernard, Washington University research scholar, points out in her recent book on sex games that for the "contracepted women" the consequences of sexual relations "need be no more significant for her than for her partner. . . . She can assume the same kind of hail-and-farewell stance as her partner can." Bernard added, "Whether many will actually want to, we haven't yet had time to learn."

On many campuses in 1966–67 a popular source of controversy was whether the university health service should issue contraceptive pills to female students requesting them. Some physicians contended that giving the pills would inevitably suggest that the college condoned premarital sex by students. Others felt that if a girl had an affair, she should at least be protected. At a number of schools, including Pembroke College, the University of New Hampshire, and the University of Chicago, pills were issued to unmarried female students at the discretion of the college physician. Meanwhile the men at Harvard were receiving mail-order catalogues, addressed to each of them by name, from a firm in Florida inviting them to purchase contraceptives in wholesale lots.

Some theologians began arguing the moral implications of advances in contraceptive techniques for unmarried persons.

One notable retort came in 1966 from Roger Shinn, dean of instruction at the Union Theological Seminary. He contended, "There is no virtue in morality if we are pure only because we fear being caught."

During 1967, while starting to prepare the manuscript of this book—and after the results of our 1966 College Survey had been processed—I encountered so much contention and speculation about The Pill on college campuses that I made a specific sampling on this issue among girls at two state universities in the Rocky Mountain area. One school has a reputation for being traditional in outlook, the other for being liberal. One hundred questionnaires were distributed among girls—50 at each campus—with stamped envelopes addressed to me so that they could respond anonymously if they chose to respond at all. I received 74 completed questionnaires.

Since approximately the same proportion of girls responded at each school, and since with one minor exception their responses were surprisingly similar (surprisingly, in view of their different reputations), I will report the samplings simply as a single survey of 74 coeds in the Rocky Mountain area. And since the sample is relatively small, I will indicate the responses only in general terms. Here in summary are the results:

• More than 60 percent of the coeds felt that contraceptive pills should be available on request at student health centers.

• About three-quarters of these coeds knew at least one unmarried female student who was on a steady regime of contraceptive pills. (Eleven knew of at least eight fellow students who were using the pills.)

• As for knowing women students who possessed contraceptive "devices," about half personally knew at least one such student.

• Only about 40 percent felt that the development of advanced contraceptive techniques had produced any significant change in either sex attitudes or behavior among women students on their campus.

• Somewhat less than a fourth of these coeds indicated that they personally had ever followed a regime of taking contraceptive pills. (The question was worded in such a way that a positive response could mean they had taken the pill specifically for contraception purposes, or as a general precaution in their dating situation, or for medical reasons.) Slightly more pill-using was reported at the supposedly traditional school than at the liberal school—one girl out of four at the traditional school, one out of five at the liberal school.

• More than three-quarters of the girls confirmed that if they wanted to obtain birth-control pills locally, they would know how to go about it.

The average age of these coeds was about 20½ years, and about half had at one time or another been pinned or engaged.

Several of their amplifying comments centered on the wisdom of distributing pills at student health centers. One in opposition said, "I would rather see our infirmary obtain the services of a dentist or optometrist than start giving out B.C. pills—this would be of much more benefit to *everyone* on the campus."

One of the girls who favored distribution said that if they were accessible, there would be fewer frantic searches for abortionists. She said, "I think that abortion has ruined more people's lives, especially regarding their own self concept, than the pills ever would." This girl, incidentally, indicated that she had thus far abstained from sex before marriage herself.

One girl who said she had never taken any "B.C. pills" said it was not because she was virginal. She said that she supposed she should be on pills right then. She explained: "We've depended on rubbers, rhythm method, vaginal foam—and luck. Oh yes, and douching. (Not all at once; quit laughing.) . . . Hopefully my period will come in about two weeks from now, but I'm never sure . . . I just might be growing a baby right now, for all I know. There wouldn't be that possibility if I had taken pills."

As for the impact of pills and other techniques of control on sex attitudes and behavior, one girl complained that the pill's ready availability leaves the coed "with no defense." The male simply asks, "Why?" She added, "The mere fact that you're not in love seems to be out these days. If your answer is a pregnancy fear, his answer is quick: 'Do you want me to pick up some pills?' Thus a coed is backed into a wall."

Others, however, do not think the situation quite that drastic. One said, "A promiscuous girl will be herself whether or not she takes the pill. I think B.C. pills have their main effect on the number of college marriages. Couples can now plan to have *no* children until they are through school."

Another girl, age 21 and going steady, commented, "Perhaps the only change in attitudes is that girls must now sit down and really think through their reasons for 'abstaining' or whatever. Fear of pregnancy can no longer be used as a reason for not having sexual relations, but I think it has always been a rather superficial one, anyway. Most have deeper and more personal reasons."

From their comments it was clear that some of the girls they knew who were taking pills really were taking them for medical reasons such as control of menstrual cycle or for skin problems.

On the other hand, medical reasons can also often be simply the reported reason for obtaining or using pills.

A New Orleans physician who teaches at Tulane University reports, "Very few single girls come in and ask me for birth-control pills, but quite a number ask me to regulate their cycle or relieve their cramps." He felt a number "aren't quite honest." At Penn State University the following casual conversation took place between a male and female student within the hearing of a number of people:

She: "Mary wants to borrow my prescription. She's going to live with this boy for a week."

He: "What are you going to do?"

She: "I can't give her any pills—I don't have them."

He: "Can't you get the prescription filled more than once a month?"

She: "I don't get them here. My mother sends them to me each month, for my skin." (Laughter.) "And I haven't had skin trouble lately." (Laughter.)

5. The growing unwillingness of collegiate authorities to serve as substitute parents

Traditionally parents have expected colleges to carry on the role of chaperonage with youngsters when they send their son or daughter to school for education. Colleges in varying degrees have accepted this role. To implement this they have developed parietal rules governing life within the walls of the college. These have been designed to assure parents—and in the case of public institutions, the state legislators—that the school is maintaining a high moral tone. The prevailing view, for example, has been that students could no more entertain persons of the opposite sex in their dormitory rooms than they could in their bedrooms back home.

For a host of reasons college authorities have found it increasingly difficult and uncomfortable to maintain this posture of substitute parents, though most schools still do.

For one thing, schools have the problem now of greater numbers of students to cope with and more of them with cars. Also increasingly there are on campus older students—either doing graduate work or undergraduates who are returned veterans—who are above the legal age of adulthood, 21.

With the growth of large universities, more and more students are living off campus in housing difficult to supervise. At Cornell, for example, many hundreds of male undergraduates have been living off campus. And at many larger schools scores and sometimes hundreds of unmarried male and female students living off campus take rooms or apartments together, some quite openly. Still another difficulty is that with the nationwide shift in new accommodations from hotels to motels, hundreds of colleges now have motels abutting their campuses for the convenience of visitors to the schools. The motels vary in their rules about whom they will accept as registered guests. But even those willing to set rules often have difficulty maintaining surveillance over who actually goes into the rooms, since guests of motels need not pass through the lobby. At the motel facing Southern Methodist University there are two outside stairways leading to rooms that are both some distance from the lobby.

A professor at Arizona State College in Flagstaff thought that one of the local motel proprietors was being unnecessarily suggestive in advertising locally that two persons could sleep in the motel's extra-large beds with no additional charge.

Added to the difficulty of school administration in setting or enforcing rules is the growing insistence by the students that they be treated as grown-up individuals (even though those making the most noise may be 17-year-old freshmen). At hundreds of schools there has been a recent clamor for easing or virtually wiping out such rules. In 1968 these rules proved to be a tempting target for restless, protest-minded students.

A writer for *The New York Times,* after checking the demands for change at six campuses, observed that some of the student demands seemed inconsistent. Students were simultaneously demanding that the college stay out of their lives as far as their bedroom behavior was concerned while demanding that the college had a responsibility to provide students with contraceptives. (Some students insist they can see no particular inconsistency in such demands.)

The mood of the students in calling for more and more freedom came in for some critical comments by college officials and spokesmen. The editor of a special issue of *The Journal of the National Association of Women Deans and Counselors* suggested that the youthful peer culture "operates in the present only, without benefit of history, and it moves on feeling and sentiment rather than logic. It has, moreover, become quite alienated from adult contact and influence."[14] And the Dean of Columbia College, speaking of the pervasive privitism of today's undergraduates, commented on their "puzzling unwillingness to confront the public consequences of so-called private actions." But he added that idealism was not absent.

On the other hand, college authorities themselves have in many cases been handling the problem of campus morals in a manner that might well arouse disrespect and inclination to rebel. Many of the schools have codes that stress the expectations that students will always demonstrate responsible behavior, but there is usually no spelling out of what responsible behavior is.

Dana L. Farnsworth, head of Student Health Services at Harvard, told the annual meeting of the American Orthopsychiatric Association in 1965 that "Until we resolve our own confusions, we will not be in a favorable position to help our younger colleagues thread their way through the devious paths of development to sexual maturity."

The Group for the Advancement of Psychiatry set up a Committee on the College Student, and this committee checked several dozen colleges on their approach to guiding students on behavior that might involve intimate physical relations. It concluded, "In no institution did we find published or printed materials that explicitly stated its views toward sexual conduct on the campus, yet institutions widely assume that student behavior will reflect the college rules and regulations."[15]

A noteworthy blast at administrative evasiveness came from

a graduate student at the University of Illinois, Roger Ebert, when the campus YMCA and YWCA sponsored a faculty forum on value formation. He asked the faculty members, "What does the university hold as its values, its system of morality, its beliefs about right and wrong in personal conduct? Nobody knows. Nobody would dare to know."

He charged that the university's disciplinary structure "is like those pathetic lists of regulations they hand out in the women's dorms. You know: 'couples in the lounge are to have three feet on the floor,' and so on. There's never any statement of what the rules are designed to prevent, and so the idea grows up among students that in practice anything goes so long as you have three feet on the floor. . . . Students are reinforced in their suspicions that the rules here are primarily for show, in order to impress parents, legislators and the other substitutes for a constituency of students."

Some officials point out that many girls need rules as an excuse to get out of awkward situations with men. They have the excuse of curfew. It does seem evident, however, that some schools which have been liberalizing their rules on room visitation have, in the absence of any clearly stated position on values related to sexual behavior, implicitly if unwittingly given their assent to fornication in the student bedrooms.

In any event, fairly dramatic changes in rules are appearing, especially at American private colleges that traditionally have been presumed to provide a cloistered atmosphere. A student at Skidmore crusading to change that school's curfews told us excitedly in 1967, "At Smith they are trying to throw out housemothers. . . . Both Smith and Mt. Holyoke have abolished their rule against staying at a motel within 30 miles of the schools." A number of colleges with women have been moving to a system of letting older students have dorm keys.

One major area of student-administration conflict concerns the hours when the girls have to be in and how many "overnights" they can have per semester. Rules have been changing so rapidly it is hazardous to report specifics here. Louisiana State University, despite its reputation for being a fun-loving school, has been requiring all girls to be in their rooms by 10 o'clock on week nights (but has been liberal on weekends). As recently as 1965, the Dean of Women at the University of South Dakota fought against liberalizing the rules requiring girls to be in their rooms by 10 p.m. week nights on the ground that any change would attract the wrong kind of girl. But at a number of state universities, dramatic easings of rules are occurring. At the University of Wisconsin now, all girls except freshmen have no hours at night when they must be in (provided that parents give such permission, and most do). Many thousands of students do not live on campus. One male student with an apartment told me in early 1968, "Any girl, even a freshman, can come to my apartment."

At coeducational schools there usually is no rule whatever setting hours for men, which some girls find galling. The strategy is that if the school can control the girl, it controls the man (at least as far as coeds are concerned).

A more sensitive area of conflict centers on whether a student can entertain visitors of the opposite sex in his or her room, which in most cases has a bed in it. At a time when Russia's University of Moscow was rescinding its rule permitting mixed visiting in dormitories, a number of U.S. colleges began permitting it. In some instances the college authorities simply were bowing to student pressure, and in others they have followed a positive philosophy that a college education involves far more than what happens in the classroom, that the student learns from his citizenship in the total campus community.

Private men's colleges, perhaps because they don't have to coax funds from state legislators, have been more inclined to permit visiting in rooms than have state institutions (or religious-affiliated institutions or women's colleges). The great majority of U.S. colleges still permit no visiting whatever, or only on carefully controlled open-house days. And even then there may be the requirement that the door be left open and that feet be kept firmly on the floor.

Smith and Vassar have been permitting men to visit in girls' rooms on certain afternoons each week. On the other hand, Bennington has permitted girls to entertain men in their rooms well into the night on weekends.

Among Eastern men's colleges, Columbia has been permitting men to have women in their rooms on Saturday nights till 1 a.m. Sunday. Harvard has permitted room visiting until 7 o'clock at night on weekdays and until midnight on Saturday. One of the more liberal arrangements in the U.S.A. has been at Wesleyan University, where men can entertain women guests in their living quarters until 2 a.m. on Friday and Saturday nights. During weekdays the girls have to be out by midnight. Even this liberality, however, does not prevent some violations. On a Saturday night in 1967, when the "community code" called for all girls to be out of college residence rooms and suites by 2 o'clock, someone pulled a fire alarm at one of the residence halls at around 3 a.m., perhaps as a prank. Three or four girls came running out of the men's quarters. One student advised us, "If it had been a big weekend, there would have been a lot more." Students and faculty alike there are uncomfortable about the way their rules and community code, which spells out a rationale for responsible conduct, are working in actual practice. Some are urging the concept of eliminating all regulations in terms of hours and putting more stress upon what constitutes reasonable conduct with a female guest in any of the 24 hours of the day. (By 1968 Princeton and Northwestern University were among the schools that also permitted room visitation until 2 a.m. on weekends.)

At schools where the rules specify the conditions under which students can have guests of the opposite sex in their rooms, only the letter of the law is often met. If the rules require that lights be left on during such visits, students may use light bulbs that have been dipped in black paint. At schools where the rules require that a door be left open the width of a book, this has been interpreted by students as meaning the width of a book of matches. Or as at Oberlin, where it has been the rule that girls entertaining male students on weekend afternoons keep doors open the width of a wastebasket, pre-crushed wastebaskets are sometimes used. If the rules require that feet be kept on the floor, couples fully comply by lying down on the floor.

An analysis of our College Survey leads us to doubt there is any clear relationship between liberality of visiting rules and the accumulative incidence of coitus, at least among older male students. (See Chapter 12.)

We made one special survey at two men's colleges in the Northeast of the behavior of students when they are permitted to entertain girls in their quarters. At these two schools not only were the students invited to respond to the general College Survey checklist used at 26 schools in the U.S.A. and abroad, but also they were invited to complete the special checklist. This, like the larger checklist, permitted wholly anonymous response, and they could ignore it if they wished. If they did complete it, the checklist was mailed directly to me in a stamped, addressed envelope. The two schools are those in our general survey labeled "An Ivy League University" and "A New England Men's College." At each of the two schools a representative sample of upperclassmen was sought. One hundred of the special checklists were distributed to upperclassmen at each school, and from each school there was better than an 80 percent response to all the questions.

Our first question asked how they felt about the relatively liberal visitation rules that were in effect at their schools. At both schools a substantial majority felt the rules were about as they should be. Those favoring change were almost entirely in favor of even greater liberalization.

In our second question we asked them to try to recall what happened the *last time* they and a girl were in their room or suite on an unchaperoned basis for more than a momentary visit. There were 10 alternatives. The first, for example, was: "There were always several of us around, talking, listening to music, things like that." Another possible response was, "We just talked." Two of the alternatives gave them the chance to indicate that in addition to any other activities that took place the student and his girl friend had experienced coitus. Approximately 14 percent of the men at the Ivy League University and approximately 26 percent of the men at the New England Men's College indicated that coitus had occurred the last time they had entertained a girl in their quarters.

Our final question was:

Viewing accumulatively your experience in inviting feminine visitors into your private quarters please check the maximum intimacy you and the girl visitor ever permitted yourselves while in the privacy of these quarters.

There were 6 possible responses. At the Ivy League University about 30 percent indicated that in their entertaining girls in their room they had never gone beyond light caresses, necking, good-natured wrestling, etc.; and at the New England Men's College about 15 percent said they had not gone beyond such activities. At the Ivy League school about 40 percent of the students indicated their maximum activity stopped short of petting below the waist; and at the New England

Men's College about 25 percent indicated their maximum activity had stopped short of such petting. As for those who checked coitus as the maximum intimacy they had ever experienced in their living quarters, the responses were as follows:

> Ivy League University—26%
> New England Men's College—49%.

In the general College Survey one item in the checklist distributed to 21 American colleges and universities stated:

Recently there has been a considerable growth of motels near college campuses. Have you had occasion to be in the room of such a motel alone except for the presence of one member of the opposite sex?   YES ___ NO ___

Somewhat less than half of all the male and female respondents answered "yes" to the question of being in a motel alone with a member of the opposite sex. For both men and women, those who had ever experienced coitus were considerably more likely to check "yes" (more than half) than did those who had never experienced coitus (about one third).

A number of students properly set us straight by pointing out that the fact they had been in such a situation did not mean they had been involved in any intensive form of sexual activity. (In fact the person of the opposite sex could have been a brother or sister.) A girl at the Midwestern Protestant University said, "Staying in a motel overnight with the boy I love was one of the richest experiences I have ever encountered—*no sex involved.*"

And a girl at a state university in the Upper South mentioned that some fraternities there rent motels for a beach weekend, and she indicated that this, in terms of pressure, can become a bit awkward.

A few students in commenting on the question said in effect, "Who needs motels?"

CHAPTER 3

The Bombardment of Sensual Stimuli

"I actually think young couples are pressured into sex today because of what they think everybody else is doing, what they see on television, in the movies, and what Madison Avenue promotes. I am not alone in these thoughts." Coed at a private university in New York City, in responding to the College Survey.

Another element of the new environment for sexual awakening and maturing that must be taken into account is a greatly increased sensual content. This escalation has been so gradual and all-pervasive that we often overlook its impact. We may forget, for example, that television didn't exist as a popular medium a quarter-century ago. The youngster today who is graduated from high school has already spent about 15,000 hours watching television, according to the director of the Center for Communications, Fordham University. Marshall McLuhan, communications theorist at Fordham, suggests that recent changes in communications are producing a new "invisible" environment with profound implications for almost every aspect of society, and are contributing to the generational gulf.

One definition of "sensual" is: "connected or preoccupied with bodily or sexual pleasure." Younger people today—whether they are teeny-boppers or older youths approaching adulthood—are bombarded from all sides with varying types of sensual stimuli. These come not only via communications media, but via new social customs.

These younger people are exposed to more frequent and more explicit depictions of uninhibited sexual behavior and are pressed to be preoccupied with sexual enticement and encouraged to cultivate a wild look. At the same time, there is a greater frankness about sex, which quite probably is healthy. But on balance the sensual content—approaching saturation —of their living environment is vastly greater than it was a quarter-century ago, and the possible impact of the bombardment of stimuli must be taken into account. A book could be written on each source of the stimuli. Here we will simply indicate, by noting the sources, the pervasiveness of the bombardment and some possible impacts.

The flickering stimuli of cinema and television. Consider the increased exposure of young people to depictions of sexual play. By the age of once-"sweet" 16 the average U.S. girl has seen depicted on motion picture or television screens several hundred demonstrations of how erotically aroused males and females embrace. And at the least this 16-year-old girl has seen a dozen illustrations of how a female behaves when she is about to have, is having, or has just had sexual intercourse.

Millions of teenagers have seen Sophia Loren disrobing to music in preparation for a coupling that the story line suggests is obviously about to occur. They have seen in *Alfie* or *Darling* or *Tom Jones* the male or female star moving gaily from one seduction scene to another. When they see these depictions at their neighborhood theaters, with money given to them by their parents, and after reading rave notices of the shows by distinguished critics, should we be surprised if they conclude that their parents take an indulgent, if unstated, view toward out-of-wedlock sexuality? (Assuming they haven't been specifically counseled to the contrary by their parents.)

In the making of motion pictures consider how things have changed since Leslie Howard, in his famous bedroom scene a few decades ago with Norma Shearer in *Romeo and Juliet,* was required to keep his feet on the floor. During the 1930s one sensational breakthrough toward boldness occurred in the film *Ecstasy* when Hedy Lamarr delicately suggested by an arm movement the completion of intercourse. In the 1940s much of the motion-picture competition was based upon showing more and more cleavage in the feminine bodice. Today such competition is pretty well passé in the movie theaters. Women often are seen bare to the waist, or entirely nude. Young people can see violent rape scenes as in *The Virgin*

Spring. They are given a clear impression of a woman masturbating in *The Silence*. In *La Vista* they see an intoxicated suitor pawing at the heroine's breasts and thighs. In *Boeing-Boeing* they see the male star comfortably established in an apartment with three airline hostesses who, because of their staggered schedules, assume they are the undivided target of his courtship. In *I, A Woman,* they may see a young actress purportedly undergoing several orgasms. They could see, in early 1968, a widely hailed film, *Closely Watched Trains,* which is a comedy about a young man wrestling with his problem of premature ejaculation. More to the point of our interest, perhaps, most of the young females of the movie were depicted as being not only willing, but eager for casual coital encounters.

In *A Stranger Knocks* they see sexual intercourse pretty specifically depicted. And in the stunningly beautiful picture *Blow Up* they see, in what some might consider to be scenes extraneous to the plot, a man and a young woman obviously in the midst of intercourse . . . and two nude girls trying to tear the clothes off the male star and in the process, at least in some uncensored versions, see a flash of the pubic hair of one of the girls. During the 1960s there have been comedies based on premarital pregnancy and movies in which the dialogue includes such picturesque phrases as "screw you!" and "hump the hostess."

Some newspapers have been trying to offer movie-goers, and particularly parents, some guidance on the "acceptability" of pictures playing at local theaters for various age groups. When I was in Wichita, Kansas, in 1967, *The Wichita Beacon* listed appraisals of 10 pictures, then showing locally, that had been evaluated by The Film Estimate Board, by *Parents Magazine,* and by the Legion of Decency. Out of the 10 pictures available in the city that Saturday afternoon only 1 was agreed to be acceptable for viewers of all ages. Six of the 10 were listed as objectionable for "young people," as well as for children. We strolled by a local theater showing a film considered by all three rating agencies as objectionable for young people as well as children. The lobby was swarming with young people and children. Apparently neither the young people, their parents, nor the theater took the ratings very seriously. On the other hand, in Texas a motion-picture trade organization has charged that the voluntary classification of films as "adult" was hurting business.

At a city in southern Ohio, school officials and parents became sufficiently concerned about the number of 10-year-old boys and girls passionately necking and petting under the trees of the schoolyard to hold a conference. Investigators have been finding that physical attraction is not entirely absent between young males and females during the latent prepuberty years; but the parents and school officials in this Ohio city were more inclined to surmise that the children were just acting out the grand passion they had recently been seeing on the screens of neighborhood theaters featuring *Thunderball* and other James Bond movies.

Most metropolitan U.S. areas have in addition to their neighborhood-type theaters one or more picture houses offering a constant diet of "exploitation films" such as *Body of a Female*. In 1967 one maker of such pictures acknowledged that nudity alone was no longer enough to attract crowds, "so we go in for violence and orgies. Orgies are very good."

In 1968 a national TV network spokesman acknowledged that in the past year the use of suggestive TV programs had accelerated.

The new explicit stimuli of song and dance. Songs heard over radio and jukeboxes and sung by millions of teenagers had such lively titles as "Sock It to Me Baby" and "Let's Spend the Night Together." They heard laments in "Too Bad, Little Girl" about the girl who failed in romance purportedly because she had not gone all the way.

The new modes of dancing in the late 1960s might reasonably be expected to reduce male shyness. To fast music the young ladies by the millions were performing modulated bumps and grinds before their male escorts. And to slow music the partners frequently wrapped both arms around each other to achieve a snug pelvis-to-pelvis fit and then swayed, somewhat as in the act of intercourse.

At a number of U.S. colleges, pajama dances became popular. In the Chicago-Milwaukee area some of the college students favored toga dances in which the male and female partners were dressed only in sheets. At some Eastern men's schools, including Yale, there has been a vogue at pajama dances to drag mattresses up to the edge of the dance floor and loiter or roll with partners of the opposite sex between dances.

The stepped-up erotic content of published materials. The kind of erotica that in earlier decades was discreetly placed on the top shelves of news stores now dominates the display cases of many hundreds of newsstands and carries such titles as *Lust Jungle* and *Lust Teen*. Newsstands in San Francisco, or many of them, featured a periodical called *Midnight*, whose front page was devoted entirely to the headline: SIXTY DOLLAR OPERATION THAT RESTORES YOUR VIRGINITY.

By the mid-1960s there was so much emphasis on obscenity and bizarre depictions of sexual relationships in U.S. fiction that the treatment of sex was taking on a depressive quality, and some were speculating that perhaps some sort of exhaustion of bold themes might produce a shift in handling the dramatization of sexual encounters.

New advances in the unveiling of the female body. Many have watched with mounting fascination in the past decade the increasing exposure or delineation of female flesh in everyday attire.

A leading historian of female fashions, James Laver, the curator of the Victoria and Albert Museum in London, points out that in the past century the erogenous zone in women's fashions has shifted from the waistline to the bosom to the fanny to the ankle to the nape of the neck to the knee to the navel and to the underarm.

At the turn of the century males were excited by the sight of a well-turned ankle. But it has been some decades since the woman's ankle has even been noticed. By the 1960s designers were hard put to find areas of the female body that had not been featured in their designs. Possibly the emergence of mass media has forever eliminated the possibility of making an erogenous zone of the ankle. Fashion designers have found that the surest way to get their new designs published is to expose new areas of the female body—or present the female body in a bizarre new setting.

During the 1965–67 period the focus shifted away from the bosom (which has long fascinated American males more than

males in most other parts of the world) and put the focus on
the female leg. Thus we had the miniskirts and microskirts—
with the highest hemlines that had been seen on civilized
Western human females in recent centuries for everyday wear
—and the trend to tight pants. Many of these slacks, also
apparently for the first time in recorded history, detailed the
female fanny in all its contours and crevices, thanks to one
marvel of technology, stretch pants. Subsidiary trends (not
involving the focus on the leg) were dresses with peekaboo
holes, feminine underwear that could double as streetwear,
and dresses with sufficient plunge in front to put the focus
on the navel, or in the rear to put the focus on the beginning
of the cleavage of the buttocks. In 1968 one designer was
featuring a blouse to be worn without bra which, it was
promised, people could "see through." Also by 1968 there
were signs that some leading fashion designers were swinging
the focus back toward the bosom (and trying to drop the
hemline drastically as a way to make obsolete the tens of millions of miniskirts they had encouraged females to buy).

On the beaches first of Europe then of the U.S.A. the
bikini which first dazzled males was becoming so common-
place that a bikini by itself was no longer sufficient to attract
the male eye. In terms of the development of sex attraction
between males and females, however, the bikini continued to
play an innovative role. It greatly broadens the area of the
female body where it is permissible to engage in casual petting,
even in public. One of the unadvertised features of sun creams
—often suggested by advertising—is that they permit the male
and female companions, under the excuse of helpfulness in
applying lotion, to caress at least 95 percent of each other's
bare bodies in public.

While I was traveling from Greece to Italy on a Yugoslav
freighter, a group of Austrian girls and young men of late
high-school age came aboard with nominal chaperonage. They
seemed to have no particular place to sleep except the decks.
One day as I cruised, a lad and girl decided that the likeliest
space on the deck for them to relax was a space about three
feet from my chair. They put down a blue air mattress. Soon
they were entwined. This was in daylight. The girl was in a
bikini and the boy was in trunks. She had one of her bare
legs thrown up over his bare legs. He had his right arm
drooped across her bare stomach. What impressed me most

was that as they nestled and fondled each other, she kept snapping bubble gum out of her mouth.

The promotion of the dissolute look. An aspect of recent feminine fashion trends that may well be affecting the male-female relationship has been the resolute straining for an uninhibited look. The pioneering fashion designer Rudi Gernreich put the change in these words: "Twenty years ago a young girl was supposed to look sweet and innocent, but that ideal no longer applies. Before they are 17 years old they cultivate a wild, consciously sexy look." (In 1967 the word "wild" was being used to sell such diverse teen products as hit tunes and soda pop.) Gernreich added that this wild look was supposed to be very unnerving to the male. Certainly it might help make the shy male less shy about making advances.

The massive promotion of the sexually provocative body. The personal-enhancement industry has been insistently advising young females that their personal success in life is measured by their effectiveness in inspiring passes from males. And these—it is suggested—are directly related to the olfactory or visual allure a girl achieves by employing advertised products. And the boy is urged to beef up his pass-making power with girls by using the advertised scents.

By the mid-1960s some of the ads for scents were quite explicit in what they offered to both the male and female user. The producers of Aztec, a toiletry for males, published three pictures of a male and female in suggestive poses, and the pictures were labeled "Before," "During," and "After." Fabergé disclosed in its advertising to young females that its bedtime perfume "Needs body warmth to release its fleuressence." The promoters of Piping Rock, an aftershave lotion, presented a girl with ruffled hair lying languidly in bed on her elbows speculating, "Was it him . . . or his Piping Rock?" Even toothpaste makers promise to give your mouth more sex appeal. An official of one product-development company confided to me that his company was embarked on a crash program to produce a spray for males that really seemed to be effective in breaking down female inhibitions.

In 1964 a *Seventeen* magazine survey indicated that whereas in 1948 only 2 out of 10 girls were regular users of mascara, by 1964, 9 out of 10 were.

The change in buying habits by age emerged from a study conducted by consultant Eugene Gilbert, who specializes in the youth market. He reported that the 15-year-old girl in 1965 was buying the same kind of cosmetics that the 16½-year-old girl was buying a decade earlier.

All this commercial pressure to be provocative was raising questions about what was happening to the image of femininity for girls in general. Girls vary enormously, of course, in physique, brains, sex appeal, and potentialities for nurturing children, and yet in the United States all are expected to become sirens and sex objects. A Norwegian university student who had spent a year as a high-school exchange student in Illinois compared relations between teen-age boys and girls in Norway and Illinois by saying that in the United States "there is a tougher atmosphere. All girls have to come up to a certain beauty standard and to socialize."

David Mace, until recently Executive Director of the American Association of Marriage Counselors, has studied male-female relationships at first hand in more than 50 countries. He thinks something pretty unfortunate is happening in the U.S.A. to the image of the female. Mace explained:

"Our whole culture is involved in a serious confusion between femininity and sexuality. . . . The truly feminine woman does not project her sexuality. She is modest. It goes against her nature to project herself sexually . . . [yet] American males, being made to feel that there is a lack of femininity in their women, are demanding that they dress and behave in a more sexually provocative way. This is really an adolescent misconception of what femininity is. The radically provocative woman is often the very opposite of feminine."

Encouraging all young females to strive to be *femmes fatales* quite probably is diverting many of them from the notion that fulfillment in life will come through achievement and good works—and destines them to become, later on, obsessive clock and wrinkle watchers. However, they don't seem to mind. We asked the women students in our College Survey:

Do you often wish you didn't have to spend so much time making yourself visually attractive to men?
YES ___ NO, I ENJOY THE EFFORT ___

About 80 percent said they enjoyed the effort, and girls in the International Sample responded in nearly the same proportion. A college girl in the surfing crowd of Southern California, where we made a special, small comparative sampling, offered this explanation of how the pattern works: "I spend much time making myself attractive. I am a girl and I must accept my half of the bargain, which is that the boy takes me out and pays for everything and I in return make myself attractive and try to be pleasing to him intellectually and physically."

Promoters of products to enhance sex appeal and enjoyment have been energetically at work in many countries in addition to the U.S.A. In Germany an enterprising businesswoman has developed a multimillion-dollar business, with several outlets, for her so-called sex supermarket. Her catalogue features such items as a tranquilizer designed to keep the male calm while awaiting his partner's escalation to passion . . . alleged aphrodisiacs for placing in cocktails, candy, and perfumes . . . and bath essences that promise to send "tender rays from heart to heart."

The pressures to be precocious in attracting the other sex. In considering the new incentives to experiment—as part of the changing environment in which sex attraction now develops—we should also note the lowered age at which young females and males are thrown into social contact with each other.

The great mobility of American families helps make many mothers anxious to assure that their daughters get noticed socially in the new areas into which they move. Girls are encouraged to date at younger ages than was true a quarter-century ago. Another possible cause of the trend is the increased amount of time that millions of mothers have today to be preoccupied with their daughters' social development. In many communities the mothers are getting up at PTA meetings to demand school dances at the fifth- and sixth-grade levels, and formal proms by the eighth grade. It is highly doubtful that such dances would be held if left to the youngsters, especially the males, who then may be shorter than their same-grade girls.

Mothers, too, tend to be secretly pleased if their daughters demonstrate they can win repeated invitations from the same boys at a fairly early age, because it offers not only proof of popularity, but assurance of escorts at important events. Market Researcher Eugene Gilbert has found that whereas a quarter-century ago only one 14-year-old girl in a thousand was going "steady," today one out of nine thinks she is "going steady."

What steadiness and precocity of dating among early teen-agers leads to has been documented by sociologist Winston W. Ehrmann in his fine study of dating behavior among students at a Southern university.[1] In his inquiry 841 male and female students recalled their early dating patterns (which had developed around 1950). He found that girls were much more likely to report dating at an early age than were boys. (Among girls 72 percent had dated by age 14.) And he observed, "Our data for both males and females show a very pronounced association between frequency of dating and sexual behavior. Those who dated frequently as compared with those who did not were much more sexually experienced. . . ." No girl who had dated frequently had by college stopped at the hand-holding stage, and college girls in reporting their current behavior were three times as likely to be having intercourse if they were going "steady" than they were if they were dating no one steadily.

It is not clear whether the American pattern of formal dating—with the boy calling for the girl and paying all expenses—produces more intimacy than the North European pattern of dating, where the young people meet in groups informally and usually on a "Dutch" basis. Probably not. There is evidence that the U.S. girls feel—and the boys expect —that if the boy spends money on his "date" he is entitled to a clear display of affection in return. On the other hand, formal dating does permit somewhat more parental surveillance over the girl's choice of boy friends. We asked students in our College Survey for their views on the merits of U.S.-style formal dating vs. European-style informal dating. The students in the U.S.A. and abroad were pretty evenly divided on the two types of dating. The one noticeable difference was that in virtually every country sampled, girls were more likely than males to favor an arrangement that made it easy for boys and girls to get together informally (rather than waiting to be asked).

The age at which dating occurs also seems to affect the

power pattern between male and female teenagers on dates. This interesting point was made by Wallace Fulton, past president of the Sex Information and Education Committee of the United States (SIECUS). He explained, "In the early teens the power rests largely with the boy in relationships between him and the girl because she is under pressure from her mother to do a lot of dating as proof of her attractiveness and popularity. This may get her into going steady as proof of her ability to attract males. Because of this the girl is under the power of the boy and he may say, 'We've been necking a while, let's start petting.' And she is scared that he will drop her and that her mother will be concerned. On the other hand in the late high school and early college years the power returns to the girl as she begins to get experience and the girl and boy can talk it out if one or both is concerned about intimacy."

A very popular girl at an Eastern women's college indicated in a remark that the quality of a girl's dating relationships often is affected by the age at which she begins dating. She had noticed that the girls who did relatively little dating during high school seemed to get a lot more fun out of their college dating than did the girls who had been in a social whirl all through high school.

The new vogues in adventure. Still another incentive for sexual experimentation in the new environment that deserves mention is the pressure to find new ways to prove one's daring which arises from the shrinking possibilities for adventure felt by many young people. David Boroff, while a professor at New York University, observed that "Sex is the last area of adventure in the quasi-welfare state in which we now live." There is often a straining to live dangerously or excitingly. Many very bright girls in the Northeast date dope addicts just for the thrill. At a number of campuses a seemingly new phenomenon is called "throwing a moon." In this a male student, when one or more female students are approaching, will quickly slip down his trousers and underwear and bend to present his bare buttocks. It is done in a flash and is aimed at shocking girls.

In the context of searching for adventure, perhaps we should note the very clear increase in use of stimulants by young people in the past quarter-century. There has, for example, been a substantial increase in drinking by people under the age of 21, despite some state laws.

Whether alcoholic intake promotes promiscuity between young people, however, is less clear. It is widely assumed that there is a relationship between drinking and sexual exploration, but certainly the relationship is not as direct as is widely assumed. Alcohol is a depressant and sedative when taken in substantial quantities. However, alcohol consumed in small-to-moderate quantities may remove inhibitions that prevent people, especially girls, from acting out desires for closeness that they may already feel. Boys who are afraid of sex may use liquor to loosen up. A high-school teacher in Connecticut heard girls discussing the fact that they liked to have boys drink because the boys were not so shy and stiff.

In our College Survey we sought to learn whether alcoholic stimulation was present at the time of first coitus for those students who indicated they had at some time in their life experienced intercourse. Two-thirds of all U.S. male and female students said they had not been drinking at the time of their first experience. About one in 8 indicated that one or both partners had been "under the influence" of alcohol at the time of first coitus. Possibly most significant was the fact that about 1 in 5 said they had had a drink or two but had felt the effect only mildly. This might lend support to the thesis that a modest amount of alcohol would not be a depressant and might loosen inhibitions.

In the International Sample the German, Norwegian, and English male students responded much as the U.S. students did, but the English girls indicated a substantially higher proportion had been drinking at the time of first coitus.

More than 40 percent had been drinking and fully a third of the English girls who had experienced coitus—and many in the sample had—said that one or both partners was "under the influence" of alcohol at the time.

A girl at a private university in California commented, "I have found that alcohol does not plant the idea of doing things, but it sure helps."

Reports from across the nation have indicated an increased use of marijuana (and some use of LSD, which apparently is genetically dangerous) among college students, with indications that at some colleges at least one-fifth of the student body has at one time experimented with "pot." This again may represent a search for adventure, but as with alcohol there is no clear evidence that it serves to stimulate sexual experimentation. Heavy users of marijuana are said to be uninterested in physical intimacy. *The New York Times* quoted one college woman in New York as saying, "I have control with pot. If I drank I might go to a party and go home and go to bed with someone. It has happened. But never with pot." The kind of person who would experiment with pot might also be the kind who would experiment with sex. Sexologists report that LSD, on the other hand, definitely produces a loss of inhibition. And there have been a number of reports that Methedrine tends either to enhance or depress interest in sexual intimacy.

These then are some of the new ways that younger people are subjected to sensual stimuli to a degree never known in recent history. Conceivably as individuals become more jaded they will be attracted to a more reticent style of life. A student at Wesleyan who had been vastly stimulated during his sophomore year when his fraternity staged a pajama dance explained that by his senior year he had concluded that pajama dances "were not all that great." Still this barrage of stimuli will apparently continue and will be a part of the preparation for life of each new girl and boy passing through adolescence.

Now let us turn to a third element in the new environment for sexual maturing that must be considered, the wilderness of counsel today about what constitutes reasonable behavior outside marriage with members of the other sex.

CHAPTER 4

The Disarray in Moral Concepts

"No one system of sex values is currently accepted in theory or in practice by the great majority of Americans." Lester Kirkendall, professor of family life, Oregon State University.

In 1967 a television network in the United States presented a long documentary on the state of sexual morality among young people. Afterward the sharp-witted television critic Harriet Van Horne commented that certain of the adult experts who participated offered an unimpressive performance. She added, "If they served no other purpose, though, they provided a clue to what has induced the mild but unmistakable moral anarchy that pervades so many campuses today." She noted that nowhere was there any hint of a "strong moral presence." In fairness perhaps she should have added that anyone taking a position of "strong moral presence" in the late 1960s could assume he would be shot at by some expert sharpshooters of a different viewpoint. On the same program a coed at the University of Michigan observed that "There is nobody saying 'no.'"

A recent public-opinion poll of Americans found that two-thirds of the persons polled felt sexual moral standards somehow are becoming "worse" than they were a generation ago.[1] (Intimacy outside marriage is of course just one aspect of sexual morals.)

Perhaps it might be well if we review very briefly how we arrived at our present state of disarray regarding what constitutes appropriate behavior as far as premarital intimacy is concerned.

Human attitudes toward premarital intimacy of young males and females have varied considerably from era to era, and from society to society—and almost constantly have been a matter of concern for civilized peoples.

Primitive people have tended to take a permissive attitude. George P. Murdock's cross-cultural study of more than 100 societies around the globe turned up evidence that about 70 percent of the societies tended to be indulgent about premarital coitus.[2] Advanced societies, however, have almost unanimously at some stage in their development taken a sterner view of full intimacy before marriage.

David and Vera Mace, family specialists, in analyzing the strong emphasis placed on chastity of the bride in most Eastern nations suggest that one motivation for this is a desire by the fathers for insurance that the quality of their family seed remain unadulterated.[3] Another thought that supported chastity was the suspicion that what a girl could do before marriage she might do after marriage, and so contaminate the seed.

Christianity placed a very strong emphasis upon both marital fidelity and premarital chastity. The moral life was seen as strongly associated with restraint in all physical intimacies, but especially those outside the institution of marriage.

This viewpoint has been especially persistent in Catholic teachings. Alan W. Watts, philosopher and student of the world's religions, notes that in one fairly recent summary of the compendia of Catholic moral theology 44 pages were devoted to a discussion of the various categories of sin, of which 32 pages, in fine print, are occupied with sexual sins.[4]

G. M. Carstairs, professor of psychological medicine at Edinburgh University, characterized the general traditional Christian position by saying, "In our religious traditions the essence of morality has sometimes appeared to consist of sexual restraint."

In North America, concern about premarital continence, at least for respectable women, has always been strongly stressed until quite recent times, though with mixed success. During the 18th century, engaged couples frequently were required to confess to their minister whether they had ever committed fornication; and the records of the Groton Church, Groton, Mass., indicate that in a listing of 200 engaged couples 66 of them (or 33 percent) had confessed to fornication.[5]

Judgments are necessarily subjective, but some observers believe the chastity ideal became considerably stronger in the 19th-century Victorian period (in both North America and England) than it was in the earlier 17th-century Puritan period. By the Victorian period a good woman was not supposed even to be interested in the sexual aspect of her life, and some to prove it boasted of their frigidity. Max Lerner, the historian, has suggested, as one explanation, that as people became less certain of the old religious certitudes, their first reaction was to impose more rigid moral codes. Others suggest the long, hard challenge of taming and industrializing a new continent was a factor. At any rate the good woman went onto the pedestal. Meanwhile, for many Victorian males, the prostitute was serving her traditional function of helping preserve the virtue of the good women of the community.

The proscription of overt expression of sexuality among respectable people in the Victorian era did not of course mean that sexual feelings disappeared. Some suggest, in fact, that sexuality in sublimated form was more evident. Alan Watts points out that in the Victorian era women's fashions did everything to accentuate the feminine body "in the very act of covering it from neck to toe in veritable straitjackets of tweed, flannel and boned corsetry." Even chairs, tables and household ornaments were suggestively bulged and curved. He added that the legs of furniture were often "so obviously thighs or calves that squeamish housewives made the resemblance all the stronger by fitting them with skirts."

This highly stylized pattern of life of the Victorians began crumbling during World War I and its aftermath. The war with its upheaval not only disrupted the elaborate network of controls over behavior, but brought hundreds of thousands of American males into contact with people, including women, in foreign lands. (To this day a great many Americans and Britons have an image of the French girls as being free, hot, uninhibited lovers.) Americans speak of tongue-kissing as "French kissing," and many Englishmen call their sheaths or condoms "French letters." Much of France's reputation for free love, I suspect, derives from the fact that millions of young, homesick American and British males encountered some of France's less inhibited girls while on leave to Gay

Paree during World War I and World War II—and embroidered their encounters when they got home. My research indicates that any reputation French girls in general have for premarital promiscuity is underserved. The French as a people are considerably more attached to the chastity ideal than either the Americans or the English, and considerably more inhibited about discussing sexual matters openly.[6]

In any case, World War I and its aftermath marked the abrupt end of Victorian-type inhibitions, especially in the United States. Advocates of free love were able to get their views widely discussed. Girls shingled their hair, lifted their hemlines from ankle to knee, took up smoking, and helped give their generation the label "flaming youth." The decade saw a dramatic change in both attitudes and behavior regarding premarital sexual intimacy. Along with the upheaval created by the war there were a host of other influences for change, and the continued weakening of the religious belief that sinners who violated the sex code might roast in a very real Hell.

The great change in sexual attitudes since 1920 was also substantially encouraged by several individuals. Their research did much to unsettle traditional concepts and weaken the old external controls over sexual behavior.

First of all in this century there was Sigmund Freud. In his work with emotionally disturbed patients he had seen sexual instincts as motivating much of human activity. At one point he wrote, "We have found it impossible to give our support to conventional morality [which] demands more sacrifices than it is worth." And at other points he concluded that a basic cause of much of the world's neurosis was repressed sexuality.

His disciples and popularizers helped spread throughout the world the inference of this, namely that the way to be emotionally healthy and to be rid of crippling inhibitions was to express our sexual instincts freely. (Widely overlooked was the fact that he modified and clarified some of his views over the decades and that he came to be cited also by proponents of sexual restraint. It is of passing interest that in his personal life Freud was patriarchal, puritanical, a man with an apparently mild sex drive who voluntarily put an end to the physical aspect of his sexual life at about the age of 40.[7])

Another remarkable individual who did much to transform our attitudes toward our sexuality was Alfred Kinsey. (It has always been a source of gratification to me that I became acquainted with this eminent scientist and was able to make a couple of very small contributions to his research.)

The publication of the massive findings of Kinsey and his associates at the Institute for Sex Research on the sexual behavior of the human male and human female had a very considerable liberating effect on the public's attitude toward sexuality. This unfettering effect was a major contribution to mental health, as well as to knowledge of ourselves. His principal associates in this vast venture were Wardell B. Pomeroy, Clyde E. Martin, and Paul H. Gebhard.

A biologist by training, Kinsey was careful in his studies to measure only the measurable. Thus he put the main emphasis upon the sexual "outlets," however attained, of the thousands of males and females interviewed; and he tried to avoid any assessment of the quality of the male-female relationships. He scorned those who tried to place moral evaluations upon sexual acts he found to be practiced by a great many people. Perhaps also because of his background as a biologist he took a naturalistic view of sexual behavior: the way things are in real life is probably the way they ought to be. Thus he was not particularly in sympathy with much of the endeavors by the society of his day to regulate individual sexual activity. All this was interpreted by many people as putting him on the side of permissiveness.

A third individual researcher who undoubtedly has been having a substantial impact in changing sexual attitudes is William H. Masters. He and his associate, Virginia E. Johnson, spent several years at their laboratory in St. Louis making color motion pictures of adult human males and females in the act of copulating and masturbating. Masters' findings, while illuminating at several points (and of considerable interest to specialists in sexology) do not compare in importance with those of Freud or Kinsey. However, his research methods —carefully assessing physiological reactions of married and unmarried humans undergoing orgiastic experiences—tended to startle and fascinate millions of people (and to appall not a few).

From Freud to Kinsey to Masters the emphasis of the research moved ever further away from the quality of sexual relationships (with their components of affection, love, and fidelity) to emphasis upon the nature of the physiological release. (All three men came from backgrounds of medicine or biology. Masters is a specialist in obstetrics and gynecology.) The tendency, finally climaxed by Masters, to see sexual activity primarily in physiological terms drew some sharp dissents from some scientists. Leslie H. Farber, as chairman of the Association of Existential Psychology and Psychiatry, was inspired by the Masters research to suggest in 1964 that some scientists in their preoccupation with physiology were forgetting "the duality previous centuries knew: namely that the body is both a natural object and not a natural object." Forgetting this, he said, many sexologists and psychoanalysts were claiming "the erotic life as their exclusive province, removing it from all the traditional disciplines, such as philosophy, religion and literature which had always concerned themselves with sex as human experience. . . . Qualities such as modesty, privacy, reticence, abstinence, chastity, fidelity, shame—could now be questioned as rather arbitrary matters which interfered with the health of the sexual parts."[8]

The interest in reducing sexual behavior to measured form, as exemplified by Masters, inspired at least one psychologist to try to develop formulas that described male-female interaction. Robert L. Karen, a San Diego psychologist, produced a paper in 1959 entitled "Some Variables Affecting Sexual Attitudes, Behavior and Inconsistency." A reader soon encountered such statements as the following:

"Both men and women engage in the more serious types of sex play as the type of dating involvement increases. The men, however, are significantly more liberal in their actual conduct particularly for the first few dates (NoK, N, PAW-PBW, SI $X^2 = 16.22$ 3df, p< 1 percent), frequent and continuous dating (NoK, N., PAWPBW, SI, $X^2 = 14.62$ 3df, p < 1 percent), and going steady (KN, PAW, PBW, SI, $X^2 = 15.62$, 3df, p< 1 percent) . . ."

It is only by a search of the author's footnotes that one discovered that "No" meant nothing, "K" meant kissing, "N" meant necking, "PAW" meant petting above the waist, "PWB" meant petting below the waist, etc.

In the past two decades the professionals in family life education, sex education, and marriage counseling, and the authors of textbooks dealing with sex behavior have come increasingly from scientific disciplines where they got their graduate training in sociology, psychology, psychiatry, or (to a lesser degree) anthropology. The public looked to them for insights and guidance. These professionals in their systematic investigations have greatly broadened human knowledge and insight. But they also often found themselves analyzing situations where values and morals had long played a predominant role. What should their attitude be to values and morality? Issues of "right" and "wrong" behavior are particularly bothersome to scientists. One school of sociologists argues that their discipline must be value-free to be scientific. Many scientists felt that their only reasonable role was to suggest what seemed to be functional at that particular moment for that particular human group. Whether what was functional might be perceived as good or bad was something for moralists to argue about.

Some scientists, drawing upon their training, suggested that any behavior should be judged simply by whether it conformed to the group's norms and would thus escape the consequences of negative group sanctions. (If we apply this reasoning to the young go-go-go sensation-seekers widely evident in the 1960s, we would have to conclude that they were indeed conforming to their group's norms, not encountering any negative sanction from people important to them—and thus were behaving appropriately.)

The dilemma on values became most visible when scientists trained to be "objective" and dedicated to being value-free were moving into "helping professions." Their job and their duty was to offer guidance to people—often young people—puzzled or troubled about issues involving male-female relations—including physical intimacy—that had in the past been deeply enmeshed in value judgments.

One of the most respected figures in family research, Harold T. Christensen of Purdue University, has sought to bring order to conflicting viewpoints on this seeming dilemma with a number of analyses of the problem of values. He points out that while scientists properly should be concerned with *what is* rather than *what ought to be,* it is impossible for a scientist to separate himself entirely from values. The scientist should be honest enough to try to keep separate his "citizen-self" and his "scientist-self." And he should recognize that in family research people's beliefs and values are "important data" to be considered, since they inevitably color behavior. He suggests that the task of the scientist is not to set up or affirm a moral system but rather to try to identify *cause-and-effect relationships* which might help all citizens in choosing guidelines for moral decision.[9]

Still some strive to remain utterly value-free while filling a helping role with the public, or they may let personal values color their professional counsel. And some in facing the problem seem to find it tempting to take a highly permissive stance.

Mary Calderone, the delightfully articulate Executive Director of SIECUS, recounted in 1966 an evening she had just spent in a Midwestern city with a half-dozen leading family-life specialists, most of whom were well known for the liberality of their views regarding sexual behavior before or after marriage. As those sexual liberals talked she noted that in their own lives they had deeply committed marriages. In talking of their own marriages there was a feeling of cherished values and deep commitment at work in their relationships at home. She asked them, "Do you make this sense of commitment clear to your students?" Most of them indicated that they did not. She asked them why not and recalls that their answers mostly added up to the idea that they didn't like to sound authoritarian. She suggested that if they believed in commitment and did not convey it they were being poor advocates of something they believed in. Some indicated she might have a point.

While the overall trend of objective professional opinion was, for whatever reasons, toward greater permissiveness, there was little consensus. Professionals with equally impressive scientific training were taking public positions on what was appropriate sex behavior that ranged from radical to traditional. A person seeking insight or guidance had available, in fact, a smorgasbord of expert opinions to choose from on what now constituted appropriate sex behavior, especially premarital behavior.

Isadore Rubin, editor of *Sexology,* sought to find some order in the great variety of sharply conflicting positions being taken, in the absence of consensus, and in 1964 tried to cite the principal viewpoints in a paper presented at the annual meeting of the National Council on Family Relations.[10]

He isolated six positions along a repressive-permissive continuum (and they did not exhaust the schools of thought).

Here are his "six major conflicting value systems of sex existing side by side in this transitional period of morality":

1. *Traditional repressive asceticism.* Rubin described this as still the basis of most of our official codes and laws. It proscribes any kind of sexual activity outside of marriage and firmly links sex to procreation.

2. *Enlightened asceticism.* In his view this is exemplified by the views of such authorities on the male-female relationship as David Mace, recent president of SIECUS. He points out that Mace takes a positive attitude toward sex and welcomes debate but tends to link coital behavior by young people with "softness" and unhealthy self-indulgence. Mace, he explained, sees youth as a time when invaluable lessons of self-control and discipline must be learned, with sex as one of the supreme areas in which self-mastery may be demonstrated.

3. *Humanistic liberalism.* Here he pointed to family-life specialist Lester Kirkendall as a leading opponent of "inflexible absolutes" who is instead concerned primarily with the *quality* of the *relationship* between the persons experiencing any particular act. It is not the commission or omission of the act, but the consequences on the interrelationships of people that should count.

4. *Humanistic radicalism.* This viewpoint, in Rubin's view, was best reflected by a veteran psychiatrist and marriage counselor, Walter Stokes, who also puts emphasis on the quality of the relationship but hopes that with proper "cultural engineering" in the future young people can enjoy relatively complete sex freedom. (Stokes made it clear to me, however, that unlike some radicals he believes that males and females usually want warmth and love to accompany their sexual activities.)

5. *Fun morality.* The most conspicuous spokesman here, Rubin suggested, was Albert Ellis, head of the Institute for Rational Living. In the view of Ellis, sex should be seen as fun, and the more sex fun a person has, the sounder he will be psychologically. Ellis feels premarital intercourse should be freely permitted and even at times encouraged for well-informed, reasonably well-adjusted persons.

Ellis has been conducting his Institute for Rational Living in a New York building that one of his critics has called a "Six-Story Palace to Permissiveness." It is in an exclusive area just off Fifth Avenue. He holds or supervises classes and seminars for laymen and professionals. In a 1967 speech to the American Psychological Association he contended that "healthy adultery can help some marriages." Ellis has termed efforts to preserve chastity until marriage an "overt display of errant masochism." And he coined the phrase "sex fascist" to refer to those people who arbitrarily believe that certain values, in terms of human behavior, are superior to others. In one debate on sex morality between Ellis and David Mace, Mace pointed out that if Ellis in an earlier century had made statements he had made during their debate, he would have been thrown in a dungeon. Instead of that, Mace chided good-naturedly, "you're on the crest of the wave. Everybody wants to hear your daring, avant-garde philosophy."

In England a longtime advocate of a position close to the "fun morality" defined by Rubin might be psychiatrist Eustace Chesser, who states, "If premarital sexual intercourse is the result of mutual desire, frankly acknowledged, without pretense or false promises, it needs no further justification."[11]

6. *Sexual anarchy.* Rubin pointed here to the late French jurist René Guyon as a conspicuous advocate. Guyon attacked chastity, virginity, and monogamy and called for the outlawing of all antisexual taboos and the wiping out of all ideas that connect sexual activity with notions of immorality.

(Rubin might have also mentioned here, perhaps, an amiable, controversial educator in England, A. S. Neill, long director of Summerhill, the ultra-progressive school that has sixteen affiliated schools in the U.S.A. Neill has advocated heterosexual play in childhood and has stated, "When children have no moralistic training in sex, they reach a healthy adolescence." He added that "Every older pupil at Summerhill knows from my conversation and my books that I approve of a full sex life for all who wish one, whatever their age." He stated that it gave him a bad conscience that he did not distribute contraceptives to students but that to do so would cause the school to be closed down by authorities.)[12]

All the stating of bold, conservative, and intermediate positions on what is appropriate in sex behavior in the U.S.A. and abroad—viewpoints ranging from sex is sin to sex is fun—by adult authorities is unquestionably a necessary phase in man's groping with his new condition. But for the moment all the groping has, as Dr. Rubin points out, placed youth in an "extremely difficult predicament."

There is a wide choice of behavioral styles, a notable absence of generally accepted guidelines, and a bewildering variety of counsel.

A German girl, in responding to our College Survey, indicated she was unhappy to be approaching maturity in such an environment. She explained:

"Many of the conventional norms, principally those of the church under which many young people grow, produce many guilt complexes. That was my own experience. However, I feel that the greater psychological danger is in a normless society."

Meanwhile we were seeing—in addition to changes in the environment for sexual awakening and maturing—other dramatic changes in the environment and relationships of males and females. We will look at some of these in the next section.

II. The Shifting World of the Sexes

CHAPTER 5

The New Look in Young Males and Females

"Sometimes someone walks by you and you wonder from the smell if it's a man or woman." A girl shopping in a New York department store, quoted by *The Wall Street Journal*.

A number of historians have suggested that fashions in grooming in any particular period say a good deal about the mood of the people involved. If that is correct, historians will ponder for centuries the abrupt, dramatic changes in grooming that came over younger males and females in the 1960s.

The strenuous efforts of the fashion industry to create styling obsolescence might account for some of the change. And the whims of homosexual designers could not be overlooked. Still the changes were so widely embraced and so bizarre when judged by concepts of appropriateness that have prevailed for most of the preceding century that one had to wonder whether the grooming changes are symptomatic of some fundamental shift in the identity of the sexes. Let us take a brief look at this grooming upheaval. Although etiquette no longer really requires it, I will take the ladies first.

James Laver, fashion historian who dates pictures by the clothing worn in them for London's Victoria and Albert Museum, contends that any good designer tries to express the collective psyche. When the female feels emancipated, there is a strong tendency to flatten her figure and shear off her hair. In cultivating a thin-hipped look, he feels, a woman is making an anti-family statement and saying that she no longer feels tied down. He feels today's women are trying to make some sort of statement about their attitude toward their femininity. Laver states, "We are at the end of a patriarchal system. Men no longer have to give the impression of being good providers by their dress, nor women of being good mothers and housekeepers."

Historian Barbara Tuchman, in commenting on contemporary fashions, complained that too many women were starting to look like Lolitas or lion-tamers. Angularity, long considered anti-feminine, was the rage in 1966-68, along with microskirts. Twiggy became a national heroine.

By the late 1960s, women by the millions were appearing at social functions in pants. Many were not just in cute slacks but in tailored trousers. Some girls in earlier decades have worn bloomers or knickers (just as in occasional periods in the past thousand years men have worn the equivalent of skirts), but never before in the history of the Western world had so large a proportion of women been wearing trousers. Fashion dictators eager for a new look certainly encouraged the trend. As early as 1965, the editor of *Vogue* was announcing, "The leg is *the* big fashion focus of the moment, and boots, patterned hose and pants express this but the pants will not disappear because they are extremely practical for women."[1]

The drive was not just to help free women physically, but to help them look like men. Stress was placed upon a lean or tough look. Hard or metallic fabrics or shiny plastic became popular. An editor of *Harper's Bazaar* announced, "There is a chic about women wearing men's clothing." Many of the more chic girls in fact were going to men's departments in stores or to Army and Navy stores to pick up their pants in order to have the real thing, not an imitation. Many young women were specifying that they wanted slacks with the male-type zipper leading up from the crotch rather than the once female-type zipper on the side. In the movie *Where the Spies Are* a girl is shown coming out of her dressing area into the room where David Niven awaits her. She is casually adjusting the zipper of her blue jeans as she approaches. Males have long been taught that such action in the presence of females constitutes inappropriate behavior.

In 1967 the maker of Captivator shoes for women advertised happily that his shoes were "blatantly boyish." The French fashion designer Yves St. Laurent produced for his new look in 1967 a woman wearing a trouser suit in gangster pin stripes, worn with shirt, vest, fedora, and open-toed clogs. At about the same time, chic New Yorkers were titillated by a report that a "female" in a raincoat shown in one of the current fashion magazines was actually the boy friend of the photographer. At a number of college campuses girls began buying aftershave lotion as perfume. In the choice of shoes, anthropologist Charles Winick points out, men have been moving to lighter, laceless, more pointed shoes at a time when women were moving to lower, square-toed, heavier shoes.

Identifying a person's sex often became difficult. In Duluth two adult companions and I in a car passed three teenagers in slacks. We could not agree how many of them were female. While standing in line for a ticket at the J.F.K. airport in New York, I saw ahead of me a young person who was wearing rough, unfinished cowboy boots, blue-jean pants, a blue-jean jacket. The person was smoking a cigarette and had shoulder-length hair. What was it? Eventually when the person turned to leave, I felt confident it was a female.

At a number of different public locations where I had time to kill, I reviewed the first hundred females coming into my line of vision who appeared to be between the ages of 14 and 40. Here were some highly impressionistic findings from each sampling of 100 females:

Cleveland, riding to airport in afternoon	67 females in pants
Beverly Hills shopping district, afternoon	58 females in pants
Greenwich Village, Saturday evening	35 females in pants
Stockholm boulevard, Sunday afternoon	33 females in pants
Denver theater district, Saturday afternoon	31 females in pants
Main Street, Mitchell, S.D., late afternoon	24 females in pants
Salt Lake City, entrance to Mormon-operated store, noon	8 females in pants

In Spain, Italy, and Argentina—all Latin countries where the male likes to consider himself the undisputed head of the family—native women in pants were a rarity.

Writer Helen Lawrenson has speculated about whether a normal man really wants as a mate a female who when strolling beside him is virtually indistinguishable from his kid brother. A related question that deserved investigation is what the modern male thinks when he finds himself dating a girl in slacks if he has aspirations to develop physical intimacy. At a number of colleges, girls have been wearing slacks not only to class but on dates. Slacks eliminate the need of the female to be dainty in her movement and so may have advantages for casual romping. But what is in the mind of the male? One question we asked just to the males in our College Survey was:

If you were dating a girl with whom you hoped to reach the petting stage or beyond, would it please you more if she was wearing: A DRESS ___,   SLACKS ___,   WOULD MAKE NO DIFFERENCE, REALLY ___.

About half of the U.S. males said it made no difference. But of those who had an opinion the males favored dresses over slacks by a margin of 2 to 1. Interestingly the preference for dresses increased with age. The males 23 years old or over with an opinion preferred dresses by a margin of nearly 4 to 1.

English and Norwegian male students were as emphatic as U.S. students in their preference for dresses. Only in Canada did the males find dress and slacks about equally preferable. As for comments:

• A male at the Ivy League university: "Some girls are squeamish about taking off slacks before they get turned on and, from an engineering standpoint it is easier to turn on a girl through panties than through slacks." But he still thought a girl wearing slacks could be just as appealing sexually as a girl wearing a dress.

• A male at the men's college in New England: "I am turned on more by girls in dresses generally. . . . For light petting definitely a dress. For petting limited to above the waist, probably a sweater and slacks offers the maximum in contact and the minimum in temptation."

• An Italian university male who happened to receive one of the checklists: "If the woman has slacks on, her more complete collaboration and decision is required."

Some have suggested that the dramatic change in feminine

garb in the past few years has not so much been anti-feminine as anti-conformist.

The spectacular change that took place in the grooming of young males during the 1960s was even more disconcerting to the older generation than changes in the female's appearance.

Males have tended to be sober in their apparel and extremely cautious about fashion changes for at least 150 years; yet in the 1960s the young males swung violently away from what had traditionally been deemed appropriate. They swung two ways:

• One trend was to cultivated sloppiness. There were the long, shaggy hair, the beards, the tattered sneakers or sandals, the grimy clothes.

In a lounge at a college in the Pittsburgh area I saw a boy and a girl on a sofa measuring the length of their hair. His was longer. And at a college in Colorado during a question-and-answer period after a talk, I made a mistake that apparently mortified me more than the student audience. A long-haired person fairly well back had a hand up, and I acknowledged by saying "Yes, ma'am?" When the person stood up so that I got a better look and addressed me in a baritone voice, I knew I had made an error in sexual identity.

While the long hair was commonly thought of by adults as effeminate, it actually was just startlingly different. Samson had a mane, and the legend is that he lost his manliness temporarily when Delilah slipped up and sheared it off. Long hair was a convenience on the U.S. frontier, where barbers were hard to find. And Lincoln grew a beard apparently because beards were then coming into vogue. What really perturbed thoughtful adults more than the long hair and untidiness were the slack jaw, softness, and slouch that many of the young males displayed—which were more flagrantly in defiance of traditional ideals of young manhood resolutely facing life.

• The other trend was to cultivate the dandified look. Much of the original pioneering for this came out of Swinging England, starting perhaps with the Beatles in their early phase. Many young Englishmen began wearing eyebrow makeup, transparent lipstick, billowy, satin shirts with floral patterns, fluffed-up hair, high-heeled boots, and lots of jewelry. One male musical group, The Pretty Things, had pink-dyed hair.

U.S. social critic Tom Wolfe, after looking over the young males garbing themselves on Carnaby Street, London, said it was as if, "suddenly mankind were bursting out of the tradi-tional old gray business sack suits like a bunch of randy roosters."

In the United States, a DuPont award for male fashion design went to a designer who came up with a velvet jump suit with ruffled shirt. Male models in skirt-like outfits began appearing in the U.S.A. and several other countries. Suits for men featuring broad hips and narrow shoulders were dis-played. A *New York Times* fashion reporter commented that the question whether or not the new male fashions were masculine didn't seem to bother people as much as it might have even a few years earlier.

Business was understandably fascinated with the U.S. male's new interest in grooming. The business journal *Forbes* reported at the end of 1966: "THE AMERICAN MALE IS START-ING TO SMELL LIKE THE AMERICAN FEMALE . . . he is turning past utilitarian things like aftershave lotions to the more feminine items like colognes, creams, hair coloring, even make-up . . . According to sales figures . . . the American male—not his wife, daughter or girlfriend—is now the hottest prospect for cosmetics. In fact, the annual volume of men's 'grooming aids' is close to $500 million: about three times what it was three years ago . . ." In 1967 at a convention of the National Hairdressers and Cosmetologists Association, Inc., demonstrations were presented on applying cosmetics to males (but you are not supposed to call it cosmetics). Men can now be sold, they were told, on highlights under the eyes to do away with circles, and creams that subdue five o'clock shadow. Major cosmetic companies began offering males lip guards, eye pads, pancake makeup, and creams to prevent rough, red hands.

There have been foppish human males, as well as males with manes, in previous centuries; but what did this abrupt swinging to both dandification and sloppiness in the 1960s signify?

Was it just restlessness . . . or alienation from the Establish-ment . . . or affluence . . . or women's influence . . . or a mass freaking out . . . or what? The merchandisers of apparel and lotions might be held partly responsible for the dandification, but hardly for the sloppiness. Los Angeles psychiatrist Ralph Greenson thought the tendency for young males and females to look alike stemmed from the fact that so many of them were afraid of the opposite sex and were actually seeking a twin, not a sweetheart. Others wondered if the wilder ventures in grooming were a symptom of the frivolousness of the times. Before the French Revolution, men in the courts were wearing rouge, embroidery, lace, and conspicuous jewelry.

The growing power of girl friends in influencing the grooming of males was also apparently a factor. In 1966 the magazine *In* for teen-age girls had a feature called "You're In If . . ." Among other things it offered readers these two tests of really being In:

". . . if your boyfriend is a real click and has long hair."
". . . if you and your boyfriend use matching colognes."

In 1967 *Ingenue* magazine also was advising its young feminine readers that the newest thing in teen-age togetherness was for steady-daters to smell alike. The president of the Mennen company, maker of toiletries, said in 1966 that the big question you ask about any new idea in his business is: "Will the girls like it?"

Two possible explanations for the male's shift in grooming behavior that seem particularly impressive both relate to modern problems of identity.

In an increasingly depersonalized, mobile world young males may be seeking visual or olfactory ways to attract attention to themselves. This is tending to make them narcissistic. While I was getting my hair cut in a Connecticut barber shop, it was invaded by teen-age males coming in after school for trims. Their dress was carefully sloppy. Most were in bare feet. They wore blue jeans and had their shirttails out. All had massive heads of hair in varying styles. As they waited their turn to get to a barber's chair they kept looking at themselves in the shop's mirrors, and several used their own pocket mirrors plus the shop's mirrors to get a better view of the backs of their heads. They primped with their combs in a way that is usually associated with femininity.

In Edgartown, Mass., a long-haired young man on summer vacation wandered into what had always been a female beauty parlor and asked if perchance he could get a new permanent wave in his now straggly hair. The feminine hairdresser, an old-fashioned type, quoted an exorbitant price and said that in any case she wouldn't handle it. He wandered out, visibly discouraged by the island's backward ways.

A more fundamental explanation may be a sensing by the males that traits and behavior long associated with robust masculinity are becoming less and less functional in modern society. There has been a shriveling of frontiers or plausible enemies to conquer or empires to build. It is possible that young males today are quite honestly searching for a new, more comfortable identity and have decided to defy the traditional masculine stereotypes regarding appearance.

A youth worker in Oslo, Norway, has concluded that the wearing of bangs by Scandinavian males represents a healthy or at least realistic trend. He suggests many young males find the he-man posture increasingly preposterous and are no longer afraid to let the softness in their natures manifest itself. There is a feminine component in all males, and there may seem to be no socially important reasons today to try to deny it. Family sociologist David Mace, who gave me this interpretation, found it impressive.

A year after hearing this provocative concept I came upon an analysis by English anthropologist Geoffrey Gorer that drew a somewhat similar but more startling conclusion. He suggested that young people nearly the whole world over had sensed a need to redefine the concepts of "a real man" and "a real woman" if we are not to destroy ourselves completely. He suggested that the long hair, dandified dress, and pleasantly epicene features that so infuriate their elders are a visible repudiation of the ideal of aggressive masculinity that has been traditional in recent generations.[2] Gorer suggested that these unconventional young people might well succeed in modifying both the value systems and the sex roles of their societies.

Certainly in our depersonalized, precarious world, masculine aggressiveness and thing-mindedness are traits that if vigorously applied could depress rather than enhance the human condition.

CHAPTER 6

The Young Female Questions the Extent of Her Liberation

"I am trying to develop some plan in life so that I won't feel pressured into marrying any creep that comes along."
A junior coed at a university in Colorado.

The thoughtful young female of the late 1960s, whether dressed demurely or like a booted lion-tamer, found herself with considerably more options open to her than the young female had a quarter-century ago. In fact, she had more options than the females of just about any era in recent centuries. And she had more options open to her than an equally intelligent male. Unless he was a complete drop-out from society, he still was expected to carve out some sort of career for himself. But she had the choice of working or not working, marrying or not marrying, working full-time or just part-time, working primarily for money, or working primarily for a sense of personal fulfillment. Still another option, if she had the assets, was that she could drift quite a few years occupying herself mainly with being a glamour girl.

If she was interested in riches, again she had more options than the male. As a Radcliffe graduate pointed out, a woman doesn't have to make money, she can marry it. Society is still scornful of the male who marries for money.

At first glance this young female of the late 1960s seemed indeed to be superbly situated. In the preceding quarter-century two changes involving the life role of females have been particularly dramatic. Females have substantially pushed forward their liberation from males. And they have developed a broad range of new skills (while many of their older skills withered from disuse). Sociologist Ira Reiss suggests that the role of women changed more in just one century than in all of the 50 preceding centuries.

During those 50 earlier centuries, it might be noted, virtually all the recorded history was recorded by males. Also during these centuries the tenets of most of the Western religions—as developed primarily by males—strongly suggested supernatural sanction for the subservience of woman. (St. Paul admonished, "Let your women keep silent in the churches, for it is not permitted unto them to speak.")

But increasingly women had begun to question the logic of their subservience. In the past century we saw the rise, decline, and a resurgence in a new form of feminism.

One important factor feeding feminist feeling was a change in what the home was all about. Vassar historian Carl N. Degler believes the feminist movement really began when men in factories began to take away women's traditional work.[1] It might also be noted that the feminists' first victories in obtaining the right to vote in the U.S.A. occurred almost entirely in the frontier states of the West, where the ratio of men to women was often more than 10 to 1. Women were prized and men gallantly gave them revolutionary prerogatives.

It is an interesting coincidence that nationally women got the right to vote in the United States in the same year that the sale of intoxicating liquors—which many women crusaded against—was prohibited, 1920. Men in those days did almost all the drinking, and used family funds to finance their pastime.

(Switzerland still hasn't given women the right to vote. Many of the Swiss women I talked with about this did not seem particularly aggrieved. One, an editor, explained that there are so many elections that men, when they go to the polls, usually do so because their wives tell them they should.)

In the United States suffrage was finally put across by the ferocious in-fighting of embattled women, many of them gallant idealists.

Historian Alan P. Grimes, of Michigan State University, in his 1967 study of the Puritan ethic and woman suffrage, advanced the interesting idea that the suffrage movement was seen by astute white Anglo-Saxon Protestant males, then dominant in U.S. society, as useful to their larger strategy of holding power and therefore encouraged it. This male Establishment, he argued, were greatly concerned about the sea of immigrants and liberated Negroes who were starting to vote in great numbers; and the Establishment calculated that giving women the right to vote would give it a longer lease on power. Their own kind of women would be the ones most likely to exercise their new right to vote.

I have tested this thesis by exploring the names and faces of many of the women most deeply involved during the 1913-1919 period in fighting for suffrage. The evidence suggests it would be somewhat unfair to imply that the women doing the battling in front of the White House and elsewhere were overwhelmingly Anglo-Saxon types. Among the women listed as being arrested at one time or another were Adelina Piunti, Jennie Bronenberg, Helen Chisaski, and Rose Fishstein. But a closer inspection suggests that perhaps such women may have been soldiers on the line. The leadership was overwhelmingly made up of women with Anglo-Saxon names.[2]

In any case, it soon became evident that women—once they had the vote—were not going to be wild-eyed radicals. If they had any impact at all, it was toward social stability and the protection of private enterprise. Perhaps it is no accident that the first three presidents elected after women got the vote were Warren G. Harding, Calvin Coolidge, and Herbert Hoover, all conservative Republicans.

During the 1920s, the decade of the flapper, the U.S.A. underwent its first dramatic break in loosening society's restraints upon intimacy between the sexes outside marriage. It would not be warranted, however, to connect this bursting out of uninhibited behavior directly with the emancipationists. Author Max Eastman, an early sexual liberal, advises me that he feels emancipation and sex freedom were two quite different movements. "Most of the emancipationists were noble, virtuous women," he says. The main impetus toward greater freedom in sexual behavior arose out of the profound shaking up of society in the aftermath of World War I, with urbanization, mobility, speakeasies, birth control, etc.

The younger feminists urging sex freedom and sex equality in the 1960s probably have more in common ideologically with the sex-freedom and sex-equality advocates of the 1920s (who are now in their seventies and eighties) than with intellectuals who underwent young adulthood in the 1930s, 1940s or 1950s. Male-female relationships moved back toward more traditional patterns during the three decades from 1930 to 1960. Perhaps the Depression, with a premium on breadwinners, was a factor in starting this reversal. Women's styles became more traditionally feminine.

During the 1940s and 1950s, feminism as a dynamic force in the world outside the home faltered. Women worked, but often with considerable guilt. A number of forces drove them to feel their proper place was in the home. Probably the fright of the atomic era had something to do with it. Then there was the massive impact of advertising, which glorified the little woman happily using her suds and appliances. And there was the affluence, which made the suburban station wagon, overflowing with children, seem like the ideal attainment.

We must not overlook, either, the impact of psychiatrists and psychoanalysts, who tend to be wedded to the idea that males and females are different and should stay different in their life roles. It was argued by some of them that women who had been crying for equality with males might be suffering from penis envy. Interestingly two of the most vehement spokesmen of the general viewpoint of stressing male-female differentiation were two women psychiatrists, Helen Deutsch and Marynia Farnham. Farnham argued that the more education a woman had, the greater the chance of sexual disorder and the damaging of children by maternal deprivation.

In the mid-1950s psychologist Nevitt Sanford and his colleagues after studying students at Vassar College became convinced that something akin to a "flight into femininity" had become common among college women.[3]

And in the early 1960s author Betty Friedan drew a wide audience with her warning to women that the popular and heavily promoted idea that fulfillment comes through being a happy homemaker was having a malignant, stultifying effect upon feminine potential and development.[4]

Sociologist Jessie Bernard, now at Washington University, has documented the fact that during the whole period from 1939 to 1959 there was a steady decline in the proportion of collegiate faculty members who were women and that those who were on faculties were less likely to be reformers at heart.

If thoughtful young women had not by the mid-1960s come

full circle from the earlier part of the century, they at least showed similarities to their grandmothers in their attitudes, including a new interest in self-assertiveness.

The new interest in careers by college graduates is attested to by Ethel Nash, former president of the American Association of Marriage Counselors. For quite a few years she has been conducting seminars in North Carolina for engaged couples. When she began these sessions 6 years ago, practically none of the engaged girls among the 12 couples was thinking of having a career. By 1964 virtually every engaged girl attending was planning a career. And there was no fiancé attending who did not want his wife to work after marriage.

While the early feminists wanted equality, the thoughtful young woman of the 1960s is more preoccupied with broadening her horizons to attain a sense of personal fulfillment. Edna Rostow, psychiatric consultant, suggests that feminism today has become an attitude that synthesizes the gains of the suffragettes and the insights of those who experienced the transition to freedom.

Some of the pioneering suffragettes take a dimmer view of the current concerns of young women. I have had many long talks with Elsie Hill, a magnificent, articulate, easy-to-anger woman in her eighties who was twice arrested during the battle for woman suffrage and is honorary chairman of the National Women's Party. Many of her surviving colleagues are falling down and breaking legs or having other incapacitations associated with the ravages of advancing age. A lawyer by training, Elsie Hill is a grandmother but still prefers to be called Miss Hill. She is busy every day battling to get a straight-forward sex equality amendment to the U.S. Constitution that will flatly state, "Equality of rights under the law shall not be denied or abridged by the United States or any state on account of sex. . . ." Many times a month she is on the phone shaming Congressmen into line. She points out that the Nineteenth Amendment only secured the right for women to vote; and the 1964 Civil Rights Act merely secured for women more-or-less equal opportunities for jobs. There is more to life than voting and job-holding, and in the latter case there are a host of state laws professing to "protect" females that in effect handicap them in competing with males.

There are laws requiring special meals for women, special rest periods, no long hours, no night work, and so on.

Miss Hill thinks it is a shame that few of the leading women's colleges (at this writing) had a course on women's rights. And she expressed disgust one day when she sat watching an auditorium full of graduates from her old school, Vassar, tittering at an amusing panel discussion on who is supposed to take out the garbage in the home. Instead, she felt, the women ought to be out fighting for women's rights. Miss Hill exclaimed, "These kids have never been to bat for anything. They are not doing a thing for equal rights!" A new national group that includes many younger professional women has been formed under the name "The National Organization for Women" (NOW). It shares Miss Hill's impatience for wiping out any and all barriers to full equality for women, now.

A quite different view of the status of women's equality is taken by Adrienne Koch, who has been chairman of American studies at the University of California, Berkeley. She states, "As we look about us in the 1960s only mop-up operations remain to complete the victory of full legal rights for women."

That, quite sketchily, is the background against which the thoughtful young female of the late 1960s was expected to try to shape her future and develop an image of her ideal role for the future.

For all her options, and liberating opportunities and opening up to liberation, the modern young female has been less effective in taking advantage of them than worried males might have expected. Some of this might be explained by a normal time lag in adjusting to a new condition, but the young female contemplating a life plan was finding her alleged opportunities beset by complications.

Morton Hunt, longtime student of the female role in Western society, is bemused by the paradox that the emancipated middle-class American woman is now free to train her mind and use it and move about unchaperoned and free to accept or refuse her mate's passion at night. She is, he says, a more nearly complete human being than any in more than a thousand years; and yet she is far from being completed or fulfilled. She is often unsure of what to do with her freedoms, distracted and intimidated by her many opportunities, fearful that she may lose her femininity if she experiments too far with them, and fretful, bored, and discontented when she limits herself to safe, traditional ways.[5]

In trying to sift out her many perplexities, the modern girl keeps coming back to three particularly troublesome questions.

1. What does she want most of all out of life?

Among the girls responding to our College Survey a number volunteered comments indicating uncertainty about this question.

• A coed at the state university in the Midwest described the way girls there become panicky during their junior and senior year: "They are preparing for a career and then seem to forget about it because all their friends are getting married."

• A college girl in the Southern California beach sample: "I think a lot of women are finally becoming individuals, and if they shy away from careers because they think they won't get married, they are mistaken. They will be the kind of wives husbands leave out of boredom."

As the modern girl ponders her future, she often senses that she really can't fix her plans too firmly until she gets the marriage thing settled. Of course she will marry, probably. But whom? When? Into what milieu will it throw her? She can sympathize with the high-school girl who said, "Gosh, I guess I haven't made any plans past the age of 24."

Family sociologist Paul Landis, now at the University of Arizona, quotes a college girl as summing up superbly the modern dilemma many face in these words: "I have a double set of life goals; one set is for if I get married, the other is that if I remain single." [6]

The thoughtful girl should be planning well past 24—but she of necessity has to do some contingency planning for the 24-year-old phase of her life.

In thinking of "the marriage thing" the thoughtful girl senses, too, that the real core of her concern is not combining husband and career, but rather developing a life pattern that will permit her to find fulfillment in the outside world and be a good mother. This raises difficult problems of accommodation.[7] One Swedish sociologist in talking about the modern female's predicament said, "Children are so important to women's satisfaction, and yet at the same time these gals want education and career and promotion. How in hell is this to be combined?"

Many modern girls have sound reasons for wondering if they can build a satisfying life today on the basis of being a homemaker alone. In our segmented, urbanized society, where production activity is usually moved far from the home, the wife is either alone a lot or spends her days conversing with 3-, 5-, and 7-year-olds. Many sense that the more creative functions in the home have been shrinking with all the prepared foods, appliances and factory-made clothes.

I recall that, as a farmboy in Pennsylvania in the first quarter of this century, my mother on a typical Sunday morning not only taught Sunday school and played the organ in church, but really prepared the Sunday dinner. She went to the hen house, selected the right chicken, cut off its head, feathered, gutted, and cooked it; used the broth for cooking the dumplings, which she started by scooping flour out of her great sack. She peeled the potatoes, hand-mashing them, picked and podded the peas before cooking them. Since those were the days before cake mixes, the cake and icing had to be made from basic ingredients. Usually she had made the bread and churned the butter the previous day. She mixed up ingredients for the ice cream, then helped me crank it to stiffness in a hand freezer. I don't know if my mother felt fulfilled from such a morning's activity—she was a former school teacher—but I do know it kept her busy.

Some argue that the average homemaker today is as busy as ever. She has more checks to write and chauffeuring to do. She is more likely to cook gourmet dishes. She, on average, is less apt to have servants (they began disappearing with the Depression 35 years ago). With the growth of affluence she has more mechanical equipment to worry about.

Still, there is a suspicion that much of her activity is makework to fill a vacuum. She may make virtually a full-time occupation out of mothering and in fact subconsciously desire to keep herself pregnant to assure herself additional years of motherhood service. But this may not make her popular in the modern suburban neighborhood. In the 1950s large families were widely glorified. By 1968 neighbors of a family with five, six, or seven children were more likely to think how much the cost of schooling so many children would add to the tax load of everyone.

The average wife today can assume her full-time motherhood service will be over by her early thirties with the departure of her last child to school. Birgitta Linnér, Swedish marriage authority, suggests that the child-bearing period has become a relatively short intermezzo in the course of a couple's life together.

Still there is evidence that many millions of women, if not the majority, see their greatest opportunity for fulfillment through being good mothers and wives. Psychologist Anne Steinmann and two associates rated 5,000 women on how they perceived the ideal path to personal fulfillment. Was it through realizing one's own potentialities or through finding fulfillment through others (i.e., children and husband)? They found the great majority not only saw their own main life goal as that of raising healthy, well-adjusted children, but also saw that as the goal of the ideal woman.[8]

2. Should the young woman of today pursue a mode of life that minimizes sex differences, or does she really want role differentiation?

Here noted fellow-women beckon her from both directions. Some female champions of the female urge young women to become uncompromising in pursuing full equality of treatment with males. A number want sex differences to be minimized to the full extent anatomically possible.

In the U.S.A., the most articulate of the new feminists has been sociologist Alice Rossi, of Johns Hopkins University. She believes the modern bright girl should not be afraid to take on the man in long-monopolized areas such as engineering, physics, and corporate management. Rossi would like to see a revival of the old feminist idealism among women. To her, full-time motherhood is neither sufficiently challenging to the woman nor beneficial enough to the child to justify making it her exclusive occupation for 15 or more years.

Among Swedes, who are now so absorbed in working out sex roles, the most celebrated and controversial advocate of sex equality is a shy, beautiful young woman, Eva Moberg.

She contends that women are still a long way from really being released from subservient roles. She calls for a rebellion against sex differentiation and proposes that after children reach the nursery state the tending of children is no more necessarily the mother's job than it is the father's.

The French feminist Simone de Beauvoir thinks that marriage is an oppressive institution and that woman can be happy only when she has achieved complete independence from males.

At the same time, we have outstanding women proposing a more moderate view. In the United States, for example, anthropologist Margaret Mead, while championing women's rights, holds that sex differences are "exceedingly valuable." They promote human effectiveness and contentment.

Edna Rostow contends that a good many young women are incapable of dealing with future long-range intellectual interests until they have proceeded through the more basic phases of their own healthy growth as women. For many women, she contends, the experience of marriage and raising a family is one in which immense growth takes place in themselves and provides the most important challenge to their resources that they will ever face.[9]

The bright girl looking forward to her motherhood period may be inclined to give less than her full talent to career preparation. At a state university in the South one of the most brilliant girls in her class was the granddaughter of a nationally distinguished surgeon. She had a 3.8 average out of a possible 4. When I asked her what she planned to do after college, she said she was studying to be an occupational therapist. She explained this involved a 5-year college program that included the study of basket-weaving as well as anatomy and abnormal psychology. I asked whether, in view of her family background and school record, she had ever considered studying to be a doctor. She said she had thought about it but she wanted to get married and have four children, and she said, "You can't be a good mother and a good doctor." I countered that I knew women who were. With that she replied that not only did occupational therapy require fewer years of training than medicine, but it made a lot of sense as a career for a woman because it could be done on a part-time basis.

3. How does a talented girl relate herself to the males she will be confronting in her world?

One very talented woman, social critic Marya Mannes, warns that, right or wrong, the average American male is uneasy in the presence of markedly intelligent women and that the woman who wishes to change this unease into love must spend a good part of her life reining in her wits. Alice Rossi, on the other hand, finds such reining intolerable.

What is the attitude of the young people themselves on this point?

In our College Survey we asked:

Do you believe that a good many bright girls consciously or unconsciously downgrade their ambition for a career because of fear that it might hurt their marriage potential?
YES ___ NO ___ DON'T KNOW ___.

Considerably more than half of all the male and female students in the North American samples (U.S. and Canadian) agreed that such a downgrading of ambition for a career did still occur among girls. On the other hand, considerably less than half the students in Norway and Germany felt such downgrading occurred in their countries.

One girl at the state university in the Rocky Mountain area made an interesting distinction. She said, "Bright girls that I have known have seemed more inclined to downgrade their intelligence than their ambition. . . . It's 'cute' to be scatterbrained but unattractive today to be lazy."

If girls do opt to pursue careers seriously, they must decide what kind of role they will play in coping with the males of their work world. Jessie Bernard in talking about academic women points out that the mode may be neuter, sexy, feminine, or womanly. She explained that the neuter mode often results in an imitation of the male role performance with anomalous results. If she is sexy, males will tend to respond to her as a sex object. If she is "feminine," males may tend to see her as dainty, frivolous, appealing. They feel comfortable in the complementary masculine role with such women. Dr. Bernard added that males also understand the womanly role, although they may feel less comfortable with females functioning in this role since, she said, the womanly mode implies a good deal of strength in the female involved.[10]

So much for moods and modes. But what is the actual state of aspiration of the nation's brighter girls today? Some observers seem to assume the great majority of modern, educated U.S. girls are aching to develop careers.

We sought in our College Survey to find how many of the junior and senior women sampled were seriously planning careers. The female students were asked this question:

Do you have seriously in mind an occupational career that you would like to pursue most of the next 20 years?
              YES ___   NO ___   UNCERTAIN ___.

The responses from the young women at the 19 U.S. colleges and universities where women are enrolled indicated that just about *one-half* of them did seriously have in mind such a career. The "NO" responses were 28 percent, and the "UNCERTAIN" responses were 21 percent.

Quite a dramatic variation in pattern occurred on the basis of regions. The greatest interest in seriously pursuing a career appeared in the East and in the West, where the "YES" responses were 58 and 57 percent respectively. On the other hand, only a third of the young women at the three Southern universities indicated that they had any career seriously in mind. Women at the Midwestern schools scored slightly below the national average.

The relatively low interest in careers that girls at the three Southern universities express suggests that they view the function of college, on average, somewhat differently than their sisters in the East or West.

In the International Sample, students at the German and Canadian universities responded pretty much as the U.S. women had responded. However, at the English and Norwegian universities there was considerably more interest expressed in careers than was expressed, on average, by the U.S. girls. The responses in England and Norway in fact were higher than those at *any* of the 19 U.S. schools (English, 78 percent; Norwegian, 77 percent).

A girl at the private university in California offered this explanation of why she hoped to attain a capacity for achievement outside the home even though she did not visualize herself as a career woman: "I want to do something meaningful as a person aside from being a mother and wife. I need this in order to respect myself."

But a coed at the university in the Rocky Mountain area said, "The only dedicated careerists here are the kids who are going to teach in elementary schools, and they are mostly mousy people."

Girls who permit themselves to feel that they are going to be hung up on "that marriage thing" as an imponderable in their early twenties face two hazards in particular. One is that if they think in those terms they may come to feel that they have failed as persons if they don't get married fairly quickly. And the second trouble is that with such a conditional approach to a career they will probably not be adequately prepared to meet male competition.

There is substantial evidence that young women in general are not making the necessary preparation to take full advantage of their liberated state, and that in fact there is presently a tremendous waste of human resources here.

U.S. government statistics on education reveal that while girls show up as being as bright as men all through high school and undergraduate college work they tend to drop out of the competition for higher degrees. In the early 1960s about 4 out of 10 students entering college were females, but only 3 out of 10 students receiving bachelor's or master's degrees were women. And only 1 out of 10 candidates earning a Ph.D. was a woman. That represents quite a drop since the 1930s when 4 out of 10 bachelor's and master's degrees went to women and 1 out of 7 Ph.D.'s went to a woman.

Marion Stephenson, a woman who has advanced to administrative vice president of the radio network at the National Broadcasting Company, is one who contends that young women today are being handicapped when they refuse opportunities for higher education, which she feels is mandatory for achievement in a technologically exploding world.

To explore this contention I requested from several of the nation's outstanding graduate schools information on the proportion of their graduate students who were female. The results:

• *Sociology.* At the University of Chicago's Department of

Sociology the degrees awarded to females during the 1960–65 period were:

Ph.D. 16%
Master's 24%

• *Architecture and fine arts.* At the University of Pennsylvania's Graduate School of Fine Arts in 1964–65 the proportions of enrolled graduate students who were female were:

Architecture 7%
Fine arts 40%

• *Religion.* At the Yale Divinity School in the 1964-65 academic year the proportion of students studying for the ministry or religious education who were female was 13 percent.

• *Medicine.* At the Washington University School of Medicine the proportion of enrolled students who were female in 1964 was 9 percent.

• *Law.* At the Columbia Law School the proportion of students who were female in 1965 was 16 percent.

• *Business administration.* At the Harvard Graduate School of Business Administration—which did not open its doors to women until 1959—the proportion of students in 1965 receiving the M.B.A. degree who were female was 2 percent.

Some overwhelmingly male graduate schools have long tended to view female students as nuisances or upstarts. A very bright girl who became the first female ever to win a degree in architecture from a large Southern school presented me with a long and convincing story of prejudices she encountered which forced her to perform far above the level expected of male students.

But such resistances to females have decreased substantially just in the past few years. Among the graduate schools listed above, Harvard, for example, has been actively seeking more feminine applicants in business administration, and Washington University has been actively seeking more young women as medical students. And of course the changes affecting the deferment from military draft of graduate students caused hundreds of graduate schools in 1968 to start looking hopefully to females to fill out their ranks.

This then suggests the status and state of aspiration of

liberated young females in the 1960s, and their puzzled mood as they contemplate their future. What meanwhile has been happening in the male-female confrontation out on the occupational front? The evidence suggests that women have been making dramatic inroads in some occupations, and have been making very little impact in others. Let us look in on these confrontations.

CHAPTER 7

Female Beachheads and Male Bastions

"We are clearly approaching a time when there will be no kinds of valuable work that cannot be performed as well by one sex as by the other." Nevitt Sanford, director, Institute for the Study of Human Problems, Stanford University.

In 1967 a number of giant corporations moved their headquarters from Manhattan to suburban communities, and one of the interesting explanations was that these corporations were seeking to locate near large pools of alert young white-collar housewives. The companies had discovered that white-collar wives might be interested in working in their offices but didn't want to cope with commuting every day to midtown Manhattan.

At about the same time, an official of the National Council for Women of Great Britain proudly advised me that the shortage of women workers in Britain was greater than the shortage of male workers.

The last quarter-century has seen dramatic shifts in the male-female division of work roles in the world outside the home and a massive overall growth of women with jobs.

Growth of women in the work force. In the period from 1947 to 1962, females accounted for two-thirds of the increase in the U.S. work force. By 1967 there were twice as many women in the work force as in 1940. Nearly half of all women capable of working actually were working.[1] Their total participation fluctuates; but the trend of female employment has been dramatically upward. Countries where a similar great growth in working women has occurred are the United

95

Kingdom, Finland, Denmark, Austria, the Soviet Union; and countries where women have been relatively slow in moving into the work forces are Norway, Belgium, the Netherlands, Italy, and Spain, according to Swedish manpower authority Per Holmberg.

The ages of women who work. The big growth has not been among the youngsters, but rather among women over 40. There are two major periods when women go to work, according to U.S. sociologist Alice Rossi. One is the years around the time of marriage; the other is when women are between their early forties and mid-fifties.

The marital status of working women. A quarter-century ago 1 married woman in 6 was working; by 1965 1 married woman in 3 had some kind of job. The majority of all working women now are, furthermore, married women living with their husbands.[2] No country in Europe, except the Soviet Union, has such a high proportion of married women in the work force.[3]

The education of working women. The higher the level of a woman's education, the more likely she will be working. Only one-third of the women who had not gone beyond grammar school were working in 1962, whereas three-fifths of the college-educated women were.[4] The Women's Bureau of the U.S. Department of Labor reported in 1966 that its study of nearly 6000 feminine college graduates 7 years out of school (and presumably near the peak of their "motherhood service" if rearing children) revealed the following: 41 percent presently married were working . . . and 28 percent of the mothers of children under 6 years old were working![5]

Where the working women work. By occupation the largest number in 1964 were clerical (7½ million). The next largest number were in service roles (3.7 million), and the third largest number were operatives (3.6 million). But among working wives the number of professional and technical job-holders doubled in 10 years. By 1964, 3.1 women held such jobs, so that proportionately, working women had as many jobs classified as professional or technical as working males.[6] (One out of 8 employed persons in each sex.)

As for college graduates, an analysis made by the Women's Bureau in 1964 showed the following rank order for all occupations commanding more than 2 percent of the 43,000 women graduates investigated:

Teachers and school workers 62%

Nurses 6%

Secretaries, stenographers, typists 5%

Misc. professional workers 5%

Social, welfare, recreation workers 3%

Biological technicians 2%

Clerical workers 2%

An analysis made earlier in this decade of women who had been deemed outstanding enough to be among the 19,000 listed in *Who's Who in American Women* indicated that the largest group (16 percent) were "club, civic, religious leaders." Of those in presumably paying jobs the top 6 vocations were writers, 8 percent . . . college educators, 7 percent . . . artists, 7 percent . . . physicians, 5 percent . . . librarians, 5 percent. A majority of the women listed not only were married, but had at least one child. About 13 percent had 3 or more children.

We have been seeing shifts in the degree to which males or females dominate occupations. In the occupations of cashier, bank teller, and bookkeeper, long dominated by men, women have been taking over. The Fuller Brush Man is now more likely to be a woman. Males, as indicated, have historically been keepers of the written record, one technique of domination. In 1966 all three top editors of the campus newspaper at the University of Idaho were females. In my hometown in Connecticut in 1951 the town's licensed realtors were divided approximately evenly between males and females. By 1966, 80 percent of the realtors were women.

On the other hand, males have been sweeping females out of their dominant positions as principals of elementary schools.

The National Council of Administrative Women in Education has deplored the substantial drop in the percentage of women in administrative roles in schools. In just 10 years, starting in 1951, the percentage of elementary-school principals who were women dropped from 56 percent to 37 percent. And there has been a considerable increase in men who are nurses. They insist upon being called "male nurses."

Two decades ago women were firmly entrenched as hairdressers in their sex's salons. Today, a majority of high-style hairdressers in urban areas outside the South are estimated to be male. Women are most likely to dominate in the South or in the outlying areas of every region. In large metropolitan areas in the more expensive shops males now command the scene, and females tend to be the assistants. It has reached the point where one suburban lady in Connecticut exclaimed, "Why, I'd feel slighted if I got a woman!"

We also have the anomaly of an occupation being identified primarily with one sex in one country but with another in another country. In Sweden being a butcher is regarded as a male's job; in Finland it is mainly a female's job. On the other hand, in Sweden bank tellers are overwhelmingly female, while in Norway they are mainly male. In Finland pharmacists and dentists are primarily women. In the U.S.A. and Great Britain female engineers are a rarity; in the Soviet Union about a third of all engineers are women.

In secondary-school teaching in the U.S.A. women tend mostly to be in the lower grades and men mostly in the upper. (In Argentina 80 percent of the primary-grade teachers are female, 11 percent of the university educators are female.) Male dominance becomes emphatic at the college level (though at women's colleges male ascendancy is less conspicuous).

One day when I happened to be in the lobby of a Kansas City hotel where about 180 U.S. historians were milling about waiting to go into conference, I made a rough count of the women in the group. It was about 1 in 10. Sociologist Jessie Bernard in her study of faculty women in colleges cites a study at 98 colleges showing that about 19 percent of the total teaching staff was female. But when the analysis was confined to full professors, the female contingent dropped to 10 percent. In a study confined to "20 leading universities" the proportion of full professors dropped still further to 5 percent.[7] Only in the disciplines of education, home economics, and library science were more than 20 percent of the total faculties female, at all ranks.

Other U.S. professional areas dominated rather overwhelmingly by males are accountants, lawyers, pharmacists, scientists, engineers, and physicians.[8]

Only about 7 percent of the U.S. physicians are female, despite the cry for more doctors. Among all the Western nations of the world the U.S.A. ranks near the bottom for female doctors. In England nearly 20 percent of the doctors are female; in the Soviet Union 3 doctors in 4 are female. One reason there are so few women doctors in the U.S.A. unquestionably is that males dominating the profession have mostly taken a dim view of female doctors, and often have created obstacles or sought to keep them out of important functions. A leading New York doctor commented to me, "I've never heard of a woman doctor being asked to serve on a hospital abortion committee, even though women are most involved by committee decisions." Further, as an obstacle to young women hoping to become doctors, there is the great amount of family money usually required to get a medical education in the United States. Writer Jean Libman Block points out that while 57 percent of young male medical students have wives who contribute to their support, very few married medical students who are female can expect financial help from young husbands.

As for the women who are natural scientists, sociologist Alice Rossi found a few years ago some dramatic variations. While less than 3 percent of the physicists and earth scientists were female, more than a fourth of the biological scientists and mathematicians were female.

Magazine editorial staffs tend to be dominated by males. At the two leading U.S. news magazines there were no feminine names among the names of the top 20 editors at both magazines in early 1968, even though at one a woman presided over the corporation owning the magazine.

The president of the Christian Science Church, a woman, observed in 1965 that women tend to be more religiously inclined than men. In that church, female practitioners of spiritual healing have outnumbered male practitioners. But among the main-line Protestant denominations only a few hundred women have attained the full status of senior pastors, and most of them are confined to the United Church of Christ, the United Presbyterian Church in the U.S.A., and the Methodist Church.[9] Women traditionally have been barred from being priests or rabbis.

At a gathering of parish ministers in 1965 one of the things deplored was the diminishing number of ministers. During a low point in all the gloomy discussion, one voice was raised to suggest that more be done to develop women ministers. (Women attending this conference were holding a separate session devoted to "women's work.") The response to the suggestion was absolute silence. Finally the presiding bishop said, "Well, I don't know how it is here, but in our part of the country we don't go much for women preachers." His quip was greeted with a general snickering.[10]

One of the areas where women have made the least progress of all in challenging male dominance is in leadership roles. In any organization that is not all-female the chances are slight that there will be women in the leadership.

There are a few notable exceptions. Author Elizabeth Janeway effectively heads The Author's Guild. The Society of Magazine Writers, after electing 16 consecutive males as president, in 1966 chose a female president, Jean Libman Block, and she was regarded as one of the best ever elected. Th advertising industry in 1967 was dazed by the fact that the most talked-about and fastest-growing ad agency, Wells, Rich, Greene, Inc., with more than $50,000,000 in billings after only one year in business, was presided over by a gay, delightful, glamorous, brilliantly inventive blonde woman named Mary Wells Lawrence. Her soft, thrilling voice, according to one observer, "makes the maddest ideas seem perfectly possible."

One day I heard on the radio George E. Moore, director of the celebrated Roswell Park Memorial Institute in Buffalo, comment that women at the institute's laboratories held mainly "supporting" roles. Wishing to confirm that I heard such a bold statement correctly, I queried him and he good-naturedly confirmed that he had been heard correctly. He explained, "In our experience women have proved to be best in supporting rolls in the laboratory. Very few women have the training, knowledge, energy, and most important, creativeness, to be successful leaders in scientific groups. I am unable to state whether or not their present achievements result primarily from the social mores of our time or whether their constitutional differences (which I enjoy) may interfere with their roles as creative scientists."

It might seem an anomaly that the great majority of the presidents of U.S. women's colleges are male, if you exclude the Catholic women's schools. Of 72 non-Catholic women's colleges in the U.S.A. only 1 in 8 was headed by a woman in 1966.

The leadership at Kelly Services Inc. is of interest since

it grew up primarily by supplying "Kelly Girls" to employers needing feminine help on a part-time or short-time basis. In 1966 all 10 of the top officers of the company were male.

The best estimates are that no more than about 2 percent of the executives of U.S. business are female.[11] In the federal government top female executives are even harder to find. One count of people in super-grade jobs indicated that only about 1 percent were held by women.[12] The rarity of women as executives is not confined to the U.S.A. A study of eight firms in England revealed that while a third of all the employees were women, only 1 in 20 women held a responsible position.[13]

A number of reasons in addition to simple prejudice help account for the small proportion of women in leadership roles, though stereotypes do abound. There is a feeling among the male business executives, for example, that women wouldn't "fit in" at the male social clubs where they profess to consummate many of their important deals. In my own assessment a few years ago of the 7 characteristics most important in the success of business executives, 5 seem to have no sexual overtones.[14] The only two that may be more common to males are:

• The ability to respond to provocation objectively It is often charged, especially by males and perhaps with justification, that most women live closer to their emotions than most men and may be more swayed by their emotions in interpersonal relations.

• The capacity for sustained, purposeful drive toward an objective. Plenty of women have drive, but the characteristic may seem to some unfeminine, and furthermore the pattern of their lives may make sustained drive more difficult.

I asked a woman editor of a women's magazine why the top editorship was held by a male. Instead of suggesting prejudice, she said she suspected that very few women were "single-minded" enough to fight their way to the top in major business enterprises. If women marry, they have the problem of phases. This was described in a report of the National Education Association when it called for more women leaders in education. It stated, "Another drawback to women's progress is their interrupted careers. In a recent survey, the NEA found that less than one-fifth of women teachers were between the age of 30 and 39, crucial years during which candidates are most likely to be considered for promotion." [15] Many women drop out of teaching in the thirties because of the demands of rearing children.

In business, women seem to do best in managerial roles that are in research, retailing, public relations, advertising.

What are the characteristics of the women who succeed as executives that seem to set them apart from women in general? A psychological consultant (female) at The Personnel Laboratory, Inc., which tests both males and females for managerial jobs, offered me some general impressions about women who succeed as executives:

They tend to be mentally assertive. They do something with their knowledge and don't just passively retain it. "Intellectually these women seem to be more incisive than average . . . more probing, questioning, and more demanding in specific answers," she said.

The energy resources of such women are often "astounding." Since the women are usually unwilling to give up other aspects of their lives, they must exert themselves far more energetically and more consistently than most people, male or female.

In family background an impressive proportion come from homes in which the mother was a passive figure and the young girl identified more closely with her father. Eager for his approval, she developed aspirations in areas she was sure he understood and admired.

Regarding motivation of such women, while the so-called "masculine protest" is not as intense as it used to be, there is still often a specific zest for competing with the male.

The area where women have perhaps had the poorest record of all in attaining leadership roles is in the labor-union movement. Not only have they been more reluctant than men to organize in the first place, but those who do rarely become union leaders. Historian Charles W. Ferguson has pointed out that in 1966 there was no woman on the 31-member executive committee governing the AFL-CIO. There is some evidence that this lack of leadership of women in unions may be due more to reluctance than to prejudice. Historian Eleanor Flexner pointed out a few years ago that in two unions where women clearly dominate the membership ranks, the International Ladies Garment Workers Union and the Amalgamated Clothing Workers, women have done little to elect their own sex to the top boards, even though they had the votes to do so. In both unions about three-quarters of the members are female, and on both boards only 1 member in 9 was female.

In political life, too, women tend to be the soldiers who ring the doorbells and stage coffee hours. Generally they do not run for, or succeed to, high office, even though they have the votes. There are about 4,000,000 more eligible female voters than male voters in the U.S.A. The number of women elected to Congress has hovered between 1 and 2 percent of the membership. A high-water mark was reached in the Congress taking office in 1959. It contained 18 women. By 1965 the number had receded to 12.

Of the approximately 150 individuals who have been appointed to the U.S. Cabinet since women won the vote in 1920 only 2, at this writing, have been women: Frances Perkins and Oveta Culp Hobby. Both served about a quarter-century ago. About 1 percent of the federal judges recently have been women.

In Western Europe women have done little better in attaining high public office. During 1965 a woman in Great Britain was named to its third highest tribunal, the High Court of Justice. She was Mrs. Elizabeth Lane. She donned the traditional wig, and lawyers were advised to address her as "Mr. Justice Lane." [16]

Perhaps the best achievement record by women in the Western world has been in Finland. There they occupy one-eighth of the seats of parliament and one-third of the seats in Helsinki's municipal council. In recent decades the only two women to be elected to head major national governments are both in the underbelly of Asia: India and Ceylon; and both these women bore names made famous by male predecessors. In the Soviet Union, where 75 percent of the doctors are women, only about 3 percent of the Communist Party's Central Committee is female.

One problem women will have to correct if they hope to improve their proportion of leadership roles is the prejudice against women leaders by other women. In one survey 640 women were asked if they would vote for a qualified woman to be President of the U.S.A. if she ran against an equally qualified male. Two-thirds of the women said either that they would not or that they would prefer not to vote for a woman President in those circumstances.[17] One woman wondered whether a fellow-woman would command respect in an eye-ball-to-eyeball confrontation with a male foreign leader. Another wondered whether a female President might make the nation's males feel a little less masculine.

One rough measure of the proportion of females who are judged to be outstandingly successful Americans is their representation in *Who's Who in America*. In a random sampling of all entries whose names began with "M," approximately 4 percent were women.

Still, women have been fighting to get into some occupations where their number is small or where they are not represented at all. They have not succeeded in getting on a space flight in the U.S.A., but did so in Russia. Major U.S. airlines, as of 1967, were sticking to their ban on feminine pilots despite protests and despite the fact that many of their male pilots get some of their basic training under female flight instructors. Arizona State College in Flagstaff finally accepted 2 girls as forestry students in 1965 after they energetically argued that the education was essential to their recognized right to earn a living as foresters.

In Title VII of the 1964 Civil Rights Act the word "sex" was inserted almost casually in listing types of people who could not be discriminated against by companies in their hiring, pay, or promotion practices. This created some pandemonium in employment circles as job descriptions were reworded from "errand boy" to "errand person." Several hundred men working at the Rath Packing Company in Waterloo, Iowa, found themselves laid off during a cutback while the great bulk of the female force remained on the job. Many of the men were more than a little upset about this. Always in the past during cutbacks it had been the women who were laid off. But Title VII decreed that layoffs be determined by seniority, and a great many of the women had begun working there during World War II, when men had departed for military duty.[18]

Some U.S. employers began describing male and female jobs differently and then offered less pay to feminine applicants. The Equal Employment Opportunity Commission set up to prevent discrimination was beset by so many questions and complaints that it began trying to hedge with guidelines such as the one stating it was all right to specify sex if it was a bonafide occupational qualification (i.e., being a Playboy Club bunny).

Another difficulty was that the Act was frequently in conflict with state laws purporting to protect women from hardship situations. A conference of the Commerce and Industry Association in New York was advised by federal officials that where there seemed to be a federal-state conflict, corporate officials might as well follow state law until the courts "say you are wrong." Elsie Hill, the spirited emancipationist, had me on the phone within hours after this statement was published to point out that this was what she had been saying all along: that the Civil Rights Act of 1964 did not really assure women equality and that there was still need for a Constitutional amendment guaranteeing equality, such as the one she had been seeking for 40 years.

Perhaps the most awkward anomaly persisting after the Civil Rights Act was that newspapers continued to divide their help wanted ads into "FEMALE" and "MALE" sections. Usually they ran a small disclaimer citing the Act's provisions against discrimination and explaining that the ads were arranged under "Male" and "Female" merely for the convenience of readers.

Other factors in addition to laws, practices, and anatomy that were preventing married females of the late 1960s from fully exploiting their purported equality in the occupational field were problems of motives and role expectations. For example:

The married career woman may still be conditioned by society to feel guilty if she is working while her child has a runny nose.

She may lack stick-to-itiveness as a careerist simply because she has a better excuse to quit and retreat to the home when the going gets rough than her husband has, because much of society thinks she ought to be in the home anyhow.

She is still expected to be a gracious hostess for her husband and a good mother.

She knows that much of her income will go for extra clothes, travel, and baby-sitters.

In our highly mobile society she knows her husband's success often depends upon being able to move where his company wishes; whereas if she is asked to move, she might feel impelled to refuse to move. Women tend to place a higher emphasis upon the importance of community roots while children are growing. Also, though the situation is changing, it is still the tradition that the husband's job comes first. Finally, it is still probable that he is making more of the family income than she is.

There are now occasional situations where it is the husband who has said, "Whither thou goest I will go." When Patricia Roberts Harris, a noted lawyer, was offered the post of U.S. Ambassador to Luxembourg, her husband announced he would close down his Washington law office and accompany her to Europe. And when a successful New York newspaper-woman was offered a chance to become a TV personality west of the Alleghenies, her husband, who works in television, ar-ranged to move to the same city with her.

But these are still isolated cases. The situation in general remains much as the president of Sarah Lawrence College, Esther Raushenbush, put it after spending years helping mar-ried women solve their career problems in our society. She said, "I think this generation still has not worked out a way of making it comfortable or in many ways possible for women to combine a top-level job with marriage. We haven't found a real solution yet."

But, as we will see in Part II, many approaches are being tested. There is growing acceptance, even by males, that the number of work roles in modern society that women can handle as well as men has greatly expanded. And much of the male hostility to having female colleagues on the job has at least become muted. With this in mind, let us turn to some of the puzzles confronting the modern young male.

CHAPTER 8

The Young Male Reacts—
and Uneasily Ponders His Future

"The question is raised as to whether we are approaching an era of more confident women and more anxious men."
Emily Mudd, Philadelphia marriage counselor, et al.[1]

While the spotlight recently has been on the "New Female," the young male in transition has been facing gnawing problems. He not only has to cope with those new females, but also must cope with other upsetting new elements in his way of life.

It is easy for the young male to perceive that masculinity counts for less in the home, at work, and even in bed. Some years ago when 18 family experts were invited to list the most important changes affecting the modern family, they listed in second place (after divorce) the "decline in authority of husbands and fathers." The decline is continuing. In 1968 sociologist Jessie Bernard observed, "There is beginning to be recognition of the fact that the change in the status of women may have a deleterious effect on men."

Some males feel the new pressures much more than others. But as a generalization, a distinction made by psychologist Theodor Reik seems fair. He said that in our civilization women are afraid that they will be considered only women— and men are afraid they will not be considered men enough.

Vis-à-vis the new females, young males are being invited to move over. They have the option of adjusting philosophically to their new role expectations . . . or pretending that nothing is happening . . . or fighting back. Meanwhile they must maintain their aplomb under scrutiny. Family sociologist David Mace suggests—as one symptom of the new condition —that the point of suspense in the modern novel is no longer focused on whether she will or she won't, but on whether he can or he can't.

Many young males not only feel their adequacy threatened, but are confused as to what really the modern world expects of them. Officially they are still expected to be strong, bold, gallant to women, masterful breadwinners, and protectors of weaker women and children. This ideal male is primarily a product of civilization. Primitive societies tend not to make so much of sex differences.[2]

In some Western societies we still have laws on the books that affirm the male to be the lord and master. In Italy the female can legally be disciplined by father, brother, or husband; and she is required to live where her husband decides to live. The Italian wife who tries to kill an unfaithful husband will be treated as an ordinary criminal in court; while the husband who murders an unfaithful wife will be viewed as having committed a crime of honor and be punished lightly, if at all.[3] Much the same double standard in dealing with husband-wife assaults prevails in the courts of Texas, U.S.A.

There is evidence that males never have been as dominant and superior-minded in coping with females as they often like to pretend. Early psychiatrists made much of the "penis envy" of women. More recently, several have been impressed by the "vagina envy" of males. Keith Fischer, psychoanalyst of Philadelphia, advises: "There is magic in the vagina and the woman's capacity to have a baby. Some men get sick when their wives get pregnant. And the man usually calls the newborn 'my baby.'" Other psychiatrists have shown a new interest in the primitive ritual called the couvade, which was reported decades ago by anthropologists working with primitive tribes. A 19th-century report on the ritual as practiced among Indians of Guiana and reported by Sir E. F. Im Thurn described the ritual as follows:

"The woman works as usual up until a few hours before birth; she goes to the forest with some women and there the birth takes place. In a few hours she is up and at work. . . . As soon as the child is born the father takes to his hammock and abstains from work, from meat and from all food but weak gruel of cassava meal, from smoking, from washing himself, and above all from touching weapons of any sort, and is nursed and cared for by all the women of the place. . . . This goes on for days, sometimes weeks."

Professor of psychiatry Bruno Bettelheim in discussing such rituals suggests that women, being emotionally satisfied by actually demonstrating their ability to create new life, can be indulgent with male make-believe. Men, he said, need the make-believe to fill the emotional vacuum created by their inability to bear children.[4] Sociologist Gunnar Boalt of the University of Stockholm suggests that women's main biological drive is to have children, not to have husbands.

In any case, young males today are seeing that many of the historic male prerogatives are now dubious. A number of psychotherapists have noted that there seems to be an increase in the number of passive, dependent males among their patients. That would not, of course, necessarily apply to the general male population. But historian Charles W. Ferguson in tracing the male's traditional sources of confidence and power states:

"Virtually all the conditions that produced and fostered masculine philosophy and sentiment have vanished. As far as their day-to-day existence is concerned, most men have moved from a physical and violent world into a sensitive and delicate one. Energy has been transferred from muscles to molecules. The new atom has replaced the old Adam."[5]

The changed world of the male arising from the liberating of women can be seen vividly in Japan, where for centuries the male has been monarch of the home. When I was in Japan a few years ago, a group of business executives were invited to discuss what aspect of the traditional way of life the Japanese most stubbornly wanted to preserve. One man blurted out, "We don't want to change our women!" Younger men in the group told me later that they, the younger ones, no longer insist that their wives follow them if they walk in public. In fact, they take their wives out to dinner about once a month and walk with them side by side. They added that they are sometimes kidded by older people the next day about being seen with their mistresses.

The new assertiveness of females arising from near-equality and such liberating influences as conception-control has probably most startled young males in the area of physical intimacy (for those who have explored that area). We might suppose that males should be delighted by evidence that millions of young unmarried females of good backgrounds are becoming more sexually playful and less inhibited. And many do count this as a very great gain. Very few societies in recorded history have witnessed such a phenomenon as a widespread pattern. Many young males, once they have reflected on the matter and contemplate the future, are not sure they should be enchanted. They hear from psychiatrists, if they haven't learned for themselves, that the sexually demanding woman can be a formidable one. Sociologist Helen Mayer Hacker, of New York University, some years ago foresaw new burdens for masculinity in intimate encounters.[6] She said:

"The ability to perform the sexual act has been a criterion for man's evaluation of himself from time immemorial. Virility used to be conceived as a unilateral expression of male sexuality, but is regarded today in terms of the ability to evoke a full sexual response on the part of the female. . . . Sexual prowess represents an alternative to economic success in validating manhood. Any deficiencies in this realm, therefore, are much more ego-threatening to men than to women."

We see this need for validation of manhood in an extreme form perhaps in the problem of the young Negro male, who has an appalling economic heritage going back to slavery, and often has trouble finding a decent job.

In any case the young male is learning that sexual intimacy is no longer just a matter of taking his pleasure. Sociologist David Riesman of Harvard suggests that many modern girls are becoming "critical consumers of male performance."

After studying the sex lives of hundreds of U.S. college males, social investigators Phyllis and Eberhard Kronhausen made the strong comment that modern women were making sexual demands on men never dreamed of by the previous generation, with many displaying a degree of sexuality unthinkable only 10 years ago.

The young females are encouraged in such expectations by cosmetic advertisers. In 1967 Coty depicted a girl dabbing perfume on her virtually bare breasts. The message to the female reader was:

"Want him to be more of a man? Try being more of a woman."

Personal effectiveness by males in intimate relations depends largely upon self-confidence. Anthropologist Margaret Mead has suggested that once the male starts considering such factors as sentiment, prestige, interpersonal relations, and the mood of his female partner, he becomes less reliable and automatic in executing coitus.

Another problem the modern young male encounters in coping intimately with the liberated female is that it is vastly easier for the female to perform adequately in coitus, and even simulate ecstasy, than it is for the male. And then there is the new uncertainty about safeguarding against pregnancy. Before the days of the pill, the intrauterine device, and the diaphragm, the male usually handled whatever precautions were felt necessary. Now with the control of safeguards passing to the female, if the unmarried female elects to test her powers to conceive, or if she elects to nudge him into setting a wedding date, he may be left in ignorance of her intent.

Young males see abundant evidence almost every night on television that the traditional image of the masterful male has been scuttled by the producers of family-comedy shows. A few facts of life about television may account for this: (1) there are more female than male viewers; (2) in homes where husband and wife are watching, the wife usually controls the selection of programs; (3) wives are about five times as likely as husbands to be potential purchasers of the products being advertised.

Mass communications specialist Robert C. O'Hara, of the University of South Florida, finds that in the typical family comedy the male is incapable of handling even the simplest tasks without making a mess of things. When, as often happens, he does something against the judgment of his wife, disaster invariably ensues, and she has to straighten things out. In *Bewitched* it is the miracle-performing wife who keeps saving her husband from disgracing himself. One investigator after a study of TV comedy formulas found that an all-pervading one was "The Jackass Formula." Under this barrel-of-laffs formula, the men cook up a scheme . . . the wives perceive it can't work . . . the men go ahead anyway . . . it doesn't work . . . the wives save the situation.[7]

In 1967 TV commercials depicted a series of baseball celebrities such as Yogi Berra beaming as they used their wives' hair spray. On one network commercial, the husband was asked why he bought Borax. He explained, "My wife told me to buy it and so I bought it." And there was the bald husband looking solemn as his radiant wife explained to viewers, "This is my husband Jim. He may not look like much to you. But I love him." And then she demonstrated why, by feeding him some Temp Tee whipped cream cheese; the bald, solemn husband went wild kissing the lovely hand that was feeding him.

All this, of course, is surface froth. There are, however, fundamental reasons for many males to be unsettled about the roles emerging for them in modern life. One is the shrinkage of ways to validate themselves in ways that have reassured them in the past. A girl wants to be called a girl as long as plausible; a boy wants to be called a man as soon as plausible. (In this book—readers may have noted—I usually refer to an unmarried male in his early twenties as a "man" but refer to an unmarried female in her early twenties as a "girl.")

The frontier and the sea have largely disappeared as places where restless young males could find self-realization. And it is becoming increasingly unsafe for society to let young males have access to those traditional emblems of masculinity, guns. One of the saddest lines in contemporary drama was in Arthur Miller's movie *The Misfits*. The character played by Clark Gable had made his living capturing wild horses, but they were now hard to find, and the best market for those captured was the dog-food industry. He muttered, "I've got to find another way to be alive—if there is one anywhere." In our new society the cow puncher is being replaced by the key puncher as the figure close to the center of free enterprise.

In the TV commercial the male still, after lighting up, heads his horse off into the rugged challenges of Marlboro Country. But how rugged is the West?

Sociologist Reuel Denney comments that no young males enjoy the imagery of the rugged individualist more than those in the arid rural states. But he added that most of these states would hardly break even if it were not for federal subsidies for farm products; metal and water resources; income from tourist bars, dude ranches, and gambling; and graft on the public lands.

There are still rugged or adventuresome jobs—as in ranching, truck-driving, carpentry, sponge-diving, piloting planes, etc.—but a more typical enterprising young male of the late 1960s is shown in the TV commercial for Sun-Up shaving lotion. He gives a Tarzan cry, leaps over the living-room balcony, and starts to work carrying his briefcase. The son of such a commuter probably has only a vague idea how Father validates himself. This raises interesting questions about what kind of men such sons will be when they grow up.

If perchance he rises toward the top of a major business enterprise, it doesn't bring much glory, because executives of large corporations increasingly are trained to be semi-anonymous, bland, soft-spoken, non-oddball team players.

Or, if he succeeds in a job requiring technical skills, he confronts the uneasy fact that with the blinding speed of technological innovation his skills will probably be largely obsolete in a decade or so and he may have to learn new skills.

The young man's image of himself as a future community leader is likely to be weakly fixed. He has observed that husbands in his neighborhood who commute to work leave much of the family's representation in the community to the wife, if there is any representation.

If he is thoughtful, the young male may also perceive that many of the traits most necessary to our society's healthy functioning today are traits long considered to be female rather than male. Margaret Mead mentions these three virtues, long regarded as more appropriate for women, as being necessary today: patience, endurance, steadfastness.

Along this same line, Richard Farson, director of the Western Behavioral Sciences Institute, suggests that women are better suited for the world of the 1980s because they are less encumbered by the Protestant ethic, under which worth is only possible by hard, painstaking work. With the electronics revolution he anticipates that less and less time or energy will be needed for hard work. There will be more emphasis upon finding fulfillment through human relationships and the enjoyment of culture—both of which, he contends, come more naturally to women.

We should note, too, the quite new conditions under which modern young males are reared. In earlier societies in the U.S.A.—where father was dominant and male relatives were near—the boy was mainly under male influences in his formative years. This is still true in many working-class homes. But in the homes of the mobile, corporate, white-collar toiler, management of girls and boys is left mainly to the mother.

Disciplining is more likely to come from mother than father, and so is more likely to take the form of a withdrawal of love than of a thrashing.

In his first years in school the young male is still in an overwhelmingly female-dominated environment, and in coeducational schools he must compete with same-age girls who have matured more rapidly than he has. His schooling—and thus usually his dependency upon parents—will extend well past the time he achieves physical maturity. As family specialist Lester Kirkendall points out, "The chances of the modern lad of 18 gaining community recognition for his masculine achievements through economic and vocational activities are severely limited."

In counting major changes in the maturing male's world we should note, too, the substantial erosion of uniquely male habitats. Australia is one of the few modern countries left where men dominate everyday life, assign women to clearly supporting roles, and congregate regularly in their sex-segregated male haunts, including pubs and clubs.[8]

In the U.S.A., clubs and restaurants still reserved exclusively for males are becoming exceedingly scarce. Women are following men into saloons; and the saloons soon become lounges. If the husband goes fishing or hunting, the wife increasingly is likely to go along and even want to fish or hunt herself.

One of the most respected of all sanctuaries for young American males, the poolroom, declined for decades and—typical of the times—its recent resurgence has involved a desexualization of the institution. It is now more likely to be called a "billiard lounge" with wall-to-wall carpeting and sexually ambiguous decor. Sociologist Ned Polsky, however, doubts the sport can thrive for long on a bisexual basis, because women simply see it as a passing fad, while to the bachelor male it has deep emotional meaning as a refuge from women.[9]

Perhaps the most startling desexualization of a sport can be seen in the journals devoted to wrestling. The magazine *Wrestling Illustrated* now carries on its front cover in small type under the title these words, "Combined with *Girl Wrestling*." One recent front cover carried the pictures of 5 wrestlers. Four were male, and the other was a female, Brenda Scott. She authored an article of lament entitled "MEN ARE

AFRAID TO DATE ME." In the article she drew upon her psychological insights to conclude that her problem stemmed from the fact that males like to think they are the strong ones.

In today's world a great many young males are getting an increasing amount of guidance from managerial young females. The evidence of this is coming from several directions. Some years ago *Science,* the respected journal of American scientists, carried an article ominously pointing out that high-school boys were increasingly being influenced in making career judgments by their girl friends and that if the girls had a poor image of scientists as potential husbands the boys were likely to change aspirations. Medical-association leaders have observed that many potential young medics are steered away from a medical career by girls who don't like the idea of waiting years and years to land a breadwinner. *The American Journal of Orthopsychiatry* has presented a paper by psychiatrist Paul A. Walters, Jr., of Harvard, who pointed out that girls who go steady often seem to pick as a boy friend someone they can mother, and the girls tend to attach considerable importance to similarities. Thus there is the open encouragement to young males to prove their devotion by wearing look-alike long hair and stylish clothing textures that females find interesting.

In 1964 the Youth Research Institute, which advises many major corporations on teen-age interests, surveyed teenagers and came up with some highly suggestive evidence that girls were taking charge of their boy friends. The head of the institute, Lester Rand, advised me, "Boys have gotten into the habit of wanting to conform to what girls think is their ideal. Fellows actually go window-shopping with girls when they buy their own clothing. This is becoming far more pronounced."

Mr. Rand leans to the idea that the male's new reliance upon the female stems primarily from the fact that girls are more perceptive about interpersonal relationships. In our confusing era with its generational gulf he explained, "The boy seeks out a steady girl in order to have someone to tell his problems to. A girl can *listen,* so she is in a better position to offer counsel. The boys are not likely to listen to problems because they are not too good at giving advice." Here are some more of Mr. Rand's conclusions:

Teen-age males are getting a good deal of advice from girl

friends on how to make and manage money. Some girls and their boy friends reported having joint bank accounts.

The survey found a number of cases where girls, indeed, were selecting careers for boy friends and vetoing career choices that seemed unpromising.

Girls often place their boy friends on rigid diets they have clipped from newspapers.

Mr. Rand surmised that the American husband in the future would be thoroughly housebroken. The institute's survey inspired columnist Art Buchwald to carry an amiable report on "The Teen-age Matriarchy." He received a large number of letters from male and female teenagers and generously sent me a batch of them for inspection.

About half of both male and female letter writers were inclined to agree the girls were managerial. Here are some of the comments:

A girl in Macon, Georgia, didn't entirely agree but said, "We do make suggestions as to what colors they would look better in, but the boys pick out their own styles in clothing."

A male from Milwaukee: "The girls got us an [*sic*] believe me they know it. . . . I have talked to my buddies and its [*sic*] all the same story. . . . What is worse, they know so much."

A cadet at Bordentown, N.J., military school: "After all they are what we want and we will do almost anything to acquire and keep their affection."

A girl in Alexandria Bay, N.Y.: "The boys seem to want us girls to recognize them more, to feel sorry for them, give them guidance. The teen-age boy doesn't get this attention at home."

Most of the points I have been making about changes in the male environment and behavior are just tendencies. They obviously don't involve all young males. Still, many observers are wondering how much demasculinization actually is occurring in young males. And some are wondering if it portends an upsurge in apprehension about heterosexual relationships that could lead to homosexuality and if such an increase in homosexuality is in fact already occurring.

This is a speculation that should be inspected warily, since there is little solid, quantified evidence to support it. At the same time there is little quantified evidence to prove the opposite.

The Committee on Public Health of the New York Academy of Medicine reported in 1964 that there is "an impression that at the present time the practice of homosexuality is increasing among the population at large. By the very nature of this condition, data about the prevalence of homosexuality are often inaccurate and misleading. . . . Certainly if there is not more homosexuality than in the past, it appears to be more open and obtrusive."

A number of studies indicate that homosexuality is considerably more common among males than females, which suggests that the strain of heterosexual adjustment after puberty is harder for the male than the female. One possible explanation is that the female has had less reason to worry whether she could perform the act of intercourse adequately. But the difference as it exists may also relate to the fact that modern-day male children tend to be exposed considerably more to their mothers than to their fathers. There is less stigma to being a female homosexual, and she is less apt to be anxious and to feel inadequate than the male homosexual commonly is or feels.

Several psychiatrists and psychologists have expressed a belief that the incidence of homosexuality is rising, but this may merely reflect a new openness in seeking counsel and treatment. In 1963 *The American Journal of Psychoanalysis* carried an article by Frederick A. Weiss, past president of the Association for the Advancement of Psychoanalysis, in which he stated flatly, "The incidence of homosexuality and homosexual trends in heterosexuals has increased very much in the last few years."[10] Homosexual trends in heterosexuals refers to people who are functioning heterosexuals but have inclinations that could lead them to homosexuality.

Perhaps the most impressive study of homosexuality on record is that supervised by Irving Bieber, clinical professor of psychiatry at the New York Medical College. In it 77 psychoanalysts supplied detailed information on 206 homosexual men. Dr. Bieber offered this conclusion about homosexuals:

"They avoid normal sexual activity because they have developed overwhelming fears of their sexual capacity and enjoyment with members of the opposite sex."[11]

Thus he would not support the popular notion that the male homosexual is eager to be like a female. Another psychiatrist, Harry Gershman, put the matter more strongly than Bieber. He said of the male homosexual:

"His love for another man is a rationalization for the desperate lack that he feels in himself. . . . A woman poses a tremendous challenge to him, for only she can expose him as defective in the role of a man."[12] Another psychiatrist quotes a male patient as explaining his homosexual behavior by saying, "Together with him I am at least a whole man."

Bieber's study convinced him that the roots of homosexuality are indeed in the early home environment and that it rarely occurs if the child has a sound relationship with *even one* of his parents. The main implanting of male homosexuality, he concluded, occurs when a mother is overly intimate, excessively possessive, and protective. Such mothers, he added, also tend to dominate and minimize their husbands. The fathers tend to be aloof or away a lot. Weiss cites a remarkable statement made by author D. H. Lawrence to explain the mother's role in fostering homosexual trends in young males:

"The love which would have been a beautiful gift for the husband she gave to the son and it became poison."

While the number of U.S. homosexual males in the late 1960s can only be guessed at, they have in a decade become vastly more visible on the U.S. scene and have taken up influential, if not commanding, roles in several fields, including fashion design. According to an analysis by *Time* magazine, deviates are so widespread in the theater, dance, and musical worlds that they "sometimes seem to be running a kind of closed shop."[13] A drama critic of *The New York Times* in 1966 mentioned that several of the most successful American playwrights of the past two decades were reputed homosexuals and that their treatment of marriage and women tended to be vicious and lurid, possibly as a sublimation of social hatreds. He suggested that homosexual artists exalt style, manner, and surface and decry artistic concern with many traditional matters of theme and substance because they are prevented from using fully the themes of their own experience. This critic speculated that the theater might be healthier if such writers were not forced to resort to disguised presentations of their feelings.

Meanwhile, there does seem to be an increase in the number of males who fear or believe they are not as masculine as they think males ought to be.

Psychologist Eleanore Luckey, of the University of Connecticut, states, "I am deeply concerned by the number of males on campuses where I have been who are concerned enough about masculinity to wonder if they are homosexual." She suspects their wondering often starts because there are so few ways they can substantiate their masculinity. Likewise sociologist David Riesman comments that boys and girls have a new fear that was less apparent a generation ago, a fear that they might be homosexual. A number of family specialists have offered the impression that young men today are often driven to premarital sexual experiences to prove their masculinity and relieve themselves of their apprehensions about homosexuality.

The need for reassurance of masculinity—and the quest for it—can be seen in some masculine pursuits and reading habits. There is substantial evidence of a compensatory emphasis upon activities and appearances loaded with masculine overtones. A large portion of the millions of males who tramp off into the woods with guns each fall—often to kill dogs, cows, or each other—quite probably are trying to prove something about themselves. The importance of the gun as a virility symbol sent hundreds of thousands of males into a vehement protest completely out of proportion to their need for guns when mild legislation to regulate the sale of guns, as potential weapons for assassination and other crimes, was considered in the 1960s.

In California many young men who make their living at such menial jobs as cemetery workmen during the week, in ordinary work clothes, get into black leather jackets and helmets with iron cross markings on them when the weekend arrives. They mount their roaring motorcycles; and quite a few spread terror as they sweep in droves through outlying towns.

The Wall Street Journal one day in 1965 devoted its lead article to the Walter Mitty syndrome of males as it shows up in the purchase of high-powered cars. It told the story of a 22-year-old male clerk in Detroit who becomes a tiger when he jumps into his Oldsmobile 442, guns the 400-cubic-inch engine and hears the rumble of dual exhausts. This clerk was quoted as explaining, "I really don't drive much, but I try to get out a little on weekends, and I have had it up to 135."

One of the best evidences we encountered of the sale of masculine reassurance was in the December, 1964, copy of *Men*. The differing images of the modern male that emerged in the editorial and advertising content was startling. The split in imagery was wide enough to suggest that many males may indeed be living a Walter Mitty life.

First, let's look at the editorial content. Featured on the cover was an article entitled, "ONE MAN MARINE ARMY WHO CONQUERED BLOODY BATU." The cover drawing showed a wounded Marine in a tree, blood about him, with a machete, knife, hand grenades, Tommy gun, and rifle. Below were a bunch of unsuspecting Nipponese soldiers. Also the cover featured an article entitled "HOW THE FBI TRAPPED GANGLAND'S BLOODIEST FOUR." And the Complete Book featured on the cover was "MADEMOISELLE HOT BLOOD." It was about a hard-nosed male adventurer who had to cope not only with Red terrorists in Malaya but with a Eurasian flame of a girl. (Apparently surveys had indicated that "blood" is a power word with males.) In any case, the bulk of the editorial content related to male conquest either in battle or in bed.

Now let us look at the tenor of the same issue's advertisements. Did they offer the male readers opportunities for adventurous work that would satisfy yearnings for glory and physical conquest? Hardly. The first full-page ad offered dealerships for cleaning soiled furniture. The second full-page ad was placed by an extension university inviting male readers to learn how to become "high-paying draftsmen." The third ad offered success in air conditioning and refrigeration. The fourth ad (full page) offered courses in musical instrumentation. And so it went. Very few of the invitations offered any kind of opportunity that would even be outdoors. Here are some of the invitations as stated in the ads:

"YOU can step into a well-paid hotel-motel position. . . ." "Meat-cutting offers you success and security. . . ." "Learn upholstery. . . ." "Be a real estate broker. . . ."

There were advertisements near the back for knives and lessons in karate. But more typical were the two ads on page 81. The first was: "Amazing invention quickly helps give you a *strong, manly voice*." And below it was an ad that stated, "Flatten that belly . . . look athletic . . . just slip on your 'wonder slim.'" Wonder Slim was described as a back supporter. It appeared to be essentially a male corset.

Meanwhile, some of the more sophisticated male magazines provided their readers with material that exhibited glowering hostility or amiable paternalism toward females. A good deal of their content seemed designed to denigrate females. The mood was often competitive or defensive and seemed to suggest a drive by the males to protect their long-dominant position.

Playboy usually presents women as playthings, pleasant to pet. On the other hand, *True* quite regularly has been depicting women either as the adversaries of man or as a breed whose come-uppance is overdue. Each month it has a regular feature, "IT'S A MAN'S WORLD," dedicated to keeping males informed and to keeping "the little woman firmly in her place."

On the front cover of its February, 1967, issue *True* asked its readers if their wives were spying on them. One of its major efforts at keeping the little woman firmly in her place was an article in its February, 1965, issue entitled: "THE FEMALE FEARS THAT BIND A MAN." It was illustrated by a cartoon of a sweating man in harness trying to move forward while hauling a nest containing his brood, with his wife looking fearfully backward. The thesis was summed up at the outset: "Women are afraid of all kinds of things. Financial insecurity is only one of them. Women are afraid of physical hardship, physical danger, illness, the dark, lizards and mice and insects to list a few." The author, Max Gunther, acknowledged that this was the way women were constituted and there wasn't much a man could do about it. But he added, "When female fears prevent a man from doing things he wants to do, it's time to blow the whistle, time for a declaration of male independence from womanish worries!"

In contrast, the leading U.S. women's magazines during the 1960s devoted very little space to trying to put the male in his place. Instead, when discussing male-female relationships they seemed to be trying thoughtfully to understand what was going on.

Considering their surgent position, they could afford to be magnanimous.

III. Trends in Premarital Intimacy:
Some Evidence of Changes
in Thinking and Acting

CHAPTER 9

From Flaming Youth to the Up-Tight Generation

"The incidence of premarital sex among college girls is somewhere between 15 percent and 85 percent." A good-natured remark by Donald Longworth, as chairman of the Sociology Department, Bowling Green State University.

The investigators of male-female relationships have had a good deal of difficulty in trying to reach a consensus on whether premarital intimacy is actually increasing, decreasing, or remaining unchanged. One might assume that unless there have been powerful countervailing forces quietly at work—such as the development in younger people of internalized controls as external controls have crumbled—the weight of forces in the new environment would produce an increase in premarital physical intimacy. If there has been any such significant shift in behavior in the past two decades, many of the best known professionals have not been prepared to say so.

The people who take positions (whether they favor "yes" or "no" conclusions about an increase in intimacy) have depended largely upon extrapolating from evidence gleaned in earlier decades, or they have offered impressions based upon observation, circumstantial evidence, or an application of logic. The few systematic surveys of sex behavior made in the 1960s in the U.S.A. are mostly small and offer conflicting findings.

In 1965, in my search for reliable data, I consulted Clark E. Vincent, then president of the National Council on Family Relations, about trends in premarital intimacy. He is greatly respected for his studies of sex behavior, especially that resulting in illegitimacy. He said, "I don't think we really know how much of this premarital sex is talk and how much is action."

At about the same time, I got in touch with a distinguished medical scientist who in addressing a national conference in 1964 regarding the sex problems of women had stated, "The trend toward premarital sex experience is proceeding with extraordinary rapidity."

Eagerly I asked him on what he had based that statement. He sent a list of four sources, and I checked each. One stated that premarital sex was "probably" increasing. Two others offered indirect, inferential evidences based on trends in illegitimacy or pregnant brides. The fourth was based on a survey by another investigator who had published a report 5 years earlier that was based on samplings that had been completed nearly a decade earlier still.

Two good examples of contrasting opinions that have been offered were in two reports published within the same week in 1966. In one a leading official of the National Association of Independent Schools was quoted in *The New York Times* as stating that students were developing "terrifying attitudes toward sex." In the same week Dana L. Farnsworth, head of medical services at Harvard and Radcliffe, told a gathering of college girls, "Your behavior and your mothers' behavior is very similar, and they were nice girls, too."

One formidably qualified observer somewhat modified his view of the contemporary scene between 1965–68. John H. Gagnon, senior research sociologist at the Institute for Sex Research, Indiana University, pointed out in 1965 that the available evidence would suggest that "the long-predicted change in American sex patterns has not in fact occurred." In March 1968, presumably on the basis of new evidence that had become available to the institute, he and his colleague William Simon wrote in *The Annals* of the American Academy of Political and Social Science: "At present, there are uneven signs of a shift in rates of premarital intercourse in our society—a shift toward increasing incidence of premarital intercourse on the part of the female."

Another formidably qualified observer, David Mace, suggested in 1965 that if changes toward increased premarital sex were not indeed occurring, then the signs were misleading. He was then Executive Director of the American Association of Marriage Counselors. He said: "Nobody's got the facts [but] we do have a whole new climate of freedom and acceptance, a removal of taboos. I see no counter pressures worth talking about. The present situation throughout the United States is one of chaotic confusion. Most generalizations can be contradicted from community to community. What is happening is that we have been moving from a fairly agreed position to an absence of position."

In the course of my research I tried to make an assessment of the available evidence by sifting the best studies I could find based on surveys, circumstantial facts, and authoritative opinion. I tried to organize the direct evidence—that based on surveys of behavior or attitudes—by decades of the 20th century. Also I placed the studies in the decades in which the surveys *actually were made,* rather than when investigators got around to reporting the results, which often occurred in a subsequent decade. Further, I sought to separate those surveys based upon samples of the general population and those based on college students' responses, since the latter offer a more homogeneous group for making decade-by-decade comparisons. Finally, I brought together, separately, a number of studies made in other countries for cross-cultural comparisons.

Investigators of premarital intimacy have devoted the most attention to the incidence of coitus not only because society has viewed it as a major break point in premarital behavior, but also because while definitions of petting may vary, definitions of coitus do not.

In the Notes for this Chapter 9, starting on page 486, I have listed more than 40 studies on which the following summary is based. In the Notes, I indicate the size of the sample and the sampling methods used. And in the Appendix to this Chapter 9, starting on page 453 you will find, if interested in a detailed examination, the principal published evidence of the incidence of premarital intimacy based on circumstantial evidence and on the direct evidence as revealed in (1) samplings of the general population and (2) samplings of college-level populations, with citations to the studies listed in the Notes from which the evidence was drawn.

What follows here is your author's impression of the highlights of the material contained in that Appendix, as far as they reflect trends, or absence of trends.

Circumstantial facts regarding the incidence of premarital intimacy

For whatever they are worth, the clues offered by trends in illegitimacy, pregnant brides, and venereal disease in the U.S.A. all suggest that the incidence of premarital coitus has been rising in the past quarter-century.

The illegitimacy rate tripled from 1940 to 1963. . . . The proportion of girls who become pregnant before marriage evidently has risen significantly (and more than a third of all girls who marry while in high school are pregnant at the time of marriage). . . . Venereal disease among adolescents more than tripled in the nine years between 1956 and 1965.

Some of this indirect "evidence" of increased premarital coitus, however, may be attributed to better record-keeping, or greater openness in acknowledging personal conditions that people in the past managed to keep secret, or carelessness caused by an overconfidence of youths in the new scientific protections.

Direct evidence on premarital intimacy emerging from surveys of behavior and attitudes

Regarding general populations. There is general agreement that there was an upheaval of sexual behavior in the U.S.A. during the decade of the 1920s when youth was said to be flaming. Some contend that any changes since then have been primarily changes of attitudes catching up with the shock waves of behavioral changes that occurred in that era, with perhaps some slight behavioral changes, too.

It has been difficult to speak authoritatively on what really has been happening in recent decades, if anything, as far as the general public is concerned, because the last systematic sampling, the Kinsey group's, was completed before 1950. (Kinsey's principal associates were Wardell B. Pomeroy, Clyde E. Martin, and Paul H. Gebhard.) Many of even the younger people interviewed by Alfred Kinsey and his associates are now grandmothers and grandfathers.

The only survey worth noting of a semi-general nature in the present decade has been that conducted by *Seventeen* magazine of 1166 teen-age girls who were recruited to serve on its Consumer Panel. While they might be deemed "typical" teen-age girls, it is doubtful that they reflect a national cross-section since, as the research report states, "the demographic data in this report conforms to tested patterns of *Seventeen* subscribers." One finding from the questionnaires they completed, however, seems worth mentioning (in the absence of other survey data). During the 1960s as many girls reported they had experienced coitus by the age of 19 as had reported coital experience by the age of 21 before 1950. In the Kinsey sample 25 percent of the females reported they had experienced coitus by 21. In the *Seventeen* sampling 25 percent of the girls in the 18–19 age group reported they had experienced coitus.

The various careful samplings, including the Kinsey one, that were made before 1950 suggest that the following trends occurred in sex behavior during the first half of the 20th century:

1. The incidence of coitus before marriage reported by females more than doubled. Before 1920, two studies show, a fourth or less of U.S. brides were non-virgins, whereas by 1950 about half the brides who were interviewed were non-virgins (again reported by two different studies).

2. For males during the early part of the century there was a modest but consistent rise in individuals reporting pre-marital coital experience.

3. The number of sexually experienced males who reported that a part of their premarital sexual experience had been with the women they subsequently married showed a dramatic rise in the decade-by-decade comparisons made by Lewis Terman. Of the males who were sexually experienced, only 1 in 3 marrying before World War I was likely to indicate that *any* of that experience had been with the woman he subsequently married. By the 1930s, 4 out of 5 experienced men were likely to report that some of their coital experience had been with their brides-to-be.

4. One of the more dramatic findings of the Kinsey group was the very considerable difference in sexual experience reported by males who went to college and those who had only a grade-school education. Only 45 percent of his "younger generation" males who went to college reported coital experience by the age of 20, whereas 87 percent of the

males with only grade-school educations reported coital experience by the age of 20.

5. Studies in France and England indicate that between the end of World War I and 1950 the percentage of wives who had experienced premarital coitus in those countries nearly doubled. (But they still remained a minority among the married respondents.)

Regarding premarital intimacy of college students. This somewhat more homogeneous group is the one that particularly interests us in our search for trends or absence of trends regarding premarital intimacy. Most of the systematic samplings, reported at this writing, were made in the 1940s or 1950s. Unfortunately there is only one survey worth noting before 1940 (that by Dorothy Bromley and Florence Britten). And a number of samplings since 1940 have been of females only. (It should be remembered that college students today include a far greater proportion of their age group than was true in 1940.)

The Bromley and Britten survey found collegians reporting premarital coital experience in these proportions: 50 percent of the males, 25 percent of the females. That same pattern, within a few percent, emerged from the Kinsey pre-1950 findings on the number of college-level males and females who had experienced coitus by the age of 21.

One of the few systematic studies reported since 1950 on the coital experience of collegiate males is that of Winston W. Ehrmann, who studied both males and females. Sixty-five percent of his collegiate males reported coital experience. But this sampling was at one Southern university (University of Florida), and as we shall note, Southern male collegians may not be typical of U.S. male collegians as a whole. A few years later, Harold T. Christensen and George R. Carpenter found among males at a Midwestern university that 51 percent reported they had experienced coitus.

On the other hand, Ehrmann's college girls reported in the early 1950s that only 13 percent of them had ever experienced coitus. Again we were dealing with a sample from one Southern university.

A glance at the surveys administered to college females by their professors reveals that in all instances less than 25 percent of the girls have reported ever experiencing coitus. One noteworthy finding emerging from such professor-administered studies is that in the 1940s and early 1950s in every instance that we have examined, less than 15 percent of the coeds reported coital experience. In those reported by the late 1950s and the 1960s the figures more commonly were in the 20–25 percent range. Many of the samples were so small, however, that a few percentage points of difference may be meaningless.

In 1965 Mervin B. Freedman wrote a paper with the rather sweeping title "The Sexual Behavior of American College Women," for the *Merrill-Palmer Quarterly*. It was based on a long-term study he and colleagues had made of 49 Vassar graduates and received a great deal of national publicity. (See Note 26.) He reported that 22 percent of these graduating seniors had coital experience. (His report did not state that his subjects were members of a class that had been graduated a half-dozen years earlier.) In connection with his finding he stated near the end of his paper, "The data presented in this paper are consistent with the findings of other studies which are almost unanimous in reporting the incidence of non-virginity among college women to be 25 percent or lower. . . ." The other studies he mentioned by name were those of Ehrmann and Kinsey.

Within a few months there appeared a report on a considerably larger though perhaps less intensive study of senior college women made by Harrop and Ruth Freeman, who have been involved in college counseling. Dr. Harrop Freeman was in law and counseling at Cornell University and is an affiliated member of the American Association of Marriage Counselors. Recently both he and his wife have been doing research at the Center for the Study of Democratic Institutions. The Freemans interviewed or sent questionnaires to young women in several areas of the country. Some interviewees had problems that had caused them to seek counseling. The Freemans' findings were reported in *The Journal of the National Association of Women Deans and Counselors*. They found (and at this writing their report seems to have attracted little attention outside the field of college counseling) that 55 percent of the senior women in their sample had experienced coitus. The Freemans did not seem to be aware that this was radically out of line with what was generally being said about coitus among college females, or with what previous surveys had shown about the sex behavior of college women.

In the various principal studies of the sex behavior of college students there were these further findings that will be of particular interest later in this section:

1. Lester Kirkendall discovered that among his 200 college males who had experienced coitus 19 percent had at some time patronized a prostitute. This was in the late 1950s.

2. In the late 1950s Eugene J. Kanin and David H. Howard reported that among wives living in housing units of a Midwestern university campus, 43 percent had experienced coitus with their husbands-to-be before marriage. (They were not asked to report any other coital experience they may have had.)

3. Ira Reiss found in comparing the attitudes of adults and students (high school and college) regarding what was acceptable in premarital sex the following: Only 17 percent of a national adult sample thought such coitus was acceptable for a girl who was "engaged," whereas 44 percent of the students thought such coitus acceptable.

4. Harold T. Christensen and George R. Carpenter made the one noteworthy, systematic cross-cultural study on record in the late 1950s by comparing the sex behavior and attitudes of university students at a Danish school, at a U.S. Midwestern school, and at a Western U.S. "Intermountain" school where Mormon influence is strong. They found that reported coitus for female students ranged from 9 percent for the Intermountain students to 21 percent at the Midwestern university to 60 percent for the Danish female students.

5. Substantial differences by schools or regions have appeared in a number of investigations made within the United States of sex attitudes and behavior of college students where comparisons were possible. For example:

• Ira Reiss found in comparing attitudes at a Virginia college and at a New York college with notably permissive attitudes toward sex that the students at the two schools differed rather dramatically on condoning premarital coitus as acceptable if a girl was "in love":

The Virginia college .... 16% felt such coitus
                                                                              acceptable
The permissive N.Y. college .... 72% felt such coitus
                                                                              acceptable

• The Freemans in their study of women students at schools in different areas (and women from different parts of the country) concluded that young women from the East and West were more liberal, with the South most conservative (except for Florida and Texas) and the Midwest somewhere between.

• Gael Greene in her impressionistic assessment of what was happening to the sex life of coeds on many campuses found as a major impression that behavior and attitudes vary considerably depending upon the location of the school and type of school.

• Bromley and Britten found in their study that at two women's colleges—one with a reputation for its liberal views and the other with a reputation for its conservative environment—the girls at the liberal school reported a coital rate twice as high as the conservative one (18 percent vs. 36 percent).

Some biologically oriented investigators, on the other hand, are suspicious of any sample if there are any significant variations from campus to campus or region to region.

And some investigators feel it is implausible that any significant change could take place in sexual behavior within a generation or two, barring extraordinary circumstances. Evidence strongly suggesting a contrary conclusion emerges from two successive studies in 1960 and 1965 at Swedish "people's colleges." Within the 5-year period, for example, the reported coital experience of female students rose from 40 percent to 65 percent.

This then is the picture of the reported research at this writing.

In the face of the scarcity of systematic studies reported in the decade ending in early 1968—when there has been so much talk about a "sexual revolution"—careful observers were left to speculate whether America in the 1960s was—or was not—undergoing any significant shift in behavior and attitudes regarding premarital intimacy.

The press featured reports of the wildness of modern youth, including pictures of nude parties staged by students in California. Perhaps partly in reaction, many of the experts in marriage and sex behavior were saying "not proven."

Some highly respected figures who have tended to the view that there has been little or no evidence of change in actual behavior in recent decades are: educational psychologist Nevitt Sanford, sociologists Ira Reiss, Robert Bell, and anthropologist Charles Winick. In 1966, however, John Gagnon, who is with the Institute for Sex Research and was, at that time, inclined to this view, emphasized that "We are distressed by how little actually is known. The lack of research is a terrible commentary."

The Institute finally obtained by 1967 substantial grants from the National Institute of Child Health and Human Development and from the Hugh M. Hefner Foundation, established by the celebrated publisher, for new research with college students. With its funds the Institute for Sex Research arranged for personnel affiliated with the National Opinion Research Center to interview 1200 college students on 12 U.S. campuses. (Washington's grant for this project is entitled "Youth Cultures and Aspects of the Socialization Process.")

Perhaps it should be noted that some of those cited above as doubting there had been any noteworthy change in sex behavior made their statements before the Freeman study of college senior women was released to college deans and counselors.

On the other hand, some other highly qualified observers were stating, or assuming, that significant changes in behavior were indeed occurring. This school of thought, confronted with the same shortage of systematic surveys of actual behavior, tended to be impressed by the circumstantial evidence in statistics on illegitimacy, pregnant brides, etc., and the social forces at work that might logically be producing a significant change at least among some groups. Here are two samples of this viewpoint offered by respected observers:

• Harold T. Christensen, who has headed family study seminars at the American Sociological Association and the National Council on Family Relations: "I have no real basis for trends, only opinions. My opinion and some research suggests that *female* premarital sex is increasing."

• Lester Dearborn, who has been a marriage counselor for more than 30 years: "I don't agree with all the talk that there has not been much change in premarital coitus. My experience is that there is much more. For 30 years I have been taking case histories of couples. A question I always ask, and note the response on a corner of the card, is, 'Did the two of you have intercourse before marriage?' Now the overwhelming majority say that they did. Thirty years ago the majority of wives would explain that their man expected to marry a virgin."

That is roughly the picture of what in recent years has been said and reported about premarital intimacy. Perhaps the most provocative statement of all was made by David Mace. He speculates that if no noteworthy changes are taking place, "then we will have to revise our whole idea of what is going on in a culture. We are being subjected to a barrage of sexual stimulation and seeing many signs of social upheaval. If this is not producing changes in behavior then we have got to reexamine our concepts about the factors that do cause changes."

CHAPTER 10

An International Sampling of Young People Regarding Intimacy

"One often gives strangers information he would never think of giving to his close friends or family." Ira L. Reiss, researcher in sex attitudes and behavior, University of Iowa.

The paucity of solid information about whether sexual attitudes and behavior were—or were not—changing and the abundance of conflicting opinion about what was happening to the sexual behavior of both males and females led us to attempt a fresh sampling that will be described here. The hope was that this might offer the possibility not only of a new late-1960s look but a chance to make some interesting comparisons not previously attempted.

It was decided to confine the main survey to junior and senior students in colleges and universities—or their age equivalent abroad—since (1) they constituted a homogeneous group, (2) they include many of tomorrow's leaders and trend-setters, (3) their education and intelligence made them more likely to have the patience to complete a 2000-word questionnaire, (4) they were accessible to us in many areas, and (5) they were now adults or close to it.

Our hope was to be able to make comparisons by regions, by types of school, by national samples, and by the career aspiration of girls, since there was reason to believe, or suspect, that premarital intimacy might vary on all these dimensions.

The idea was to ask identical questions of both males and

133

females at many different types of institutions in the U.S.A. and abroad. As indicated, the exploration grew beyond expectations as it crossed first regional and then national boundaries until responses were in from 21 U.S. schools and 5 universities in other countries.

One does not have to be a cynic to inquire how anyone can possibly arrive at anything approaching the truth about the real feelings and behavior of college students or anyone else in such a sensitive area as physical intimacy. Questions of validity and reliability have plagued just about everyone who has attempted research in this area.

The first question any survey-maker encounters when he tells acquaintances he is investigating sex attitudes and behavior is: "How do you know they are not lying?" It is a reasonable question.

If people were colored marbles in a well-mixed bowl, statisticians assert, you could develop a reasonable national sample on the basis of perhaps a thousand drawings. Poll-takers and TV-raters achieve results that satisfy their clients when they draw national behavioral pictures on the basis of sampling 1000 to 2000 carefully chosen individuals in various parts of the country.

Getting a picture of collegiate behavioral habits on the basis of, say, 1000 individuals presents a host of difficulties. To mention just one complication, some school populations are drawn primarily from their area, others are semi-national institutions.

Assuming you could arrive at some accurate cross-section of the nation's students by choosing 1000 of them, you would then have to make sure that those among them who finally agreed to provide you with information about their sexual behavior were still representative. The odds are heavily against a 100-percent response in a large-size sex survey without some element of coercion. (We came close at *one* school, for *one* sex. At the Midwestern Protestant university we got a 96-percent response from all the girls who received checklists.) Coercion under whatever guise not only violates a student's privacy but, further, it increases the probability that he or she will not be truthful. Even assuming that those freely responding are still representative of the original carefully chosen sample, you would still have the problem of making certain that each person who responded was truthfully describing his behavior and attitudes. Here if you demand absolute certainty you would have to administer a truth serum.

Beyond this you would have the problem of making certain that your questions were phrased in ways that would really measure what you thought you were measuring.

The various investigators cited in the preceding chapter tried to cope with these problems in various ways, and some were less successful than others in pleasing either themselves or critics.

Some have depended upon volunteers. Others have sought to reduce this process of self-selection which threatens distortion by asking for volunteers from within specified groups of eligibles. This was the Kinsey procedure. And a few have tried by various ways to achieve true randomness.

Also, various techniques have been used to try to assure that information given by willing respondents is truthful. Traditionally males in talking about sex have been notoriously inclined to boast, while females have been inclined to understate experience. In recent years, however, this has declined as a problem in sampling collegians because of their increased openness in discussing sex. Ehrmann commented in his study, "A surprising fact discovered in the interviews was that in a few instances the individual was more willing to discuss his or her sex behavior than to reveal the identity of the father's occupation when it had a low social prestige value."

Some investigators have sought to arrive at truth by assembling the willing respondents in a room and administering a questionnaire. Terman did this and was criticized by Kinsey for doing so. Some professors have passed out questionnaires to willing students in their classes with assurance of anonymity (and a few have passed out "anonymous" questionnaires involving sex behavior to *all* students). Unless such sampling is carefully handled, there may be a subtle element of coercion or pressure in any case, since the students are under the influence of the professor to make a good impression by volunteering, or may regard the professor as a father figure. Or the students if asked to do any writing may wonder about the anonymity since the professor has access to samples of their handwriting. Another difficulty has been that often the questionnaires have been handed out entirely or primarily to students in family-living classes, who are no more representative of the student body than a survey confined to engineering students would be.

A few investigators of attitudes have used polling techniques of going door-to-door on a street, which is probably the very least likely way to elicit candor on matters relating to sex. Others have used face-to-face interviewing techniques with individual subjects.

There are some good reasons for favoring this face-to-face interviewing approach when it can be afforded. The interviewer if competent can, from knowledge of the respondent, evaluate his or her responses and probe for clarifications. Also if a great deal of information is sought, there is a greater chance the respondent can be induced to stick with the interviewing until it is completed than that he would stick to the completion of a lengthy questionnaire. It is arguable, however, whether in face-to-face interviewing situations respondents will be as matter-of-factly truthful about their sexual behavior as they would be when responding privately to an anonymous questionnaire. There would seem to be the theoretical probability that more respondents might be inclined in face-to-face discussion of their sexual behavior to protect their self-esteem or blur over uncomfortable aspects of their lives. (We will see in Chapter 21 that females, far more than males, are sensitive to—and often preoccupied with—the nuances of relationship when talking with another person even about non-sexual subjects.) Another inherent shortcoming of the interview when a person is invited to describe his or her sexual experience is that full anonymity for the respondent is obviously not possible. There will always be one person, the interviewer, who knows what the respondent confided.

Some interviewers have sought to minimize possible embarrassment to the respondent by using only males to interview males, and females to interview females. Others such as Kinsey have concluded that a skilled interviewer will arrive at the facts whatever his sex. Even assuming that interviewing is the preferred approach, there is a practical difficulty. The cost of conducting careful, private, standardized interviews with many hundreds of carefully chosen individuals about their sex behavior and processing the results is—as the Institute of Sex Research can testify—high indeed, in time and money.

Finally, there is the problem of getting a good response from those you have singled out for questioning. This is especially a problem with college students, since they have many things on their minds and they are surfeited with requests to fill out forms or questionnaires about some aspect of their lives.

What is an acceptable response rate? We were given expert opinions ranging from 20 percent to 85 percent. A psychologist at the University of Rochester wrote a paper on attitudes of students toward coeducational dormitories on the basis of a 10-percent return from the students who were given questionnaires. Burgess and Wallin in seeking to get responses from 1000 recently engaged couples had students distribute questionnaires among 6000 such couples they knew.

Kinsey and his associates in depending upon volunteers drawn from designated groups reported that about one-fourth of all their case histories came from groups where everyone contributed a history, and about one-sixth of the female case histories used in their book on the female came from such 100-percent response groups. They added that "a considerable portion" of the rest of all their case histories came from groups where they had gotten histories from 50 to 90 percent of the individuals in the group.

Back in the late 1930s Bromley and Britten (see Note 15 in Chapter 9) made a sampling of college students on sexual attitudes and behavior, and based their report on a 20-percent response.

In the May, 1965, issue of *The Journal of Marriage and the Family* two investigators reported making a study on the attitudes of school principals toward high-school marriages. They sent out 490 questionnaires and reported, "The response was good . . . 57%."

At this writing the Institut für Sexualforschung at the University of Hamburg in Germany is analyzing results of a massive survey of sex attitudes among students at 13 German universities. Several thousand returns have been received. (Paul Gebhard, Alfred Kinsey's successor as Director of the Institute for Sex Research in Indiana accepted an invitation to help in the analysis of the data.) The director of the German study, Hans Giese, reports that the total response rate from the 13 universities is 59 percent, which he describes as "very high indeed."

In the present survey being reported we decided arbitrarily to set aside, or treat with extra wariness, any individual samplings that did not produce a response rate of at least 50 percent. (Eleanore Luckey believed that given the procedures used, 60 percent would represent a good response.)

These then are some of the kinds of problems any investigator in the area of sex attitudes and behavior has to cope with.

Let us look then at the samplings we made and the way we made them.

THE SAMPLES

The "College Checklist" was originally distributed to 2100 junior and senior students at 21 U.S. colleges and universities along with a letter of explanation and a sheet entitled "Regarding Protective Procedures" spelling out the assurances of confidentiality and anonymity. (See Appendix 10-A.) At each of the 21 colleges, 100 students received the checklist. If the schools were coed, 50 of the checklists went to males and 50 of them went to females.

Of the 21 U.S. colleges 7 are in the East, 5 in the Midwest, 3 in the South, and 6 in the West (4 in the Southwest and 2 in the Northwest). Thus in terms of population distribution of the country the South is a bit under-represented and the Southwest is substantially over-represented. However, because results are reported in terms of percentage of responses made, these disproportions present no serious problem. The main point to be noted is that each of the four main regions of the United States is represented by at least 3 schools that include at least 1 state university located in a small town or city and that include at least 1 private university located in a large metropolitan area.

In the total sample there are 2 all-male colleges and 2 all-female colleges. Although these are all in the East where one-sexed schools are more characteristic than in any other region, all 4 draw their students from the national arena.

Of the 21 U.S. schools, 2 are specifically church-related. One is a Protestant university, the other a Catholic university. Both happen to be in the Midwest, a point we will allow for later. (In retrospect I would be happier if we had taken samples at a minimum of 50 colleges. Not only do there appear to be regional patterns, but in each of the major regions of the country there are at least 15 basic types of 4-year college, and most of these vary considerably in their environment on such possibly significant variable elements as rural-metropolitan, protective-permissive, scholastically easy-tough. We recognize that the responses from our 21 schools can only be suggestive, not comprehensive, nationally.)

Substantially the same checklist was distributed to 300 students (150 male, 150 female) at major universities in England, Norway, and Canada. For technical reasons a larger number (450) was distributed at a German university.[1] These 4 samplings constitute the International Sample whenever we refer to it as an entity.

It should be added that originally universities in both France and Italy had been included and that a distribution was made according to plan to 150 girls at an Italian university. Because the response rate was low, their responses have not been included in the analysis of the International Sample. However, where it has seemed appropriate or is of interest I will refer to them. The Italian male sampling was inadequate and has not been included beyond taking note of a few of the comments that were made on some of the response sheets. This is also true for the French sample whose checklists, because of shipping delays, arrived during the students' all-or-nothing year-end exam week and a full distribution as planned could not be made.

In seeking a Scandinavian sample there was an equal opportunity to distribute in either Norway or Sweden, and Norway was chosen because (1) there were already 3 fairly large college-level samplings available on Swedish students and (2) some U.S. sociologists have stated that the United States is moving in its sex patterns toward the "Scandinavian" pattern and I wondered if Norwegians were similar enough in their sex behavior to Swedes (and Danes) really to support a generalization about "Scandinavians." (I have no information on Finns.)

In order to keep the comparableness of the International Sample and the U.S. Sample as reliable as possible, the international subjects were selected by age (between 20 and 22), rather than according to their year in the university. The mean age of U.S. students was just under 21 years of age; and an averaging of the mean ages of the international samples yields a mean age of about 21 years for both the males and the females.[2]

It is impossible of course to choose from all a country's many universities one that typifies the nation's students. The difficulty was especially apparent in England, because it now has a great variety of university types ranging from its ancient world-famous centers of learning to the new "red brick" schools. We did in each country at least choose a large university drawing its students from many parts of the country.

Our 3 non-college samplings involved the distribution of a modified form of the college checklist to 200 Army enlisted men, to 100 young males and females in the beach area of southern California, and to 100 recently married wives living in campus housing at a university in the Rockies. In this last sampling the aim was to search for any indications that attitudes held by women might change with marriage.[3]

HOW THE SAMPLING WAS CONDUCTED

In developing a pattern for distribution a primary concern was to respect the privacy of each individual who might be invited to participate. In early 1967 the journal *Science,* published by the American Association for the Advancement of Science, carried a summary of the findings of a White House panel created to investigate problems of privacy posed by behavioral research. The panel stated, "The right to privacy is the right of the individual to decide for himself how much he will share with others his thoughts, his feelings and the facts of his personal life."

Earlier a fine detailed analysis of how privacy should be protected in research appeared in the *Columbia Law Review,* November, 1965. The article "Privacy and Behavioral Research" was by Oscar M. Reubhausen and Orville G. Brim, Jr. Mr. Brim was the president of the Russell Sage Foundation, and Mr. Reubhausen was chairman of the Special Committee on Science and Law of the Association of the Bar of the City of New York. The authors emphasized three conditions in particular that any researcher should strive to meet, and indicated that in some types of research meeting all three was difficult. These three conditions were assurance of consent, assurance of anonymity, and assurance of confidentiality. The sampling procedure that was used in the survey being reported here was designed to meet all three of these tests absolutely.[4]

A triangular method of inquiry was employed. At each college or university arrangements were made to have a student known or recommended as being especially responsible and conscientious supervise the distribution, and 100 checklists were mailed to him or her. On coed campuses the student in charge arranged for a member of the other sex to work with him or her in handling distribution to the other sex. Distributors were all paid on an hourly basis. The distributors were instructed in approaching a prospective respondent to explain in a quite general way that your author was making a survey of attitudes and behavior of students regarding the male-female relationship and then to ask the student if he or she would like, at the student's leisure, to examine the checklist and complete it or not as he or she chose. A stamped envelope addressed to the author at his home in Connecticut was attached to each questionnaire. Each questionnaire could be completed simply by making check marks.

Students distributing the forms were instructed to make no record whatever of the identity (when known to them) of students accepting the checklist for examination. All forms received have been kept within a special file arrangement.

Students making the distribution were instructed to seek as representative a cross-section of their student body as feasible. Instructions and suggestions were offered on how to do it. (The instruction is in "Procedures for Distribution" reprinted in Appendix 10-B.)

Upon completing distribution, each supervising student completed two reporting forms on which he or she explained in considerable detail precisely how the distribution occurred and the percentage of students approached who accepted the checklist for inspection. (The U.S. acceptances-for-inspection ranged from 75 percent to 100 percent, with an overall average of approximately 91-percent acceptance.)

It was hoped that by the distribution procedures employed, which enabled students to respond to the checklist privately and anonymously, we would minimize any tendencies that the students might have toward either bragging or understating. It should be noted in any case that the findings are based on questions which gave all students in all regions and countries precisely the same opportunity to tell the truth or to exaggerate. The patterns of responses by schools varied considerably (as your author suspected they would), but they varied in patterns that were consistent and in fact in ways that became roughly predictable.

THE RESPONSE

The returns totaled 2259 checklists, 2202 from unmarried students, as follows:

	TOTAL	MALE	FEMALE
1. U.S. College Sample	1,393	665	728

   (The original distribution to 21 colleges)

| 2. The International Sample | 809 | 436 | 373 |

   This included: 245 English university students (142 male and 103 female); 233 German students (120 male and 113 female); 152 Norwegian students (86 male and 66 female); and 179 Canadian students (88 male and 91 female).

3. Recently married wives living in a Rocky Mt. state university's student housing .... 57.

In addition, occasional reference will be made to the 48 Italian university girls who responded.[5]

I have mentioned earlier that the Institute for Sex Research, in its recently undertaken investigation, has sampled 1200 U.S. students at 12 colleges. Perhaps it should be stressed now, if comparisons of the two studies are made, that approximately half (or 600) of the Institute's 1200 students were freshmen and sophomores and thus were at lower academic class levels than the juniors and seniors that comprise our entire U.S. College Sample.

The rates of return for those samples that will be regularly used in the analysis were:

The U.S. College Sample 67%
The Canadian university sample 60%
The Norwegian university sample 51%
The German university sample (unmarried)[6] 62%
The English university sample[7] 82%
The recently married Rocky Mt. wives 57%

Here is a list of the U.S. colleges and universities where 2100 checklists were originally distributed with the response rate (at time of tabulation) by the students at each school:

The East (Total return: 493)

New England Men's College 84%
Private University in New York City 53%
Ivy League University 81%
State College in New England 59%
Private Women's College in Northeast 83%
Private Women's College in Northeast with liberal
    parietal rules 65%
State University in New England 68%

The Midwest (Total return: 364)

State University 65%
Catholic University in Metropolitan Area 71%
Protestant University in Non-Metropolitan Area 78%
Private Coed University in Metropolitan Area 70%
Private Coed University in Non-Metropolitan Area 80%

The South (Total return: 185)

Private University in Metropolitan Area 76%
State University 37%
State University in Upper South 72%

The West (Total return: 351)

State University in Rocky Mt. Area 69%
State University in Southwest 47%
State College in Southwest 64%
State University in Northwest 53%
State University in California (one campus) 56%
Private University in California 62%

In the U.S. colleges more girls than men responded. The reverse was true at all the European schools. The greater responsiveness of U.S. girls showed up even more clearly on the blank sheet for "amplifying comments" that accompanied each checklist. (It could be sent in with the checklist or separately.) The girls not only supplied comments in greater numbers than males, but in total words they volunteered more than twice as much comment as the U.S. males.

It has sometimes been suggested that only the bolder, more worldly, more sexually experienced people tend to respond to surveys of this nature. That might apply to interview-type surveys that rely on face-to-face encounters. There is no evidence that it applies in our survey. The highest single rate of response from all the distributions (96%) came, as noted, from girls at the Protestant Midwestern university, yet their reported attitude and behavior were relatively conservative. The girl handling this distribution was delayed a week because of her work in connection with "Christian Emphasis Week." Also it might be noted that the most conservative female student sample in the entire survey—that of the girls at the Catholic university in the Midwest—was based upon a 72-percent return—or substantially above the average return of the 21 U.S. schools.

As for the comments students were invited to make, about a third of all the students did add comments, some running to 1800 words. A dozen or so made caustic comments. A number set us straight or scolded us for ways certain questions were phrased. One male complained that the wording of several of the "yes" or "no" questions "hung me up."

Primarily, however, students in their amplifying comments simply tried to offer the benefit of their thoughts and experiences; and where there was any particular tone to the comments, those that were friendly considerably outnumbered those that were not.

So much for the description of the samples and sampling methods. Let us look now at some of the findings of our sampling of attitudes and behavior of students at 26 colleges in the U.S. or abroad, made under the conditions described. Many of the results of our College Survey, as the reader has already perceived, are being reported throughout this book at points most pertinent to the subject under discussion. But here in what immediately follows we shall focus on the responses to questions directly relating to sexual attitudes and behavior.

First, for the reader's orientation, is a brief preview of the results. Then, in the two chapters that immediately follow, readers will find a more complete presentation of the survey results, with a breakdown of the students' responses to each question relating to sexual attitudes and behavior, along with some of the amplifying comments from students that seemed particularly interesting.

THE SURVEY RESULTS—A PREVIEW

Until a solid body of information about the sexual behavior and attitudes of the present younger generation is built up through extensive, systematic research we must be content with suggestive evidence. I will here try to sum up what our College Survey suggests about the behavior and attitudes of one particular group of young males and females: approximately 2100 junior and senior college and university students at 26 schools in the U.S.A. and abroad who responded to our inquiries. At points I will indicate how these findings seem to relate to earlier research.

Regarding the sexual behavior of the college males. Our U.S. college males indicate slightly—but only slightly—more accumulative incidence of coitus than the college-educated males interviewed by the Kinsey group in the 1940s. Kinsey's college-educated "younger generation" males reported that 51 percent of them were coitally experienced by the time they were 21-year-olds. Our 21-year-old collegians reported that 57 percent had coital experience.

Our findings for males are even closer to the findings of Ehrmann regarding the sexual behavior of Southern college males. Ehrmann, who did his sampling at one Southern university around 1950, reported that 65 percent of the male students were coitally experienced. The students were drawn from the general undergraduate body. The average of the coital incidence at our three Southern universities was 69 percent for junior and senior males.

Regarding the sexual behavior of the college females. Our U.S. college females report a far higher proportion are non-virgins than has been reported in any of the better-known investigations of college women made prior to 1960.

Consider again, for females, the benchmarks provided by Kinsey and Ehrmann in the samplings they made 15 to 20 years ago. About 27 percent of Kinsey's college-educated females reported they had experienced coitus by the time they were 21-year-olds. In contrast, 43 percent of the 21-year-olds in our U.S. college sample reported they were coitally experienced. That is an increase of nearly 60 percent.

At Ehrmann's Southern university, 13 percent of the coeds in his sampling of undergraduates around 1950 reported they were non-virgin. In our sampling at three Southern universities an average of 32 percent of the junior and senior coeds reported they were non-virgin. Thus while our figures and Ehrmann's seem almost identical for males, our females report more than twice as much non-virginity as Ehrmann's coeds reported.

Our findings support the surmises of a number of observers who have stated that if there has been any change in the sexual behavior of young people in recent years it has involved primarily females. (Among expert observers offering this opinion have been David Mace, Isadore Rubin, Harold Christensen, Albert Ellis, and Andrew Hacker, who has probed student attitudes at Cornell University.) And our findings are in at least the same upward direction in incidence of non-virginity that was found in the one reasonably substantial study of college women made in the 1960s by the time our own study was undertaken—that by Harrop and Ruth Freeman, which was confined to senior women.

On the other hand, our findings do not support the contentions made by those who say there has been little or no change in sexual behavior in recent decades. And they conflict particularly with the statements made in 1965 by Mervin B. Freedman, when he reported on his study made in the 1950s of 49 Vassar senior women, and with statements by psychologist Nevitt Sanford, who had been involved in three Vassar-type studies of college women. Freedman, readers will recall, said his findings were consistent with the findings of other studies which are "almost unanimous" in reporting that coital experience among college women was "25 percent or lower." (See Note 26 and Appendix, both for Chapter 9.) And Sanford reported to the educators of the United States that he found there has been no "revolutionary" change in the rate of pre-marital intercourse since the 1920s, and added, "We find be-tween 20 and 30 percent of the women in our samples were not virgins at the time of graduation." [8]

In our sample of junior and senior women more than 40 percent report, as noted, they were non-virgins. Only 4 of our 19 schools enrolling women produced responses that conform to Freedman's sweeping statement about the existing situation. And only 4 of our 19 schools fell within the 20 to 30 percent range cited by Sanford.

Three other points might be made about the sexual behavior reported by our female respondents.

• We found no indication that copulation has become rampant among college women in general (or males either), which news accounts focusing upon extreme situations of promiscuous behavior might imply. A solid majority of our total sample of junior and senior women reported they were still virgins. (And more than 40 percent of the upperclass males did, too.)

• There was little evidence that modern girls approach male-female physical intimacy in the passive or submissive spirit frequently reported for women earlier in this country. Note for example that 58 percent reported they had engaged in mutual genital petting, which suggests an equalitarian ap-proach to petting.

• There is evidence that the U.S. girls in our college sample were substantially more inclined to have premarital intercourse with males other than their spouses-to-be than was evident in research earlier in the century. Fifty-three percent of the non-virgins in our sample had *already* engaged in intercourse with more than one man, and more than a third of the non-virgins said they had experienced intercourse with "several" or "many" males.

Regarding the sexual attitudes of college students. The traditional ideal of chastity until marriage for both males and females did not command majority support from either sex in our U.S. sample. A majority of the males were ready to regard premarital coitus as reasonable if the parties were past their 18th birthdays and were tentatively engaged. Females were more conservative. Majority support among females was offered only if the coital pair were 21 years old and "officially" engaged.

Females are still much more concerned than males that some kind of ongoing relationship exist before premarital coitus can be acceptable.

At the same time, about half the respondents from both sexes are not committed to the ideal that one's partner in marriage should not have previous coital experience with another person. Such previous experience by a partner would not "seriously" trouble a majority of either sex, but would trouble a majority of males at least "some."

Our U.S. respondents offered little support for the traditional norm of a double standard of behavior for the two sexes. The double standard commanded most support among females, and particularly among Southern and Midwestern females. There nearly half of them accepted the idea that a sexually experienced male might still reasonably expect virginity in his bride.

There are notable exceptions, but to a large extent groups that ranked high on permissive attitudes also ranked high in the incidence of reported behavior.

Regarding the college male's use of prostitutes. Our figures suggest a spectacular decline may be occurring. To see the apparent decline we might place our figures beside two benchmarks: Kinsey's findings on the percentage of college-level males who had ever patronized a prostitute by the age of 21 and Kirkendall's findings in the late 1950s of patronage among 200 sexually experienced males at one university.

	PERCENT WITH PROSTITUTE EXPERIENCE
Kinsey (before 1948)	22
Kirkendall (1950s)	19
Our U.S. male sample (1966)	4

These figures seem to lend support to Winston Ehrmann's concept that one of the dramatic changes in premarital sexual behavior of Americans in the last 40 years is the "marked increase in petting and coitus among social equals. . . ."[9]

Regarding possible regional differences. Our data suggest that striking differences exist according to the region in which the schools are located. The Eastern students were clearly the most permissive in their attitudes, and the Midwestern students most restrained.

In actual behavior the pattern was substantially the same, except that Southern males replace Eastern males at the top of the regional-rank order in reported coital experience. This would lend support to the concept that behavior does not necessarily correlate with verbalized attitudes.

Regarding possible national differences. The differences among the national samples likewise proved to be striking, both in behavior and in expressed attitudes. The North American samples—U.S. and Canadian—tended to be relatively conservative, with Canadians in general appearing as the most conservative of all the national samples. In behavior the German university females appeared substantially less restrained than the German university males.

Our evidence about Scandinavia as revealed by the Norwegian students—both male and female—indicates that sexuality is far from rampant among university students there. Norwegians were just one place above the U.S. males and females in reported coital behavior in the rank order of the national sample and were far from appearing in an extreme position. The Norwegians strongly scorned the double standard. But more Norwegian than U.S. girls favored the concept that one's first coital experience should be with the person one would subsequently marry. On the other hand, Norwegian males ranked second only to the English in favoring casual sexual liaisons.

The major surprise (to us) in the International Sample was the extreme freedom of behavior and permissiveness of attitudes reported by the English students, both male and female. They headed the list in virtually all cross-national comparisons. Our findings lend support to the statement of the English political commentator Henry Fairlie in 1966, the same year we did our sampling, that "Britain, at least in its public behavior and public exhibitions, is now the most immoral country in the West." [10] And a possible clue to explain what appeared on the surface at least as a bursting forth from traditional restraints was offered by Sir Denis Brogan, University of

Cambridge political scientist, in writing about "The English Sickness," in 1967.[11]

He suggested the young were unsettled by the nation's delayed shock in adjusting to the reduction of responsibility that came with the loosening of ties to what had been history's largest empire.

Regarding the effect of career aspiration upon the sexual behavior of women. The young women in our U.S. sample who were career-oriented tended, for whatever reason, quite clearly to be more permissive in their sexual attitudes and to be more free from restraint in engaging in sexual activities.

Regarding the role of age in sexual behavior. U.S. students in particular seemed to feel strongly that age and emotional maturity have to be taken into consideration in weighing the appropriateness of sexual acts.

In their own reported behavior, males showed a substantial increase in reported sexual experience between the ages of 20 and 22, whereas the females showed very little difference in experience at these three ages most common to junior and senior women.

Regarding possible differences by type of school. In the U.S., students at schools in rural locations were on the average clearly more conservative in their reported sexual behavior than students at schools in or near metropolitan areas.

Both male and female students at private colleges and universities were more permissive in their *attitudes* regarding premarital intimacy than students at public colleges and universities. However, a somewhat higher proportion of males at public institutions were coitally experienced than the males at private institutions (which could reflect differing patterns by social class).

Our evidence suggests that colleges with liberal rules tend to have a somewhat larger-than-average proportion of coitally experienced students than do schools with conservative rules. There are, however, exceptions in both directions that suggest that factors other than rules undoubtedly account, at least partially, for the difference noted.

Students at the Eastern women's college with liberal rules reported a very high proportion were coitally experienced. On the other hand, both the two men's colleges in the Northeast with liberal rules about entertaining female guests in rooms were down at the midpoint of the rank order of coitally experienced male samples.

There was no apparent substantial difference in the social-class origins of the girls at the women's school with liberal rules and men at the men's schools with liberal rules. Do liberal rules affect men and girls differently? Is public reputation a factor? Does a school that has a reputation for sexual liberality attract unconventional or sexually liberal students in the first place, or cause students enrolled to try to live up to what they perceive the school's reputation to be? Or are the liberal rules the result of the demands of students who are already high in coital experience? Is high academic aspiration an inhibiting factor, where a student can behave pretty much as he wishes? We know that academic requirements at the two men's schools are extremely high. It is tempting to speculate on such questions; but at this point it would seem imprudent to surmise any specific cause-and-effect relationship between rules and behavior.

Students at church-affiliated schools reported a quite low level of sexual experience. At our Protestant university the level was relatively low; at the Catholic university it was conspicuously low.

That, then, is the general picture. Let us look at the specific responses of our young adults in the two chapters that follow.

CHAPTER 11

The Sexual Attitudes of 2200 Young Adults ...

"Ideally I think a girl's first full sex experience should be with her future husband. But one of the couple ought to know what they are doing. Who wants to marry a fumbling incompetent?" A coed at a state university in the Rocky Mountain area.

One of the first questions put to the students responding to our college checklist that explored specifically their sexual attitudes was in two parts. It asked:

Do you feel that ideally it is still true that a man and girl who marry should have their first full sexual experience together? YES___ NO___
And only after they are married? YES___ NO___

Just about half of the U.S. students, both male and female, checked "yes" to the first part of the question. Or to put it conversely, about half of the students did not feel that it was necessarily ideal that the man and girl who marry both have their first adventure in coitus together.

As for the second part of the question—dealing with the full-chastity ideal that the first coital experience of both partners should occur only after marriage—male support dropped to 35 percent. The girls, however, remained almost as strongly in favor of the ideal of waiting until marriage (47 percent) as they were for having the first experience together whether married or not.

In comparing responses of students by the major regions of the U.S. where the 21 schools are located, it appears that the strongest support for the ideal that prospective mates should have their first coital experience together comes in the Midwest. And the least support is offered by students in the East. (For amplification see Appendix 11-A.)

All 3 of the schools attended by girls (whether coed or all-female) that were least insistent that prospective spouses have their first full sexual encounter together were in the East. And all 4 of the schools where the girls were most insistent that the partner's first experience be together were in the Midwest. In the rank order, from most to least insistent of the 19 schools with girls, the five Midwestern schools ranked 1, 2, 3, 4, 9. This gives evidence that the strong conservative bent of the Midwestern students is not confined to the two church-affiliated schools in the U.S. sample, which both happen to be in that region.

This same contrasting pattern—with the Midwesterners most conservative and the Eastern students most permissive—persisted on the ideal that the couple should also wait until marriage. The full-chastity ideal for both mates was supported by 72 percent of the Midwestern girls versus only 34 percent of the girls at Eastern schools.

It should be noted that students, both male and female, at the two church-affiliated schools offered some of the strongest support for the ideal that the first experience of two people who may marry should be together. The Catholic university topped the rank order for both males and females; and the Protestant university ranked third among the 19 schools enrolling girls and second among the 19 schools where men are enrolled.

At the state university in the Rocky Mountain area we sampled not only coeds, but also 57 recently married wives living in student housing. Interestingly the recently married wives were almost twice as insistent that a couple's first experience be together as were the coeds in the samples (about two-thirds vs. one-third).

Among the international groups sampled, the English students were the least committed to the ideal that prospective marriage partners should have their first coital experience together. Thirty-seven percent of the men and even fewer of the girls—29 percent—thought so. The small sample of Italian university girls were the most conservative of any national sample in believing that coital experience not only occur first together, but also that it occur only after marriage. Three-quarters of the 48 Italian girls said "yes" on both points.

Canadian girls were next most conservative: 66 percent favored the ideal of first experience for both being together and 40 percent favored waiting until marriage. Interestingly among the supposedly free-loving Scandinavians, 60 percent of the Norwegian university girls favored the ideal that first experience for both be together. (Only 51 percent of U.S. girls had favored this ideal.) However, the Norwegian girls were as reluctant as the English girls to endorse the ideal of waiting until marriage: in both national samples only 28 percent of the girls favored this even as an ideal. And the Norwegian and English males also were in almost precise agreement in their low regard for the ideal of waiting until marriage: 20 percent of the males in both national samples favored this ideal.

Those students offering amplifying comments were inclined to suggest that while it was a nice idea for both the prospective mates to have their first coital experience together, it was in these days not very practical. The question seemed to pose a dilemma for some girls. A few indicated that while they liked the idea, they also felt a girl should be initiated sexually by a man who was not a bumbler.

Some comments from females. A girl at the private university in California said, "For myself, I would rather wait until I marry. I am very emotional and deep physical involvement with a boy could be the end of me. I would like my husband to have a little experience because I am very naive about sex."

• A girl at one of the state university campuses in California: "I don't want to marry until I am 24 years old, so if I still were a virgin I think I'd be lacking in life-learning. And if my husband was, I'd really worry about him!"

• On the other hand, a girl at the Catholic university suggested that the male virgin, while "a fairly remarkable phenomenon," would bring a great amount of self-discipline and high standards to his marriage.

• An Italian university girl said simply, "For the man no, for the girl yes."

Recently married wives living in school apartments at the state university in the Rocky Mountain area were, as indicated, much more strongly in favor of having first experience together and waiting until near marriage than were unmarried college women on the same campus. Here are two of their comments:

• "I feel that intercourse between two virgins is so much more meaningful and less apt to make the woman feel self-conscious. I think a great many girls are kidding themselves when they say they want a man with experience or think that a man is abnormal if he hasn't had intercourse with other women previously. . . . In some ways I am glad my husband and I had intercourse before we were married, because we became adjusted to each other fully."

• "I think a couple should have sexual experience before they are married [but] *only* if they are officially engaged and will be married soon. . . ."

Some male comments. A Norwegian male: "Nobody should marry without having experienced coitus together, before the decision of marriage becomes final."

An American male at the Ivy League university said in regard to the ideal of prospective mates having their first experience together, "I answer a very strong yes, even though both myself and the girl I am going to marry had intercourse before we met. Until I had met her, I had always thought that I would not care whether or not my wife had had intercourse with another person besides myself. . . . But as I fell in love with this girl I began to change my mind. Now I would give anything if she could be made a virgin again."

Do you think it is reasonable for a male who has experienced coitus elsewhere to expect that the girl he hopes to marry be chaste at the time of marriage?
YES ___ NO ___ PREPOSTEROUS ANACHRONISM ___

The question was designed to explore the state of the so-called "double standard" sex code today. A "yes" answer would lend support to the double standard by agreeing that the rules regarding premarital sex relations be more permissive for young males than for young females.

Interestingly the girls in the U.S. supported this seemingly discriminatory standard more than the males did. The "yes" responses:

U.S. girls 36%
U.S. men 21%

But for both girls and men the great majority did not think such a standard was reasonable (and 10 percent called it a "preposterous anachronism").

Girls who indicated on their checklist that they were seriously planning a career in the years ahead were much less willing to accept the double standard (32-percent acceptance) than were the girls who either had no career plans or were indefinite (45-percent acceptance).

Viewed regionally, the least support for the idea that a double sex standard was reasonable came from students at schools in the East, and the most support from students in schools in the Midwest and in the South, especially Southern girls.

Not a single one of the 7 Eastern schools was in the top half of the rank order of U.S. schools attended by either males or females when it came to supporting the double standard.

The recently married wives living in student housing at the Rocky Mountain university offered virtually no support for a double standard. (About one in 10.)

Among the university groups outside the U.S.A. the largest contrast was between the university girls of Norway and the small sample of Italian university girls. Three-quarters of the 48 Italian girls supported the double standard, whereas in Norway less than 7 percent did.

In the German sampling this question was somewhat rephrased to specify who, if anyone, should have "sexual experience" before marriage. The majority of both men and girls (66 percent of the men and 57 percent of the girls) felt "both should have experience."

This question probing ideas about double standards drew an unusually large number of amplifying comments. Many indicated that their responses might seem confused and contradictory. They seemed to be trying to harmonize the equalitarian ideal with the idea, as stated by a German girl, that "the man by all means should be sexually experienced," and with the idea often implied by the men that it seemed natural for them to be more sexually assertive.

Some female comments. A girl in Canada: "I think an experienced male can bring a more commanding personality to a couple's sex life. He will thus appear to be more manly in the eyes of his wife. I would actually prefer a man with some sexual experience, not necessarily coitus. . . ."

• Several girls indicated they had problems involving a reverse of the traditional pattern. A girl at one Eastern women's college said, "I am not a virgin; I have fallen in love with a boy who was a virgin before he met me. He is 21 and it upsets him terribly that other boys 'had' me. We will overcome this with time . . . but his ideal of a virgin for his wife has been difficult for us."

• A girl at the state university in the East: "I am now engaged to a wonderful man. . . . He has never had intercourse but I have. . . . I pray this does not affect our marriage. If I could erase my past I would. Women should have the same rights as men because women are equal to men, *but* when it comes to sex women are too emotional to accept the single standard."

And an Italian girl explained, "It is absurd to think that a man has reached a marriageable age and has his first sexual experience with the girl he marries; but it is not absurd for the girl, given the difference between the physical needs of the two sexes."

Some male comments. A man at the Eastern state university: "One who has had coitus with a number of girls cannot really expect his wife to be a virgin." However, he added, "If she isn't a virgin she should come up with a pretty good answer why she isn't." (This might be called an updated version of the double standard.)

• A male at the Rocky Mountain university: "I certainly do not want the girl that I marry to have a promiscuous background. At the same time I feel I cannot hold it against her if she had once or twice experienced coitus with someone else."

• In the deep South an idealistic male said, "I want or prefer my wife to be a virgin, so I should try to do my part and see to it that girls with whom I go out don't lose their virginity because of me."

• Some males were forthright upholders of the double standard. A man at the private university in the South said, "I will go as far as I can with any girl. The girl I marry *will*, however, be a virgin."

And a Canadian male agreed: "A girl holds a higher position of respect by fellows who know or suspect that she has not 'gone down for the boys.' This point of view is held by all my friends (who are always talking about their next piece)."

Would it trouble you to marry a person who had experienced premarital coitus with someone else before becoming seriously involved with you?

NO ___ SOME, BUT NOT SERIOUSLY ___
YES, SERIOUSLY ___

This question revealed even more sharply an apparent double standard of judgment. In the U.S. sample the females were considerably more broadminded about a prospective mate's past sexual experiences than the males were.

More significant perhaps is the fact that less than one-fifth of the students—either male or female—acknowledge that they would be "seriously troubled." (See Appendix 11-B for amplification.)

If we combine the scores of those who would be troubled "seriously" with those who would be troubled "some" we have these approximate totals for the U.S. respondents who would be troubled to some degree:

Males 70%
Females 39%

When the data were analyzed according to regional patterns in the U.S.A., the Eastern students both male and female showed the least evidence that they would be troubled about a prospective marriage partner's previous coital experience. And Midwestern students, both male and female, showed the most evidence they would be troubled. (For details on responses from the 4 major U.S. regions see Appendix 11-C.)

A major surprise (to us) was that next to the Easterners the males most untroubled by the idea of courting a non-virginal girl were the Southerners (36 percent responding "no"). This may indicate that the males in the South are not now as strong for the double standard on chastity, at least intellectually, as has long been believed to be the case.

The recently married wives living in university housing at the Rocky Mountain school were more than twice as likely to say such previous experience would trouble them "seriously" as were unmarried girls in general in the U.S. sample.

Among the international groups, the English men and the Canadian men and girls responded much as the U.S. students did, whereas very few Norwegian students, male or female, and few English girls stated that a partner's premarital experience would be a matter that would seriously trouble them. Only 2 percent of the Norwegian males and 7 percent of the Norwegian and English girls said they would be seriously troubled.

Some female comments. A girl at the university in New York City criticized the use of the word "troubled" in the question as ambiguous. She explained, "It might make me jealous as hell but I'd still prefer ultimately to marry a sexually experienced man."

• A feminine rationalization of a double standard might be seen in the comment by a girl at the Catholic university (and it may be an old saying): "A girl likes to be a man's last romance and a man likes to be a girl's first love."

• On the other hand, a girl at the Midwestern state university: "I don't think I could respect a man who had had relations with other women. I would feel that some day I might not trust him."

• An Italian girl said she would be troubled if her man had experienced a "profound and complete love" involving coitus with a previous girl, but that she would not condemn any casual sex experiences.

Some male comments. A number of young men in their comments seemed to be saying, "No, but . . ."

• A German male: "It would make no difference. It would interest me however to know who the earlier partner was."

• And a man at the Ivy League university professed little concern but then threw in the qualification that he would not want a girl who had had sexual affairs with other men that were "too recent."

• On the other hand, a man at the Catholic university said he would be seriously troubled unless "she told me all the circumstances."

Do you feel a person can have numerous sexual affairs and still bring a deep, enduring emotional commitment to the person he or she marries?

YES ___   NO ___   AM NOT SURE ___

Slightly more than half of both the male and female respondents at U.S. schools checked "yes." Of the remainder more were less likely to say "not sure" than a flat "no." There were no distinct regional variations on this question, and few noteworthy variations in international samples. Only the Italian girls were overwhelmingly dubious.

The question produced only a few dozen amplifying comments, mostly ambivalent. A girl at the Eastern women's college with liberal rules said it was all right if a person was just sowing his wild oats before settling down, but it would be bad if the person had developed "a primarily loveless attitude towards sex 'which might' become so deeply a part of one's attitude that an honest and enduring commitment would be impossible." Some of the men indicated it might be all right if their future wife had one or maybe even two sexual encounters, but they certainly didn't want to marry a girl "who had been sleeping around."

Do you feel that most male acquaintances are more strait-laced about sex than they might like to acknowledge?

YES ___   NO ___

In the U.S. college sample more than two-thirds of both males and females checked "yes," and interestingly more males responded affirmatively than the females. In the German sample, 87 percent of the males and 72 percent of the females checked "yes"; but a minority of the Norwegian students checked "yes." Possibly this could be attributed to the greater openness about sexual matters in Scandinavia.

A girl at the Eastern state university commented that when a recent very frank movie with couples wrestling on beds and girls naked from the waist up was shown locally, the boys in the audience were vastly more embarrassed than the girls. And a man at the state university in the upper South questioned the stereotype of ego-centered males bantering about their sexual exploits. He said that at recent bull sessions at his fraternity a number of highly conservative attitudes were expressed.

What kind of relationship should prevail before a male and female should consider coitus as personally and socially reasonable? Four age groups are listed below in case you feel your response might vary depending upon age.

(a) *Age 14–17*
Only if married
Officially engaged
Tentatively engaged
Going steady
Good friends
Casually attracted

Age 18–20
If married
Off. engaged
Tent. engaged
Steady
Friends
Cas. attracted

Age 21–23
If married
Off. engaged
Tent. engaged
Steady
Friends
Cas. attracted

24 or over
If married
Off. engaged
Tent. engaged
Steady
Friends
Cas. attracted

(b) *Regardless of age (after 16) or the stage of formal commitment do you feel that full intimacy is appropriate if both persons desire it and they have a sense of trust, loyalty, protectiveness and love?*

YES ___ ONLY IF OF MATURE AGE ___,
MATURE EMOTIONS ___. DOUBT ___
DEFINITELY NOT A SUFFICIENT BASIS ___

The first part of this question—the (a) part—seemed to annoy the U.S. students more than any other item in the checklist. Many felt that everything depended upon the quality of the "relationship" between the two people. If the two people feel that it is right and meaningful for them and they are prepared to meet the consequences, then it is all right and it is no one else's business. The respondents seemed to want to eschew traditional labels on stages of relationship. Several pointed out that what might be personally reasonable might not be socially reasonable. And a number fussed that the phrase "going steady" was kid stuff now. Perhaps "going steadily" would have been a more acceptable phrasing. In any case, midway in the survey, we added part (b) to the question. After that there were fewer expressions of annoyance.

But back to their responses . . .

Investigators of sexual attitudes have only occasionally sought to check whether the age of a prospective participant is important in assessing what kind of sexual experience might be appropriate. The responses of the U.S. students indicates that age is a crucial factor in the thinking of the students. And a consistent pattern based on age pervades their responses.

Even with the males, two-thirds of them in the U.S. student sample felt that coitus is reasonable "only if married" when the participants are under the age of 18, whereas only one-fourth of them made that specification if the participants were over 21.

Likewise and more emphatically (87 percent), college girls felt that the only reasonable basis for coitus by youths under 18 was that they be married. But only 46 percent of them specified that marriage was the only reasonable basis for coitus if the participants were over 21.

At all age levels, however, the girls were willing to condone coitus outside of marriage only if there was some sort of *ongoing relationship* that might lead to marriage or serious courtship. Even for possible participants in the 21–23-year-old group, only 5 percent of the college girls would condone coitus as reasonable if it was engaged in merely with a friend or with someone to whom you were "casually attracted."

Five times as many males were willing to condone coitus as reasonable under identical circumstances. (See Tables 1 and 2 in Appendix 11-D for a detailed report of responses on appropriate behavior for various age levels.)

Quite pronounced regional differences showed up among the U.S. students who felt that coitus is reasonable "only if married" at various age levels.

Note below the variation in the proportion of U.S. girls who specified that coitus was reasonable "only if married" for possible participants who would be in the 21-to-23-year age group:

> Girls at Eastern schools 24%
> Girls at Midwestern schools 73%

This contrast shows up even more dramatically when the 19 U.S. schools where girls are enrolled are listed in their rank order. All 4 of the highest ranking schools in insisting that people in the 21–23 age group can engage in coitus "only if married" are in the Midwest. And *all* 8 of the lowest-ranking schools are in the East or West.

We also see a clear variation by type of school among students feeling that coitus would be reasonable for people in the 21–23 age group "only if married." Both male and female students at public institutions were more conservative in insisting that a married state exist than were the students, on average, at the private institutions. And students at church-related schools were most insistent of all. (For an analysis of female responses at these 3 types of institution see Appendix 11-E.)

If we are correct in assuming that in general students at private institutions come from a higher socio-economic family background than students at public institutions, this might suggest that those with somewhat lower socio-economic backgrounds are more conservative in their sexual attitudes. This does not necessarily conflict with the Kinsey findings that males, at least, who go to college are more restrained in their sexual behavior than those who do not. First of all, we are here talking about *attitudes*, not *behavior*. (We will see in the next chapter, as indicated, that among male students it is the private-college students who are the more restrained in reported behavior.) Furthermore, there is the good possibility that Kinsey's college-level students were delaying gratification because of the severe challenge that often was posed in going to college in the pre-1950 period, and the controlling element may have been educational aspiration, rather than socio-economic level.

A solid majority of the U.S. girls in our sample who had no certain career plans were insistent that girls in the 21-to-23-year-old range reserve coitus for marriage, whereas only two-fifths of the career-oriented girls were of that opinion. (See Appendix 11-F.)

A glance at the responses from Norwegian, English, and Canadian students shows that the English students, both male and female, were most accepting of premarital coitus among the "casually attracted" for every one of the 4 age categories. The percentage of English girls who accepted the reasonableness of such coitus between people only "casually attracted," if they were in the 21–23-year age group, was 15 percent.

The part (b) to the question asked whether, regardless of age or stage, full intimacy would be considered "appropriate" if both persons desired it and had a "sense of trust, loyalty, protectiveness and love." Here were the reactions.

Neither for males nor females did a majority of the U.S.

college sample accept the appropriateness of coitus under such conditions. Their "yes" responses were:

U.S. male students 32%
U.S. female students 19%

However, when the ingredient of maturity (chronological and emotional) was added, the proportions who were ready to regard such premarital coitus as appropriate were:

U.S. male students 70%
U.S. female students 60%

The remainder checked either "Doubt" or "Definitely not a sufficient basis."

In the international groups, the Canadians and Germans responded approximately as the U.S. males and females did to part (b) of the question in expressing reservations if maturity was not an ingredient. But the English and Norwegian students were substantially more liberal in accepting such a situation with an unqualified "yes" as a basis for full intimacy. In both those countries close to half the male and female students approved of intimacy under such conditions, without adding any conditions about "maturity." (See Appendix 11-G for response rates of females at the 4 universities in the International Sample.)

Some female comments. A girl at the state university in the Midwest pointed out, "There is a type of relationship that involves love without the progression to marriage."

• A girl at the university in New York City: "A girl doesn't have to be madly in love with every boy she sleeps with." She thought that sometimes intimacy with a boy to whom she was only "casually attracted" could be "very important to her development. Then when she meets the man whom she plans to have a serious affair with or marry she'll know the difference between love and physical attraction. And the latter won't be so important." (Her school, it should be noted, was the one that had by far the highest percentage of females approving coitus if "casually attracted.")

• A senior girl at the Rocky Mountain state university who had not experienced coitus was critical: "There seems to be a growing trend to regard sexual intercourse as a necessary experience before complete maturity can be reached." One of her friends, she said, had engaged in coitus only out of intellectual curiosity.

• And a sexually experienced girl at one of the Eastern women's colleges said ruefully, "We profess to accept premarital sex, perhaps even to encourage it in others. . . . But beneath this facade of sophistication is the still very impressionable . . . young adult who is still very insecure. I don't think it is any wonder that embarrassment and shame are the more basic feelings experienced by many girls in colleges. . . . In four years of college my moral standards have shifted; they are more conservative now." She said she now felt that sex must be kept "sacred, personal, intimate" and must be shared with only one person rather than many. She felt her own coital experiences had been "a kind of impatient searching for love outside the home."

Some male comments. A male at the "men's college in New England" insisted that his attitude toward sex depended mostly upon the particular female and very little on the nature of the relationship.

• Another man at the same school said that he considered "no coitus before marriage" as right for him and "no serious petting or necking until we have become seriously and emotionally attached" as right for him; however, he then added, "but I see no need to try to apply the standards and inhibitions which I keep for myself to other people."

These then are some of the attitudes of our respondents. But it would be an error to assume that the attitudes young adults reveal necessarily reflect the ways that they are behaving. For one thing, there can be time lags between attitudes and behavior. Sometimes experience has modified in a person what was a liberal attitude into what is now conservative behavior, and vice versa. For another thing, there may be a need to appear liberal or bold. Some girls, for example, seem more interested in being *seen* in the room of a male student than in taking advantage of the private facilities available for anything approaching full intimacy. As we will see, also, young people may be very liberal in accepting a wide range of behavior for others while they confine themselves to conservative limits.

Let us then turn to what approximately 2100 students report about their behavior in intimate encounters.

CHAPTER 12

... and the Sexual Behavior Reported by 2100 Young Adults

"Many men—especially the younger ones—seem really surprised if a girl keeps going." Student at a women's college in the Northeast in commenting upon the traditional male assumption that the girl is the one who applies the brakes in intimate situations.

Both the young men and the young women who responded to the College Checklist had an opportunity to indicate types of physical encounter they had happened to have with the opposite sex up to that point in their lives.

A listing of some of the various possible forms that premarital intimacy takes was in the checklist. There were 12 types of encounter listed (with an additional one—sex with prostitute—addressed to males only)—and a choice to indicate that none of the types of encounter had been experienced. The types of encounter were not listed in any clear way by intensity of the intimacy. (For example, several types of petting were listed below the item for coitus.)[1]

Approximately 93 percent of the students in the U.S.A. and abroad who returned a checklist to us supplied information about their sexual behavior. The unmarried students in the United States, Canada, England, Germany and Norway supplying information totalled 2057 (and there were 40 Italian university girls who provided information).

Below, the types of behavior presented to students are listed by the percentage of students who reported they had experienced them, with those types of behavior most experienced at the top and least experienced at the bottom.

First, here are the percentages for males and females in the U.S. college sample. The data are based on the responses of 644 males and 688 female students who were, as stated, in their junior and senior years.

TYPE OF SEXUAL BEHAVIOR	MALES	FEMALES
Light embracing or fond holding of hands ..	99%	98%
Casual goodnight kissing	97%	97%
Deep kissing	96%	97%
Horizontal embrace with some petting, but not undressed	90%	83%
Petting of girl's breast area from outside her clothing	90%	78%
Petting of girl's breast area without clothes intervening	83%	68%
Petting below the waist of the girl, under her clothing	81%	61%
Petting below waist of both man and girl, under clothing	63%	58%
Nude embrace	66%	50%
Coitus	58%	43%
Engaged in one-night affair involving coitus and did not date person again	30%	7%
Involvement in whipping or spanking before petting or other intimacy	8%	5%
(For male respondents only) Have experienced sex on a pay-as-you-go basis	4%	

It might be noted first that both males and females participate just about equally in the first three items down through deep kissing. From there on, the girls show somewhat less participation than the men, but not dramatically less until we get to the item "Engaged in one-night affair . . ." Here male experience exceeds that of the female by a ratio of more than 4 to 1.

The much lower experience of the female in one-night affairs is compatible with the finding, reported earlier, that the girls tend overwhelmingly to view premarital coitus as reasonable only if there is some kind of ongoing relationship involved that might lead to marriage or serious courtship.

We noted in our summary in Chapter 10 that while coital experience of U.S. college males seemed comparable to that of males 15 or 20 years ago, the college females reported a quite significantly higher rate of experience. While U.S. males substantially exceeded females in the percentage who reported they had ever experienced coitus there were three exceptions at the 21 schools in the U.S. sample: the state college in the Southwest, the state university in New England, and the state university in the Rocky Mountain area.

An inspection of the male and female incidence of coitus reported at the 21 U.S. schools reveals a further indication that coital experience of male collegians today may not be so much higher than that of female collegians as is generally assumed. (Virtually every earlier study has encouraged such assumption.) At 6 of the 19 U.S. schools attended by males, *fewer* than 50 percent of the males reported that they had ever experienced coitus. And at 6 of the 19 schools attended by females, *more* than 50 percent of the females responded that they had at some time experienced coitus.

A considerable variation in sexual behavior is reported from school to school. For example, among males reporting that they had ever petted a girl's breast under her clothing, the incidence ranged from an overwhelming majority at the state university in the Southwest to a modest majority at the Catholic university in the Midwest. The same 2 schools were at the top and bottom extremes in rank order for male schools on the item of coitus, with more than three-quarters of the men at the state university in the Southwest reporting such experience and less than a third of the men at the Catholic university so reporting.

When the 21 U.S. schools are grouped by regions, it develops that the males at the Midwestern schools have the lowest percentages *in all types* of listed sexual behavior. Of the 5 Midwestern schools sampled, 4 are in the lower half of the rank order on coital experience among the 19 schools sampled where men are enrolled.

This Midwestern conservatism is even more pronounced in the reported coital experience of females. Four of the 5 Midwestern schools were at the *very* bottom of the rank order (#16, 17, 18, and 19) of the 19 U.S. schools enrolling females. And of the top 11 schools in the female rank order on coitus *all but one* were either in the East or the West.

It should be emphasized that for any U.S. school the percentage that emerged for each sex can at best be viewed as a very rough indicator of what may be the general level of experience for that sex at that particular school in view of the size of the samples at the 21 schools. It is the patterns that emerge that seem noteworthy. The responses at any particular school will be indicated only in broad terms, rather than in specific percentages.

For girls, the lowest incidence of coitus was reported at the Catholic university. On both the original distribution and on an exploratory re-run, less than a fifth of them reported coital experience. The highest reported incidence for females was at the Eastern women's college with liberal rules, where more than three-quarters of them reported coital experience.

The coital experience reported at that Eastern women's college with liberal rules was so much higher than at any other college enrolling women that we sought the opinion of a young professor there known for his good rapport with the students. Without indicating what the survey response might have been, we asked him to estimate what percentage of the junior and senior women there probably were coitally experienced. He replied, "Seventy percent, probably more." And he explained that there was among the girls at this school "a premium on experience." He said the girls there discover early in their freshman year that coital experience is an expectation and "usually in one way or another they get it by the end of the freshman year."

Obviously both this women's college and the Catholic university represent extremes in environment. However, even when we eliminate both these two schools at the extremes, there is very little change in the total picture. The reported female coital rate for the remaining 17 schools—achieved by averaging school scores—comes out to 41 percent. The pattern holds that somewhat more than 4 in 10 of the U.S. college upperclass females sampled reported they had experienced coitus.

The South has the nation's strongest reputation for a double standard in regard to sexual behavior. That reputation receives support in the survey results. In the male responses all 3 of the Southern schools are in the *top* half of the rank order in reported experience. And in the female responses all 3 of the Southern schools are in the *bottom* half of the rank order.

An averaging of the school percentages for coital rates would present this rank order by regions:

FOR MALES		FOR FEMALES	
1. The South	69%	1. The East	57%
2. The East	64%	2. The West	48%
3. The West	62%	3. The South	32%
4. The Midwest	46%	4. The Midwest	25%

And an averaging of the regional percentages would yield these national averages for coital experience:

Males	60%
Females	40½%

The above regional rank order of the two sexes persists in reports on nude embrace. For men it still persists in reporting of petting above the waist under girl's clothing. But among the girls the Midwest rises above the South on skin petting above the waist.

An analysis of the students who reported they had ever taken part in a one-night affair involving coitus and had never dated the person again suggests that for males this is most common in the South and the West. The East and Midwest ranked third and fourth. Among young women, the reported one-night affairs are practically insignificant—except in the East—and the East's figure is created largely by the very high percentage, relatively, of girls from the university in New York City who reported such one-night affairs (more than a third).

We have noted the possible regional distortion created by two schools reporting extremely high and low coital scores: (1) the women's college in the Northeast well-known for its liberal parietal rules and (2) the Catholic university. If in regional comparisons we eliminate these two schools, there is no change in the rank order of the regions, although the reported coital incidence of the two regions involved is affected somewhat. (See Appendix 12-A.)

Considerable national attention has been given to the antics of the "young generation" in California and their presumed uninhibited, live-it-up approach to sex and life. And the doggerel goes: "What California is today, the rest will be tomorrow." By averaging the two California schools in our sample we see that in reported coitus the California universities, considered together, rank just slightly above the West as a whole for each sex, and for each sex precisely 6 percent above our national average. The combined California score would leave the sampled male collegians in that state substantially below the Southern males. And the California girls would be about the same as the female average for the East (even after the Northeastern women's college with liberal rules had been eliminated).

Does the location of a school in a small community more than 30 miles from any major metropolitan area affect the sex behavior of students as reflected in reported coital scores? There were 5 such schools in the 21 U.S. school sample. For both males and females the reported coital rates of these schools on average were about 10 percent lower than the national average. As a group they had these coital rates: about 50 percent for males and 31 percent for females.

The 21 U.S. schools also were divided into those that were private institutions, those that were public, and those church-related. Among males, students at public institutions such as state universities showed the highest evidence of coital experience. Among females, students at private institutions ranked highest. Students at church-related schools for both sexes ranked lowest. (See Appendix 12-B for an analysis by types of institution.)

The U.S. girls who were career-oriented not only were more permissive in their views, as indicated in the last chapter, but also reported a substantially higher level of participation in various physical intimacies than girls without clear-cut career aspirations. For example, the career-oriented girls reported higher levels of participation in petting below the waist of the girl . . . in mutual petting below the waist . . . in nude embrace . . . and in coitus than did the girls with no plans or uncertain plans about careers. In coital experience the contrast was especially marked: 50 percent of the career-oriented girls reported experience, while only 32 percent who had no definite long-term career plans reported experience.

Do students at schools that permit the entertaining of guests of the other sex in student rooms (on more than a ceremonial basis) report a higher incidence of coital experience than those who do not? Our overall evidence suggests that they do, but any relationship between rules and behavior is far from being a clear-cut one. There are exceptions both ways. And the picture is also obscured by the fact that some big schools with strict rules have many students in off-campus apartments —or have rules but make little effort to enforce them. In our U.S. sample of 21 schools, only 4 officially permitted room-visiting by the other sex. All 4 were in the Northeast. For the 4 schools involved, an averaging by sex of the reported coital rate at the 3 schools enrolling males and at the two schools enrolling females (one is coeducational) shows a somewhat higher rate of coital experience for both males and females than does an averaging of the Northeastern schools that do not permit such visiting. We will take up two interesting exceptions, however, later in this chapter under *Number of partners in intercourse*.

It might also be of interest to note the pattern at the one state college in New England. It has conservative parietal rules. Its girls report a very low rate of coital experience, but its males report a very high rate.

Sexual behavior is clearly affected by the age of the male students. Coital experience of 20-year-old males was reported to be 51 percent, while for 22-year-olds it was 69 percent. But for the junior and senior girls at the three most common ages in our sample (20, 21, 22), there was no comparable increase by age. (For a detailed presentation of the proportion of male and female students at different ages who reported they had experienced various types of heterosexual intimacy, see Appendix 12-C.)

What explanation can be offered for the fact that approximately the same percentage of females age 20 reported coital experience as did the females age 22? One explanation might be a technical one. The sample of 20-year-old females was three times as large as the sample of 22-year-olds, which included only 60 individuals. Even so, we would have expected some sort of increase to appear between age 20 and 22 for girls. Why did no indication of a rise appear?

Gilbert Nass, sociologist at the University of Connecticut, who supervised the tabulation of the survey results, suggested that "The data indicate that if women choose to be sexually intimate during their university experience, they decide during their freshman or sophomore years and continue their chosen pattern during the junior and senior years."

Support for this suggestion might be found in a comment made to me by the Dean of Women at a college in western Pennsylvania. She said that freshman girls there tended to be more liberal sexually than upperclass girls. These freshman girls get the rush from upperclass boys who are looking them over during the first months of college. As this rush eases up, the girls start trying harder to attract the men. Also they come to college expecting from what they've heard and read that college is pretty wild sexually, so they may try to live up to the image. After a year or two in college, they develop more realistic concepts of male-female relations. (It might be noted that Winston Ehrmann in his survey of sex behavior at a Southern university reported finding very little difference in coital rate from the youngest to the oldest groups of females.)

When the responses of U.S. students are compared with the reports on sex behavior of students from the 4 universities abroad comprising the International Sample, a number of patterns emerge. (As previously indicated, far larger distributions were made at each of these 4 foreign universities than at the 21 individual schools in the U.S.A.) A total of 725 university students in these 4 countries provided information on behavior. These included 208 Germans, 209 English students, 135 Norwegians, and 173 Canadians.

Consider, for example, how the females responded to the identical items on behavior presented to U.S. students. It develops that a larger proportion of American girls reported light intimacies than did the girls at any of the 4 universities abroad. By this I mean such activities as deep kissing or horizontal embrace with some petting. But in reporting on intense intimacies such as nude embrace and coitus the U.S. girls ranked in fourth place among the 5 national samples. Here were the results for females at the universities in the 4 countries:

• Canadian girls substantially paralleled the U.S. girls in their responses, though at a somewhat lower level of participation.

• The reported behavior of Norwegian girls is of particular interest, since many observers have contended that the U.S.A. is moving toward the Scandinavian approach to sex. Norwegian girls were at the bottom of the rank order of 5 national samples on 7 of the 12 types of intimacy. However, on the more intense intimacies, nude embrace and coitus, the

Norwegian girls ranked in third place, above the U.S. and Canadian girls.

• The girls in the German university sample were relatively conservative in reporting the less intimate types of encounter, but ranked second in both nude embrace and coitus.

• The national sample where the most sexual encounters were reported by the girls was the English group. The English girls ranked first in 8 of the 12 types of intimacy listed, including nude embrace and coitus. They also reported by far the most experience with "one-night affairs involving coitus and didn't date person again" (34 percent). The number-2 national group on one-night affairs by females was the Norwegian (13 percent).

Here is the rank order of the U.S.A. and 4 international samples on the percentage of students reporting they had engaged in coitus at some time:

MALES	PERCENT HAVING COITUS
1. The English university	75%
2. The Norwegian university	67%
3. The U.S. student sample	58%
4. The Canadian university	57%
5. The German university	55%

FEMALES	
1. The English university	63%
2. The German university	60%
3. The Norwegian university	54%
4. The U.S. student sample	43%
5. The Canadian university	35%

As indicated, we were able to obtain a sample of only 48 Italian female students, and of those, 40 supplied information regarding sexual behavior. Obviously such a small sample can at best only roughly suggest a situation at one particular university in Italy. We indicate their responses only because they are so dramatically different.

Italian girls showed the lowest rate of reported experience in every single category where they supplied information. And in virtually every type of intimacy their reported experience was less than half that reported by the other national groups (i.e., coitus 10 percent, nude embrace 13 percent, mutual genital petting 23 percent, deep kissing 35 percent). This suggests that their acceptance of the double standard in reporting sexual attitudes (see previous chapter) carries through to their actual behavior.

For a comparison of the incidence rates reported by male and female students in the United States, Canada, England, Norway, and Germany on a dozen types of intimacy, see Appendix 12-D, Tables 1 and 2.

One interesting fact that emerges from a comparison of the responses of the national groups is that the German males so consistently exhibited sexual restraint, relatively, in their reports. In almost every category of sexual intimacy, including coitus, they rank as the most conservative of the 5 national male samples.

In three of the most intimate types of encounter—coitus, nude embrace, and mutual genital petting—these German males report somewhat less experience than the German females at the same university.

The English males, like the English females, were considerably more prone to have "one-night affairs" than the males of any other national sample (43 percent). And as with the Norwegian females, the Norwegian males ranked second, with 33 percent reporting such experiences.

On the item of "pay-as-you-go" sex (use of prostitute) the English student sample was the only national sample where more than 10 percent of the males reported ever having such experience. (Fourteen percent of the English males so indicated.) The men at the German university ranked second with 10 percent having paid for coitus. Canadians were in third place with 5 percent of the males reporting use of prostitutes. The U.S. students were fourth with 4 percent so reporting. And the Norwegian males were lowest with only 3 percent acknowledging sex through prostitutes. (In contrast, 28 percent of our small sample of U.S. Army enlisted men reported they had patronized prostitutes.)

Some female comments. Girls in the U.S. sample, despite the fact that their reported premarital coital experience was high compared with survey findings in previous decades, indicated a variety of feelings about their experiences. Some seemed gratified, some seemed uneasy. None seemed as need-oriented as a hippie maiden in San Francisco who explained to me why she had left a sexually inadequate male communal partner: "I had to get me a new old man because I like sex— I'm a chick." A troubled tone pervaded some of the comments offered by female students responding to our checklist. (But perhaps the troubled were more likely to supply comments.)

• A girl at the private urban university in the Midwest who indicated coital experience said, "I did not regret what I had done at the time. However after we broke up . . . I felt terrible about it. I always believed that it should be limited to the one man—husband or definitely future husband."

• A coitally experienced girl at the state university in the South: "I only wish I knew then what I now know about . . . how to handle situations that I really did not want to be involved in."

• A girl at the state university in the Northwest: "I feel I have done wrong in going as far as I did. But somehow I must prove myself. . . . Perhaps I'm afraid of being frigid."

• A girl at the state university in the Northeast revealed this interesting pattern of experience: "I have slept with several males, but none of the experiences have involved coitus because I want to remain a virgin for my husband—I suppose because of the damned double standard."

• And a coed at the state university in the Midwest, in explaining why she was still a virgin, said, "I am extremely lucky to have dated the type of boy who has not taken full advantage of my rather weak will power."

More positive were these comments from females:

• A Canadian girl: "I like to experience orgasm from deep petting—everything but having penetration or intercourse."

• A California girl explained she had never experienced orgasm but that she had participated "in the coital act sometimes uncomfortably, sometimes quite beautifully."

• A Norwegian girl explained: "With us lovemaking is something that more or less happens on the spur of the moment when the right feeling for the person is involved. Maybe we don't regard it as so dead serious as you Americans seem to."

As for how to handle males when the female feels disinclined, we got these two conflicting viewpoints from girls:

• A girl at the Midwestern state university: "Most boys would go as far as the girl will let them but respect her enough to stop and be satisfied wherever she sets the limit."

● A girl at a women's college in the Northeast: "Why can't they leave you alone when you ask!"

Some male comments. The males, both in the U.S.A. and abroad, were considerably more taciturn than the girls about offering comments, and a few were somewhat boastful. A German male seemed to consider it an achievement that he had deflowered three virgins. But most of the comments from Germany and elsewhere were more matter-of-fact.

An Ivy League male in talking about the fact that his only experience in coitus had been with a prostitute explained, "Several friends and myself went down to see this girl with the expressed purpose of losing our virginity. It was worth $25 to have the act behind me." (Kirkendall reports that the great majority of his male students who had visited prostitutes did so in groups.)

● A male at the state university in the Upper South stated that he had engaged in a one-night affair but did not feel happy about it. He said, "I found the aftermath to this to be highly distasteful, and the experience itself rather colorless."

(Incidentally, the reported coital experience of the California beach group, Army enlisted men, and recently married wives—all involving small samples—can be found in Appendix 12-E.)

Age at first intimacy

The males in our U.S. college sample who had ever engaged in petting had their first petting experience, on the average, a year earlier than the females. The mean age for reported first petting:

Males .... 16.3 years
Females .... 17.3 years

Those males and females who went on to experience coitus by the time of our sampling had their first coital experience about 1½ years after they had begun petting, on the average. This was true for both males and females. The mean age for first coitus among experienced U.S. students:

Males .... 17.9 years
Females .... 18.7 years

The boys probably were seniors in high school, the girls freshmen in college.

In the International Sample mean age of first petting in Canada and Germany appeared to be about the same as in the U.S.A. On the other hand, the English and Norwegian university males began petting nearly a year earlier than Americans (both 15.6 years of age). Much the same pattern applied to the girls in the International Sample. The English university girls were the earliest to start petting, at 15.8 years of age.

Those students abroad who had also experienced coitus had tended to stretch the period between first petting and first coitus more than students in the U.S. sample did (except for Canadian females). The English students reported on average a 2-year interim between first petting and first coitus; the Germans 2½ years; the Norwegian males 3 years; and the Norwegian females 2½.

The male and female students of Europe, unlike the male and female students of North America, tended to have first coitus at approximately the same age. In England, for example, both male and female students who had ever experienced coitus tended on average to have the experience while they were 17.5 years old. And experienced German students, *both* male and female, reported, on average, that their first experience had occurred while they were 19 years old!

Number of partners in intercourse

In the U.S. student sample one-fourth of all the male students who reported having coital experience had that experience with only one partner, whereas nearly half of the U.S. females reported their experience had been confined to one partner.

Among the sexually experienced U.S. male students, 58 percent reported having "several" or "many" partners, while 35 percent of the experienced females said they had several or many partners.

The region where experienced female students were conspicuously more likely to report more than 2 partners was the East. When the 19 schools that enroll girls are ranked in the order in which girls reported more than 2 coital partners, all 5 of the Eastern schools are in the top 7 schools in rank order.

And all 5 of the Midwestern schools with female students are in the bottom half of the rank order!

For male students the number-1 and number-2 schools in the rank order of reporting more than 2 partners are both in the South, both Southern state universities.

The coital experience reported by males at the two men's colleges in the Northeast—the Ivy League university and the New England men's college—deserve special notice. Readers will recall from Chapter 2 that these schools permit men to entertain women in their rooms, and for a substantial number this entertainment has included coitus. Yet on the rank order of coitally experienced males at each school these 2 men's schools fall almost exactly in the middle for the 19 U.S. schools enrolling men. They stood tenth and eleventh. And now we see something even more interesting. When the 19 schools are ranked in terms of promiscuity—more than two coital partners—the students at these 2 schools ranked seventeenth and eighteenth, or very near the bottom. At both of these men's colleges only 2 out of 5 of the sexually experienced males reported having experience with more than 2 partners. The only school where experienced men indicated a greater tendency to confine experience to 1 or 2 partners was the Catholic university.

There appeared to be much more of a double standard regarding more-than-one in the U.S. sample than in the university samples abroad. While experienced U.S. girls were twice as likely as U.S. males to report they had confined their experience to 1 partner there was conspicuously less contrast between males and females in reporting in Canada, England, Norway and Germany. In Norway, for example, the experienced males and females were precisely the same (32 percent) in reporting they had confined their sexual experience to 1 partner.

The most active national group in terms of having a variety of partners was the English university group. Both males and females who were experienced showed the lowest percentages in terms of confining their coital experiences to 1 partner. Of the English students who had experienced coitus, 74 percent of the males and 65 percent of the females reported they had engaged in coitus with several or many partners.

In contrast, nearly half of the German males and females had confined their coital experience to 1 partner. In the Nor-

wegian group for both males and females, nearly half those
who were coitally experienced said they had experienced coitus
with several or many partners.

Who initiates intimacy?

The fact that the majority of college girls sampled in the
U.S.A. and abroad reported engaging in mutual genital petting suggests that the modern female has moved considerably
away from the turn-of-the-century model of passivity and
resignation during sexual encounters. How many females
actually take the initiative? Males are probably poor wit-
nesses on this point since initiative is traditionally a male role
in sexual encounters. We asked the question of the males.
Only a small percentage indicated the female was the more
likely initiator. But what may be of interest is that about a
third of all our males checked "About even" to describe who
was more likely to initiate intimacies. (A professor and his
wife at one Midwestern university included in the survey have
a house on a knoll overlooking what is otherwise a secluded
stretch of lakeside beach and can observe love-making patterns, including coitus, of young couples on the beach. The
professor said, "It is astonishing. Most of the boys just loll
there and let the girls tease them sexually.")

Assessments of the other sex

On the college checklist members of each sex were given
an opportunity to classify *"most"* of the people of the other
sex they had dated in regard to interest in intimacy. Respondents were invited to review in their minds the persons they
had dated in the past year.

The girls were invited to check from these 4 statements
(which of course do not exhaust the possible situations) the
one that best described the attitude toward intimacy of most
of the males they had encountered:

1. *I think real intimacy would frighten most of them.*
2. *They seem content with gestures of intimacy such as the
   farewell embrace.*
3. *If their hands can wander that seems to keep them happy.*
4. *They are disappointed if you don't want to go all the way.*

Most of the girls at the U.S. schools certainly did not perceive their escorts of the past year to be wolf-like characters. Approximately 55 percent checked either number 1 or number 2. (Fourteen percent of the girls indicated that they felt "real intimacy would frighten" most of the males they had dated.)

On the other hand, one-fourth of the girls checked number 3. ("If their hands can wander that seems to keep them happy.") And one U.S. girl in 6 (16 percent) felt that most of their dates were disappointed if "you don't want to go all the way."

It may be significant that the girls who were coitally experienced were twice as likely to find male dates disappointed "if you don't want to go all the way" as were the girls who had never experienced coitus. This might indicate that a girl's reputation gets around. Also perhaps the experienced girls may gravitate to different kinds of males than non-experienced girls. Another possibility is that such girls might be offering a rationalization for their own behavior.

In every respect the Canadian girls responded approximately as the U.S. girls had in these assessments. The girls of both North American groups appear to be under less pressure or expectation to engage in the more intimate forms of sexual intimacy than the girls in all 3 of the north European samples. Only a minority of the girls at all 3 of these north European schools checked number 1 or 2 on this item.[2]

The clearest evidence of the greater pressure on, or expectation from, the north European girls is seen in their response to "They are disappointed if you don't want to go all the way." This was checked as follows:

German university girls 24%
Norwegian university girls 31%
English university girls 44%

It might be noted that this response by the English girls was made at a time (1966) when the young people of England seemed to be near a peak in their recent "swinging" style of life.

Perhaps it should be noted, too, that Norwegians in particular have a different concept of the word "date" from that of Americans. They tend to "date" only persons with whom they are going steadily. Otherwise it's just an outing. One Norwegian girl said, "I simply don't have dates with men I don't like good enough to go to bed with."

And another Norwegian girl, sexually experienced, said of the question that it was "kind of strange because to most of the boys I know sex isn't the most important part of the relationship." Then she added, "If I really like a person and he likes me as well, it is a question of mutual agreement, not of *me allowing* him to do this or that."

One of the French girls who received a checklist said, "It is easy with a bit of intuition to know what a boy one goes out with will want." She added she had personally not encountered a boy in the past year content with "a farewell embrace."

Some comments by U.S. girls

• A girl at the state university in the Rocky Mountain area: "To put it bluntly the college guys are on the make and will take what they can get, but they don't want to accept the responsibility for their actions."

• In contrast, a girl at the private university in the South: "Many men want a girl to say no. They are honestly happy when she does. They want to respect somebody."

• A girl at one of the Eastern women's colleges offered a category not on our list: "Most of the men I have dated in the past year have made overtures at going all the way but are not disappointed if you refuse."

Some of the special kinds of problems that some girls in the late 1960s encounter are suggested by these comments:

• A girl at the state college in the East pointed out that a girl might enjoy the roaming hands but because of her upbringing "can't admit the pleasure."

• A girl at the private university in the South acknowledged a leadership role in intimacy: "I often have to initiate the first sex move on a date."

• A girl at the state university in California said she needed to plan "how to pass out with clothes on to avoid complications."

• A girl at the Eastern state college: "I have been dating a homosexual for a year."

• And a girl at the university in New York City suggested that many couples find themselves copulating simply because they have no other way of communicating successfully. Sex, she said, had become a "sort of skin language. . . . People don't commit themselves verbally because they are afraid of being misunderstood and so they try to say with their bodies what they can't say with their words. Everyone seems to be afraid of blowing his cool."

The men were invited to respond to 5 somewhat different statements as a way of classifying *"most"* of the girls they had dated in the past year in terms of affectional behavior. The five statements, which again obviously don't exhaust the possibilities, were:

1. *They are pretty conservative beyond perhaps a goodnight kiss.*
2. *They will usually go along for fun up to a point of light petting.*
3. *They resist real intimacies unless there has been talk of love.*
4. *They seem happy to go as far as I want to go, short of coitus.*
5. *They seem to want to go all the way if we have a chance.*

Since men could reasonably check more than one of these, the total percentages add up to more than 100 percent, so we will simply indicate which items were checked most and least.

Only one-fifth of the U.S. males thought of their dates as being "pretty conservative beyond perhaps a goodnight kiss." On the other hand, even fewer—or 15 percent—agreed that "they seem to want to go all the way if we have a chance." Nearly half of the males checked both items 2 and 3, meaning in essence that girls will go along for fun up to light petting and that they resist real intimacies unless there has been talk of love.

Here is how the U.S. males compared with university males in the International Sample in checking "They seem to want to go all the way if we have a chance": U.S. 15 percent; Canadian 25 percent; English 34 percent; German 37 percent; Norwegian 41 percent.

In all the samplings outside the U.S.A., men also were

less likely to feel that girls would resist real intimacy unless there was talk of love.

In the U.S. group, men with coital experience were four times as likely to check "They seem to want to go all the way if we have a chance" as were the U.S. males who had not experienced coitus.

The men as usual were considerably less voluble in amplifying their thoughts about classifying dates than were the girls.

A male at the Ivy League university said, "A girl can often make a boy behave as she wants him to without him necessarily realizing that she is 'leading.' "

The confusion of modern U.S. males about their expected role regarding sex behavior was perhaps best, if unintentionally, stated by this male at the Protestant university in the Midwest. First he explained, "I am somewhat troubled because I am not really looking for a wife but sort of take advantage of nice girls who assume I am. It is just too much for me to turn down a chance to go all the way. Soon thereafter I begin to become afraid of being trapped and usually drop the girl, and try to do it in a way to ease the hurt for her. If a girl I think I love would say, 'You can go all the way with me because I love you,' I don't think I would."

But he also seemed to yearn for a world in which girls would not be available for the kind of exploitation that he himself practiced. He lamented: "If girls would wait until marriage, as hard as it may be, I feel that the sexual morals and the number of happy marriages would go up."

Well, that is the situation as it shows up in the responses to our checklist.

We cannot assume that trends in sexual attitudes and behavior that appear to be developing among college students would necessarily reflect trends taking place with young people in general. Some assume that as more and more of the young go to college they will adopt a relatively more restrained pattern of sexual behavior, such as Kinsey found among his college-educated subjects. Others believe the converse: that as colleges continue to draw from a broader socio-economic spectrum and also draw in more students with only a modest level of scholastic aspiration, the college students will tend more closely to reflect the sexual patterns of younger people in the general populace. Your author leans to this latter view.

IV. Changing Patterns in Mate-Seeking Behavior

CHAPTER 13

New Problems—and Solutions— for Boy Meeting Girl

"The big city is losing the confidence of the female . . . the opportunities for boy meeting girl (have become) fewer." Charles Abrams, urban planner, New York.

Until quite recent decades the U.S. girl tended to fall in love with the boy she had grown up with. He lived within a mile or so of her. Their folks knew each other. They knew each other so well that physical appearance faded into a minor factor in their reasons for liking each other.

This pattern of an easy drift into the male-female courtship survived the buggy and even the Model T, but not the Thunderbird. In the past quarter-century the accelerated rate of family mobility, urbanization, the growth of vast real estate developments, great employing organizations, consolidated schools and going away to school, obsession with "looks," and fast cars have made falling in love with the boy next door an exceptional situation.

Today's youths are exposed to more young people of the opposite sex and so presumably have a greatly widened range of choice. But this is partly an illusory expansion, because they have more problems in establishing enough of an acquaintanceship for a deep, continuing, and solidly based attraction to develop.

Girls by the hundreds of thousands are becoming disillusioned with the assumed advantages of the big city as a place to meet interesting men. As urban planner Charles Abrams puts it, "the urban mechanisms for convergence have become defective." The more tightly people are packed together, the more likely they are to set up walls against strangers in order to maintain their privacy. As we all know, apartment dwellers often do not know the tenants next door.

Sociologists in earlier decades developed theories about the crucial role of residential propinquity, or nearness of homes, in mate selection. They found that even in major cities one-fourth of all marriages were contracted by people living within 5 blocks of one another. Propinquity is still relevant; but factors other than the accident of residential propinquity are usually bringing young males and females close enough together for an emotional fusion to take place.

A good deal of ingenious thought in recent years has gone into optimizing one's chance of having the kind of encounters with members of the other sex that could become serious.

A good many girls weigh the romance-potential of jobs or careers they are considering. Vocational guidance people often fuss about the fact that girls are inconsistent, indefinite and unrealistic about their career plans when in fact they are being, from one viewpoint, quite realistic. They are rating the job on its "transfer value to the home," to use a phrase coined by personnel people. Some years ago I sat in with a group of guidance people at the Vocational Advisory Service in New York. The director had this to say of the factor of transfer value: "It is a serious consideration for many girls and should be given just as respectful attention as any other factor affecting their selection of a job." A placement official in Radio City advised her that many girls being interviewed bluntly asked, "How many men are working in that office?"

From discussions with such guidance people it appeared that the following kinds of jobs were considered to be low in romance-marriage potential: Elementary-school teaching . . . dressmaking . . . telephone operators' jobs . . . working for feminine service groups . . . insurance-company jobs, where tens of thousands of female clerical workers are needed. A personnel official of an insurance company in Boston advised me that a good many of the girls at that company did complain about the on-the-job male shortage.

On the other hand, some jobs were viewed by the guidance people as having a high marriage potential. For example: secretaries in engineering and advertising firms . . . airline hostesses . . . working in department stores that hire lots of men . . . being buyers for stores . . . nurses in veterans' hospitals.

Some observers have assumed that being a nurse in a hospital attached to a medical school is a marvelous place to work in terms of romance-potential because of all the single medical students and interns with probably affluent futures. A recent sociological study by James K. Skipper Jr. and Gilbert Nass, however, raises a serious question about this assumption.[1]

They found that the situation is a little more subtle than simply achieving physical propinquity with desirable males. (This finding undoubtedly has application in other vocational settings.) Their study focused on the dating problems of 120 student nurses at a large medical center in Chicago. These girls were in frequent contact with medics of all sorts. The girls' dating experiences were to a surprisingly large degree characterized by disillusionment. The girls tended to become more promiscuous than they ever had been and to develop a sense of being exploited.

It seems the difficulty was that people have different motivations in their dating. The authors mentioned these: (1) for recreation; (2) for socializing with members of the other sex; (3) for status achievement; (4) for beginning a courtship.

The researchers found that nurses tend to be extraordinarily courtship-and-marriage-minded in their dating. On the other hand, the medical students and interns rather overwhelmingly viewed the dating of nurses as a recreation, a chance to cut loose and find release from the intense pressures of their work and study. As one intern explained, "We don't have much time to fool around, so when we do date we want a girl who is pretty lively and ready to go. I mean a real swinger." Further, the medics seemed to expect the nurses they dated to obey their wishes just as they were required to do in the on-the-job relationship. Many of the medics, with years of financial skimping ahead, were in no mood to think about serious courtship. The result of these conflicting motivations of nurses and medics gave the male a controlling role in the dating relationship to an unusually large degree. He had less to lose, was usually less emotionally involved. The investigators concluded, "The student nurse was in a poor bargaining position and forced to make concessions (being more sexually permissive than she would normally) in order to maintain the relationship. This situation caused the girls much distress."

Girls surveying the masculine world of eligibles may also be acutely aware that some areas of the United States have fewer mature males than other regions. The shortest supply of males over 18 is in the District of Columbia, Massachusetts, New York, Alabama, and Pennsylvania. The presence of Washington, D.C., and New York on the list is noteworthy, since Washington and New York City have long been assumed to be the most inviting places for a girl to go if interested in appealing, eligible males.

The states with the greatest surplus of males over females tend to be those in the West and closer to the ruggedness of frontier life. The only U.S. states with an actual surplus of males over females in the 18-and-over age group are, in descending order: Alaska, Hawaii, Nevada, Wyoming, North Dakota, Montana, Idaho, South Dakota, and New Mexico. Not one of these male strongholds has a great metropolitan area.

During the 1960s a number of business entrepreneurs—sensing the magnitude of the modern problem of boy meeting girl—began developing substantial enterprises that promised such meetings. These entrepreneurs have thrived mainly by appealing to inhabitants of great metropolitan areas. Many of the big resort hotels in the Catskills began featuring in their New York advertising "Singles Weekends," and some offered particularly attractive rates to unattached males, since more females than males had tended to respond to ads. One resort energetically catering to "singles" had strolling violinists to serenade guests checking in and promised that on its premises "a solitaire is a diamond, not a game."[2]

"Dating bars" catering to the young singles crowd have sprung up in Chicago, New York, and a number of other cities. They often feature the fact that they are run by young people, and they have youthful, virile bartenders. Considerable efforts are made to reassure respectable unescorted girls that it is socially acceptable for them to congregate there. Among the numerous dating bars in the Rush Street area of Chicago in early 1968 were The Store, The Jail, and The Spirit of '76.

One of the more spectacular new social mechanics of the 1960s for getting the still-single sexes together has been the great growth of apartment complexes catering to the "singles" trade. They usually are built around pools or face beaches. The idea apparently evolved in Southern California and may have been inspired by the fact that a great many young females and males there were starting to move into beach apartments that had a high concentration of "singles." In some instances, the single tenants evolved arrangements that amounted to communal sex.

By 1964 apartment complexes such as the South Bay Clubs in the Los Angeles area were specifically catering to singles in their billboards and other ads. The idea of apartment complexes for singles—sometimes known as "go-go apartments"—has spread to Chicago, St. Louis, Atlanta, San Francisco, Phoenix, Baltimore, Washington, Detroit. In Dallas alone, thousands of unmarrieds live in complexes catering to singles.

The advertised emphasis at most of these places is on "fun" rather than marriage. An official of South Bay Club boasting a singles tenancy of more than 99 percent has stated, "People can do what they want, when they want and with whom they want, as long as it doesn't offend the others. The only rules you'll see posted are safety rules by the pools."[3]

Another technique for getting singles together has involved the direct approach of announcing availability for courtship. Americans still are a little reluctant to take out advertisements for this purpose, as is common in Egypt.[4] It is also common in West Germany, where many hundreds of classified ads appear each week, and where matchmakers have long flourished.[5] The late authority on marriage, Abraham Stone, spotted a fascinating advertisement in an English newspaper which stated, "Gentleman owning a tractor wishes to correspond with a lady owning a thresher." The gentleman added, "Please send picture of thresher."

Americans first began feeling comfortable announcing their desire for companionship with the other sex when would-be matchmakers began proclaiming that they were using scientific techniques. Somehow it seemed more respectable when the computer or psychological assessment techniques were put to the challenge of bringing allegedly compatible males and females together.

As with the singles apartments, scientific matchmaking in the U.S.A. first flourished in the great metropolitan areas, and particularly in California, with its fantastic influx of strange newcomers. One of the pioneers in scientific matchmaking, in the 1950s, was Karl Miles Wallace, who did a doctoral dissertation on the prediction of marital adjustment. In the course of his research in California he set up (under the name of Karl Miles) the Personal Acquaintance Service. He began classifying each client by assigning him a socio-economic index score ranging from 0 to 9. He also assigned each client one of 5 personality trait scores and had 29 other items of information. He fed all the data on each client into an electric card-sorting machine (this was before the computer was harnessed to matchmaking). Several thousand people became clients at some point. Out of his experience Miles (Wallace) began advising the clients not to try to find a "one and only" or "perfect" mate, but to be content with having one's opportunities for mate selection enhanced. One problem he repeatedly encountered seemed related to this counsel, for he observed that "the introduction club may selectively attract the perfectionist, the super-critical, the intolerant, and the inflexible, who expect too much from other human beings and are therefore isolated and lonely."

Inspired in part by the success of Karl Wallace, a sociologist in New York, Eric Riss, in the late 1950s set up the Scientific Marriage Institute. He combined interviewing and testing and developed about 70 factors that were punched onto IBM cards (computers were now available). This Institute, too, began placing great stress on flexibility. Riss said a lot of people "have some fantastic ideal that can't be fulfilled. This is the cultural sickness of our time." The Institute at last report claimed clients in all 50 U.S. states.

Another of the more ambitious efforts at scientific matchmaking was launched in the early 1960s in Toronto, Canada, under the name of Scientific Introduction Centre. It had 8 social scientists working as part-time consultants. It too uses IBM cards and psychological testing and asks also quite a number of practical questions, presumably based on past difficulties, such as:

"Would you meet someone who smokes heavily?"

"How important is it to you that your wife be 100% sexually faithful to you after marriage?"

"How important is it to you that your mate take a bath or shower every day?"

Other questions are: "Annual income——? Savings——? Property——? Please describe."

By the late 1960s matchmaking services claiming the aid of science have sprung up in several parts of the U.S.A., with Southern California still the area of most conspicuous activity. One Los Angeles company called Human Inventory, Inc., reportedly with 6000 clients, is headed by the former executive of an aerospace company. A longtime matchmaker with less scientific pretensions is Clara Lane, who has "Friendship Centers" in 10 Western cities, with headquarters in Los Angeles. She advises that her organization has experimented with mating by UNIVAC at its Denver center, but she wrote, "Honestly, Mr. Packard, a machine is a machine, and it cannot take into account the things that are most important, and I think I can state the most important briefly—chemistry or physical attraction to each other. Only personal contact by a trained observer can take that into account successfully." She said that at first her business had been badly hurt by the "computer thing" but she has been counterattacking with the slogan that "A UNIVAC can't kiss."

Since psychologists, sociologists, and psychiatrists are far from agreement on what causes one male and one female finally to single each other out for a lifetime partnership, Miss Lane's wariness is probably warranted.

But meanwhile computerized matching took off in an entirely new direction: arranging blind dates for collegians. These enterprises have promised only an interesting evening, not a possible lifetime partner. Ingenious collegians at Harvard, M.I.T., and Wesleyan with access to computers began the trend with Operation Match and CONTACT. For a few dollars they promised the client 5 names of collegians whom their computer verified to be compatible dates. Both organizations soon claimed they were servicing more than 100,000 customers. My daughter, while still at college, subscribed to a computerized dating service for collegians and got the names of 8 compatible males—7 months after she had paid her fee. By that time she had met enough interesting males so that she had become only mildly interested. Also she found that another girl subscribing at her school had gotten most of the same male names. My daughter heard by telephone from 5 of the males on her list and was sufficiently interested to write to one. But another who called and said he was attending a nearby college turned out not to be enrolled there. But she still argues that if a girl is careful, the general concept of com-

puterized dating is a good one: "You meet people you otherwise never knew existed." The primary appeals of the collegiate computer-dating operations seem to be that (1) they
offer a male and a female an excuse to get together for a date
without being introduced and (2) they provide an excuse for
girls to be assertive in seeking dates.

The collegiate entrepreneurs of CONTACT began moving
in a large way into high-school dances with a "Computer
Dance." They promised: "A count of the mutually punched
tabs will instantly tell you how compatible you are" to any
prospective dancing partner. By 1968 CONTACT reported
it had been the ice-breaker at 2000 high-school dances.

By late 1966 an organization called Data Dating, in Wayne,
N.J., was advertising nationally and had girls in cowboy boots
passing out application-questionnaire forms to people on the
streets of New York City.

A young executive of CONTACT, located in Boston, generously supplied me with a computerized analysis of information supplied by male and female subscribers. In a sample of
6000 college students in the Northeast chosen for analysis,
here are some of the computer's findings:

- College men most commonly are 5' 10" in height and college women 5'4", or a 6-inch difference. (If we are to accept
the collegians' own report of their height.)

- Men are considerably more willing to accept dates with
Orientals or Negroes than are women. (For example, 21 percent of the men said they would accept dates with Orientals,
but 5 percent of the girls said they would.)

- Ninety-four percent of the men and 97 percent of the
women considered themselves "average" or "better" in looks
(which suggests an inherent difficulty in matching on the basis
of self-analysis).

- Only 12 percent of the men but 17 percent of the women
said they prefer to have a date who is "sexually experienced."

- Forty-two percent of the men and 32 percent of the
women reported that they "almost always" kiss on first dates.

- Both men and women had a choice of 20 qualities that
they might consider important in a date. The men most often
checked "physical attractiveness," "friendliness," and "honesty." The women most often checked "sense of humor,"
"intelligence and knowledge," "emotional maturity," and
"honesty." In a blind-dating situation it is understandable why

both stressed honesty. But for the rest we see evidence that girls, more than men, were taking the long-term view of traits that would be important if a marriage developed. The men, by stressing looks and friendliness, were apparently not thinking much beyond a pleasant, ego-enhancing evening.

As for the high-school students who were sampled, the responses of 20,000 boys and girls were analyzed. Here are a few of the computer findings:

• There were approximately twice as many blonde girls as blond boys, which would suggest the role of cosmetics in modifying nature for the girls.

• The weight of a prospective date seemed of enormous importance to the boy: 91 percent wanted a girl who was "average" in weight, and less than 2 percent said they didn't care about the date's weight.

• Seventy-three percent of the boys and 70 percent of the girls reported that they were definitely planning to go to college.

If more than 70 percent of male and female high-school seniors, indeed, start going to college, one may wonder who in the future will be developing the vocational skills to become the plumbers, electricians, carpenters, cooks, secretaries, retail clerks, and so on. But in any case this is one more evidence that a vast number of our present high-school students, male and female, aspire to go to college.

This brings us to the principal meeting ground that U.S. society has evolved for permitting the young men and women who are either moderately intelligent or come from affluent families (or both) to develop affectionate relationships. John Finley Scott, as a sociologist at the University of California, Davis, puts it this way: "College and matrimony . . . combine to render the campus the most active marriage market in modern times."

Millions of students are performing the exertions of scholastic pursuit primarily for career preparation or for the challenge of serious inquiry. Nonetheless, for millions of other students (and their parents) the fact that the college campus provides a pleasant setting for romance and a promising field of eligibles makes the cost and effort of college seem bearable.

On a 5-minute stroll across the campus of the University of South Florida at dusk your author counted 14 couples who were walking arm in arm or hand in hand or were lying partially entwined upon the grass.

In a survey conducted by the Educational Testing Service of 13,000 entering freshmen at 23 public and private colleges the students were asked to list their top-priority reasons for going to college. Slightly more than half, or 51 percent, gave top priority to the fun aspects of college, such as the social life, rather than to academic reasons. They were asked to state which of four philosophies most accurately described their own philosophy concerning higher education. Philosophy C stated that besides all the occupational training and/or scholastic endeavor, "an important part" of college life was the "outside" part. The statement concluded: "Thus while not excluding academic activities, this philosophy (C) emphasizes the importance of the extra-curricular side of college life." It was this philosophy C that got twice as many checks as any of the others. One of the conclusions of investigators, from the survey, was that "large numbers of the youths are lacking seriously in academic (or even vocational) commitment." [6]

One significant aspect of the growth of college enrollment is that the number of women attending has risen much more rapidly than for men. In the decade ending in 1966 there was an increase of 83 percent of freshmen women enrolling, whereas during the same period the increase for men had been 57 percent. By 1964 about 38 percent of all college seniors were women.

While many hundreds of thousands of these women students are seriously bent on career preparation (either for a lifetime career or for insurance), the majority of college girls have romance and eventual marriage much on their minds. A survey at a major Midwestern university of freshmen women asked what they hoped to get out of college. About 70 percent included in their objectives the possible happy encounter with "*the* man for me" or the desire to meet boys and have a lot of fun.[7] (The girls also indicated a desire for personal growth, a search for status, a different style of life, and the wish for exotic experience.)

A publication released by the U.S. Office of Education suggested the majority of young men go to college to help them get jobs and the majority of girls go in the hope that it will lead sooner or later to marriage.

One girl at the State university in the Midwest in responding to our College Survey wrote this comment: "Living together as girls do in a college environment they sense a drive toward marriage. The atmosphere is so marriage-directed that one becomes involved in it even though your career plans aren't favorable toward marriage. In a group of college girls, one who isn't 'dying' to become pinned, engaged or married is an oddity."

The manual *Where the Girls Are* prepared by staffmen of *The Daily Princetonian* said of the girl going to Smith College, "Always keep in mind that a Smithie is looking at you not only as her date, but also as the man who may some day be footing the bills to send her daughter to Smith."

Even in casual dating situations, girls tend to weigh, if unwittingly, the marriage potential of the dating partner more than the young man will. This was demonstrated ingeniously by two sociologists while they were at Iowa State University, Robert H. Coombs and William F. Kenkel.[8] By using a computer they arranged blind dates between 500 college males and 500 college females for a dance. The couples were paired on the basis of what they had, in questionnaires, said about themselves and their desires in a dating partner. (Female students in describing desirable partners put much more emphasis on socially desirable characteristics such as fraternity membership, whether he was a good student, his race, religion, etc. The only factor that men listed more emphatically than the girls was looks.) After the dance, it turned out that the men were more likely to have thought the date a great success, and the girls were distinctly more cautious in saying what they thought of it. The authors concluded, "The woman is likely to be more serious minded than a man about the whole matter of mate selection and to view dating partners in the broader social context of marriage. . . . Since she cannot afford to err, a girl is more likely to be reserved in her evaluations. . . ."

More recently, in 1967, possible support of this thesis came from University of Pennsylvania sociologist William M. Kephart, who analyzed the reported romantic encounters of 1079 college students. He concluded that, "contrary to rather strong popular impression, the female is not pushed hither and yon by her romantic compulsions. On the contrary she seems to have a greater measure of rational control over her romantic inclinations than the male. This control manifests itself in a kind of matrimonial directness. . . ."

This marital orientation of women students is not peculiar to the U.S.A. On a television panel discussion in Japan— where 16 percent of the university students are now female— the majority of the mothers on the panel said they regarded higher education as a means of improving one's opportunities in marriage. Girls with a serious career orientation and who pursue careers through much of their life, furthermore, may well marry a male they encountered while in college. Radcliffe —high in career-oriented women—is a coordinate college of Harvard; and, while the local folklore stresses the antipathy between students of the two schools, a survey at Radcliffe's class of 1949 revealed that 42 percent of the women who had married had Harvard men as husbands.

Students at all-male colleges, who for decades and even centuries have been content with their all-male status, are now clamoring, "We want girls." Even in England, men at the austere University of Cambridge are calling for a higher proportion of female classmates.

In many areas of the U.S.A., the administrators of all-male or all-female colleges are moving to go coed or at least coordinate. The president of Princeton, saying he was bowing to the inevitable, announced that some arrangement would be made for coeducation within 10 years. Wellesley College and M.I.T. are undergoing a trial marriage of joint classes, even though the schools are more than a dozen miles apart. It is not just the playboys and playgirls that are seeking out schools where both sexes are represented. Consider the first choices of the National Merit Scholarship winners. A heavy majority of the males in 1965 chose coed or coordinate colleges, such as Stanford University, Cornell University, Harvard University, and the University of California (Berkeley). And for the female winners their choice of schools where males would be present was overwhelming. Twenty-one of the 25 most popular with these female scholars were coeducational, and 3 other schools were very close to colleges enrolling males. The only school in the top 25 chosen where there wasn't a good college enrolling males nearby was Vassar (Vassar and Yale went far to try to arrange a marriage of their schools, but in 1967 found practical considerations too formidable).

The surge across the country away from single-sex schools has so much momentum that some observers are starting to wonder if a single-sex school not near a school enrolling the other sex can survive. The monastic concept of education is in full retreat. Even Notre Dame is developing an exchange arrangement with nearby St. Mary's College.

And within coeducational schools, furthermore, the surge is toward bringing the male and female students closer together in their daily living arrangements.

When I was an undergraduate at Penn State, the male and female dormitories were on opposite sides of the campus, nearly a mile apart. Today, with the "community" concept spreading, male and female dormitories are adjacent, often with common lounges and dining facilities. This pattern is repeated across the country. At Ohio State they call such linked male-female dorm arrangements "coeducation residences" and feel they brought a noticeable improvement in dress, language, and manners. The Dean of Student Relations, John Bonner, Jr., advises that the arrangement has been quite successful, with no problems except "for the age-old game of aggressive young males attempting to sneak into women's quarters." (And he might have added the now common game at some schools of young females sneaking into men's quarters.) In 1966 Ohio State moved from having coed dorms with horizontal separation (side-by-side) to also having coed dorms with vertical separation in high-rise towers. At the Morrill Tower the men have been on the lower floors, the women on the upper. At the new Lincoln Tower there will also be vertical separation. Bonner advises there have been no significant problems with coed residences, whether they are divided "either horizontally or vertically."

Among U.S. colleges, the University of Rochester has perhaps gone further than any other major school in pioneering coeducational living. It began a twin-towers program in 1964 with men and women living in each tower, on separate floors. The students live in 6-person suites with each student having a small private bedroom off his suite's lounge. Students of each sex are permitted to have students of the other sex as guests in their suite's lounge. Adult residential advisors were eliminated so that each suite runs its affairs pretty much as desired in terms of visiting arrangements involving the other sex. There is, however, one rule that has produced a great deal of grumbling from students. That rule prohibits heterosexual entertaining in one's private bedroom off the small lounge of each suite. A university psychologist studying the arrangement concluded there had been a substantial amount of ignoring of the rule in some suites, which students tended to justify by alleging that the university had published that rule simply to protect itself against public criticism.

At Fairfield University in Connecticut the campus newspaper carried a report speculating on the desirability of putting male and female students in alternating rooms so that the students—the argument went—would not have to dream about sex any more and could think more about their studies. And at Stanford University the 30 brothers of Lambda Nu arranged for 20 coeds to become "associates" and sleep at the fraternity in a special wing.

Even the most permissive U.S. schools still have some way to go to achieve the casual closeness in living quarters of male and female students at Scandinavian universities. There, coed dormitories are usually run pretty much like hotels and in some instances are run by the students themselves. At some, the students are separated by floors, but this is more to permit wandering unclad in the corridors than to prohibit intermingling, because movement on the stairways between floors is generally unsupervised. Family life specialist Lester Kirkendall while at a student hotel at the University of Oslo relates there had recently been a great deal of hilarity because of a mix-up in assigning students to rooms. A girl had been assigned to a room with two men. She was reassigned.

For the schools that remain single-sex in the U.S.A.—and they are primarily in the Northeast—the traffic between male and female schools has become heavy and well-organized on weekends. A common pattern for a woman's college such as Skidmore, where there are schools with men enrolled in several directions, is for 6 or 7 girls to rent a car for the weekend—or to use a girl's car—and take off, for example, down through Massachusetts and Connecticut. The driver is usually the one going the farthest. If she is going to Yale, she may drop off passengers at Williams, Amherst, University of Massachusetts, Trinity, and Wesleyan. The cost per girl runs between $5 and $8.

In earlier decades the men tended to go to the girls' schools; now many girls prefer to leave their own campus and go to the men's school for the weekend, even though they must pay the transportation to get there. (The usual etiquette is for the male to pay for her room at a local rooming house.) As a

Wesleyan student explained it, "Boys never pay transportation for a girl, especially if she is crossing a state line. There is the Mann Act, you know."

Both male and female colleges have frequent "mixers," especially for freshmen and sophomores. Girls by the busloads take off for mixers at men's schools, and men come in droves to the girls' schools. Freshman girls of course are of special interest to males at most of the Northeastern men's schools, since the girls represent a new crop. Most of the women's colleges have "baby books" showing a picture of everyone in the freshman class. The various fraternities and clubs at the men's schools try to build up a library of these baby books. Fraternity brothers who have had specific experience with specific babies may helpfully scribble next to a girl's picture such information as "Dog," "She does it," or "Don't bother—sawdust between those gorgeous eyes."

In the 1965–66 period a number of the New England men's schools held symposiums on sex with talks by theologians, philosophy professors, etc. At one Connecticut school the adult speaker distinguished between "neat sex" (spur of the moment) and "sex with a history" (meaningful relationship). It was suggested that if there was sex, the latter was preferable. Here is a report that one student provided on the discussion that took place back at his fraternity after one such symposium:

"Most of the discussion dealt with life at a college weekend . . . which was analyzed to be a ritual where everything is pointed toward sex, especially on Saturday with a football game, then a cocktail party, getting a bit high, dinner which on some weekends is served without silverware with a sort of Viking, savage theme and with tempestuous music with continual strong beats in the background. This plus the liquor, it was agreed, gets you a little bit hot. This is followed by a dance, parties, drifting from one house to another . . . more drinking. About 1 o'clock the band stops and there is just nothing left to do . . . everything is pointed toward sex, taking your girl to a room and having sexual relations. In this situation, it was agreed, it is pretty hard to have 'sex with a history' because it is hard really to get to know the girl. You really don't have the basis for a talk."

In our College Survey the females were invited to respond to this question:

It is being said in some areas that college weekends have become a ritual built around developing sexual tension. Has this been your observation?   YES ___ NO ___

Thirty-seven percent of the girls responding checked "Yes." A girl at the private university in New York City amplified by saying, "Not only was it my observation, it was my downfall!" The females were also asked in the same connection:

Do you feel that on weekends a girl who dates has to spend too much time and energy being on the defensive?
                                        YES ___ NO ___

The "Yes" responses ranged from 18 percent by the girls at Midwestern schools to 40 percent by girls in the Northeastern sample, which included the only two all-girl colleges in our survey. One girl at an all-girl school, however, commented, "Sexual tension on college weekends, and being on the defensive, seems to be the predicament only of those who do not have a meaningful relationship with their dates."

Sororities, fraternities, and college clubs still play their traditional role in bringing the socially select or homogeneous together in dating situations. Sororities in particular screen girls with the ideals of the older generation (which rules the sorority) very much in mind. At the University of Arizona, where there is more interest by girls in sororities than by males in fraternities, proportionately, one student said, "It is difficult to get a date with a girl who is Greek if you are not a Greek." A man who had been at the University of Arkansas recalled a strong feeling among fraternity and sorority members that fraternity men should date only sorority girls, and vice versa. He added, "It was tough on me because I was dating a sorority girl and we liked each other a lot. But she would go out with me only if we went someplace where she would not be seen."

Sociologist John Finley Scott after making a study of the modern sorority concluded that it is primarily an institutionalized way to control marriage. He pointed out that membership is much more rigidly supervised by alumnae than is the membership of male fraternities by alumni. He found that the sorority system flourishes in particular at the big state universities where all sorts of students can attend and where there are "opportunities to be met and dangers to be guarded against."

With the explosive growth of brand-new colleges there is so much demand upon the better-known fraternities for local chapters that they often set up a "colony" on the campus at first. At the colleges with the highest academic standards the fraternity-sorority system seems to be taking on somewhat less importance, partly because of the spread of the equalitarian ideal and partly because entrance test scores and grades have more to do with who gets into the school than charm or Daddy's prestige.

A number of colleges by their environment and their admissions policies succeed in making their schools particularly appealing as dating-mating grounds. At Illinois Wesleyan, for example, students are convinced that there is a deliberate policy of maintaining a 50–50 balance between male and female students enrolled. An official at Thiel College in Pennsylvania, which in 1965 had a 50–50 ratio between men and girls, said, "We're working toward 60 boys and 40 girls as a ratio. The 50–50 ratio is hard on the morals and the morale of the girls." She explained that a number of men are not interested in dating at all and then "there are also a number of men who have a girl back home or elsewhere so that some of the girls in competing for available boys become more free sexually." Rollins College in Florida has, for several years, maintained an enrollment in which there are approximately 100 more males than females.

The most romance-evoking environment for dating-mating at any U.S. campus visited by your author is DePauw University. It is a relatively high cost, high academic standard school (coed) that was once affiliated with the Methodist church and is located in the small hamlet of Greencastle, Indiana. It has stiff regulations regarding cars, drinking, and room visitation.

A considerable number of local customs have developed to promote romance between male and female students on campus. Fraternities and sororities—whose members include about 85 percent of the student body—play an enormous role in this promotion of romance. And the administration is certainly not unaware that the possibility of romance is one of the school's numerous appeals. The college has maintained a ratio of about 7 males to 5 females. Because of the attractive sex ratio, a girl, to get in, usually has to be in the top 10 percent of her high-school class, whereas the boy can usually get in if he is in the top 20–25 percent.

To be invited to be a member of some of the more prestigious sororities at DePauw you need a recommendation from not only an alumnus, but one who is from your hometown or from Greencastle.

A handbook entitled *Fraternity and Sorority Practices at DePauw 1964–65* spells out the important role that fraternities and sororities play in promoting romance. It has a stamp across its cover reading "This is not an official publication of DePauw University." One paragraph reads: "The social prestige and advantage of the house are enhanced by exchanges and serenades." It went on, "A serenade is an exchange after closing hours for women's residences, often on the occasion of a pinning of a member from each house. Preparation for serenades takes place at song practice, which, in some cases, consumes up to three hours a week and may be required."

I happened to be at a sorority house at the 12:30 A.M. closing hour on a Saturday night, and about 30 couples were in the foyer and out on the terrace kissing goodnight with various degrees of enthusiasm. Obviously the girl who simply wanted to say goodnight to a so-so date was under considerable pressure to go beyond.

One of the first rituals that the sorority or fraternity pledge at DePauw encounters is the kiss-in. When the sororities induct their pledges, each pledge walks up the sidewalk with a man. On one side of the sidewalk are the sorority sisters and, on the other, the brothers in the fraternity providing the escorts. Male escorts are drawn by their fraternity from the freshman class and are assigned to girls on the basis of height. At the end of the march up the sidewalk, each boy kisses the girl being pledged and hands her a rose.

A number of the sororities, including the Tri Delts, have what they call the Candlelight Service when a sister becomes either lavaliered, pinned, or engaged. (Lavaliering is the lowest form of commitment.) The girl confides the wonderful news to the president of the sorority, and the president calls a gathering of the sisters around a table. A candle is passed around the table from sister to sister. No one but the president knows the lucky sister involved. That is the suspense. The candle may go around once, and when it comes to the girl in question and she blows it out, it means she has been lavaliered. If, however, the candle goes all the way around without being blown out, it is sent around a second time. If the unidentified girl blows it out on this trip, it means she has been pinned! But if it is not blown out on the second trip and goes around a third time before she blows out the candle, it means she is engaged! ! ! Later, usually after hours, the girl who is pinned or engaged will be serenaded by the brothers of the lucky male.

Finally, there is the custom of the pansy ring. One of the sororities stages this each spring near graduation. Girls on campus who are graduating seniors and have become engaged parade through this ring made largely of pansies. In 1964, nearly half of the senior girls went through the ring. A girl cannot step through the ring unless there is an actual date set for the marriage.

All of this ritual to promote romance may seem quaintly old-fashioned to students at some of the multiuniversities where unstructured male-female relationships prevail, and many couples, who like each other a lot, casually begin sharing the same bed for weeks at a time at an off-campus apartment.

In terms of our survey, however, the main thing that is of special interest about the DePauw situation is this: 75 percent of DePauw students marry DePauw students.

CHAPTER 14

Why Marry—and When?

"All societies recognize that there are occasional violent, emotional attachments between persons of opposite sex, but our present American culture is practically the only one which has attempted to . . . make them the basis for marriage." Ralph Linton, U.S. anthropologist.[1]

Since Ralph Linton made that observation three decades ago, the basis for mating he described as peculiarly American has become common throughout much of the Western world, and is catching on in much of the Orient. It has also grown still more widespread in the U.S.A.

The rush of young male and female lovers in the U.S.A. to join together in till-death-do-us-part partnerships—largely on the basis of "violent, emotional attachments"—has been increasing in popularity all during this century. Figures released by U.S. Census officials reveal that the proportion of marriageable people who are indeed married has never been higher in the history of the U.S. Census.

Census figures of 1964 when contrasted with census figures in 1940 show how much more popular marriage has become. By the time U.S. males and females reach the 35-to-44 age group the never-marrieds have come close to disappearing from the population:

	1940	1964
Males still single	About 14%	8%
Females still single	About 10%	5%

Furthermore, young people of the U.S.A. have been plunging at ever earlier ages into marriage until very recently. In 1940 only 12 percent of all females listed themselves as married by the age of 19; by 1964 more than 27 percent of the girls in the 18–19-year-old group listed themselves as married.

Much the same enthusiasm for marriage has appeared in England and a number of other Western nations.

In our survey we asked college and university students in the various national samples:

Can you visualize a happy, satisfying life for yourself that might not include marriage?
YES ___ NO ___ UNCERTAIN ___

Of the U.S. females only 15 percent gave an unqualified "Yes." Most girls who added comments indicated they could visualize such a life, but they would rather not. A much higher percentage of the English university girls checked "Yes" (26 percent). And a still higher percentage of "Yes" responses— 29 percent—came from the Norwegian university girls.

On the other hand, the male students in all three countries (U.S.A., England, Norway) were about equal in their "Yes" responses (about 24 percent).

The U.S. girls who had no serious career aspirations were considerably more likely to check "No" (84 percent) than were the girls who did have career aspirations (62 percent checked "No").

We know why young males and females want to be together; it is less clear why they want to stay together.

At first glance, this recent great popularity in the permanent ties of marriage might seem incomprehensible and even indicate that some sort of loss of rationality was sweeping the Western world. The institutions of marriage and family have rapidly been losing many of their traditional reasons for being.

In the mid-1950s, sociologists W. F. Ogburn and M. F. Nimkoff reported a survey in which 18 experts on family life were invited to list what they thought were the most significant changes taking place in the American family. Of the 21 changes cited, 8 involved a loss of function. For example, here are the 8 losses of function they indicated:

• Loss in the importance of marriage as the only acceptable

setting for sexual intimacy, as a result of the increase of sexual intercourse outside of marriage.

• The transfer of the protective function of the family to police and to social organizations and to medical facilities.

• The increasing transfer of education of the young to schools.

• The transfer of much of family recreation to the movies, the automobile, to sports spectacles (and most recently, to television).

• Transfer of the family's productive functions largely to factories, offices, and other places of employment beyond the boundaries of the home.

• Increasing transfer of religious worship, when it occurs, to churches.

• The loss or reduction of the family as an insurance for aging parents. (Traditionally, aging parents could assume their children would care for them.) Today with mobility, plus pension plans and security programs, children take a more unfavorable attitude toward the idea of supporting elderly parents.

• The lessening importance of many traditional functions of homemaking, with the advent of mechanical appliances.

Sociologist Otto Pollak, of the University of Pennsylvania, has suggested that even more significant than such specific losses, for many, has been the loss of a family's self-control in "setting its own standards." The views of government experts on what is appropriate in education, health care, etc., for family members, may leave a family feeling it is losing both power and competence.

Even that most fundamental of all family functions, reproduction in order to perpetuate blood lines and the species, is becoming considerably less obvious as a need, with overpopulation becoming the world's most acute problem.

Clark Blackburn, head of the Family Service Association of America, recalls that only a few decades ago, an American woman had to marry for economic survival. She was barred by social convention from working, and more effectively barred by her lack of education. Today both job opportunities and education are available.

Economic urgency is not likely to impel most modern young women into marriage; and the need of the male to have a good hard-working wife to help him fulfill his role efficiently has become less widely felt. As anthropologist Margaret Mead pointed out, the modern Western male, unlike the Eskimo male, does not need a wife to chew his boots.

Some decades ago Dr. Mead observed, "In every known human society, everywhere in the world, the young male learns that when he grows up, one of the things which he must do in order to be a full member of society is to provide food for some female and her young." [2] In recent years, some adult males have been opting out on this traditional requirement and have been getting encouragement from marketers. *The Wall Street Journal* featured on its front page in 1967 an article about the way that American businessmen are exploiting the fad for a "Swinging Singles" life. Some unmarried, job-holding grown-ups, both male and female, between the ages of 20 and 34 are creating a new, carefree, fun-loving life based on single-hood. And quite a few young women in the U.S.A. and Scandinavia are deliberately opting out of the traditional female role. They are embracing motherhood while rejecting wife-hood, by declining to marry the fathers of their children.

Still, as noted, marriage has never been more popular than it has been in the past few years. In view of the loss of so many traditional functions served by marriage, how can we account for its increase in popularity? Sociologist Harold T. Christensen offers one clue when he states, "About all that is left to hold today's family together is the servicing of the sexual-affectional needs of the spouses and the personality formation needs of the children." These have traditionally been considered the bare minimal excuses for family formation, and yet today, these affectional-personality needs and certain other psychological intangibles have taken on enormously enhanced importance. This is because of the changing nature of the society in which young males and females come to maturity. Here are some apparent reasons why marriage has taken on greatly enhanced importance.

• *The intensified need for the warmth that can come from attachment to a person of the other sex.* Hegel contended that love is a quest for completeness. Psychiatrist Erich Fromm defines love as the overcoming of human separateness, as a fulfillment of the longing for union.

Several dozen French women were asked in a survey what a woman needs in order to be happy. Nearly all of them mentioned, in some way, an attachment to a man, to a husband.

But the need for "love" was mentioned explicitly by only about 20 percent of them.[3]

In the modern world, attachment to individuals is extremely difficult to maintain for very long because of all the mobility. University of Michigan sociologists Robert Blood, Jr., and Donald Wolfe, in their extensive study of husbands and wives, pointed out that "The only friendship which is guaranteed to survive mobility is marriage. Because husbands and wives move together they can count on each other in strange communities." And they added that for today's male, "his wife has become a man's best friend." [4]

Marriage then is often an escape from aloneness and a search for warmth and predictability in a dependable close relationship. Edna Rostow, as consultant in psychiatry at Yale University, put the situation vividly when she stated, "The idea of marriage. . . which seems to be emerging, is one in which central importance is attached to a relation of all-embracing intimacy with another person."

In 1965, students at the University of Illinois staged a symposium designed to help them get concepts of love and morality in perspective. The thought of one eloquent male, which was read, was: "I think I want to fall in love . . . the temptation of someone really knowing me and understanding all of me, the bad and the good, the strong and the weak . . . of someone I can squeeze and hug and who can squeeze and hug me is strong."

This hugging . . . this attachment . . . this enduring friendship . . . this escape from loneliness . . . this achievement of completeness . . . this all-embracing intimacy is most likely to be achieved by mating with a congenial member of the other sex.

• *The need for identity in the face of the new difficulties in achieving it.* The depersonalization of the outer world, the confusion about "who am I" that plagues so many millions of late adolescents, the swallowing up of communities by spreading megalopolitan areas, all have made it more difficult for many young adults to feel much sense of relevance as citizens. One good way of establishing identity in today's world was stated by sociologist Paul H. Landis, of Washington State University, in these words, "Marriage today is one of the most certain ways to fulfill the need to feel significant." Through marriage you become important to someone, and through parenthood, important to a number of individuals.

• *Marriage offers, for many, a sense of anchorage in an uncertain world*. For many, marriage is a refuge. New York psychologist Theodor Reik commented, "Although the home has been stripped of many functions, it has kept its unconscious meaning as the continuation of man's first domicile, which was the womb."

This view of marriage as the one safe refuge in an uncertain or hostile world took on great significance for many young Germans who were seeking a meaningful life in the turbulent years following World War II. One of Germany's leading behavioral scientists, H. Schelsky, has noted that, "Seen from the viewpoint of the insecurity and crisis of modern public order . . . man's essential expectations of security are deflected from social organizations external to the family. He then looks once again for security within the family." He suggested that the family in such cases is felt to be "the last stability factor in our disintegrating, modern world." [5]

In addition to these three emotion-gratifying reasons for marrying noted above, a number of young people today get married for quite specific needs:

• Many teenagers rushing into marriage are seeking an escape from unpromising life situations.

• A new reason for young men, aspiring to be managers, to get married is that the company they work for expects them to marry.

• And then, of course, there are the hundreds of thousands of young people who drift into the attractive trap of marriage after an impregnation.

• The desire to bequeath a part of ourselves to posterity. This desire for children remains a powerful factor driving many to marriage. The temptation remains, despite statistics about overpopulation, to create someone in our own image.

• Finally, we should not overlook a massive effort to persuade young people that marriage is the ideal state they should aspire to. Industry is still delighted by the prospect of increased sales when family formations are on the rise.

Sociologist Leslie Koempel, of Vassar College, who deplores our overemphasis on marriage, suggested that if the family disappeared because it was no longer economically functional, married love would have to be invented all over again to move goods off the store shelves.

One interesting aspect of the appeal of modern marriage is that while women are substantially more preoccupied with the thought of marriage than males before marriage, it is the males who are most likely to express contentment after marriage. Our College Survey, as indicated, showed that a substantially larger proportion of our unmarried males thought they could get along fine without marrying than did the unmarried females. Yet once married, males tend to be the more pleased with their state of wedlock.

A national survey by Peter H. Rossi, while he was director of the National Opinion Research Center (University of Chicago), concluded after examining thousands of interviews that while marriage is one of the wellsprings of happiness for a man, it is not so clearly so for a woman. She is more likely to suggest some discontent, perhaps because of the tensions of bearing and rearing children.

A similar picture—as far as males are concerned—emerged from a study financed by the National Institute of Mental Health. Genevieve Knupfer, as a psychiatrist at the Mental Research Institute of Berkeley, Cal., interviewed 785 adults in the San Francisco area. She concluded that bachelors, in general, turned out to be more unhappy and maladjusted than either single or married women. And married men were the happiest, in general, of all 4 groups. She found the single males three times as likely as single females to report they were unhappy. Dr. Knupfer surmised that males unable, or unwilling, to marry might be more likely to be psychologically impaired to start with, since men still usually do the proposing. Older single women, in contrast, may be self-assured, gifted, and have strong personalities, which led to their being bypassed because many men still want to feel superior to their wives. These mature single women are far more apt to lead happier, well-adjusted lives.

Despite the fact that men seem to get more contentment from marriage, it is, as indicated, the single girls who seem more eager to imagine themselves moving into a situation that can lead to marriage. This greater interest of the female in assuring herself she is developing an ongoing relationship toward marriage with a male is reflected in the discrepancies between males and females in recalling their brushes with love.

Researcher Evelyn Duvall in a study of adolescent love found that 36 percent of the girls questioned said they were in love at the moment, whereas the figure for boys was 25 percent.[6] (The fact that girls tend to have their first romances earlier than boys and marry at an earlier age might account in part—but not wholly—for this discrepancy.)

Ernest Burgess and Paul Wallin in studying recently engaged couples reported that the men seemed considerably less apt to recall they had ever discussed marriage with another possible partner than did the women. They observed, "The men do not think of themselves as having seriously discussed getting married whereas the women do."[7] The same situation showed up in a 1966 survey of 1000 Americans on the subject of love.[8]

ROMANTIC UNIONS VS. ARRANGED UNIONS

The fact that emotional rather than practical reasons increasingly account for marital unions probably helps explain why romantic dialogue has continued to replace family arrangement as the process for getting males and females together in wedlock.

A student at the New England men's college, in responding to our College Survey, wrote of his generation, "There generally seems to be an attitude that if love doesn't conquer all, it at least justifies all."

While love has long been heralded in songs, poems, and letters, it has only recently received widespread support, as Linton indicated, as the basis for wedlock. Marriage was too serious a business to be left to love. Psychologist Ernest van den Haag comments that, "Love is a very unruly horse," which is why, in the past, people seldom thought of harnessing couples in marriage on the basis of asserted love. In the past, there have been a number of sound reasons for discouraging matters based on feelings of love:

• Parents have assumed that their own decades of adulthood, in which they could observe life, have given them a superior basis for judging the suitability of possible unions.

• Family arrangement offers a better guarantee that the girl of exceptional character and background will achieve a "good" marriage than is still the case if she is thrown into open competition for males on the popular basis of looks and wiles.

Family specialists David and Vera Mace in their study of Asian marriages, where family arrangement still plays an important part in most countries, made this interesting comment: "In general, there is about the average Eastern woman a poise, a serenity, an impression of inward contentment, that stands out in contrast to the bewildered, restless, anxious demeanor of Western women today." One Asian told them, "In the West you fall in love, then marry. In the East, we marry and then fall in love."[9]

A few decades ago, U.S. sociologists tended to view romanticism as disfunctional as a basis for forming marriage. The belief was that romanticism tended to contribute to family disorganization. More recently, a number of sociologists have been concluding that, in our peculiar kind of society today, romanticism as a basis for forming marriages is indeed functional, and has positive values.

Columbia sociologist William Goode puts the functionalism of love today in this way: "In a rootless society, with few common bases for companionship, romantic love holds a couple together long enough to allow them to begin marriage."[10] This might be called the adhesive function of love.

With the lessening of family arrangements in marriage there has been in the U.S.A., at least, an increase in the acceptance of love-based marriages between young people of different religious backgrounds. Inter-religious marriages have steadily been increasing, and now nearly one-third of all marriages are interfaith.[11]

There is a feeling among many behavioral scientists that romanticism is furthered by the repression of overt sexual outlets. Thus, one conceivable reason why there has been a seeming decline in the romantic mood in the 1960s, despite the growing importance of love relationships, is that the increased openness about sexual discussion may have brought a reduction of mystery and sentiment. Van den Haag contends that love is longing. Thus, he argues that when sexual objects are easily and guiltlessly accessible, romantic love seldom prospers.[12]

In our College Survey we tried, not too successfully, to probe the feelings of students in the various countries on this whole area of romanticism, coolness, love, and meaningful relationships. Students, in commenting, quarreled more over definitions on this question than any other question in the checklist. At any rate, here are the questions and their responses. Our question was in two parts. First we asked:

Do you wish there was less stress on "coolness" and more on sentimental romanticism of the assertedly old-fashioned type in today's dating relationships? YES ___ NO ___
HAVE NOT THOUGHT ABOUT IT ___.

About half of the U.S. men and girls said "yes," they did wish there was less stress on coolness. Those who had never experienced coitus were substantially more inclined to check "yes" than were those who were coitally experienced. In the International Sample, the English university students showed the least interest—only 1 in 4—in placing less stress on coolness and more on sentimental romanticism. The second half of the question asked:

Or does the deferment of marriage until long after puberty now make it more sensible to be concerned about "relationships" than about love? YES ___ NO ___

Somewhat less than half the U.S. students agreed the focus might better be on "relationships" than on "love." Abroad, Norwegian university students were quite emphatically in favor of putting the emphasis on "love," while the English students wanted the main emphasis on "relationships." In the United States, a girl at the university in New York City commented, " 'I love you' is a very hard thing to say if you've mastered the art of cool. It is a very sad state of affairs; verbal affection, if not overdone, would be a nice thing to have."

At the same time, there does seem to be an increase in real companionship between young men and girls who have developed a serious admiration for each other. It can be noticed in college lounges where a man and a girl may be engrossed intently in conversation for more than an hour. And often the conversation is just a sharing of thoughts. In our survey, a male at the Catholic university said, "I am looking forward to the time when I have my companion in life."

Modern courtship has a high content not only of talk, but of equalitarian talk. A study made by sociologist Jerold S.

Heiss at the University of Connecticut in 1962 indicated that the closer males get to a committed relationship with a girl, the less they dominate the talk.

In modern collegiate courtships, the displayed symbols of the various stages of commitment vary and tend increasingly to be individualized, but frequently the first sign of commitment is when the young man gives his girl friend his college sweatshirt or a lavaliere chain. A girl at Bowling Green State University mentioned she had acquired seven male sweatshirts. These acquisitions can mean very little emotionally. If the couple's affair becomes more serious, they may exchange nightgowns with school or club symbols on the gowns. (At some schools, however, nightgowns are viewed simply as good party favors.) When they reach the "engaged to be engaged" stage and start thinking at least in general terms about planning their future together, the male surrenders to the girl his fraternity pin (or a special pinning model of it) or his college ring.

One problem of symbols if couples become fully committed, i.e., engaged, is that students who marry while undergraduates or going to graduate school often do not have the money to buy the traditional symbol of engagement, a decent-looking diamond ring. Since at current prices this would cost hundreds of dollars, the engaged campus couples have become more casual and may settle for simpler rings or the gift of possessions known to be cherished, or they keep using the pin; and some just don't bother buying anything. Others permit the ring to be provided by funds supplied by the groom-to-be's parents.

Even engagement in today's fast-shifting scene is far from being a certain thing. Breach-of-promise suits would be greeted with guffaws. Harrop and Ruth Freeman found in their study of 800 college senior women that a third of them had had fiancés to whom they were not now committed.

TRENDS AND PROBLEMS
IN THE TIMING OF WEDDINGS

In the United States the median age for marriage for both males and females reached its lowest point in recent decades just before 1960. Since then it has risen slightly. But still census figures indicated that between 1940 and 1964 the median age for first marriage for girls dropped from 21½ to 20½ years and the median age for men from 24 years to just about 23 years—to leave them with a difference of about 2½ years of age at marriage.

By 1967 teen-age brides appeared to be on the decline. This decline may become abrupt for a demographic reason. Robert Parke, Jr., and Paul C. Glick of the U.S. Census stated, "The relative over-supply of young women will tend to produce a further rise in the next ten years in the age at which women marry for the first time."[13]

Their reasoning should give marriage-minded girls pause for reflection: since "women marry men who are two or three years their senior, on the average, there has been in the past five years a drop in the number of males per 100 females in the main marrying ages. . . . In the early 1950's there were, in the average year, about 104 males per 100 females in the main marrying ages. . . . In the latter half of the 1960's it will average only about 93 [males per 100 females] and will subsequently return to 99 per 100 in the early 1970's," they predicted.

"These figures describe, in broad terms, the 'marriage squeeze' that has resulted from the fact that the girls born in the post war baby boom come of age [for purposes of marriage] sooner than the boys."

Perhaps of equal significance to the "marriage squeeze" is the fact that "average" age of marriage is increasingly derived from two groups in our society marrying at significantly different ages. With millions of high-school graduates now going on for higher education each year, we have one large group of the younger generation theoretically committing itself to postponement of marriage. Meanwhile, those who do not go beyond high school or who drop out of high school have been marrying in far greater numbers while still in their teens. The Population Reference Bureau reported in 1964 that, on the average, there is a 4-year difference in the age of marriage for women who become college graduates and those who do not pursue education beyond high school.

Traditionally, young people—especially males—have based their marriage readiness not upon their chronological age but rather upon their readiness for independence. Today many collegians who have not achieved this readiness for independence have been marrying anyhow.

Some observers have searched for explanations for the fact that, overall, young people, of whatever education, have been marrying earlier. They point to such social changes as increases in exposure to the opposite sex, social mobility, increased employment of women, the loosening of youth ties to the family created by urban living, increased economic affluence, and increased emphasis on romance.[14]

Society's frequent warning to girls to hurry before they lose out also is probably a factor. Though these girls have a half-century of vigorous life ahead, many are made to feel nervous if they don't marry by the end of adolescence.

The new ability to marry on the installment plan or with substantial parental help also has encouraged early marriage regardless of education. *The Wall Street Journal* at the beginning of 1966 reported that most economists believed the young adults of tomorrow will be getting an ample reserve of financial help from Mom and Dad. It reported, "Through loans and gifts from their parents, these youths will become important consumers even while they are still trying to settle into their first jobs."

Sociologist Marvin Sussman of Case Western Reserve University found some years ago that young marrieds were already getting a substantial amount of help from their parents.[15] He interviewed 97 families in New Haven, Conn., that had 195 married children and found that 79 percent of the parents had established a pattern of giving moderate help and services to their married children.

The role of unplanned pregnancy, which has been on the rise, is, of course, a conspicuous goad to early marriage, especially in high-school marriages.[16]

Another incitement to early marriage is the eagerness of the marriage industry in several states to perform instant unions day or night. In Nevada's Las Vegas about 80,000 persons were married in 1966, or more than the city's total population. Justices of the Peace can readily gross $100,000, primarily from marriage ceremonies, during their 2-year terms. One vivid description of a marriage there, lasting 90 seconds, read: "The young bride wore a pink, blue, and yellow polka dot pants-suit. The teenage groom wore a leather jacket and wrap around sunglasses."[17]

One test of marital success is its stability. On that test, teen-age marriages are notoriously unsuccessful. The divorce rate for those marrying in their teens is more than twice as high as for couples marrying at later ages.

We asked students in our College Survey—who on average were approaching their 21st birthday—this question:

What would you consider to be the ideal age for a person such as yourself to marry, if the person desired to and had a completely free choice?

Following the question was a list of numbers from 17 through 29. The ages most preferred by the U.S. girls for marrying was in the 21-to-23-year range. About two-thirds checked one of these years. But the other third indicated their ideal was in the 24-to-26-year range. The mean age checked would be 23.1 or presumably about a year after completing undergraduate work. Girls who said they were seriously planning careers tended to choose an ideal age nearly a year older than the girls with no career plans or indefinite career plans.

As for the males, they most frequently checked the 24–26 year range. Half checked one of these years. The mean ideal came out as 24.4 years.

As for the international samples, both males and females in most countries tended to favor marrying about a year later than the mean ideal ages of U.S. students.

In the U.S.A. the actual median age at marriage in 1960 for collegians who had completed *4 or more* years of college was 26 for men and nearly 24 for women.[18] Those who did not finish 4 years of college married earlier. Gerhard Neubeck, of the Family Study Center at the University of Minnesota, in citing these facts, took note of the fact that a larger proportion of collegians are marrying while still in college. On some campuses nearly a third of the student population are married, and he suggested that increased sophistication in controlling conception through oral contraceptives was a factor. The couples are assuming that if they are careful they can continue their studies without any serious risk of pregnancy.

Before 1945 college marriages were relatively unusual, and at some schools marriage was grounds for dismissal. The percentage of married students in 1944 was about 6 percent.[19]

At state universities and state colleges, ingenious couples by part-time and summer jobs can often raise most of the finances themselves, since tuitions are low and loans and often scholarships are available. But if the young husband and wife are going to a private school or aren't job holders at a state school, and if both of them try to continue their studies, family subsidies are often the only answer. Marvin Sussman and Lee Burchinal in studying parental aid to married students concluded, "Young couples today exhibit a much more casual attitude toward economic readiness for marriage. . . . Even if the most extreme concessions are made, these students by their marriage decisions, have rejected the norm of a reasonably assured financial status before marriage. . . ."

Many of these married students are, in effect, starting married life as playmates rather than as self-sufficient mates. One father, a television executive in New York City, lamented that he didn't mind too much paying the cost of his son's getting married and supporting the marriage, but he was upset that he now had to pay for his son's divorce.

We asked the students in our College Survey this question:

Do you think it is a good idea for a man and girl to marry while still undergraduates if they are in love and the parents of both are willing to continue financing their schooling?
YES ___   NOT SURE ___   POOR WAY TO START OFF
A MARITAL PARTNERSHIP ___

Twenty-seven percent of the U.S. males said "yes," as against only 19 percent of the females. Nearly a fourth of the respondents were "Not sure." On the possible "Poor way to start" response, the females were somewhat more emphatic: 59 percent of the females checked this, as against 50 percent of the males. Approval of such marriages was somewhat stronger in the West than in any other U.S. region. In the international samples the strongest support for the idea came from English university students: more than 40 percent of both males and females checked "yes."

The 57 recently married wives living in university housing at the U.S. school in the Rocky Mountain area were more in favor of such marriages (35 percent said "yes") than coeds at that campus or coeds in general, but some of them may have been influenced by a need to justify what they had already done.

Most of the amplifying comments from U.S. students came from the females and were quite strongly opposed. One girl said she saw nothing wrong with the idea of couples marrying before graduation if they work "as much as possible" and are not "totally dependent" on their parents. That was about as close as any came to supporting the idea. Those opposing the idea offered such explanations as these:

• "The idea that one should be dependent upon one's parents for support when married is contrary to the meaning of marriage. Marriage is a stepping forth with someone you love to start a life of your own independently for better or for worse."

• A girl at an Eastern women's college in deploring the idea added, "Same pertains to rings. I think it outrageous for parents of a boy to buy the diamond. Rather no ring. . . ."

The voices of experience coming from the recently married wives we sampled who were living in university housing in the Rocky Mountain area were of special interest. Those who commented were strongly opposed to such undergraduate marriages as a rule, but some approved in certain situations:

• One thought it was all right if the students worked and paid most of their expenses.

• "My parents think my husband is using them and myself for money because he is the only one of us in school."

• Another said she was very familiar with marriages that were completely subsidized and added, "Most of the partners feel little challenge and no responsibility. It is especially a blow to most of the males because they can't find any masculine values if they don't contribute at least partly to the support of their wives."

Those are some of the cautionary comments. But with more and more students going to college and more and more becoming committed to advanced study in graduate school, the question whether to marry or not marry is going to become an increasingly common one for students in the coming decade. Those who are marrying in large numbers are creating a major new type of young marriage—and society might do well to decide what it thinks of such marriages and to start setting up some ground rules.

V. The Married Confrontation: Coping with Some Novel Patterns

CHAPTER 15

Shifts in the Power and Duties of Husbands and Wives

"An overwhelming majority of both boys and girls agreed that the man was not to be considered the 'head' of the family." Clark Blackburn, Executive Director of the Family Service Association of America, in citing a survey of 500 Louisiana teenagers.[1]

Such an equalitarian view of marriage represents quite a change for humans since Confucius admonished, "The woman's duty is to prostrate herself submissively before her husband in such a way as to have no will of her own, but to demonstrate a perfect form of obedience."

In fact, it represents quite a change from the master-of-the-hearth concept of the husband that was common in the United States until recent decades. Early in the last century a well-known publication of that time, *The Ladies' Book,* quoted a minister as admonishing the bride: "Your duty is submission. . . . Your husband is, by the laws of God and of man, your superior; do not ever give him cause to remind you of it."[2] Many living Americans can remember wedding ceremonies in which the bride vowed she would "obey" her husband. In England until the past century, the official hierarchy of a family ran from father to eldest son, then other sons, and only then to mother and daughters.

Today with millions of women earning their own incomes, going to college, and wearing pants, it should not be surprising that the egalitarian ideal is spreading in marriage. When John Hancock and 55 other good and true male patriots stated, in

1776, that all men are created equal, it is doubtful they were thinking much about females. But the ideal went on record and is today close to being a reality in the relationship between husbands and wives.

The trend has been encouraged by the fact that today's husbands and wives, far more than in the past, must work out their married roles without having elder kinfolk to guide or admonish them. When revolutionary regimes in Russia, China, and Cuba introduced dramatic changes liberating women from male dominion, one can speculate that idealism was not their sole motivation. They may well have perceived that their own precarious position of power could be augmented by shaking up the whole fabric of male-dominated kinfolk structures so powerful in the villages. At any rate, a number of family specialists doubt that the patriarchal family will be able to develop and flourish in the kind of advanced technological societies we are seeing today.

Investigators of married relationships have long pondered how to measure real power within a marriage. Obviously, appearances can be deceptive. In some U.S. regions, wives still ceremoniously defer to their husbands in public. Sociologist David Heer, of Harvard, has found that when you ask a husband and wife together who wins out in arguments, the wife is the more likely to exaggerate in attributing greater influence to the partner.[3] And psychologist Eleanore Luckey found in a study of 80 married couples that when a person is dissatisfied with his or her marriage he (or she) is more likely than average to describe the partner as domineering.[4]

The best way to measure real power, apparently, is to assess how the husbands and wives really deal with each other at home.[5] But that of course is not easy to ascertain. One of the better descriptions of the *source* of married power was offered a couple of decades ago by the sociologist Willard Waller, a genial, acerbic skeptic who greatly whetted my own interest in human behavior while I was a student of his at Penn State. In Waller's view, marital dominance derives at least initially from how the partners would stand in courtship desirability if again free. He advanced the "principle of least interest" to account for marital power. In his concept, power is maintained by the partner more willing to rock the boat (i.e., being more willing to quarrel before outsiders, being quicker to offer to call the marriage quits, being last to try to make up).[6]

In earlier days, husbands jocularly explained they maintained power by keeping their wives barefoot and pregnant. It is still true today that the pregnant wife is in a weakened position to apply conjugal power. But today the wife can control her pregnancy and, as the controller, has some extra leverage of power if she knows her husband greatly desires offspring.

Also in older days, the husband had a legal right to maintain his authority by beating his wife as long as he didn't use a stick thicker than his thumb.[7] Today with wife-beating frowned upon (and riskier to the husband) many a male, in taking a mate, tends to seek out one who obviously will defer to him because she is less educated, or younger, or substantially smaller, or lower in social status.

As in most human affairs, money can be a major source of power in marriage. Who supplies it? Who handles it? When both partners have substantial incomes, their views toward power tend to move in an equalitarian direction.[8]

Social scientists Robert O. Blood, Jr., and Donald M. Wolfe, of the University of Michigan found in their extensive study of about 900 husbands and wives in the Detroit area that the spouse handling the family money was more likely to have a high "mean power score," a doubly appropriate phrase.[9] If the husband always handled the money, he had a considerably higher power score than if the wife always did. In the opinion of your author this, however, is not invariably the situation. At our house, the power struggle focuses upon who can push the most problems of handling finances onto the other's lap.

This type of unending power struggle over money at our house is more consistent with Barnard sociologist Mirra Komarovsky's distinction about power in decision-making. She has found that the power is not so much with the person who makes the decisions as with the person who decides who is to make the given decisions. She finds that a whole field of decision-making can be relegated to a weaker partner by the dominant mate.[10]

Some suggest that another way to measure power in a marriage might be who has the most to say about the choice of friends. Sociologists at the University of Nebraska tried to

determine who does the most—the husband or wife—to initiate friendships and who has the most to say in the selection
of people that will be close friends of the couple. When the
husband and wife agreed on the facts involved, it turned out
that husbands were reported to be about three times as likely
as wives to initiate friendships.[11] But again, this might merely
mean that the wives, in responding to the investigations, had
leaned toward deference to the male ego. My own investigation some years ago of friendship patterns among Jewish
couples indicated that, no matter who initiated the friendship,
it was the wives who handled most of the week-to-week social
arrangements that got couples together.

Still another way to measure power might be who is the
more influential when a couple must reach a decision. This is
difficult, however, to ascertain with certainty in laboratory
situations. Sociologist William F. Kenkel, of the University of
Kentucky, conducted studies—which he concluded were not
definitive—with young married couples to see how various
couples arrived at a decision when asked how they would
spend an unexpected windfall of $300. Evidence emerged
which clearly indicated that men did most of the talking and
introduced most of the ideas; but the evidence also indicated
that most commonly the final decisions were in accord with
ideas the wife had advanced.[12] Was this feminine influence?
Or was it simply evidence that husbands will want to do the
gallant thing when invited to spend $300—especially when
the $300 is hypothetical?

In recent years, the main public arguing on how to measure
marital power has been between Blood and David M. Heer
(who studied the power relations of 138 married couples in
the Boston area). Blood advances what he calls "the resources
theory," and Heer advances what he calls the "exchange
value theory."

Under Blood's "resources" concept, the greater power is
with the partner who brings the more resources to the marriage. By resources, he has in mind such things as money and
property, educational level, and social status.[13] Heer acknowl-
edges the importance of resources but claims the crucial factor
is the value placed on these resources *outside* the marriage. In
the crunch, where one or both of the partners contemplate
the possibility that a divorce or separation may develop, who
would be in the better position on the open market to make

a good remarriage?[14] In short, he accepts Waller's "least interest" principle and tries to put it into the context of the values each partner would be able to put on the block in seeking remarriage.

My impression is that while both the "resources" and "exchange-value" theories have merit, they are inadequate to explain the power situation in many of today's marriages, since both are resources-oriented. Socio-economic strength, personal competence, and attractiveness are relevant but are not the whole story. Today much of the adhesion of the two people is often based upon the meeting of emotional *needs*. It seems to me that power in a marriage today is significantly affected by the intensity of the emotional needs of each spouse. How much does the male or female need to be married to someone? And more specifically, how much are his or her *needs* being satisfied by the person with whom he or she is involved in wedlock? Considerable power in a showdown would reside with the partner whose felt needs (emotional, social, or economic) are least met by the marriage. A comprehensive theory should assume that spouses would take both resources and needs into account in contemplating what kind of situation they would be in if the marriage were dissolved. The one least disturbed by the prospect would have more theoretical power.

All the major theories recently advanced assumed that either the wife or the husband can now be the more powerful figure and so, by inference, reject any automatic assumption of male superiority in power. Clark Blackburn, in speaking to the International Family Conference in Rome in 1965, flatly asserted that American marriage had moved swiftly from an authoritarian structure to a democratic framework where wives—and sometimes even children—have an equal say in family decisions.

Blood and Wolfe asked the wives of their survey which partner usually gave in after an argument. A fourth of the wives said the husband gave in. And about 40 percent gave equalitarian responses.[15] Two noteworthy studies have been made of husband-wife power as perceived by their own adolescent children. One might have reservations about how competent many adolescents are to judge the true power relationship between their parents; but at any rate, both studies found teenagers predominantly convinced that the power relationship between their mothers and fathers was equalitarian.[16] Sociologists Charles E. Bowerman and Glen H. Elder, Jr., in reviewing studies of the trends in marital power—including those by Blood and Wolfe—for the August, 1964, *American Sociological Review,* stated:

"Recent data indicates that equality between spouses is increasing and that women are more frequently stepping into the primary role in the family."

Does more power gravitate to the wife who works than to the wife who does not? The answer would seem to be yes. When David Heer asked the married partners he studied who usually won out if there was disagreement, there was a somewhat greater tendency if the wife was working for both partners to report that it was the wife who usually won out. A study in Paris, France, of 300 marriages found that in all social classes, wives who stayed home were more likely to be dominated by their husbands than were the wives who had jobs.[17] The tables developed by Blood and Wolfe indicate that the husband's "mean power"—a statistical phrase with that interesting second meaning—is likely to become less, the longer the wife holds a job.

What about the effect of the presence of children on husband-wife power? David Heer found a significant positive association between the number of children in the family and the influence of the husband in decision-making.[18] This would suggest that the wife not only loses power temporarily if she is pregnant but also if she is tied down with the responsibility for small children. The Blood and Wolfe tables indicate that the husband's "mean power" is consistently higher where there are children than where there are not children, and that it is highest of all where the children are of preschool age.[19]

Does husband-wife power vary by social class? It apparently does. The lower-class wife, whether working or not, will usually have a more dominant influence in the marriage than her equivalent in the middle class. (Possibly because the husband is less of a success by the standards of a materialistic world.) In terms of income, the Blood and Wolfe tables showed the husband's power rising through each of five levels of income and was highest for husbands who had incomes of $10,000 or more. This pattern, however, does not necessarily apply in countries where there is a strong patriarchal tradition, such as Greece and Yugoslavia. There, the more educated man is more likely to be more thoughtful in granting his wife relatively equal status.[20]

Some sociologists focus their attention primarily on what is happening to the "roles" of husbands and wives, rather than to their theoretical power. Talcott Parsons and Robert Bales, of Harvard, developed the thesis some years ago that any husband-wife team has two basic roles to perform. One is the "instrumental" role of bringing home the bacon, handling the family's relations with the outside world, etc. The other is the "expressive" role, the inside job of holding the family together. The instrumental role, of course, has traditionally been the husband's; the expressive role, the wife's. Parsons has suggested that the wife is being pulled over more toward the instrumental role but is still more involved with expressive functions than the husband.

Another way to assess what is going on between husbands and wives today is to examine the *tasks* each performs. Blood and Wolfe were able to compare city couples with farm couples and concluded that city husbands were substantially more domesticated than farm husbands. The city husbands were much more likely to get their own breakfast, help with the dishes, etc.

The wife in America still has primary responsibility for food, laundry, children, and home, and the husband most likely has charge of major repairs, handling important outside matters, earning the bulk of the income. But lines are blurring. A half-dozen studies show that, where the wife works, the husband tends to take on a greater share of the housework. At my house the one remaining task that is invariably sex-typed and assigned to the husband is taking dead mice out of traps.

The sharing of tasks gained in general acceptability after World War II, because of the new kinds of marriages young couples going to college developed then. If both were studying, care of the baby might fall to the partner least pressed at the moment in his studying. Before they marry, males at the modern day mega-university may be picking up skills that will make it seem natural to help with the cooking—or be better connoisseurs of their brides' cooking. Tens of thousands of students living in off-campus apartments are learning to cook their meals as a way to save money. At the University of Wisconsin a male and female student were casually comparing recipes for beef Stroganoff.

Worried observers may mock the young husband who holds the ladder while his wife paints the ceiling, but the young husband and wife involved usually have little thought that the male is being placed in an inappropriate position. Recently a bride reported to me that her new husband had been helping her with the ironing. He beamed as she made this revelation. In the new kinds of marriages held together so largely by emotional feeling, such activities may strengthen the needed sense of companionship, at least in the early years. And it would be wrong to assume subservience in a husband who frequently does the dishes. It may be a simple act of consideration for a working wife who, he knows, has had a tough day; or it may be simply that he is bored watching television and, having spent the day at a sedentary job, feels the need to stir around.

Care of the family automobile has, for most of this century, been one task the husband invariably handled. This often was where he felt proudest of his prowess. A majority of U.S. husbands still take the larger share of the care of the family's car or cars; but the situation is rapidly changing. A major oil-company survey found that 43 percent of service-station customers today are women. Even the matter of taking cars to garages for substantial repairs and maintenance is being handled increasingly by wives. I put the matter to William McConnell, service manager of the garage I often patronize in Connecticut. I gave him a chart and asked him to keep track of all the people who brought cars in for servicing during one week in November, when much of the winterizing of cars is done. Of the customers known to be married, 40 percent proved to be wives.

This did not surprise Mr. McConnell. He said, "We're seeing many more wives than even four years ago. Their proportion is getting higher and higher. If it is a big heavy job involving lots of money, the husband will bring it in. But the woman brings the car in for winterizing. The men seem to forget that, and the women have been sold winterizing on television." He said he would much rather deal with women than men because it is easier to sell them preventive maintenance than it is men. Also they seem more likely to be aware that snow tires need changing; and they are more conscious of appearances (possibly because of a greater concern for making a good impression with acquaintances). They want scratches fixed.

Some months later, he invited Mrs. Packard and me to attend one of his "Ladies Only" seminars on automobile ailments and maintenance. There were 35 women in attendance. Mr. McConnell that evening gave them a lesson on what makes cars run. He held up a carburetor and said, "This little honey can give you a lot of trouble in the wintertime." Then he explained the distributor, the fuel pump, the battery, and the troubles all could cause. During the question period some queries put by ladies were:

"What is a ball joint?". . . . "What is a disc brake?" . . . . "Why is it that my car goes clank even when I'm parking?" To the last question Mr. McConnell said, "Lady, you've got trouble."

The role of taking care of the family car, or even driving it, would still appall most French housewives. Mme. Rose Vincent, editor of the French women's magazine *Femme Pratique,* reported to me that she had been trying to get her feminine readers to use the family car, and by using it, to shop once a week instead of shopping every day on foot. She explained, "The French man still does the driving for the most part, and he is not at all used to taking his wife to the market. And the wife is so far away from the idea that she wouldn't dream of asking him."

Other French observers also report that French women still are very traditional in their ideas about family roles and tasks. The French author Menie Grégoire states, "Even when French women work, we know that they rarely accept their husband's help in household chores . . . French women love being women and they love men to be men . . . It is the women who set the limits unconsciously . . . with all kinds of excuses: 'Get out of the kitchen: you're in the way.' "

Russians, for all their pioneering in opening up career roles for women, still tend to be traditional in assuming that household tasks belong to the wife. When the Russian wife gets home from her long day's work, she spends about three times as much time as the husband in coping with household tasks. The Russian astrophysicist Alla Masevitch states that the thing that impressed her most about her visit to American homes was the way husbands helped their wives. She exclaimed, "What a help they are, especially in entertaining and dish-washing! I am trying to popularize this in the Soviet Union."

In England the dramatic change that has come over the division of household tasks was reported by two psychologists at the University of Nottingham, after investigating the behavior of 700 fathers with their year-old babies. More than half fell into what the psychologists called the "highly participant group." The psychologists pointed out that 3 decades ago, the number of highly participant husbands in baby care was probably negligible.

But there were some distinctions on what the fathers would undertake in caring for their babies. The vast majority played with the baby and often helped get it to sleep. But only 57 percent said they had ever changed a "nappie" and still fewer had ever given the baby a bath. Possibly those were tasks involving skills that made them nervous. The psychologists noted that a number of the wives took evident pleasure in the masculine clumsiness of their husbands. As for the ultimate test, appearing in public places pushing a pram, two-thirds of the husbands indicated they would, if necessary, take the baby out without the mother; but more frequently they explained they didn't mind pushing the pram "if we go as a family."

One interesting study of the distribution of both power and duties between husbands and wives was conducted in the U.S.A. by family sociologist Reuben Hill, Director of the Family Study Center at the University of Minnesota. He made an analysis of couples representing three generations of the same family lines. There were 120 couples from each generation: the grandparent generation, the parent generation, and the married-child generation.[21] Hill found a clear shift from authoritarian to equalitarian patterns as he moved from the oldest to the youngest married groups and also much more sharing of tasks in the youngest "married-child" group.

While Hill found role distinctions between husband and wife were much more blurred in the youngest group, he reported that the youngest couples were considerably more skilled in communicating with each other. Older couples tended to be reluctant to enter into disagreements or to express hostility, but they also proved to be poorer at working out a consensus, when confronted with difficult questions. The young marrieds were quick to express conflicting opinions but also were deft in locating a basis for agreement and in moving to help the partner losing an argument save face.

In view of all the shifts in power, tasks, and roles, how much of the husband's traditional position as "head" of the household remains?

The power situation in up-to-date homes looks as ambiguous to an outsider as it does in many up-to-date corporations. The husband has been given the newly created title of Chief of the Executive Committee. Meanwhile, the wife has moved into the presidency. Which one actually has the more say about the running of the enterprise varies, as with the corporations, from house to house.

CHAPTER 16

Some Contemporary Styles in Wedlock

"That husbands and wives like as well as love one another, enjoy one another's company—this is a very exalted conception of marriage. For many if not most marriages the 'natural' course of events leads . . . [to] a parallelism in which each goes his or her own way." Research scholar Jessie Bernard, Washington University.

The young couples conjoining into marriage in such great numbers today must each decide what they want their marriage to mean to them. The model of their parents may seem either quaint or irrelevant. The needs to be met in the marriage have become different and less specific. The union has been substantially freed from surveillance by kinfolk and neighbors. And old patterns of deference, as just indicated, can be ignored.

In this new context, the young marrieds are searching for a plausible style for their legal partnership. Despite the new freedoms of choice, one can sense that their marriages are taking root in less than an idyllic setting. Freedom may also mean isolation. And isolation is a conspicuous element shaping millions of recent marriages.

Some observers take the bleak view that young husbands and wives confronted with the modern condition and its shrinkage of community life are trying to create a community in microcosm by their own marriage.[1]

This sense of isolation felt by young couples also appears widespread in much of Western Europe. English psychologists have noted a trend to isolation; in Germany sociologist H. Schelsky sees the modern family unit being isolated and dispersed in large urban centers with abundant entertainment and recreational amenities available. Schelsky also suggests that young marrieds are relatively more preoccupied with consumption and less with their creative roles in life. In fact, he speculates that modern technology may reduce the family to a "mere consumption unit." If TV commercials in the U.S.A. are symptomatic, then this trend to a consumeristic marriage is far along in the United States. On TV a young husband and wife are shown trying to control their hysteria in the face of a modern kind of crisis; their "Right Guard" aerosol deodorant can is empty.

The presidential address at the 1965 meeting of the National Council of Family Relations had the provocative title: "Familia Spongia: The Adaptive Function." The president, Clark E. Vincent, was half-humorously suggesting that our technological era calls for families that have sponge-like characteristics. In a period of rapid social change, he contends, families need to be adaptable and resilient in order to facilitate the changes for society. He suggests the family may even serve the sponge-like function of absorbing the blame for many of our current social problems from delinquency to drop-outs.

Vincent has refused to be pessimistic about the family, even if it is sponge-like. He too takes note that it is no longer a producing unit as in earlier times but adds that it has become "a viable consuming unit." He asks, "Is it any less important in terms of function that it consumes houses, cars, camping equipment, hi-fi equipment, and so forth?"

Other behavioral scientists, like Vincent, believe that changes in the family can be for the good as well as for the bad. Talcott Parsons, the Buddha-like eminence of American sociology, argues that the changes we have been seeing involve gains as well as losses. And Columbia sociologist William J. Goode stresses the mediating function of the modern family. It acts as a mediator in being a buffer and strainer between the individual and the larger society.

While family specialists are pondering what is happening, younger males and females involved in wedlock are testing a variety of possible marital patterns. These range from frivolous to thoughtful, and from fragile to deeply meaningful. Their tone ranges from desperation to devotion.

With all the millions of couples experimenting with married confrontations, the results are far too varied to attempt any arbitrary, all-inclusive classification. For example, there still are Mom and Pop marriages, marriages held together for "the sake of" the children, marriages that begin on a binge or at the prodding of a shotgun. There are the running-battle kinds of marriages in which the couples meet their inner needs through in-fighting. Some marriages appear to be held together by hatred. And there are the plaything marriages in which the male maintains his languorous, buxom bride in her high-rise dollhouse.

But in looking over contemporary styles of marriage, six types seem to be especially noteworthy as the last third of the 20th century begins. Most of the six reflect—or meet needs or desires created by—recent social changes.

In describing them I will put the emphasis upon the one most conspicuous element that seems to characterize the relationship. Many couples can undoubtedly see themselves in more than one of these six types of marriage. There is overlap. And the elusive element of love, in varying intensity, can be found in several of these types.

Viewed as types, the six fall into two quite different categories. In the first group the most conspicuous element is the *style* of the marriage. In the second group, the most conspicuous element is the *quality* of the married relationship. Here then are the two groups. First let us look at three interesting modern types of marriage distinguished by style:

1. *The fun marriage.* Here the preoccupation of the partners is on having a good time, planning outings, holidays, parties, and excursions. Both enjoy being on the go in search of the glamorous Good Life as defined by the more restless and hedonistic members of their peer group; being married adds to the convenience and fun that they can have by doing all this together.

The mood of a couple involved in the Fun Marriage shows up best perhaps in the choice of a home. After World War I, returning servicemen and their sweethearts by the millions were singing "Home, Sweet Home" and yearning to build a nest somewhere in the West. After World War II and the Korean War there was a similar enormous popularity among the recently married for having their own little house, even though it was now likely to be on a vast tract of Cape Codders or split-levels.

By 1958 the popularity of these single-family houses started to fade. A number of economic and demographic reasons were advanced for the drop (such as a recession and a decline in families with pre-adolescent children), but as those conditions changed, the fading in popularity of "singles" still continued, especially among young marrieds. Meanwhile there was a great upsurge in the popularity of apartments, especially the very posh types.

A clue to what seemed to be going on was offered by a top official of a great steel corporation in addressing home builders at an October 1965 meeting of the National Association of Home Builders. He stated:

"I have checked with my own children and with their friends. I find them, upon marriage, feeling that they need a place to live; but it is a secondary thing . . . compared with having a new automobile, a weekend at a ski lodge . . . or what have you. They are motivated entirely differently than my generation was. When I got married, the first thing I needed was a house, and I wanted to own it. But in Pittsburgh today among the children of my friends this is not the reaction I get at all. My own children . . . couldn't care less. They want to enjoy life today and look at the morrow when and if it gets here. My oldest daughter is now 40 with four children. Until this year neither she nor her sister nor her brother, who are younger, wanted a new house or the things that go with it. It's simply flabbergasting."[2]

A leading consultant to home builders, James Mills, of Home Facts Research, Inc., found this steel executive's comments confirming a married mood he had been tracking for some time. Mills feels the changing market for housing is symptomatic of important changes in values and in the American mood: "rather basic changes having to do with youth and sex and sensation-seeking." He explains: "Primarily what I am finding is the premium placed on pleasure."

What are the changes that have created this new mood among many young marrieds? Perhaps the fact that many are expected to thrive in a highly transient society makes it seem preposterous to yearn for the stable and solid. Perhaps they as growing children had too good a look at the alleged dream-fulfilling quality of modern suburban living. Perhaps some are finding their careers so highly rationalized in bureaucratic institutions that they think of life satisfactions primarily in terms of living it up off the job. Perhaps it is the affluence, and concomitant advertising. Perhaps in this era of the generational gulf they still manage to identify with the younger generation and associate home-owning with the fuddy-duddies of the adult world.

Mr. Mills contends that the single-family subdivision-type house as it has been built in recent decades conflicts with the "youth, sex, fun-loving, romantic cult of our times." He points out that the kinds of apartment houses that move fastest with young marrieds are those with sex appeal, much like those that appeal to the new singles groups. The buildings are built around pools with balconies overlooking a water fountain illuminated by multicolored lights at night. Apartments have step-up access to the master bedroom with many sensuous touches including high-fashion bathrooms, private, mirrored dressing areas, oversized beds. (The Sealy mattress people advise me there has indeed been a trend to "king-sized" and "queen-sized" beds, especially on the West Coast. Twin beds, on the other hand, have an above-average appeal on the East Coast.)

2. *The colleague marriage.* This relatively new type of marriage on a large scale has its greatest popularity among the more sober, thoughtful, achievement-oriented couples. The most conspicuous element is the interest of the partners in each other's outside careers and their joint approach to achievement. It may begin while they are both graduate students where they begin planning their careers together. Those already embarked upon careers are likely to have careers with related professional interests (such as teaching) and often work in the same field. Thus we have husband-wife theology professors at Boston University . . . a number of married sociologists . . . married marriage experts such as Evelyn and Sylvanus Duvall . . . many married lawyers . . . and many married doctors.

Two young Michigan doctors, Donald and Bonnie Norris, stood at attention in 1967 as they were sworn into the U.S. Army, shook hands with the colonel who administered the oath, and then kissed. They had both just finished their internships and were to be made captains the next day. An

Army spokesman explained that the wife would automatically be given an honorable discharge if she became pregnant.

A fine example of a colleague marriage is that of Alva and Gunnar Myrdal, both internationally famous as social scientists and as Swedish political leaders. She introduced the phrase "a pair of careers" to describe those congenial marriages where the couple's work interests strengthen the bonds of sociability and a sense of partnership. Although they are Swedes, the Myrdals command seven and a half inches of type in *Who's Who in America*, each receiving approximately the same amount of space. They have three grown children. Their careers take them separately or together to many parts of the world. I was fortunate to find them enjoying a brief work holiday at their lakeside summer home in the picturesque village of Mariefred, Sweden. They were staying in a modest second-floor apartment, and she prepared the lunch as we chatted.

The phrase "colleague marriage" apparently was first advanced in 1958 by sociologists Daniel Miller and Guy Swanson to describe the marriage of co-workers, with equal, interdependent, but distinct and mutually recognized, competencies.

One difficulty of the Colleague Marriage, if they are in the same line of work, is that some organizations, especially colleges, frown upon husband-wife teams. In cases where there are rules against such teams, the rules often go back to Depression days when there was a strong feeling that one job per family was plenty. Also there has been the feeling that if a husband-wife team work in the same department they have undue weight in interoffice politics. The University of Kansas at this writing permits husbands and wives to be on the faculty as long as they are not in the same department. Another difficulty in the academic world is that it is unusual for a department to have two openings at the same time.

A more serious problem confronting the husband and wife in the Colleague Marriage is mobility. If both are employed by a college in a small community and one gets a better opportunity elsewhere, they have a problem. There is usually less strain, and more opportunities for maneuver, if they live and work in a large metropolitan area offering a variety of opportunities for both. An example of how the mobility problem was recently handled successfully was the simultaneous move of Peter and Alice Rossi, both distinguished sociologists, from the University of Chicago to Johns Hopkins University in Baltimore, he as a department chairman, she to continue her work in research under that department's sponsorship.

Married colleagues with a shared profession have an easier time if their work permits them to be flexible about relocating. The article-writing team Jhan and June Robbins and the mystery-adventure writers William and Audrey Roos have flexibility as to where and how they work and live. The Rooses can usually work as well in Spain as in New York City or Martha's Vineyard or Westport, Conn.

One husband and wife involved in a Colleague Marriage revealed that they negotiate all possible employment moves as a team. The wife added, "Our individual career interests and ambitions were very much a part of our exploration of each other before we married. Had we not been in agreement, we would not have married. I think one of the tragedies about the way in which girls are socialized in American society is that they do not learn to think ahead."

3. *The nestling marriage.* The central element of this type of marriage is the importance to the partners of the emotional warmth of being able to take shelter with each other and to lie close and snug. Males may enter it primarily to seek a haven, females primarily to seek protection. The male seeks nurture; the female seeks support. In a lonely or confusing world both find gratification in the male-female interaction. Most married couples seek this to some extent, but for couples in the Nestling Marriage the need to be met is intense.

This intense desire for closeness through marriage and family seems especially to be associated with people whose environment has been churning or has become atomized. The social turbulence and uncertainty in life roles for Germans during most of the past half-century may help account for the fact that this type of marriage seems particularly to be sought by many Germans. This was implied in the comments we noted earlier by H. Schelsky, the German sociologist.

U.S. sociologist Lee Rainwater, at Washington University, compared attitudes of German and American husbands.[3] He found that in both the U.S.A. and Germany the "togetherness" aspect of marriage was particularly important to men in the lower-middle class, but he concluded that German men in general were more intensely interested in their families as havens from the outside world. He offered this impression of his findings: "The German men reflect more emotional involvement with their families at all levels . . . They seem to want more intense attachments among family members, and they do not show the same tendency to dampen intense feelings in family relationships, to gloss these over by an emphasis on activities and a kind of bland friendliness that is apparent when American men speak of their wives and children." Rainwater suggested that the German husbands' attachments "are used to ward off a sense of loneliness and deprivation by an uncertain world."

Let us turn now from marriages distinguished by their style to three prevalent types distinguished by the *quality* of the married relationship.

1. *The high-companionship marriage.* Here the central feature is that the man and wife still enjoy very much being together, plan their lives together (whether she is working or not), seek to be together as much as possible, and get considerable gratification from sharing both confidences and physical intimacies. They are best friends and tend to resent any intruding activity that keeps them separated beyond the ordinary demands of their work.

They may quarrel as much as any couple, but a prolonged quarrel would be intolerable. They have so much empathy and concern for their relationship that they would never let a fight spill over into another day.

This idea that a man and woman could be best friends, author Morton M. Hunt points out, would have thoroughly offended St. Paul, bewildered Tristan, and amused Don Juan. Jessie Bernard, however, found in her review of textbooks on marriage that the books were devoting twice as much attention to the companionship aspects of marriage in 1963 as they were in 1934.

Some people who may have identified themselves with one of the three earlier types of marriage mentioned undoubtedly could also identify with the High-Companionship Marriage, but most married people in the United States could not. One study of blue-collar marriages indicated that a third of the husbands and wives studied wouldn't even qualify as "friends," let alone companions or best friends.[4] They showed little evidence of wanting to share one's hurts, worries, or dreams with the other.

The sociological team of John F. Cuber and Peggy B. Harroff, of Ohio State University, studied the marriages of 437 notably successful Americans and concluded that in a majority of marriages examined, the element of companionship was not conspicuous.[5] The husbands and wives were more likely to take casual, cool, detached views of their mates. The relationship was more likely to seem useful than vital. But Cuber and Harroff did come upon some couples who felt intensely bound together in a vital relationship. One such husband explained:

"The things we do together aren't fun intrinsically—the ecstasy comes from being *together in the doing*. Take her out of the picture and I wouldn't give a damn for the boat, the lake, or any of the fun that goes on out there."

2. *The minimal-interaction marriage.* These are the marriages that stay together out of inertia or economic convenience or social necessity, or "for the children," or because that's the way things are.

In these marriages the talk is perfunctory and usually relates to essential family arrangements. For the most part, couples live in parallel grooves and they go their separate ways—as most husbands and wives have since the dawn of history. In Greek villages today, hundreds of men can be seen in the coffee shops, but the women are off in the side streets chatting on their balconies or stoops. In Japanese nightclubs, at least until very recently, there were all-male tables and all-female tables, and the husband who would be with his wife was a rarity.

In the United States the Minimal-Interaction Marriage is especially common among two quite contrasting economic groups: (1) the lower and working-class groups and (2) the ambitious executives of industry and government.

One probable reason why this pattern is so common in the working classes is that they tend to be closer to Old Country traditional patterns. Another reason is that working-class people, especially males, are often not good at communicating across sex lines. If the working-class partners are mobile and find themselves living in a strange community, they may be thrown upon each other as the only alternative to the TV set for companionship. But in more stable working-class neighborhoods, the husbands belong to their all-male cliques, the wives to their all-female cliques.

Sociologist Mirra Komarovsky in describing the sex-segregated social life of many blue-collar marriages said that one cause of the segregation was lack of any mutual interests. The interests and talk of the opposite sex often seem trivial or boring. And the husband who shows signs of domestication may be chided by his male cronies. Other sociologists suggest that at the working-class level an above-average apartness will be found in marriages in most of the world's industrialized societies.

For quite different reason the marriages of business and governmental leaders and hard-driving professional people have an above-average tendency to be nominal. Many business executives of course have intense, happy marital lives; but the obstacles are formidable. The executive is usually a man in motion. He spends a third of his work-month on the road, and if he is in sales it is higher. He is expected to move his household to whatever distant town may be designated by his management. If he is moving upward in the company's ranks, he often will be expected to maintain friendships appropriate to his rank and shed friendships no longer appropriate. Beyond this there are the long hours, the commuting, the expectation to be active in community affairs, and, at all times in public, the expectation that he will present a good image of his company. His wife often feels lonely, unemployed, or oppressed. And since her husband has hundreds of people demonstrating deference and polished efficiency when within his gaze at the office, he may be chagrined to come home and find a lack of deference or order.

On May 10, 1967, *The Wall Street Journal* devoted its lead article to the impact of the executive life on marriage, and it began its report with this paragraph:

"The corporation is taking the place of the 'Other Woman' in the so-called eternal triangle—and the staggering impact on executive marriages suggests that big business is the most demanding mistress of all."

This pattern of Minimal-Interaction frequently appeared in the Cuber-Harroff study of successful Americans of many fields. The most common style of marriage they encountered was one they called "utilitarian." They explain that by "utilitarian" they mean any union that is established or maintained for purposes other than to express an intimate, highly important, *personal* relationship between a man and woman. Such couples spend little time together, share few activities beyond those required by the amenities. Some engage in a good deal of conflict. Others are just passive. The interests of both partners have turned elsewhere. The woman's interests may be in the children or in club activities. But both are likely to report that this is the way they want it. The investigators cited a dedicated doctor who explained, "I don't know why everyone seems to make so much about men and women in marriage. I think marriage is the proper way to live. It is convenient, orderly and solves a lot of problems."

3. *The peripheral-husband marriage.* This type of marriage is different from the Minimal-Interaction Marriage only in that the husband's role in the total picture is more diminished. The marriage that presumably began with devotion has eroded to the point where he is a bystander. He is economically useful but stands outside the basic family unit as perceived by his wife. This basic unit consists of herself, *her* children, and *her* home.

In such a marriage, "Mum's great moment"—to use the English phrase—is seen by the wife, in retrospect, not as the day she married, but rather the day she brought forth her first child.

U.S. husbands can obtain a great deal of food for thought by pondering a survey that was reported in 1965 by Helena Z. Lopata, sociologist at Roosevelt University.[6] In the study, lengthy interviews were conducted with 622 housewives, virtually all mothers, in the Chicago area. About half were suburbanite mothers who had been married about 10 years and were full-time homemakers. The rest were older urban housewives whose children were grown, so many of the wives now had jobs.

All the women in both groups were asked, "What are the most important roles of a woman, in order of importance?"

A third of the women never even mentioned their roles as the wives of their presumably beloved husbands. And only one-third of all the women put the role of "wife" in first place in importance. The role they rated considerably more important than "wife" was "mother." Nearly half of the younger suburban wives put "mother" in first place as their most important role. Three-quarters of all the women interviewed put the role of "mother" in either first or second place.

Interestingly, the older urban wives were more likely to attach high importance to their roles as wives than were the younger suburban wives. An explanation might be that the younger wives were still very much preoccupied with their motherhood service function whereas the older women, with the children out of the house, were now thinking in greater numbers about the importance of having relationships with their husbands.

The wives in general attached as much importance to the role of homemaker as they did to the role of wife. And their discussion of the homemaker role made it clear they were thinking primarily of their activities in supervising the physical arrangements of their homes.

From the male standpoint an even more devastating response came when the women were asked, "What are the roles, in order of their importance, of the man in the family?"

Overwhelmingly the women saw the man's role as being that of "breadwinner." This was mentioned by nearly nine out of ten wives, and two-thirds of all the wives put it in first place. The second most-mentioned role of the man of the house was "father," which again suggested responsibilities rather than any interpersonal relationships with the "mother." In third place in terms of mentions was the man's role as "husband." Altogether, somewhat less than half of all the wives thought to mention the man as a husband at all. And only one in eight thought the man's role as husband deserved to be ranked as first in importance.

The wives, then, saw the husband primarily as a supplier of income for the home—and they attached considerable importance to their own homemaker role of arranging things in the home. Social critic Marya Mannes in commenting on the Lopata findings about wives seeing husbands primarily as breadwinners wondered whether our consumer economy is making the wife a queen of things. She asked, "Does not [this wife's] endless appetite for goods, endlessly fostered, reduce a husband to a cash register?"[7]

It would appear that many if not most of the women in the Lopata study were the kind of women so lovingly described by marketing researchers as "Mrs. Middle Majority." Found primarily in the lower-middle and working classes, Mrs. Middle Majority is absorbed in doing nice things to her home, and the advertisers endlessly cultivate her with selling messages. At least twice a night on most TV stations the Mrs. Middle Majority wives (and all other wives watching) are shown such scenes as a wife kissing and embracing a box of Fab . . . or saying ecstatically that Glad Bag wrappings saved her marriage . . . or anxiously using Lysol spray to kill any germs that might be on the telephone receiver.

Some advertisers apparently are offering the wife something more than cleanliness and nice things for the home. An official of the company producing Ajax White Knight, symbolizing power and strength, was reported in *Advertising Age* as confiding, "Every housewife has been waiting for a white knight since she was a little girl." The official explained what the Ajax White Knight slogan "Stronger than dirt" meant in these memorable words: "Actually we are saying to her 'Stronger than your husband.' "

(It might be added that upper-class wives with more money to spend than Mrs. Middle Majority may plunge into buying antiques, paintings, furs, and houses as a way to satisfy yearnings for recognition and admiration from others outside the home.)

Altogether then, the modern woman entering marriage has many choices in both style and quality of married relationship. She can, for example, work at being the playful mistress, the working partner, the nurturing keeper of the nest. She can, on another dimension, work at being the loving companion, the wife who goes her own way, or the wife who finds fulfillment through her nice home and children—with an amenable man around to keep her in bacon and Ajax White Knight.

CHAPTER 17

Developments Within the Conjugal Bed

"This concept that the act of sex fixes everything is such a cheater. So many married people look for that night in bed to fix up the great lack in their marriage relationship." Mary S. Calderone, Executive Director of the Sex Information and Education Council of the United States.

Tens of thousands of married couples in the U.S.A. have never experienced intercourse. The wives remain virgins. An investigator at the Mental Health Clinic in Bristol on the Virginia-Tennessee border was able to find 100 such wives. Many were examined by a gynecologist for confirmation.

When asked why their marriages had never been consummated by a uniting of the bodies, some mentioned fear; some mentioned a general dislike of the idea; some disliked men in general, but married one for social or economic reasons; some had impotent husbands; some assumed such an action automatically produced pregnancy. But several dozen confessed ignorance about how the coupling was supposed to take place.[1] They were confused about the location of their organ. A few marriage counselors have encountered couples who had led such sheltered lives that they didn't even know that married couples customarily did such things.

Such couples would be surprised to know that the typical wedded husband and wife marrying by the age of 25 experience the act of coitus more than 1600 times in the first two decades of their marriage. That at least is what the Kinsey findings would indicate.[2]

The biological function of frequent intercourse is, of course, to assure perpetuation of the species; but beyond this, in modern marriages, frequent coitus can serve to give the man and woman a sense of emotional warmth, a release from tensions and, at times, a delightful diversion.

But coitus would appear to be somewhat overrated as an aspect of marriage, at least among the more successful citizens. John Cuber and Peggy Harroff in their studies of the sex lives of successful Americans did not contest the Kinsey findings on the quantity of marital intercourse that occurs; but they found that a great many of their couples did not view the sexual aspect of marriage as particularly important. One man referred to it as "a damned nuisance." And a wife referred to the sexual aspect of her marriage as a much overrated activity, not important to either partner. An awkward situation arises if coitus is important to one partner but not to the other. Sociologist Robert Bell found in his study of college-educated wives that, before marriage, more had overestimated than underestimated the importance that physical sex would assume in their marriage.[3] A study of the attitudes of French women indicated that married women were somewhat more likely to agree that physical love should occupy a "small" or "no" place in life than did single women.[4] Many U.S. wives tell marriage counselors that what they miss, after marriage, is the romance and tenderness that was involved in their premarital intimacies with their husbands-to-be. Some complain that the only time their husbands say "I love you" now is when they want sexual intimacy.

At one of the national conferences I attended on marriage and the family, a simulated interview was staged in which two highly experienced experts on marriage played the roles of man and wife while being interviewed by a professional counselor about their alleged marital problems. The improvised exchange went on brilliantly for more than an hour. Here are a few excerpts to indicate the kind of points raised by the middle-aged couple:

Husband: "We don't have intercourse very much."

Wife: "What do you mean 'very much'!"

Husband: "We have intercourse once or twice a week."

Wife: "We have it two or three times a week. I ought to know. I'm there."

When she was invited to comment on her husband's behavior in coital situations she called it "stylized."

Husband: "I don't think she ever comes to climax."

Wife: "That's not true. Sometimes I do and sometimes I don't."

Husband: "Sometimes you just lie there."

Wife: "You mean I am supposed to wiggle and twitch and show I'm having a better time?"

Husband: "Lots of times she doesn't come to bed until one or two o'clock in the morning."

Wife: "Sometimes maybe I am avoiding him, but sometimes I was hoping he would get up and come and get me."

In this century and particularly in the past quarter-century, a considerable change has taken place in the roles played by married males and females during their acts of physical intimacy, however much a particular couple may enjoy it. D. M. Gallant, Tulane University psychiatrist, recently dramatized the change that has come by recounting, in the journal *Medical Aspects of Human Sexuality*, a favorite story of the Victorian era. On the wedding night the groom found his bride stretched out on the bed, unconscious from chloroform. A note to him beside her read: "Momma says you are to do what you like."

Partly the change today is due to the increased element of sexuality in the environment. Possibly the situation has been affected by the fact that modern women compete with, as well as complement, men, and in any case are more equal in marital status and feel more liberated.

Possibly all the advertisements advising women that they too can be sexually devastating have encouraged them to be more uninhibited. There may even be the fact that increased leisure and frequent boredom may give wives the energy to be more demanding. Perhaps equally important has been the open acknowledgement that females, as well as males, have sexual feelings.

Then there have been the synthetic hormones. But perhaps the most important change altering the mood and perhaps the form of marital intimacy has been the dramatic improvement—and increasing unobtrusiveness—of procedures for conception control.

All such factors have produced a surgency in sexualization of many wives that colors their in-bed relationships with their husbands. Sophia J. Kleegman, gynecologist and marriage counselor for 4 decades, finds that in recent decades there seems to have been a very sharp decrease in frigidity reported by wives. Another counselor with long experience, Lester Dearborn of Boston, finds wives today much more likely to explain that they enjoy the intimacy that goes with coitus. And psychoanalyst Rollo May, speaking of male and female patients in general, explains that therapists today rarely have patients exhibiting repression of sex in the old-fashioned sense. He states, "In fact we find just the opposite: a great deal of talk about sex, a great deal of sexual activity. . . . But our patients do complain of lack of feeling and passion; so much sex and so little meaning or even fun in it."

A social worker in New York City, a quarter-century ago, asked one wife if she was familiar with birth-control devices and received an affirmative reply. The woman went into the bedroom and showed her a 2-foot-long stick lying on the floor on her side of the bed. By 1966 more than a fifth of all U.S. wives, both Catholic and non-Catholic, had used birth-control pills.[5]

In addition to the chemical methods of birth control already available, there have been the new intrauterine devices, and the great increase in acceptance of surgical birth control by the husband or wife.

Further, a number of U.S. states are starting to ease the punitive laws on abortion that have been driving more than a million U.S. wives each year into the criminal conspiracy of secretly seeking out an abortionist. These wives have had to pay anywhere from $300 to $1500 for a simple medical procedure requiring a few minutes. The vested interest of some medical men in maintaining the status quo on abortion laws has been noted both in the U.S.A. and abroad. At a population conference in Strasbourg, France, in 1966, it was pointed out that in France, where abortion is illegal, one costs $400, whereas in Czechoslovakia, where legal abortions are readily available, the cost is $200. In the U.S.A., it should be noted in fairness, a number of individual doctors have been in the forefront of the fight to liberalize abortion laws.

In homes where the pills, the intrauterine device, or the diaphragm is used to control conception, the responsibility for control has passed to the wife. Also, it would appear that in a great many homes, initiative for starting intimacies that lead to coitus begins with the wife. There is some evidence that the wife, if she has a job, is more likely to be the one who often takes the initiative. A study of more than 100 husbands in a Western town, at least, indicated this. Those husbands who had working wives indicated a greater willingness to slacken their control of the sexual aspect of marriage and to let mutual inclination determine the time when coitus should occur.

Another new factor that undoubtedly is playing a role in altering the nature of coital encounters of husbands and wives has been the dissemination, in recent decades, of millions of marriage manuals. The book *Ideal Marriage: Its Physiology and Technique* by Theodor H. Van de Velde was in 1965 in its 45th printing. Typically, the manuals prescribe how to squeeze the last bit of erotic feeling out of the sexual encounter, and devote a good deal of the text to techniques and descriptions of anatomical acrobatics. One widely advertised book promised a frank disclosure of 546 aspects of sexual love.

Any value of the information delivered by the authors, usually medical men, quite probably is more than offset by the heightened self-consciousness generated in both partners. As noted earlier, self-consciousness can be particularly disconcerting to the male.

One concept most insistently disseminated by the manuals is that the whole encounter must be rated a fiasco unless the husband, through prowess and iron control, succeeds in effecting an earth-shaking simultaneous orgasm of the partners. Otherwise the wife has been cheated. If a married couple did indeed enjoy an explosive, split-second transport into ecstasy in each of their 1600 encounters or so, over a 20-year period, they might be nervous wrecks by the age of 45. Morton M. Hunt, a student of modern women, comments, "If a woman has been assured that she will, that she ought, and she *must* see colored lights, feel like a breaking wave, or helplessly utter inarticulate cries, she is apt to consider herself or her husband at fault when these promised wonders do not appear."[6]

In speaking of the wife's general need for orgasm during coitus, the Van de Velde manual sternly admonished, "Above all, I wish to impress upon all married men that every erotic stimulation which does not conclude with orgasm for the wife implies that the man inflicts harm." And Maxine Davis in her enormously popular book, *The Sexual Responsibility of Women,* stressed as one responsibility that "The wife must make her husband realize, as he gladly will, how important it is that she be satisfied . . . wholly satisfied." She stressed that the wife must not accept compromise.

Within a century, Paul H. Gebhard, director of the Institute of Sex Research, suggests, the pendulum has swung from under-concern to over-concern with orgasm. He wonders whether it is partly an outgrowth of the modern woman's feeling that orgasm is her due as a symbol of her equal stature. Anything the man can do, she can do as well.

One might wonder whether biology, at least, would support the logic of a male-female parallel in respect to equal need for orgasm. In the sub-human world, orgasm is virtually unknown among females. And unlike the male, there is nothing in the reproductive apparatus of the human female that requires an orgasm.

Young females of the Western world, until very recently, have been trained to control their impulses. Then on their wedding night they are expected to be perfect at the uninhibited, suddenly awakened bodily responses that climax in orgasm. Half of the married women interviewed by the Kinsey group indicated that they did not experience orgasm at any time during their first month of marriage. On the other hand, by the 10th year of marriage, about 3 out of 4 coital experiences reported by the wives interviewed in the Kinsey research resulted in an orgasmic experience for the wife.[7] Some learning evidently had taken place.

Recent experiments indicate that mature women who are already experienced in achieving orgasm can, given proper conditions and stimulation, achieve an orgasmic release at least as rapidly as males. This was one of the more noteworthy findings of the study by William Masters and Virginia Johnson, who spent some years at Washington University photographing several hundred males and females engaged in coitus or self-stimulation. All women who volunteered for their study, it should be noted, were already experienced in orgasm. Masters and Johnson concluded that their particular female subjects tended to respond faster, longer, and often more intensely than did the male subjects who were on camera. Furthermore, the women were more capable of multiple orgasms than the males. Masters and Johnson comment, "The incredible swing from yesterday's Victorian repression to today's orgasmic preoccupation has taken the human female but a few decades."[8]

From the male standpoint, one of the more deflating of all findings of Masters and Johnson was that the intensity of the female orgasm tended to be higher when achieved by self-stimulation than when achieved by intercourse with a male.

Many married women do find that physical intimacies associated with their marriage, especially if frequently climaxed by orgasm, are of enormous importance to their sense of having a good and happy marriage. But many of the happy ones are a little confused as to what constitutes orgasm. Sociologists John Cuber and Peggy Harroff found in interviewing hundreds of wives who were far above average in intelligence that many seemed to confuse a true orgasm with the generalized excitement of aroused passionate feeling. On the other hand, some of the wives who were experiencing true orgasm, they reported, still had an apathetic or negative attitude toward the whole business of sexual intimacy.[9]

And while the husband is busy proving his manliness by striving to bring his wife to orgasmic abandon, she faces the problem of either achieving or simulating that state, or leaving the impression that she is frigid or that he is inadequate. Masters has told males that if their partner has a big smile on her face near the peak of intercourse they may well suspect her report that she experienced a marvelous orgasm. A person, male or female, who is undergoing genuine orgasm is more likely to have a strained, contorted look. (See *Harper's*, May, 1968.)

The result of all the endeavors encouraged by the manuals often leads to a dialogue in the master bedroom along the lines of the fascinating one concocted by psychiatrist Leslie H. Farber. He has been chairman of the Association of Existential Psychology and Psychiatry. In a provocative article entitled "I'm Sorry, Dear" in the November, 1964, *Commentary*, he presented this dialogue (in part) with the man speaking first.

"Did you?"

"Did *you?* You did, didn't you?"

"Yes, I'm afraid I—Oh, I'm sorry! I *am* sorry. I know how it makes you feel."

"Oh, don't worry about it. I'm sure I'll quiet down after a while."

"I'm *so* sorry, dearest. Let me help you."

"I'd rather you didn't. . . . . My tension always wears off eventually. And anyhow—maybe next time it'll be different."

"Oh, it *will*, I *know* it will. Next time I won't be so tired or so eager. . . . But about tonight—I'm sorry, dear."

We were curious to know what assumptions today's college students have been led to believe about all the interest in the simultaneous orgasm. In the College Survey we asked,

Have you gained the impression that a good lovemaking relationship is almost always consummated at the physical level by simultaneous orgasm by the partners? YES ___ NO ___ HADN'T THOUGHT ABOUT IT ___.

More of the U.S. college males than the females had been led to assume that a simultaneous orgasm almost always occurs in a good relationship. About half of the males thought this, but only one-third of the females did. Among the girls who had actually experienced coitus, considerably more responded with an outright "NO" (52 percent) on the question than did the girls who had never experienced coitus. Among both males and females, students in the East were least likely to feel that simultaneous orgasm almost always occurred in a good relationship. In the International Sample problems of definition may have been involved, but the only group responding much differently from the U.S. students was the English group. There both males and females showed a higher assumption that simultaneous orgasm would occur.

A girl at the university in New York City said she had often heard the "almost always" opinion expressed but added, "I disagree emphatically on the basis of my own experience."

A recently married woman living in campus housing at the state university in the Rocky Mountain area offered this opinion based on experience, "Orgasm, simultaneously, is played up to a great extent . . . but I believe it is entirely unnecessary since those who strongly love each other and the other intimacies which they can share should find lovemaking delightful even without it. I do not come to orgasm with my husband, but am perfectly happy when *he* does." (A great many women, of course, experience orgasm in many of their coital encounters but not simultaneously with the partner. They may experience it before or—more likely in single-climax encounters—somewhat after the partner.)

Aside from the matter of orgasm, we know that married women today are more openly taking a more affirmative attitude toward intercourse than was true a few decades ago. There is now a general feeling that intercourse is something they can and should enjoy and something that can contribute to the happiness of their marriage.

The change has been best demonstrated perhaps by sociologist Robert Bell, who compared reports from different generations of wives on whether husbands were too demanding sexually.[10] Back in the 1920s, he points out, an investigator found that two-thirds of the married women reported they desired sexual intimacy *less* frequently than their husbands did. A later study around 1940 found only 1 wife in 6 reporting any feeling she was expected to engage in intercourse too frequently. And in Bell's own study reported in 1964 the proportion of young wives who felt a "too frequent" expectation to engage in coitus had dropped to 1 in 13. On the other hand, 1 in 4 of his young wives felt that their coital experiences were too infrequent!

In the United States our culture has tended to equate sexual intimacy with youthfulness. This is implicit in much that we see in films, in advertising, on TV, and in the newspapers. This has tended to build up a stereotype of the "sexless older years." Sexologist Isadore Rubin, who has studied sex of people in the 50-to-75-year range, suggests that this stereotype tends to act as a "self-fulfilling prophecy" in causing guilt or an unreasonable decline in interest in sex. He contends that a growing body of research makes it clear that there is no automatic cutoff to sexuality at any age and that sex interests, needs, and abilities do indeed continue to play an important role in the later years.

The substantial evidence that wives today have a greatly increased capacity for enjoying their sexuality raises a question as to whether it is producing any alteration in the husband's gratification in intercourse. Some see the husband's sense of sexual adequacy threatened.

A study conducted by two sociologists a decade ago concluded that it was acceptable to the married partners if they had equal sex drives or if the husband had the stronger sex drive.[11] An official of Family Service of Westchester, N.Y., has stated that his organization has been getting an increasing number of women complaining that their husbands are sexually uninterested.

Marriage authority David Mace, who has counseled wives for 3 decades, told me he had witnessed 3 different phases that wives seemed to have experienced over that period in terms of sexual encounters with their husbands:

"In the first phase the wives tended to come to the counselors complaining about their husbands' excessive sexual demands and wanted us to tell their husbands to let them alone. They at times spoke of their husbands as being sexual maniacs.

"In the second phase there was the discovery of the female orgasm pattern and this brought a change overnight. Now it was the husbands who began coming in and complaining that their wives were not responding the way they should and achieving the promised orgasms when they, the husbands, had pushed all the right buttons. Now we are in the third phase—that of the wives complaining that their husbands' performance is so poor that they are unable to achieve the orgasm to which they are entitled."

Perhaps husbands are gradually learning—or soon will learn—to tolerate wives who are more interested in sex than they are themselves.

Robert Bell, however, states, "It is possible that in the near future there will be an increasing number of problems in marriage centering around the lack of sexual satisfaction by the wife. This is an ironic switch from the patriarchal past, but it is not merely an equivalent reversal of the past situation. The basic differences required of the male and the female for sexual intercourse may make the results far more serious for the sexually inadequate or uninterested male than they were for the personally unfulfilled female of the past."[12]

In the meantime, despite all the talk of drives and techniques, what seems to count most in building a good husband-wife relationship in bed is the quality of their day-to-day interpersonal relations. We have heard that the lower classes are most "natural" about making sexual love. And we have heard that business executives are especially picked for the virility they reveal in psychological tests. Yet mates in both categories tend to be notoriously poor lovers and the explanation seems to be, as indicated, that they are prone to have Minimal-Interaction Marriages.

Sociologist Lee Rainwater in his study of lower-class sexual behavior found few couples in this class who had many activities and interests in common. They did vary, however, on whether there was a high degree of separateness in their daily patterns or only a mild separateness. He found that with both husbands and wives—and with both Negroes and whites—enjoyment of sexual intimacy was higher when there was only mild separateness than when there was a high degree of separateness. (Interestingly in both categories a somewhat higher proportion of Negro wives indicated they enjoyed the sexual aspect of their marriage than did the white wives of comparable social class.)

Unless there is the day-to-day warmth and love, sex is a matter of mechanics. There is no evidence that an adequate, tension-releasing relationship in bed will sustain a good marriage; but there is an abundance of evidence that if there is a good personal relationship, the in-bed aspect of marriage will improve with the years.[13]

The well-married couple know that sexual intimacy is a lot more than erotic feeling. It is also, as Mary Calderone points out, warmth and graciousness and humor. Engaging in sexual intimacy is, when you think of it, a pretty preposterous way for rational beings to behave. That, perhaps, is why it can be so much fun.

CHAPTER 18

The More Brittle Bonds of Wedlock

"The clerk of Los Angeles County caused an uproar recently by disclosing that for every five marriage licenses issued he had recorded four divorces or annulments."
Peter Bart, The New York Times, August 7, 1966.

A lovely bride was explaining to a friend at a Philadelphia restaurant recently how she and her new husband had scouted around until they found a minister who would let them amend the usual wedding ceremony. Instead of simply saying "I do," this bride and groom had, without prompting, each addressed a vow of fidelity to the other. And in describing the length of their commitment they had substituted the word "forever" for the more conditional phrase, "Till death do us part." They wanted it on the record that in all eternity they would be joined only to each other.

Their idealism is refreshing. If most young couples tried to modify their wedding vows nowadays, they would undoubtedly insert "if's" and "maybe's" and "as long as we can make a go of it."

A coed at a college in western Kentucky won a scholarship, but in the meantime she had decided to get married. She asked the college authorities whether, if her marriage didn't work out, she could come back to school and still get that scholarship. In England more than 2000 married people were asked whether they had considered the possibility, before marriage, that they could always get a divorce if things didn't work out. For those willing to acknowledge the thought, the people who had married in the late 1950s were more than

255

twice as likely to say they had considered such an eventuality as were those who married in the 1920s.[1]

All through the Western world divorce rates have been rising during most of this century. In the last thousand years there have been few civilized societies that could match the rate of marital dissolution of Americans in the past quarter-century. Roughly 1 out of every 4 marriages in the U.S.A. has been ending in divorce or annulment. Divorce has been disrupting the lives of about 1,300,000 men, women, and children each year.

The U.S. rate reached an all-time peak in 1946 during the untangling of many marriages undertaken during the war. Those inclined to optimism about marriage point out that the U.S. divorce rate is below that peak, though rising again in recent years. This recent level of steadiness is still close to the highest on any civilized country. United Nations figures for countries with available statistics indicate that no Western European country has a divorce rate that even approaches that of the United States. In some primitive societies where marriage is casually undertaken, there are still higher rates; but in general the rate of divorce for Western Europe is about half that of the United States. (On the other hand, in some of these countries the mistress rate undoubtedly is higher.) In early 1968, *Time* reported an upsurge of divorce rates in several Communist-bloc countries of Eastern Europe with rates now close to that of the United States.

Divorce and annulment are only the more visible forms of marital breakdown. Sociologist Harold T. Christensen estimates that for every divorce there is another breakup by desertion or separation. He states, "The United States is experiencing close to one million marital breakups each year— or about half of the number of marriages that are taking place."

In other words, a marriage made in the United States in the late 1960s has about a 50–50 chance of remaining even nominally intact.

Differences in divorce rates as between states are affected of course by the wilderness of state laws, but people in some regions seem clearly more prone to divorce than in others. The U.S. Office of Vital Statistics found that in 1961 the 14 states where divorce occurred most frequently were primarily in the West, with the rest of the 14 all in the South. On the other hand, virtually all with low rates were in the Midwest or the East. Robert D. Grove, chief of the Division of Vital Statistics, pointed out to me that the divorce rate for the West is more than four times as high as the rate for the Northeast. The 9 states with the highest divorce rate in 1961 were, in descending order, Nevada, Alabama, Arizona, Oklahoma, Florida, Idaho, Alaska, Wyoming, and Texas. The 9 states with the lowest rates were New York, New Jersey, North Dakota, Connecticut, Wisconsin, Massachusetts, Minnesota, South Dakota, and Pennsylvania.

Most of the publicity about divorce has involved notables, which has led many to assume that divorce-proneness increases with conventional success in life. People in professions like acting do have high rates of divorce. But in general, the truth is just the opposite. The disruption rate goes down as the educational level of the partners (and the vocational level of the husbands) goes up.[2]

Sociologist Judson T. Landis suggests divorce occurs because some marital ties are more brittle than others. He states, "Some couples experience a series of crises in their marriage and yet they continue married, whereas other marriages are quite brittle in that a much less serious crisis may result in their divorcing."

Quite probably, however, the modern condition has encouraged an overall increase in the brittleness of marriages. It is even possible that a relatively high rate of divorce is an inevitable concomitant of the modern condition in which married Americans find themselves.

When marriages are formed more on the basis of emotional needs and less for economic or other practical considerations, you probably have a greater hazard. With the passing of time, what was gratifying emotionally may become significantly less gratifying, and there may seem less reason to go on. The hazard of the emotion-based marriage is complicated, as sociologist Willard Waller pointed out, by the fact that when romantic attraction starts evaporating and love is not present, the partners may tend to develop overwhelming egos.

A further difficulty of the modern condition is that if the married couple fall into a divisive mood, there may be no one whose good opinion is important to them that gives much of a damn what happens to their marriage. The parents and kinfolk may be 800 miles away. In a city, most of their neighbors probably don't know them. Several of their good friends are already divorced. If they go to church regularly, and they may not, they probably have a minister who has learned to be broadminded about divorce. They may feel that the children are too young to know what is going on. (Actually, scientists are finding that even tiny infants can sense emotional upheaval in a home.)

The situation is different, of course, for couples living in genuine communities. And it should be noted that, for the first time in history, there are now in hundreds of cities and towns professional marriage counselors and family-service agencies that can be of enormous help to troubled individuals or couples that go to them for insights.

Also the situation is different for couples if the husband works for a sizable corporation and aspires to rise in it. At most such institutions the folklore persists that executives should be people whose profiles include stable marriages, and so efforts are made to maintain an image of marital stability.

Here are some further aspects of the modern condition in American life presumably contributing to the spectacularly high rate of marital breakups:

• The increased number of years that a death-do-us-part partnership must survive. When Walter Pitkin wrote his classic book *Life Begins at Forty* some decades ago, he was offering consolation to 40-year-olds who felt over the hill in age. But since 1920, with approximately 2 decades added to life expectancy, married couples have about 20 additional years in which to have a chance to become discontented with each other. Furthermore, for a larger part of their marriage they will be together without the presence of children in the house. A census official has speculated that there may be an increase in divorce of parents when children reach maturity, but any increase is so slight that it is difficult to identify. In general, about 40 percent of all divorces occur in the first 5 years of marriage; and the rate shows a fairly steady decline for each 5-year period thereafter. About 13 percent of all divorces occur with couples who have been married at least 18 years. What is more likely is that the older couples simply separate. Marriage counselor Lester Dearborn of Boston finds that today couples are much more willing to think of separation if the children are grown.

• The chance that a divorced person can remarry has increased in recent decades, and less social stigma is attached to people involved in remarriages. Such remarriage on the average occurs about 2½ years after the person is divorced. About two-thirds of divorced women, and about three-fourths of divorced men, remarry. (And more than a third of those who remarry eventually go through the divorce mill again.) Divorcees also appear to find it relatively simple to find new sexual partners whether or not they remarry immediately. Morton Hunt found, in a study of 169 divorced or separated individuals, that more than 80 percent of them were having intercourse within the first year after divorce.

• The increase in working wives has created more marriages where the wife knows she is not necessarily stuck with a husband she no longer likes simply because of economic necessity. (This fact of greater financial independence of the wife has still not significantly changed the fact that the vast majority of divorced husbands must pay alimony or go to jail. In a great many courts, the size of the award is largely shaped by the success the rival lawyers have in discrediting the spouse of the other's client.)

• In a society where people are told many times a week about the delights of model-changing, it is easier for a person to wonder why his or her attachment to a used spouse should be any more enduring than that to a used station wagon.

• Any society that permits young people to marry impulsively on the spur of the moment while immature must assume a high rate of marriage failure even where there are laws making actual dissolution difficult. Immaturity, of course, is not confined to young people. A large Midwestern family-service agency found in a survey that more than half the couples involved in troubled marriages were arguing about money, yet very few of the couples were in financial difficulty. It noted that in nearly 9 out of 10 cases the man and woman showed considerable emotional immaturity, and concluded, "Sex and money differences become the battlegrounds on which immature personalities strive."

An anachronism of our situation is that while marital breakups are widespread and are usually regarded by counselors as a failure of adhesion, most state laws make divorce an adversary proceeding. One partner must be proven by the other to be guilty of gross, cruel, or otherwise indecent behavior as a person. Unless one agrees to pose as the villain or villainess, evidence of villainy must be marshaled. This demand by society for a villain of course vastly reduces the possibility that the two can part with minimal wounds to themselves or any children involved.

Barring a basic shift in attitudes toward marriage, ever higher levels of divorce seem inevitable, if only because divorce tends to beget divorce. Children of divorcees are nearly twice as likely to undergo divorce themselves, when they marry, as the average U.S. newlywed.

A dread of the pain of a breakup plus a variety of temperamental or practical considerations, however, causes a great many discontented couples to proceed as husband and wife, though the emotional bond is gone. Their fondness and sense of devotion fade. Some search for new lovers in their fantasies, others find a real sexual partner on the side, furtively or openly.

The rarely enforced laws of more than 40 states say such persons are criminals; yet in a great many social circles, a person is now not likely even to be cut socially by acquaintances who know he or she is carrying on an extramarital affair.

Societies down through history have taken a sterner view of extramarital coitus than premarital coitus. Extramarital coitus is a clearer threat to the family and the propagation of blood lines, and also it usually is a violation of a contractual vow.

The Kinsey findings of two decades ago indicated that by the age of 40, about half of all husbands, and about one-fourth of all wives had engaged at least once in extramarital coitus.[3] An analysis of about 1100 married women by the Kinsey group also indicated that about 16 percent of all these women had engaged in extramarital petting but not extramarital coitus.

It should be stressed that of the one-fourth of all wives who had engaged in extramarital coitus by the age of 40, about two-fifths of them had been involved in infidelity during less than a year of their marriage. The Kinsey figures indicated that infidelity by females had been increasing during the 1920–1950 period.

More recently in the mid-1960s, 154 agencies of the Family Service Association of America responded to a questionnaire exploring the present state of infidelity in the United States. They were asked, for example, whether they had witnessed any particular trend in infidelity. Two-thirds of the responding agencies reported that infidelity had become more common during the previous 10 years.[4] Many felt infidelity would become even more prevalent in the years to come.

A wife is most likely to be unfaithful—if she is going to be—during her late thirties, the Kinsey figures indicated. The likelihood of a husband being unfaithful tends on average to decrease from his twenties on. Presumably the difference in patterns might be explained partly by the fact that during the thirties a wife's interest in physical intimacy is rising, while that of the husband is very gradually waning. Also in her late thirties, a wife who has depended upon her looks for ego gratification may seek proof outside the marriage that she is still attractive.

In speculating why infidelity in general seems to be increasing, marriage counselors mention not only the various factors already cited that contribute to divorce, but such additional ones as:

• All the emphasis upon sensual expression in our culture tempts and gives married people implied permission to try out their attractive powers.

• Improved contraceptive techniques may make illicit affairs seem less hazardous.

• There is often a felt need by males to assuage feelings of inadequacy, and a felt need by women to hit back at a mate or to relieve loneliness.

• Some are searching for substitutes because of an ailing marriage.

• The increased loneliness of many unchallenged wives whose husbands are traveling a great deal may make them vivacious, if not flirtatious, with attractive males they encounter.

• There is increased exposure by married couples in our mobile society to new acquaintances (who may seem very attractive), both because more wives are working with male colleagues and because of the greater geographical mobility of couples. And there are more opportunities in cities for an unobserved rendezvous. The French Institute of Public Opinion found from interviewing women in various parts of France that women in urban areas were more likely to believe adultery was common in their area than women from smaller cities and from towns and villages. The Institute stated, "The greater the population of a woman's place of residence, the more likely she is to believe that adultery is common."

• The increase in social drinking by married women. Marriage specialist Evelyn Duvall points out that one's conscience tends to be soluble in alcohol.

Knowledge that a married partner is being unfaithful has different meanings to different people. The impact varies, for example, according to how much importance the husband and wife attach to the emotional ties between them, and according to the extent that extramarital relationships are accepted or winked at in the community or society.

There is some evidence that French women see infidelity on the part of either their husbands or themselves as less of a threat to the marriage than do American women. Regarding unfaithful husbands, for example, they tend to be forgiving if the affair does not appear to be serious.

The French Institute of Public Opinion found that about half of the married women it interviewed thought it was "excusable" for a married man to have "a short, casual affair with another woman."[5] When the women interviewed, both married and unmarried, were asked what a wife should do if she found out a husband was having such a short, casual affair, some of their responses were:

Close her eyes to it	25%
Be diplomatic	20%
Forgive him	17%
Talk it over with him	16%
Deceive him to get even	7%
Leave him	6%

In the United States, men tend to be more stricken by knowledge that a partner is unfaithful than women are. Sociologist Robert Bell states, "Many men feel that adultery on the part of their wife is an irreparable blow to their marriage, but women are often less inclined to see male adultery in the same extreme ways." These are only tendencies. About 40 percent of the unfaithful women in the Kinsey study who believed their husbands knew of or suspected their affairs felt the knowledge had created no difficulty (perhaps because the husbands were carrying on their own affairs). A double standard on infidelity is less recognized today than in earlier decades.

The survey of U.S. agencies of the Family Service Association produced the estimate that in 1 case out of 6 involving infidelity, both the marital partners were being unfaithful. In such situations husbands were far more likely than wives to initiate the infidelity. John Cuber has concluded, after interviewing many successful Americans, that the assumption that adulterous behavior is necessarily furtive does not square with the facts. He found that "A considerable number of spouses have 'leveled' with the mates, who cooperate in maintaining a public pretense of monogamous marriage." In some such cases the couples succeed in maintaining good relations with each other.

One bizarre recent development has been a new openness of mate-swapping in some areas. It is an isolated phenomenon but common enough to be discussed at a seminar on adultery at the national Groves Conference on the Family in 1966. One participant indicated that in some of these cases both the husband and wife, after a swapping, talked about their experiences and compared notes. It has also become common enough to cause a leader of the nudist movement in the United States to protest that mate-swapping was giving nudism a bad name and, where practiced at nudist gatherings, was a clear "betrayal of nudist ethics."

In the past, in both primitive and civilized societies, wife-lending has occasionally been practiced. This usually involved a male whose cooperation the husband needed, or to whom he felt friendly.

Today in the U.S.A. we hear little of males lending out their wives, but more about certain husbands and wives mutually agreeing to exchange partners with another cooperative couple. The male may now feel it is necessary to encourage his wife to participate so that he may in good conscience do so himself. In some countries a game is made of mate-swapping. Two different women in Zurich, Switzerland, told me about "key parties" that had gotten some notoriety among well-to-do couples of that area restlessly searching for new sensations. At these parties, the men throw the keys to their houses or apartments in a pile. Each wife pulls out a key and then goes off with the owner of the key.

In the United States, the couples who have been reported

engaging in mate-swapping seem to come from most of the social classes. Most appear to be involved in a Fun Marriage that has burned out.

Psychologist Albert Ellis, who takes an indulgent view of mate-swapping if the husband and wife are "bright enough" to handle it, reports that in his 20 years of counseling he has heard of many more reports of wife-swapping in the past 5 years than in the preceding 15. Quite a few people, knowing he is sympathetic, have asked him if he happens to know couples in their area who would be interested in a swapping episode. It is his impression that while there is quite a bit of mate swapping occurring in New York City and in the Midwest, the big center of it is on the West Coast.

A reporter for *The San Francisco Chronicle*, Paul Avery, and his wife Emily spent 2 months looking into mate-swapping in California.[6] They reported, "We met and corresponded with more than 100 couples who, unaware that they were talking to representatives of a newspaper, unashamedly admitted to being wife-swappers." Most of these couples, they said, preferred to call themselves "swingers" and boasted of being "broad-minded" or "fond of fun in any form." Typically it was the husband who had introduced the idea as a way of solving problems that had developed within their marriage. The Averys reported that a number of publications had sprung up which carry classified ads placed by people interested in switching. *The Chronicle* inserted the following ad in one of these publications:

> Attractive couple in late 20's, bored with conventional friendships, wishes to meet with couples or singles to exchange unconventional experiences in the unusual/exotic/unique. Both bored.

The Averys reported that this ad produced 300 replies, about 100 from married couples indicating an interest in sexual adventures. While most of the answers came from Californians, there were letters from the East, South, and Midwest.

The serious magazine *Sexology*, edited by professionally trained sexologists, published a letter in 1964 from a male reader who reported that he and his wife had engaged in exchanging mates with other couples "delicately." He added that, as a result, he felt he had come to love his wife more, that both were "happy," and that they both felt no guilt or jealousy. He said he hoped his experience would help others satisfy their desires. His letter was turned over for reply to psychiatrist and marriage-counselor Walter R. Stokes, who is well known for his liberal views about sexual morality. Stokes set aside questions of conventional morality but said he felt impelled to be highly skeptical of the man's report. He felt the letter-writer had made it all sound too simple and pleasant. Stokes stated:

"I have known of several couples who have engaged in this type of behavior by mutual consent and for the same reasons given here. But in each instance, unhappy and tragic complications have ultimately arisen and the marriage has broken up." He suggested that couples who feel a need for such stimulation often seem to represent ungratified childhood sex curiosity or unconscious homosexual urges.

Family specialist Gerhard Neubeck, of the University of Minnesota, after comparing notes with other investigators on incidents of mate-swapping, concluded that such couples are usually the bohemian type and are searching for variety. Often the couples come into a room and pair off in a calm manner. It is all very antiseptic. These people, he said, are not necessarily sick people, but often are in therapy.

Neubeck has, in his studies of infidelity in general, been impressed by the fact that some playfully inclined persons cannot find enough opportunities to play within their marriage. One common direction playfulness takes is flirtation, which means "making love without meaning it." Neubeck explains:

"It is obviously not possible to flirt with a spouse, a spouse is not a candidate for consummation; spouses have already consummated. Reintroducing elements of courtship into one's life can only be accomplished by the courting of someone new." (In early 1968 Neubeck was finishing work on the first serious, scholarly study of extramarital intimacy in recent decades.)

It is noteworthy that the Kinsey investigators found that males who were involved in extramarital relationships tended to engage in more extended courting, and more extended sex play, when involved in extramarital affairs than they did when engaging in coitus with their own spouses.

But novelty, too, can wear off. John Cuber reported, at the

1966 Groves Conference, that he was surprised to find how many of his successful Americans were carrying on extra-marital affairs that had become boring. He said that some of the males had settled into an apathy that made one wonder why the affair went on, since no institutional obligations were involved. Cuber said of individuals he interviewed who were involved in extramarital affairs, "Overwhelmingly these people expressed no guilt with respect to what they were doing, although sometimes some regret over practical consequences was acknowledged. The 'offended' spouses are often not offended at all, sometimes were even relieved to be 'out from under' a relationship which was personally frustrating, and they were able, because of the adultery, to maintain the marriage for other reasons."

Neubeck and an associate, as part of a larger study, analyzed the personality patterns and needs of 9 young married people who acknowledged they had already become sexually involved outside of marriage. The thing that stood out was not dissatisfaction with their marriages, but rather that most of them scored low on strength of conscience.[7]

He has concluded, "Persons must either experience relatively little guilt or a high degree of guilt tolerance to participate in extramarital sexual affairs."

Given the modern wilderness in which male-female relationships must function, we probably should be surprised that there is not more infidelity than there evidently is, in the United States. Social observer Morton Hunt offers two interesting reasons why infidelity is not more widespread. First, American women in general are not really good at conducting affairs. He explains that the adultress in America tends to make a rather poor mistress, even when she is responsive and flattering, because she wants too much of her lover. Hunt explained, "She wants him to be her mainstay in life, her be-all and end-all, and, inevitably, her legal mate. It is enough to frighten any sensible philanderer away."[8] His second reason is more basic. He suggests that the whole character of modern marriage—its importance to the participants, its legal fragility—tends to impel most married men and women to brush aside temptations.

If, however, we combine all the evidence of infidelity and faltering marriages with the evidence that nearly half of all U.S. marriages ultimately become clearly disrupted, we see an institution that appears more brittle than sponge-like. We must wonder whether the mechanism for bringing males and females together into permanent, family-building unions has become seriously defective. Or is this just the way it is going to be from here on out?

Part II

ASSESSMENTS AND
POSSIBLE DIRECTIONS

I. How the Future Might Look

CHAPTER 19

Some Forecasts, Prospects, Experiments

"The scope for social modification of the relations of men and women is very large." John MacMurray, British philosopher.

Thus far in our exploration of what has been happening to male-female relationships, we have turned up as many questions as answers. We have seen evidence, if it was needed, that all change is not necessarily progress. And we have seen reason to inspect warily pronouncements put forward as flat Truths. But let's move on and see what reasonably solid opinions can be reached about the trends we have been examining. In this speculation and assessment we must allow, of course, for the fact that personal values may at times color opinions, including those of your guide.

Where are the changes we have been examining, then, leading us? What goals in male-female relationships should we strive toward? Are there possible norms and social mechanics, possible patterns in sex behavior and roles, in courtship and marriage, that promise a better fit of the needs of the decade ahead than we have been seeing?

Some of the changes are so profound that at this point we can only guess at their implications. William Genné, family specialist at The National Council of Churches of Christ in the U.S.A., suggests that it may take 50 to 75 years to assess the impact of our new scientific knowledge on our moral responsibilities in the realm of sex, marriage, and family life.

There are obvious hazards in trying to predict the future on the basis of a straight-line extrapolation of trends of the recent decades. It may be that recent trends toward sex freedom and uninhibited behavior will shift to a more restrained mood. In the past we've seen periods of permissiveness and laxness replaced by periods of strictness and emphasis upon ideals. There is so much sensual stimulation being thrown at the young that they may become jaded, and then reticence— and even an idealizing of females—may become attractive to them.

It is possible that the increase of working women may be slowed or reversed in a peacetime economy where automation could bring a sharp increase in the unemployed. In the past, at least, when unemployment pressures have developed, public opinion has supported the idea that male breadwinners should have first chance at available jobs.

A Swedish sociologist, Joachim Israel, has predicted that the family may disappear in 200 years. Back in the 1930s and 1940s two of America's most distinguished sociologists, Pitirim Sorokin and Carle Zimmerman, of Harvard, were taking an exceedingly gloomy view about the possible survival of the family as a viable institution. Yet we have seen that though the family is being dramatically modified in its functions, males and females are joining together in marriage at an unprecedented rate.

Recently a Harvard professor of population studies has suggested that in future decades, as population pressures mount, we will be impelled to reduce the eroticism in fashion, theater and mass media as a way of reducing the birth rate. It is dubious, however, that there is any correlation between the amount of sensual stimuli and family size. A century ago when Victorian prudery was in force, families with 7 to 9 children were very common; and today with sexual stimuli rampant, the birth rate in the United States has being easing downward.

Still we are being pushed into a historically unprecedented situation under the impact of technological, scientific, and economic changes. There are indeed a number of forces of change persistent enough to permit us to conclude that in the decade between now and 1978, they will continue to alter the way that males and females meet, court, work, and live together. Let us start with the force with the most momentous potential.

By 1978 there will be far more simple and certain methods to control conception, methods that can be applied either before or after coitus by married or unmarried couples.

Historians are likely to agree that one of the two or three

most important developments of the 20th century in terms of mankind's evolution is the spectacular success that is starting to be achieved in ushering in the Wanted Child.

The present pill, marvelous as it is, still is a primitive, worrisome thing to use, since women must keep track of the days, by taking the first pill on the 5th day after the onset of menstruation and continuing daily for 20 days. Several drug companies are finding, experimentally, that it is feasible to prepare an injection which will prevent ovulation for a month or even several months. Experimentation at a less advanced stage is also proceeding with long-acting compounds that can be taken in pill form. Another long-lasting contraception under development is a time capsule which, when implanted under the skin, could steadily diffuse a hormone creating contraception for months or years until the woman chose to have the capsule removed. Still another good possibility is that within a few years there may well be a vaccine for husbands that will suppress sperm production.

Perhaps the most watched race among researchers is that to develop the so-called "morning-after" pill. John McLean Morris, one of the two Yale doctors who have been researching the development of a morning-after pill, suggests that eventually it could be taken monthly at a time that would cover any intercourse that may have occurred during a woman's few fertile days that month. Speaking of this pill's potentialities, Dr. Morris said that, if a girl is caught off guard, "she can wake up in the morning and know that there is available a retroactive contraceptive."[1]

Most of the current pills act to prevent the female egg from being released on schedule into the Fallopian tube and this prevents a conception-producing encounter with the male sperm. The morning-after pill, in contrast, would prevent an egg that has already been successfully fertilized from planting itself, as it normally would, within the lining of the uterus. This nesting normally occurs during the week after intercourse. The fertilized egg instead would be washed out of the body.

In addition to moral implications of the morning-after pill in reducing the hazards of careless premarital coitus, there is a theological definition which may make such a pill less acceptable to followers of Catholic doctrine. Catholic theologists have contended that life begins at the moment of fertilization and anything done thereafter as a birth-control measure is abortion. On the other hand, the American College of Gynecology and Obstetrics holds the view that life begins when the fertilized egg is finally implanted firmly in the uterus.

A good deal of research is directed to finding a way to control conception that might more clearly be acceptable to Catholic theologians (while the theologians themselves have been pondering the various pills). The American Electronics Laboratories, Inc., has developed a transmitter weighing a third of an ounce. If placed in the vagina while the woman is asleep, it transmits temperatures to a stylus outside the body marking on a time-calibrated roll. This can identify quite precisely the time when the "thermal shift" occurs that precedes and accompanies ovulation. A mouth thermometer, as many have sadly learned, has low reliability in pinpointing this thermal shift. A family specialist at Ohio University advised me that some medical research has been going into trying to activate our olfactory senses, which are strong in animals but relatively very weak in humans. This could provide warning. In women, at least, research reports have indicated that sense of smell is related to the sexual cycle and is highest when estrogen levels are highest.

Interesting progress also is being made to increase the safety of women using intrauterine devices such as loops and coils. A hazard has been that a small percentage of women expel the device without knowing it. Danish scientists have developed an intrauterine device with a tiny magnet attached. A woman can, at any time, assure herself her device is still in place by holding a compass over her lower abdomen and noting that the needle points north.

The use of pills by women is starting to raise psychological questions. There is a long-acting pill now feasible, for example, that would suppress menstruation. Women for ages have spoken of their period of menstruation as a curse; yet, when it comes to the possibility of eliminating this curse, a great number of women are reported to be unhappy about the prospect. They feel a strong emotional need for the monthly purging. A woman's body each month prepares itself for the possibility of conception by building up a blood-enriched lining of the uterus where the fertilized egg would nest. When the nesting does not occur, the lining is sloughed off in preparation for the next monthly cycle. Thus menstruation is associated with women's capacity for conception, and for many women it seems important to their sense of well-being.

Investigators find some women even unhappy about taking the currently available pills, which assure them they will not conceive. Thorsten Sjövall, of Sweden's National Association for Sex Education, commented to me, "This whole business of contraception is hard on women. It is easy to tell them to use contraceptives, but the problem is that with the biological urge to create, the urge is not easy to stop. What happens psychologically to the woman taking pills who is not married? I think a lot." Also possibly a lot happens to the married woman. Sjövall speculated that the ideal pill, psychologically, is the morning-after pill that can be taken on the responsibility of the wife herself *after* intercourse. This would leave open the possibility of conceiving. The woman would have the option of ending it. (But this might increase the uneasiness of the males. Will she or won't she?)

Contraceptive pills seem certain to alter relations between unmarried males and females and perhaps the age of marriage. Pills may produce a postponement in age of marriage by taking pressure off the couple engaging in premarital coitus. The girl will not start pressing for marriage simply because of pregnancy or fear of pregnancy. There is the possibility too, as noted, that pills if taken widely by unmarried girls may increase their self-assurance. As for the morning-after pill, one's first inclination is to assume that it will greatly encourage premarital coitus by providing safety even for the careless. But another possibility is that, with such a pill, the act of premarital coitus may lose so much of its daring, illicit character that those motivated by quest for adventure may be less interested in the experience. Coitus would be meaningful only for those seeking sensual stimulation, tension reduction, or an opportunity to convey affectional feelings.

It is much too early to say what the long-term effect of the widespread use of the contraceptive pill will have upon male-female intimacies in marriage. One obvious change is that it has deprived the wife of her major excuse for saying "no." She can not plausibly cite the fear of unwanted pregnancy if she is a pill-user. The evidence strongly suggests that the pill has a liberating effect upon the wife sexually, makes her more interested in, and responsive during, intercourse. Whether this should be credited to greater peace of mind or an actual stimulating effect of the chemicals in the pills is still being tested. (As of 1968, some of the pills still in use seemed to increase slightly a user's chance of suffering certain ill side effects.)

How is the husband reacting to this greater display of sexuality in the partner since the pill? A number of psychiatrists have been reporting, in journals such as *Psychosomatics,* cases where the interest of the husband in the sexual relationship with his wife diminished after she had been on a regime of pill-taking. In a number of the instances, the doctors were undoubtedly dealing with male patients who were emotionally insecure to start with.

Mary S. Calderone, while medical director of the Planned Parenthood Federation of America, took a different view. She stated, "Our present day contraception with its far less sexually obtrusive methods may sometimes serve to bring the patient face-to-face with her own sexuality or that of her husband—a confrontation that often results in anxiety or panic on the part of husband or wife." The more traditional forms of contraception were so much a part of the preparation or experience of coitus, she points out, that they could be blamed if the encounter was not a delightful one. The pill is so unobtrusive that it can't be blamed in the same way.

Some investigators have reported finding that the wife's use of contraceptive pills has had a positive effect upon both the husband and the wife. There are also some cases reported where the woman's sexual responsiveness, for whatever reason, has declined after she has taken pills over a long period. Most of the reports and studies still must be viewed as fragmentary.

One of the more impressive studies, though small, was reported at the 1967 annual convention of the American Medical Association. A Cleveland psychiatrist, Frederick J. Ziegler, reported on a study of two dozen married couples in San Diego who were described as typical middle and upper middle class husbands and wives. They were not psychiatric patients, but simply people who had asked their physicians about contraceptive methods. They were given a series of psychological tests over a period of 4 years while the wife was on pills. They were compared with other couples where the wife, for one reason or another, had not recently taken pills. Ziegler concluded that those women who continued taking the pills over the whole period were more sexually responsive than the wives who were not taking them. But more significantly, he found that the husbands of those wives who stayed regularly on the pill showed up on the tests as having an enhanced sense of well-being and improved psychological functioning. He did note that notwithstanding this enhanced sense of well-being, the husbands of pill-taking wives estimated that on average "their wives desired more frequent sexual relations than they did themselves."[2]

So much for the implications of advances in birth control techniques. Let us now look briefly at 9 other persistent forces that surely will be at work in altering male-female relations by the year 1978, assuming there has been no nuclear holocaust.

• In a decade ahead, life expectancy for females will be approaching 80 years and for males 75 years. And there will be a very great increase in recently married women in their twenties who will be in their primary childbearing phase.

• Young men and women will be having increasing difficulty planning ahead in terms of careers because of the rapid obsolescence of job skills. Those working will be much more likely than today to be working for great bureaucratic organizations, private or public, which will demand highly mobile families.

• There will be many more millions of young people remaining in classrooms until they are in their twenties. Women, increasingly, will be dominating the liberal arts departments devoted to the social sciences and humanities. It is therefore possible that by 1978 we will be seeing the beginning of an era when women will be providing most of our philosophers and social thinkers. In this connection, California psychologist Richard E. Farson has commented, "I believe women are better suited for the world of 1980 and beyond. It is traditional and natural for women to enjoy beauty, culture, leisure—to be interested in human feelings and human relations—in people, not things. This will be important in the future more than ever."

• The material abundance available to the typical family will be at least 30 percent greater in 1978 than today. One socially disturbing related factor is that there will be a more-than-comparable increase in the already immense pressures upon males and females to be self-indulgent and impulsive in order to move all the goods that exploding technology can make available.

• Automation will be bearing down particularly upon people in clerical and lower management jobs. At the same time, there will be an explosion of jobs in service areas such as teaching, government work, therapy, catering, real estate, and other people-dealing jobs, where women will be in considerable demand, barring a depression. Some are suggesting, too, that rapid advance in automation may tend to push most of the U.S. populace away from being achievement-oriented to being enjoyment-oriented.

The United States, with about 40 million more people added to the population by 1978—and most of them congregating in urban areas—will be dominated by vast megalopolized areas, clusters with far more high-rise apartments, and less cubic feet of living space available per household.

• Husbands and wives who work will have about 300 more hours of free time a year in 1978 than today, and they will be thrown even more upon each other for companionship.

Given such persistent pressures as these for modifying the environment in which males and females will be relating to each other, what kind of family units can we expect in the future? While the family will continue to be popular, it will decline in prestige and importance. With conception control, the need that most humans have for new experiences most probably will substantially reduce the fidelity of married partners. Most families in the Western world have been based on such fidelity. And if women continue to gain in their emancipation and sexualization, it is still possible that fewer males in the future will feel comfortable in taking them on as lifetime partners, or, more importantly, feel obliged to do so. Sexual relations between youngsters may be more casually undertaken. Mary Calderone of SIECUS suggests, "It may well be in ten years that girls will be more genitally-centered too [as boys have long been] and be able to respond as quickly and easily as boys."

Speaking specifically of the family's child-rearing function, biologist Robert S. Morison, of Cornell University, foresees a decline in the importance of families in future decades. He points out that with the increased knowledge of the plasticity of the human nervous system in early life, social planners of the future will be increasingly tempted to take over functions of the home—especially where parents are conspicuously doing a poor job, in their view. This will be done in the name of insuring "equality of opportunity." Morison reasons that it is idle to talk of a society of equal opportunity when that society abandons its newcomers solely to their families for their most impressionable years, since families are not equal in their ability to train children for the opportunities of life. (The federal program Operation Head Start might be viewed as a commendable beginning of such federal efforts to implement equal opportunity.)

Some are suggesting that since many of our social ailments are traceable to home training, full-scale national programs should be developed to upgrade the quality of family life in the national interest.

In Great Britain, philosopher John MacMurray has speculated that the family has become too small a unit for the burdens it is expected to carry. He predicted, "I should expect to see a growth of experiments in the enlargement of the family by artificial means; by combination of families, for example, in a single house; or by adoption not of children but of adults into the family group" (so that there would be extended families living together that would not be based entirely upon ties of blood). He adds, "After all, the traditional family life is disappearing fast, and the family itself is nearing collapse under the strain. Yet without a vigorous and satisfactory family life, no civilized society can long persist."

However, we should not underrate the appeal of family life or overrate the appeal of promiscuity on the basis of our current confused state of affairs.

Sociologist Harold T. Christensen, of Purdue, who has been studying the family for several decades, is confident that the family, however it evolves, will remain the primary group within society and not be replaced by any Brave New World type of system of state control for reproduction and child-rearing. He feels the family will persist because "it is needed for both personal contentment and social stability."

The ways in which males and females will group together in the future to form families—and handle intimacies before marriage—offer opportunities, however, for tantalizing speculation.

It is doubtful that in the foreseeable decades there will be a drastic change in the structure of the nuclear family (wife, husband, and any children), though wedlock may well become increasingly tentative. We have seen in the past half-century several notable experiments to modify drastically the male-female relationship, inside marriage and out. The Soviet Union, Israel, and Sweden have made such experiments. In the first two countries there have been systematic, large-scale efforts to overhaul the family, to free males and females from conventional marriage roles, and to introduce sex equality. The results have been interesting.

The Soviet Union

In the whirlwind of the Russian revolution of 1917, monogamy and the bourgeois family were all but swept away, and male-female relationships in or out of marriage became socially unsupervised. Some leading Russians of that day argued that the need for sexual gratification should be treated as casually as the need for a glass of water. Divorce then could be gotten simply by dropping a postcard to the partner to notify her or him the relationship was terminated.

A particularly vivid example of the new sexual liberation was contained in a decree for the nationalization of women passed by the City Soviet of Vladimir in 1918. It called for all unmarried girls over 18 to register at the Free Love office. Those registering would have a choice of males; and the men in the community, in turn, were granted the right to choose among the girls. The selection of husbands and wives was to take place once a month. Males apparently were given some advantage in the decree, because it was stated that they could, in the government interest, choose their partner "regardless of the latter's consent." The decree added that any children born of such unions would become the property of the Republic.[3]

The mood of license was so rampant that Lenin warned against promoting sexual anarchy under the name of Marxism. Starting in 1926, civil registration of marriages was restored. Soviet policy toward sexual intimacy and toward marriage and the family started becoming increasingly conventional, puritanical, and even prudish. That trend has continued almost to the present day. By 1936 the family was proclaimed to be the social unit whose permanence and well-being was crucial to the survival of the country. In 1939, an official Soviet journal contended that sound moral ideas must be inculcated into the minds of young persons. Marriage became idealized, abortion illegal. The divorce laws were tightened and retightened until by 1944 obtaining a divorce became an extremely complicated and costly procedure requiring hearings in two courts, a posting of notices, and a payment of stiff fees.

Leading U.S. sociologists such as David Mace and Pitirim Sorokin have reported that since 1950 Soviet Russia has had a more monogamous, stable, and Victorian family and marriage pattern than most Western countries.[4] Mace has commented, "Throughout extensive travels in the Soviet Union, I found a complete absence of sexually stimulating materials in newspapers, magazines, and books; on stage and screen; on radio and on television."

One can speculate what caused such a complete turn-around in the Revolutionists' policy. At first perhaps a change from sex freedom was inspired by the simple need to bring order out of the chaos of trying to keep track of people. It is known, too, that within a decade juvenile delinquency had become an acute national problem. And during the crisis of World War II, there was certainly great concern about replenishing the great population losses of the war. But overriding all, undoubtedly, was concern about the need of the regime for order and control. When the anti-sexual revolution was in its fourth decade in Russia, critic Ernst Pawel stated, "The Soviet government still regards sex as a capricious, explosive, intractable element in the social fabric, one singularly resistant to centralized planning, and therefore to be controlled as far as possible by other means."[5]

We might also surmise that a society embarking on the vast industrialization of a still quite primitive country could not afford to permit a hedonistic mood among the people to continue. Sociologist Jessie Bernard commented, in this connection, "All the disciplines which at close range look as though they were designed only to frustrate and deprive, at longer range look indispensable for shaping the kind of clock-regulated, gratification-delaying, sober, responsible people that an industrialized society depends on." She suggested the about-face of the USSR with respect to the family was a classic example of a functional relationship between industrialization and the so-called Protestant Ethic of self-discipline and hard work.

Today the planners of the Soviet Union are starting to move very cautiously to introduce sex education and have somewhat eased the obstacles to divorce. But marriage and the family are still idealized. A vast amount of state money has recently been spent to build "marriage palaces" around the country that have chandeliers, rugs, stained glass windows, fountains, and banquet balls to add splendor and the old solemnity of the largely displaced church to the launching of marriages. Soviet sociologist A. G. Kharchev found in interviewing 500 young couples who were marrying at the Leningrad Wedding Palace that 80 percent of the couples had asked parental consent to marry even though it was not required.[6] The rate of divorce in the Soviet Union, at least until very recently, has been running at less than one-half the U.S. rate.

A second goal of the Russian revolutionists in 1917 that merits our inspection was to wipe out all legislative traces of sexual inequality. They decreed equal work opportunities for women. Lenin said that woman must be delivered from "the necessity of spending three-quarters of her life in a stinking kitchen."

This emphasis upon sex equality, unlike that of the early emphasis upon sex freedom, has persisted throughout the entire half-century that the Soviet Union has been in existence. One might surmise that, in addition to ideology, one reason for this continued support has been the urgent need of the regime for every able-bodied human it could get to help meet the challenge of quickly industrializing a vast, backward country. The married woman in Russia is not required to work outside the home, and many don't, but at least until very recently there has been some stigma of dependency attached to those who do not. And there are nearly as many women as men in the Soviet work force.

The Soviet Union has gone further than virtually any nation in the modern world to help mothers work without feeling guilt that they are neglecting their children. Considerable expenditure has gone into nurseries and kindergartens for the children of working mothers. Such a mother is awarded four months' paid vacation at the time of the birth of a child. For older children, the schools arrange classes, study periods, and school activities into late afternoon so that the children can remain at school instead of being loose on the streets while their mothers are working.

After breakfast in a typical Soviet household, David Mace found, the mother takes her baby or toddler with her and delivers the child to a nursery attached to her place of employment. Here the child is carefully cared for, Mace found, by well-trained doctors, nurses, and other attendants. The mother knows that she is within call. While nursing the child, she can take a half-hour off from work every 3 or 4 hours, at full pay.

Despite assumptions by many people in the West that all this working by mothers must be producing emotionally disturbed children, this does not seem to be the case. Mace concluded that Soviet children as a whole were given a high degree of emotional security. And Bruno Bettelheim, professor of psychiatry at the University of Chicago, comments, "Many visitors to Russia . . . have been struck by how well-behaved Russian children are to their parents, and their parents are to them."

The sex equality does not seem to extend fully into the homes of Russia. Mace gained the impression that there was still a fairly rigid differentiation of masculine and feminine roles in the home, with marketing, cooking, and tidying up nearly always handled by the wives. He found this arrangement tacitly accepted.[7] Other evidence indicates that the Russian wives, or many of them, feel this is the way it should be.

A recent development, which still has to be evaluated, is a considerable interest of Soviet girls and women, in the late 1960s, in developing slim figures and feminine graces. The scorn for concern about appearance is past. A Russian poet has made a plea that the women be placed on a pedestal and that males recapture a sense of chivalry. Reporter Charlotte Curtis, of *The New York Times,* reported in the month of the 50th anniversary of Soviet rule that the Soviet woman "no longer finds it either noble or exhilarating to work side by side with men in heavy industry, construction, mining, and shipping. She is increasingly distracted by food, family, furnishings, and fashions. . . . And there are even times when she is downright frivolous." Perhaps the Soviet people are simply developing enough individual prosperity and getting far enough away from the original revolutionary fervor to be interested in a more elaborate style of life.

The kibbutzim in Israel

Most utopians in drafting plans for model societies propose first of all that children be raised institutionally. They also usually propose to institutionalize food-serving. These ideas not only seem efficient, but have a certain appeal to parents harassed with diapers and dishes. In modern times, the boldest experiment in liberating married males and females from their usual homemaking and child-care tasks has been in the kibbutzim, collective settlements, of Israel.

In a kibbutz, marriage between the adult male and female is relatively informal. They ask for a doubling of living quarters and keep their original names. Housework is nominal, since they dine in communal dining halls. Child-rearing tasks are relatively nominal since, from infancy, the children are reared in special houses: infant houses, toddler houses, etc. Each age-group of children leads its own life, under the guidance of a teacher, or a nurse who is usually responsible for just 6 or 7 infants.

During the first year, a child will see a good deal of its mother and probably will be breast-fed by the mother. At some settlements, the nurse will raise a flag over the nursery when a baby seems to want to be fed and this is a signal to its mother, who is perhaps working in the fields, to come and feed the baby. But after the first year, the parents see their children usually only during the early evening hours and on holidays.

As the youngsters mature, they are given a room of their own in which to live. When they are awarded their own room as a mark of maturity, sex relations are considered permissible for the young people. If a young man and girl fall in love and wish to become a couple, the community usually approves their uniting and grants them a double room. Later, if a child is about to be born, they are officially declared to be married.

Swedish sociologist Gunnar Boalt wondered why the young male and female bother to move in together since their sexual needs can be met anyway. He concluded, "It seems as if both of them are tired of casual relationships and want to have a relatively permanent union, with comradeship, affection, and so forth. It is this psychological closeness that distinguished the permanent couple from those more temporarily associated."[8] It would appear, if he is correct, that there is a drive toward union of males and females even where there is little functional need for it, as we surmised earlier.

One thing that has interested investigators has been the effect of such a child-rearing environment upon the children. A number of investigations have been made. The children themselves seem to come out extraordinarily well in the kibbutzim system. Bruno Bettelheim, after completing a study of the whole body of evidence, suggests that perhaps communal rearing of children has gotten a bad name because so often it has been done carelessly with large numbers of children institutionally bunched together and left under the care of untrained, indifferent adults. In the typical kibbutz, he concluded, the children are reared in small groups and cared for by a skilled and devoted staff.[9]

Bettelheim concluded, "The children turn into exceptionally courageous, self-reliant, secure, un-neurotic and deeply-committed adults who find their self-realization in work and in marriage. Though most have some previous sexual experience, they marry in their early twenties and soon have children who in turn are brought up in the communal nursery schools. There are almost no divorces . . . and adultery is rare and severely censured."

There have been reports of high rates of bedwetting and nightmares among some kibbutzim children, but it has been suggested that this has been due to faulty arrangements at individual collectives. In one study, made by an investigator from Michigan State University, in which kibbutz children were compared with same-age children not reared in a kibbutz, the kibbutz children were unusually friendly, frank, generous, and sharing. They were likely to be more trusting than non-kibbutz children, less reserved, and to have a higher level of intellectual development and emotional maturity. And by the adolescent level, the kibbutz children seemed to have a stricter code in regard to sexuality than did the control group.[10]

What has been more difficult to ascertain has been the impact upon the fathers and mothers of being largely relieved of child care. This will apparently require observations over a longer period than has been available. Bettelheim noted that relations between parents and children were comparatively lacking in intensity and added, "Blood simply is not thicker than shared emotional experiences; it is the latter that ties people together." He noted that the "kibbutz children were not beset by parents' typical anxieties—the hopes and fears we harbor about children who are ours."

There apparently is a good deal of affection between parents and children at the collectives. They have fun together in recreational hours, and the parents lavish attention on their children. The question, however, is whether the parents themselves are progressing in their growth as adults without the fighting, disciplining, aching, worrying, and loving that attends normal child-rearing.

New York psychologist Howard Halpern from his study has suggested that in the kibbutz, parent-child relationships are much like grandparent-child relationships in American society—with all the fun and none of the anguish. He wonders whether for the parents the kibbutz arrangement could really satisfy their desire to create, to guide, and to shape a new individual. He contends that in the process of parenthood, individuals develop an expanded capacity for giving, sacrificing, protecting, and loving. In short, he suggested that, at its best, full parenthood is a powerful influence in causing people to shed tendencies toward immaturity, self-involvement, and narcissism.[11]

But it may not be possible in future decades to analyze this impact of the experiment upon parents themselves, so that we may be left to surmise. Americans who have recently spent time at settlements of the kibbutzim advise me that the settlements as traditionally organized are starting to decline, apparently for reasons that have little to do with their unique arrangements for marriage and child-rearing. With prosperity, the young are going off to college and often don't want to come back to the kibbutz. While in the early days, half of the youngsters reared in a kibbutz would return, now less than 10 percent do.

Another factor that has to be taken into consideration in assessing the unique arrangements for marriage and child-rearing that have emerged in both Israel and Russia is that they evolved in societies that were intensely involved in a struggle to achieve social ideals. Both the Israelis and the Russians were trying to give birth to a new kind of society. In such a struggle normal aspirations of marrying and rearing children were perhaps less compelling.

Sociologist William Goode, in studying family patterns around the world, comments, "No communal family pattern in the modern world has ever evolved naturally, without political force and revolutionary fervor, and both Russia and Israel have already retreated toward the conjugal family after considerable communal experience."[12]

A quite different kind of pioneering in male-female relationships, however, has been taking place in one of the most stable, secure, and prosperous of all regions: Scandinavia, and particularly Sweden. In Sweden the population has moved a considerable way toward both sex freedom and sex equality, with strong support from new kinds of social arrangements that seem designed to encourage their development. We will look at the Swedish experiment in the next chapter.

CHAPTER 20

The Swedish Approach to Sex Freedom and Equality

"We are on our way toward a society which we have never experienced before." Lars Gustafsson, Swedish editor and novelist.[1]

A number of U.S. authorities on trends in sex behavior—including sociologists Ira L. Reiss and Harold T. Christensen—have concluded that Americans are moving toward the Scandinavian model in their sexual mores.

There are some variations in the sexual mores of the various Scandinavian countries. The Norwegians, for example, seem to become more conservative the farther they are from the Swedish border or the farther they are up in the mountains. The church influence, too, is somewhat stronger in Norway. Also the Norwegians, while quite liberal sexually, tend to take their pattern of sexual behavior for granted. Until recently, at least, Danes were probably the most permissive of all the Scandinavian groups.[2]

It seems fair to state, however, that the sexual mores today of the three countries at the heart of Scandinavia—Denmark, Norway, and Sweden—are quite similar in their high degree of permissiveness. This is the view of Norwegian social scientist Harriet Holter.[3] My own talks with Swedes, Norwegians, and Danes left me no basis to quarrel with that assessment.

The outside world has heard primarily about the Swedes, who traditionally have been more reticent and formal in their general behavior than the Danes or Norwegians. Matters of sex are now very much debated on the airways and in the press in Sweden. What is less known, perhaps, is that the

Swedes link sex freedom with sex equality in their debating. And they are more resolutely pursing true sex equality and trying to put it into practice than any other society in the world. They are seeking equality not only on the job, as in Russia, but also in the home, in the school, and in all interpersonal relations between the sexes, intimate or otherwise.

In 1965, for example, young Swedish political liberals made a strong campaign to require compulsory military service for all women as well as men as a recognition of the equality of the sexes. To the Swedes, specific sexual behavior is just one aspect of the turmoil of overhauling relationships between males and females. Such leading feminine observers of the Swedish scene as Alva Myrdal and Birgitta Linnér insist that the so-called sex freedom of Swedish girls should not be viewed simply in terms of permissiveness but rather be viewed in terms of the increased independence, individual life, and self-confidence of Swedish girls.

One of Sweden's more radical advocates of sex freedom, Kristina Ahlmark-Michanek, makes her argument for the acceptability of coitus-for-friendship's-sake on the grounds of promoting equality. She feels such friendly coitus would end the double standard in morals and break up the pattern of dividing people into male and female roles. The male liberals, too, tend to equate sex freedom with sex equality. They want the woman to be subject to her own desires, not just the object of man's desires.

Three apparent reasons why the argument over sex roles and sex behavior has been so intense in Sweden, apart from general interest in the subject, are: (1) the Swedes with their high level of well-being and history of political neutrality probably have fewer national and international problems to worry about than most societies; (2) many of the so-called radicals in the sex debate have key positions in the mass media where they can present their views; and (3) Swedish television has a great many panel-discussion shows, which are relatively inexpensive to produce, and questions of sex behavior and sex roles provide lively subjects for debate.

It is true, as often alleged, that Swedish girls do smile at strangers in lobbies and elevators, but usually they are practicing human relations, not flirtation. Birgitta Linnér contends that in the U.S.A. a part of the popularity game for girls is to be sexually provocative and yet not have sex relations. In

Sweden, she explains, that is not the pattern. Instead, the girl is seeking "the individual life."

Stockholm has its share of exotic teenagers, male and female, called "raggare," searching for thrills. They gather in the evening in Kings Garden Park. One evening (during my visit) the girls were in Viking sandals with thongs wrapped up their legs, and many wore rain jackets even though it was not raining. The garb is taken as an announcement that they have come prepared for a romp in the woods outside Stockholm if a reasonably attractive boy comes along in a car. The "raggare" boys were wearing bell-bottomed trousers, turtleneck sweaters, and had Viking-like manes, often artificially curled.

A boy and girl who evidently were strangers approached each other in the park, stared in admiration for a moment, carefully laid aside their guitars, and then both, with their hands behind their backs, leaned forward and soulfully kissed. The great bulk of the crowd, however, were amused Swedes watching the activities. Some were young men and girls on dates, conventionally garbed.

One explanation for the greater premarital sex freedom in most of Scandinavia is that it has traditionally been permissive where *serious* courtship is involved. Four centuries ago in Sweden, if the families of a prospective bride and groom staged a feast, it was assumed to be the beginning of the couple's union, and it might take the families a long time to formalize it with a religious wedding ceremony. Until the 18th century, the region covered by southern Sweden and Denmark officially regarded engagements as a legal institution. The beginning of intercourse during this phase was legalized. After engagement was legally abolished as a special status, most committed couples continued to live or sleep together before marriage. The late Kirsten Auken, Danish sex researcher, advised me that a search of records in Denmark showed that in 1880 two-thirds of all brides already had children at the time of marriage or were pregnant. For a large number, undoubtedly, the conceptions were a test of fecundity.

Many observers, including Auken, have contended that, while there is today a great deal of premarital intercourse in Scandinavia, it is not promiscuous in the American sense, but rather is closely linked to courtship. This, however, may now be an outdated concept. Some Swedes now acknowledge that the situation there is changing very rapidly with more youths having casual coital experiences. The Norwegian sociologist Harriet Holter in summing up the Scandinavian situation today states:

"The usual pattern . . . can be described as follows: From the age of 16 to 20 most youngsters have some casual sex experiences with various partners. In their early twenties, they establish more stable relationships with the intention of getting married within a few years. During this time . . . the partners have fairly regular sexual intercourse, sometimes acknowledged publicly, but more often kept private as a matter of discretion. Parents often close their eyes, or declare the affair to be the private business of the young couple."[4]

Other explanations which may help account for Scandinavia's reputation for sexual permissiveness are:

• Those long, cold, snow-bound winter nights.

• The fact that the church plays a small role in everyday life, especially in Sweden. The tide of Christianity as it swept north over Europe was quite late in obtaining a foothold in Sweden—around 1100 A.D. The Vikings had been quite free sexually. Today, almost all marriages in Sweden take place in churches, and there is a posting of banns. But the number of regular church-goers in Sweden is about 5 percent of the population.

• Traditionally Scandinavians have married late in their twenties. The average age has been declining but still is substantially higher than the average age of marriage in the United States. In Norway and Sweden average age for men is 26, for girls 23. The Scandinavians have reasoned that if they can have some sex freedom, they don't have to marry so fast. One practical reason that marriages occur relatively late is the difficulty in obtaining a suitable dwelling. When Swedish sociologist Jan Trost asked couples why they married at a particular time, the first explanation offered was that they had finally gotten an apartment. (The second was that the bride-to-be had become pregnant.) In Denmark some unwed couples deliberately arrange for the girl to become pregnant, since that will improve their chance of getting an apartment.

• Another factor may be that historically there has been less prudery about nudity in Scandinavia than in most regions, with some sharing by the sexes of steam and other public baths. At the Vigeland sculpture garden in downtown Oslo, a giant phallus made up of entwining sculptured nude figures rises 56 feet. It is surrounded by nude family groups.

Some of the better indicators of what has been happening to the premarital coital behavior of Swedish young people during this decade of the 1960s show a very high degree of incidence by U.S. standards. And those indicating changes in recent years all indicate a trend toward more and earlier experience. The findings:

Teen-age behavior. In 1964 a study in the city of Örebro indicated that among students averaging about 18 years, 57 percent of the boys and 46 percent of the girls were coitally experienced (as noted elsewhere [5]). A more recent report in 1967 by Gunnar Inghe and Joachim Israel, of Stockholm University, involved the sex histories of 3000 young Swedes between 15 and 25. The investigators concluded that first coitus was occurring earlier for both males and females than was the situation before World War II. More than two-thirds now were experiencing coitus before the age of 20. The same study shows that for young adults in the 21–25-year group, more than 80 percent had experienced premarital coitus.

The behavior of college students. Georg Karlsson, while a sociologist at Uppsala University, made two samplings 5 years apart of the coital experience of students at several "people's colleges" (roughly comparable to U.S. junior community colleges). For girls the incidence leaped from 40 percent in 1960 to 65 percent in 1965. For males the increase was from 72 percent to 81 percent.[5] As for university students, the best Swedish study available at this writing was made in the late 1950s of 117 sociology students. The coital rate was 45 percent for females and 65 percent for males.[5] Our own finding for university students in nearby Norway about 8 years later in 1966 was a coital experience of 54% for females, 67% for males.

Coital experience by day of marriage. At this writing the only survey information available on Swedes indicates that around 1950 about 80 percent of Swedish brides were non-virgins.[5] However, sociologists Georg Karlsson and Jan Trost, in 1965, offered me this informal estimate: for both males and females the percentage of virgins at marriage was about 5 percent, or close to the vanishing point. Swedish marriage counselor Birgitta Linnér suggests that today premarital sex is virtually taken for granted, with only a small minority of Swedes considering it "absolutely" wrong.

Pregnant brides. Specialists in marriage have estimated that in the 1950s about 30 percent of all brides in Sweden were pregnant, whereas in the mid-1960s the estimates were closer to 40 percent.

What an observer from North America may find more startling than the statistics is the widespread openness of acceptance of premarital sex in Sweden (though polls at least still indicate a substantial proportion of adults disapprove of premarital coitus). There is wide acceptance of social situations that Americans would assume would promote premarital sex experience. In Sweden it is quite accepted that couples in their late teens take off together around the country on biking expeditions. Some will sleep together, some will not. Even in Norway, where there is more of a residue of puritanism, especially among older people, there is general agreement that it is all right for a boy and a girl to go off on a skiing or hiking trip together and sleep in the same room in one of the many skiing or hiking cottages of the country. A staff member of the Institute for Social Research in Oslo explained, "Oddly enough, the older people are not too concerned. They are in favor of sport, and they are ready to allow sex life if you ski 50 kilometers together beforehand. Sport is seen as a very positive value." In Sweden, only a small minority would disapprove of premarital intercourse between couples who intend to marry.

And if students go off to universities, there is little concern (as indicated in Chapter 13) that male and female students may at times sleep together in the dormitories. At the University of Stockholm there is a rule against bed-sharing, but it is generally regarded as a quaint anachronism. At the University of Oslo a major dormitory complex is organized by flats, with girls in one flat and boys in an adjoining flat. There is a regulation that students should not have visitors, male or female, after 11 p.m., but this is primarily to reduce noise. A faculty member commented, "If you are quiet there is no problem." At the technical institute in Trondheim, Norway, students often have responsibility for room assignments in dormitories where boys and girls are mixed. A student leader, himself married, offered this general philosophy of the way these dormitories are run: "If a girl is in a boy's room, it is just a case between them and nobody else. . . . It is strictly up to them whether they spend nights together. But if he is forcing his way, he will be expelled. It is not unusual to spend nights together, but lots of girls wait for the man they are going to marry."

Even among teenagers there is little inclination on the part of girls in Sweden to explain away coital experience as something they had to do to be popular or to hold a particular boy. In the Örebro study, the great majority of the girls who had experienced coitus gave as their reason for first intercourse that they wanted to experience it. Not one indicated she had acquiesced to an imploring partner.[6]

What startles a visitor from the U.S.A. even more than the general acceptance of premarital coitus in Scandinavia is the frequent specific acceptance by parents that their own unmarried youngsters, male or female, are engaging in, or likely to engage in, premarital coitus. Mrs. Carin Colliander, head of the marriage counseling bureau of Stockholm, explained, "In lots of households where the parents have a 20-year-old daughter there is a steady boy friend living in the house with them. This is quite accepted."

A group of 8 married Swedes, most with children, who were active in the dialogue on male-female roles were in almost complete agreement in advising me that most Swedish parents accept premarital sex for their own children if there is "an equal relationship."

One evening, I had the following conversation with a thoughtful, amiable Swedish father who is a government official with an international reputation. We were in his living room in a wooded suburb with his two sunny, polite children aged 9 and 14 amusing themselves in a nearby room. I inquired whether it was or was not true that most of the parents in his suburban area would assume that their children would have intercourse before marriage. Matter-of-factly he responded, "Yes."

To probe his attitudes I asked at what age the parents might expect that intercourse would happen. He responded:

"It shouldn't be too early. Certainly not before 16. The greatest tragedy in Sweden is for the girl to marry too early, before she is at least 20." His wife nodded agreement. (Note that he was deploring early marriage, not premarital intercourse.) Marrying early, he thought, was a tragedy because a girl would be missing much of the good and necessary experiences of life. I asked at what stage in a relationship, assuming appropriate age, would intercourse be assumed by the parents for their daughter. He said it should occur only when the boy and girl had gotten to know each other well and were over 18. He explained, "After 18, we assume our children have a right to be considered as independent individuals and to experiment with life. We would rather that they made their mistaken choices before marriage than after marriage. It is said that a person may seem to change after you have intercourse with him or her. It is better that this discovery be made before marriage rather than after marriage, when it is too late."

I asked what advice he would give his own children before they came into their late teens. He said, "First, of course, we will talk about the facts of reproduction and contraception and the possible complications. Then we will talk to them about ethics. We will, as friends, try to see that they get all the information that they need to be sensible individuals."

Later I raised the same question with a Danish businessman, the father of two children under 14. He said he had already talked with his children about the fact that at some point it might seem very important to them to go to bed with someone of the opposite sex. This man added that he has tried to indicate the importance of personal responsibility and that there is an advantage to romance. Some Scandinavians want their sex laid out flatly, he said. "I think there ought to be a sense of yearning and hope." He added that he had already told his children how to protect themselves from undesired conception.

Social workers in family-planning clinics in Sweden report it is not uncommon for parents to call and ask the clinic to advise an adolescent son or daughter on questions he or she may have about contraceptives or sexual decision-making. Family life specialist Lester Kirkendall reports an instance in Sweden in which a 17-year-old girl who had reached a point where she and her boy friend were discussing possible intercourse asked her father for advice. The father was uncertain he could handle the question adequately, so he arranged a meeting at the clinic in which he and his wife, their daughter, and the daughter's boy friend discussed with a social worker the pros and cons of premarital intercourse, the effectiveness of contraceptives, etc.[7]

Perhaps the most significant aspect of the Swedish approach to sexual permissiveness has been the effort to make social arrangements that reduce the immediate—if not long-term—pains and hazards of all this sexual freedom to the individual and to society. Swedish sex laws are not, as in the United States, aimed at combatting and punishing sin, but rather at safeguarding children and other dependent persons from the sexual behavior of persons who might try to dominate them.[8] Maternal health clinics must provide information about contraceptives to any woman inquiring, regardless of marital status. Throughout most of Sweden, you can buy condoms in automatic machines along the sidewalks. Swedish law is still moderately strict on abortion and requires substantial justification on grounds of health. But pregnant mothers can go to nearby Poland, where abortions can be had simply on grounds of social desirability and some do. A Swedish commission is now preparing a liberalization of abortion laws.

If, despite all arrangements for birth control, an unwed girl does have a baby, arrangements make the event socially acceptable. Newspapers routinely carry birth announcements for children where it is clear the mother is unmarried. The girl may report "my son" has been born; or less commonly, a girl and boy not wed announce "our son" has been born. Free infant care is provided by the state, regardless of marital status. Hospitals register a new mother as "Mrs.," whether she is married or not; and all children born out of wedlock are assigned a guardian to protect their basic interests, and to establish paternity and assure support from the fathers.

One effect of such arrangements is that there is little pressure on the girl to marry simply because she is pregnant. Many, in this situation, elect to wait until after the child is born before deciding what to do about marriage. About 50 percent of unwed girls who have babies eventually marry the father, according to Birgitta Linnér; about 30 percent marry another man; and about 20 percent don't marry at all. Quite a few young Swedish women with careers have been opting to fulfill their biological yearnings for motherhood and child-rearing without taking on the burdens of finding or coping with a husband. They set up one-parent families. Under national law, unmarried mothers can qualify for home-furnishing loans.

The attitude of school officials confronting a pregnant student is not one of dismay and a feeling that the girl must be banished (as often occurs in the U.S.A.) but simply that arrangements must be made that will be of the most help to the girl.

Efforts at sex education, both in schools and the environment outside, are massive in Sweden. In many areas, billboards remind the young to be prudent if they are having sexual affairs. These may show a handsome young man and girl smiling at each other. One billboard asked, "Think now; can she count on you?" Another stated, "Babies?—yes, but when we want them!" The National Association for Sex Education provides special shops where contraceptives can be bought and information can be obtained. As an experiment, teaching machines have been used in intermediate grades in Göteborg, perhaps as one way to ease teachers' reticence or embarrassment in talking to youngsters about physical intimacy.

Sex education in the schools has been compulsory for more than a dozen years. All instruction is given coeducationally. Virtually all students and most parents are enthusiastic about the idea of sex education if not the details of how it is handled.

Psychiatrist Gosta Rodhe, director of the national program, explained the objectives in these terms, "For children age 7 and 8 we simply try to give them a sense of belonging in the family, and the father's part in the family, and that the child came from the mother. At ages 11 and 13 when they are very interested in the facts of anatomy, menstruation, and masturbation, we try to get into anatomical aspects more thoroughly. And then at ages 14 to 16 we also get into psychological and ethical behavior." There is no discussion of sex techniques.

The sexual radicals in Sweden contend that the Handbook on Sex Instruction (Board of Education series #28) and its implementation by teachers has been too negative, with too much talk of ethics. They contend that the sex life of a person is a private affair. Rodhe explained, "I answer that in sexuality you are very seldom alone. You always get into ethics as soon as two are involved." The official position is that young people should abstain while still growing. In class discussions there is usually some attempt to include mention of good reasons for holding back from physical intimacy, including possible emotional disturbances—and to use Rodhe's phrase—"the fact that maybe the girls are not very eager to start." A national commission has been reexamining what should be taught about sex in the schools and how far the schools should get into teaching sex morality.[9]

The handbook on instruction that has been in use for a decade or so runs to 95 pages of guidance to teachers. Interestingly, the closest it comes to explaining either intercourse or how the father's sperm happened to meet up with the mother's egg is in an anatomical description of the penis, which, it is explained, is the carrier of the sperm cells "to the female sex organs."

There is no solid evidence that Sweden, with its permissiveness toward premarital sex, has an accompanying high incidence of infidelity after marriage. Swedish women become annoyed by the concept widely publicized in other lands that Swedish men lend their wives to houseguests for sexual pleasure. This seems to offend them not on the ground that a woman might participate in intercourse with someone not her husband but rather that the husbands would have any right to do the lending. They want it clearly understood that, if the wife goes to bed with another man, it is her decision, not her husband's. Polls, for what they are worth, indicate that both adults and youngsters still strongly support the concept of marital fidelity.

While most Swedes seem, in general, pleased with the amount of sex freedom before marriage that prevails, quite a few are worried about some of the problems that have developed, and apparently with good reason. A group of 140 doctors have issued a statement that is highly critical of the sex mores developing in the country and have called for firmer sexual norms. Some of the most impressive reservations we heard came from Thorsten Sjövall, head of the National Association for Sex Education. He stated, "Sweden is not the utopia that it is often pictured in terms of sex. There are questions of psychological problems that develop in intimate relationships. People are discovering that freedom can be a terrible burden."

Those people looking for specific problems to worry about can find them in such indicators as these:

• A number of Swedish experts on sex behavior are concerned about the high rate of one-parent families. About 1 child in 10 under the age of 16 in Sweden has only one parent. Rodhe feels there is a very big risk to the child in being reared in a one-parent home.

• Venereal disease rates have been rising very rapidly in Sweden.

• The divorce rate, while only 60 percent as high as that of the U.S.A., still is one of the highest in Europe and has been rising since 1950.

• The proportion of out-of-wedlock births has been rising.

On the other hand, it might be noted that prostitution has virtually disappeared in Sweden. A sociologist pointed out to me the principal corner in Stockholm where prostitutes still flourish and said that being a prostitute in Sweden today is a nasty business. He explained, "It is so easy to get a nice girl that a very large proportion of the clients are sadists or others with problems that make it difficult for them to establish conventional kinds of sexual relationships."

The Swedish experience suggests we should reexamine the often-stated assumption that interest in pornography and sensual detail is produced by the inhibitions of a puritanical environment. Throughout much of Sweden, novels and other books detailing sexual intercourse have been selling at a great rate. The book *Fanny Hill* is exhibited on newsstands. Some major stores have special basement sections with such labels as "Sex Grotto" or "Sexy Shop."[10] And Swedish film-makers have pioneered in breaking new ground in boldness in depicting intercourse and masturbation. In 1964 a radical group called Sex and Society staged a filming for a semi-public conference that was specific rather than suggestive in depicting an instance of human intercourse. By 1967, a number of Stockholm theaters were showing the Swedish-made film *I Am Curious*, which has several scenes in which the male and female stars are nude and clearly engaging in coitus.

Most startling is the finding that in the presumed heart of sexual funland a very considerable proportion of Swedish wives are not transported to states of ecstasy by their romps in bed with their husbands. In fact, intercourse seems to be one of the less satisfactory aspects of their marriages. In a study of the home life of 222 Stockholm boys, 2 Swedish sociologists asked the boys' mothers about the "sexual satisfaction they were receiving from marriage."[11] These women were mostly in their late thirties and so might be less affected by the new mores than youngsters. But in any case, here roughly is how they described the sexual aspect of their marriage:

Horrid, disgusting, etc.	13% of the wives
Feel nothing, but no trouble	16%
Have feelings, but no orgasm	28%
Orgasm sometimes	34%
Orgasm practically every time	8%

On the other hand, when these same wives were asked about the "general harmony" of their marriages, only 18 percent indicated any particular feeling of disharmony or difficulty. About a third simply said their marriages were "like most others," and an even larger number (41 percent) were enthusiastic about the harmony of their marriages. Working mothers, incidentally, seemed substantially more positive in their attitudes toward their marriages than were the non-working housewives.

Finally we should note that when the debate raged over institutionalizing a permissive outlook toward sex behavior a decade or so ago, some critics argued that if young people found it easy to get sexual companions they wouldn't bother to marry. As it has developed, marrying has become more rather than less popular among young Swedes.[12]

As indicated, much of the momentum of the Swedish movement toward sex freedom arose from the Swedish woman's concept of herself as emancipated. She wants the same freedom as the male. This conviction has led her to question domestic arrangements in marriage that would leave her in charge of nurturing children and housework and thereby inhibit her right to participate freely in the outside world.

Thus much of the argument about sex in Sweden today centers on the drive by women (and their male allies) to eliminate all social sex differences. There are still rather glaring sex differences persisting in national life; but in Sweden today a strong drive is underway to eliminate these differences. Mrs. Linnér, for example, states without qualification that Sweden is in the process of striving to attain "a degree of equality between the sexes to an extent perhaps unmatched anywhere else in the world."

Sweden's marriage code, adopted in 1920, set the stage for this drive by decreeing that when a male and female enter marriage, they are entering as independent and equal partners; both partners have a financial obligation to support each other and their children, and it specifies that housework is regarded as equal to a financial contribution.[13]

The debate on sex roles in Sweden gathered momentum in 1956 when the distinguished family specialist Alva Myrdal wrote, with Viola Klein, a book called *Women's Two Roles*. It proposed that a married woman see her opportunities in terms of phases, with one major phase devoted to her nurturing and creative life with her children, and then, when the children were grown, the woman might move into another phase that might include work outside the home. It was argued that society should seek to remove, as far as possible, the conflict between the two roles and leave women the possibility of choosing both or either.

Five years later, this concept was challenged by the gentle, lovely, then unmarried Eva Moberg, who wrote a ringing essay that is still argued about and cited in Sweden. She had gone to school in California, was the daughter of a noted Swedish novelist, and had herself attained a doctorate in literature. She argued that any release of women from male domination had to remain conditional as long as women were expected to play two roles in life. She explained to me, "It is purely mathematical. If one sex has two roles and the other sex has one role, they can never be compared. There can be no real release for women as long as it is taken for granted that being a woman means being a nurse and housewife for a great part of her life, and that her biological equipment gives her a primary responsibility in terms of children."

In her view, while the bearing and nursing of children until they can be put onto bottle-feeding necessarily is a feminine function, washing a baby's clothes, spoon-feeding it, and rearing it are not any more feminine than masculine as functions. And people who hold to the stereotype that these are women's roles, she reasons, prevent women from achieving true equality with males.

Her logic leads her to admonish women that they can't expect equality while they are expecting the male to cherish and protect them. She explained, "If you want equality, you can't ask for any favors because of your sex, and it is very devastating for the relations between the sexes if the man looks upon the woman as something precious." Many of the more violent attacks upon her and her thesis have come from women. But today Eva Moberg and Alva Myrdal are closer together in their conception of woman's role than they were earlier in the decade.

The logic of the sex equalitarians has led them to call for drastic social alterations to make the equality of the sexes feasible. This includes building more apartment complexes that offer services that minimize the household chores that the wife and husband must perform and setting up an extensive network of high-quality child-care centers.

Kai Blomquist, who has conducted research on sex roles for the Folksam insurance company in Sweden, summed up for me several of the primary objectives of the radicals in the campaign for sex equality. These were:

• Part-time work should be available for men as well as for women (so that men, too, can handle home duties, if necessary).

• The elimination of male and female job classifications.

• Fathers should have as good a chance for contact with children as mothers and have opportunities of choosing between working in the home or outside.

• Home roles must be divided equally between husband and wife.

• Education for careers must be shorn of sex-oriented overtones.

• The cost of children should be paid more by society through child allowances, and there should be a great expansion of "day houses" for children so that both parents can work.

How well are the equalitarian ideals actually being implemented in Swedish life? In some there are only beginnings. Here is what I found:

In education. During the past 15 years there has been a dramatic shift away from separated school classes for boys and girls. Coeducation is virtually universal, and even boarding schools are going coeducational. A good many boys are studying courses long assumed to be female—such as crocheting and cooking—and girls are getting manual training. At the

9th-grade level both boys and girls are given 10 hours of instruction in child care. Home economics is compulsory for both boys and girls in the 7th grade. Leadership roles in student councils still seem, however, to be overwhelmingly male.

At the university level, about a third of all students now are female, or still a slightly smaller proportion than in the U.S.A. Business administration and engineering courses are taken almost entirely by males, but nearly half of all dental students in Sweden now are female.

In the world of work. There has been a great deal of experimenting in Sweden with the concept of two women sharing one job and splitting the hours. Women are serving as crane operators on the docks, as bus drivers, and as operators of machines in iron mines. Still the proportion of women in the labor market is about the same as in the U.S.A., and less than in Denmark, Austria, or England.

Women are weakest in leadership roles. A list of the top executives in Swedish insurance companies consisted in 1965 of 348 names. All of them were male. The textile industry has an almost entirely male leadership, even though 80 percent of the employees are female. The Folksam company found in surveying attitudes that the women themselves preferred male leaders, but this was apparently because they were used to them. After they had had experience with female leaders, they reported female leaders just as good as male. Folksam also found that women in general were less interested in promotion than men. The company launched a campaign to get female employees to start thinking of long-term careers, so that more might reach the top.

In public affairs. The situation for women in Sweden is somewhat stronger than in the U.S.A., but only somewhat. In 1965 about 14 percent of the members of parliament were female, and there was one woman in the cabinet, the Minister for Family Affairs. The Prime Minister, Tage Erlander, has for years been driven each morning to his office by Mrs. Erlander before she goes on to teach her classes in physics.

Slowly, social arrangements are developing in Sweden to make a reality of the ideal of equality for husbands and wives in terms of activity in the outside world. There are now quite a few apartment houses in Stockholm where many of the homemaking functions are handled by the management. There is a great demand for such apartments and a long waiting list.

One of the fortunate couples was Eva Moberg and her husband. Their apartment house has a restaurant. She can leave laundry to be cleaned at the apartment. There is a nursery in the apartment house complex, though it is quite crowded. But it is handled by well-qualified people. There is, at the apartment building, a person who spends 4 hours a week cleaning Eva Moberg's apartment. And there is a person who takes messages and packages when nobody is home. She has a kitchen where she can prepare meals when she and her husband prefer. She exclaimed, "I think it is perfect. I never thought life could be so easy." Some of the other apartment complexes in Stockholm include resident baby-sitters and dumb-waiter elevators that deliver prepared food that can be eaten in the apartment.

Sweden is only slowly developing nursery facilities for working mothers. In many blocks in Stockholm the mothers are getting together and hiring one of their group to be the Day Mother to take care of several children while the other mothers go to outside jobs.

Working wives in Sweden are given paid maternity leave up to 6 months when they leave their jobs to have a baby, and they often have the option of 6 more months' leave without pay. By law they cannot be fired for having a baby. In some situations husbands, as well as wives, can take leaves of absence from their jobs if they are needed at home to care for children.

Until quite recently Swedish husbands have been fairly traditional in viewing homework as primarily woman's work. In the last few years, however, younger married husbands have increasingly been sharing household roles with their wives. A male insurance executive told us with pride that when his 2-year-old daughter awakens in the morning, she is just as likely to call out "Daddy" as "Mommy." Conceivably the wife helped develop this pattern. She is a child psychologist.

In a few instances men are taking care of the home while a wife works or studies. Birgitta Linnér tells of a male writer whose wife is a librarian. Since his income is lower and it is easier for him to stay at home, he handles the great bulk of the homemaker chores.

One outstanding figure in the debate over sex roles has been Bjorn Beckman, scholar and lecturer. When I talked with him, both he and his wife were engaged in advanced studies.

He said they share homemaking tasks completely. One of his regular responsibilities has been to take charge of their child during the afternoon. He explained:

"Every afternoon I'm in the park with the mothers. If occasionally a man comes along with his pram, he will not take part in the games with the children as I do. I shocked even the mothers by digging a giant hole and burying my daughter up to her neck."

In assessing possible directions that male-female relationships might take in various technologically advanced countries in the future, it will help if we know the special potentialities (and limitations) of each sex. We will consider a number of these in the next chapter.

II. Possible Approaches for Sharing the Same World Amicably

CHAPTER 21

The Sexes: How Opposite Are They Really?

"Every standardized personality test provides evidence that male and female personality scores are systematically different." J. Richard Udry, University of North Carolina sociologist.[1]

Man has been puzzling about the nature of women at least since Eve's day and, to a lesser extent, women have been trying to understand man. I say "lesser" because women tend to be more perceptive in figuring out people than men are.

How should we view femininity and masculinity in our rapidly changing world? Are the essential natures of males and females different enough to warrant essentially different life roles? How far can we reasonably go toward a single mode of life for both sexes?

We hear speculations that in a few hundred years males and females are going to look a lot more alike, with both breasts and muscles becoming less conspicuous as they become less functional. At conferences on the family in 1967, there was a clear tendency for soothsayers from U.S. universities or "think tanks" to forecast a growing similarity of life roles for males and females.

Should our society start planning for a more androgynous populace? Should we adopt the ideal of the sexual radicals in Sweden to work for as much equality and sameness of function between males and females as is anatomically feasible?

Or should we adapt the philosophy of the American author Phyllis McGinley, who contends, "By and large . . . the world runs better when men and women keep to their own spheres. I do not say that *women* are better off, but *society in general* is."[2] Another possibility is that we strive for something between these extremes of arrangement. We should always consider the possibility that some of us in our equalitarian idealism for the sexes have accepted without warrant the view that the two sexes are essentially similar, or can be made so.

It may help our reflections if we examine what is being discovered by scientists and others about the natures of males and females. Where there seem to be important differences, how much are these due to biology and how much to social conditioning? And even where due to biology, are they necessarily immutable?

The ardent U.S. feminist, Alice Rossi, in advancing proposals for sex equality *and* similarity suggests that the principal areas of dissimilarity between the sexes can readily be removed by cultivation of the characteristics of the opposite sex. Tenderness and expressiveness should be cultivated in boys; and achievement need, workmanship, and constructive aggression should be cultivated in girls. She adds, "By sex equality I mean a social androgynous conception of the role of men and women in which they are equal and similar in such spheres as intellectual, artistic, political, and occupational interests and participation, complementary only in those spheres dictated by physiological differences between the sexes."[3]

One problem in trying to understand how males compare with—and differ from—females is that there is a great variety in patterns and needs amid both sexes. Dorothy Cook, of the National Marriage Guidance Council in Great Britain, said, "Women both want to dominate and be dominated. Man wants to be mothered and not to be mothered." And Benjamin Spock, U.S. authority on child care, states, "Man has been a cruel warrior, a lace-trimmed dandy, a monk, a disciplined scientist. Woman has been a plodding farmer, a dancing girl, a novelist, even a bullfighter."

At first glance, the biological differences between males and females might seem nominal. Of the 48 chromosomes characteristic of the human species at conception, only one is different as to sex.[4] Some of the feminine track stars in Eastern Europe are so sexually ambiguous that even a nude parade past female doctors is not considered a sufficient test of sex. Officials increasingly are demanding an analysis from skin scraping of the star's chromosomes.

Yet sociologist Robert Bierstedt, of New York University, has stated that in no society in the world are men and women treated alike, nor do they engage in identical activities or dress alike or do essentially the same kinds of work.[5] And psychologist David C. McClelland, of Harvard, reports that in the short history of psychology, literally thousands of studies have shown significant sex differences.[6]

We know that males and females have many traits in common as humans (such as having 5 senses and 10 fingers), but let us assess males and females in a number of less obvious traits where they have been measured or compared and where interesting differences seem to persist. (We will postpone until Chapter 24 a comparison of their erotic behavior.) Interestingly, males and females appear to be exceptionally well-matched in general intelligence and in the speed with which they show their intelligence.

Differences in physical durability. While women require a special forward tee on golf courses and don't compete with males in the shot-put, they show a greater biological toughness. To keep things in balance Nature has had to arrange that considerably more male babies are conceived than female babies. Even by the time of birth there are about 105 males for each 100 females. The United Nations Demographic Yearbook of 1963 shows that out of 83 countries, the male's life expectancy exceeds that of the female in only 5 countries.

Differences in assertiveness. We can all think of individual females who are notably assertive. By and large, however, one of the clearest ways in which males in general differ from females in general is on this trait of assertiveness. Some social scientists go so far as to surmise that it may be related to the anatomical differences involved in physical intimacy in which the female is the receptor and the male the intruder. Those who favor the idea that male-female differences can be explained by social conditioning contend that from caveman days down, males have been encouraged to be assertive. In any case, the difference is there, and most societies encourage it. One analysis of 30 different studies of male-female behavior revealed that, in the great majority of the studies, boys turned out to be significantly more aggressive than girls.[7]

This assertiveness seems to show up in group discussions involving persons of both sexes. One evening while I was chatting with a group of Swedish men and women who were active in pressing for greater equality of the sexes, I noticed that it was the men who did most of the talking. The present president of Skidmore, a women's college, served earlier as an administrator at an all-male college. He comments that while his feminine students are more lively than most, in general, male students tend to show a greater degree of vigor in provoking discussions.

I tried to test this out by keeping score during question-and-answer periods when I appeared before audiences that seemed to be quite evenly mixed as between males and females. At 11 auditoriums—mostly at colleges—where I kept score, males asked 81 of the questions, females asked 29 of them. At an all-women's college in northeastern Pennsylvania, there were 1200 women in the audience with about 25 males in the back of the room who had been invited to come over from a nearby men's college. During the question-and-answer period, half the questions were asked by the handful of men at the rear of the auditorium.

The greater tendency of males to be assertive, aggressive, active, and pushy practically from birth has shown up in many studies. At the University of California, a study of 252 children showed that from the age of 4½ years on, boys tended to be more destructive than girls.[8] Benjamin Spock, who has spent some decades watching small children, finds that, on the average, the boys are substantially more striving and restless than girls.[9] As young men, the males still are far ahead on rambunctiousness. McClelland notes that at colleges, males tend to wreck more furniture in dormitories than women do.

Differences in the kinds of situation that absorb their interest. Almost every major newspaper has a "women's page" but not a "men's page" (although the sports and finance pages are read mostly by men). The main point is that recognition is given in newspapers to the special interests of at least the female sex.

Some years ago, human development expert Erik Erikson kept watch of 150 male children and 150 female children as they were invited to pretend they were movie directors. They could construct their movie scenes from a variety of toys and blocks that were equally available to both sexes. It soon became apparent to him that boys used space quite differently and created altogether different kinds of scenes with the available materials than girls did. Most of the girls emphasized inner space. They created interior scenes in which their people and animals were within an interior or enclosure. On the other hand, the boys were oriented outward. They were concerned about building outer protrusions onto castles they had built. The animals they used were usually outside the enclosures. Many of them made scenes involving movement, accidents, and coping with the hazards of imminent catastrophe. Erikson has recently speculated that this external orientation of the boys and the internal orientation of the girls might have a parallel in the somatic design of their differing genital areas. The male sex organ is external and intrusive while the female in her somatic design harbors an inner space.[10]

Studies by child psychologist Evelyn Goodenough Pitcher, now at Tufts University, compared the reactions of male and female nursery children to brightly colored plastic chips. The boys were fascinated and began to make things with them. The chips tended to bore the girls. When boys and girls were asked to draw pictures and explain what they had drawn, most of the girls explained they had drawn persons. Only an occasional boy said he had drawn a person. Instead, the boys drew cars, parks, trains, etc.[11] Benjamin Spock finds that even by age 1, boys are more interested in mechanical things than girls are. Sociologist Jessie Bernard thinks it significant that academic women tend to be drawn into fields characterized by interest in people.[12]

This separation of interests seems to extend down even to interests in animate vs. inanimate objects. An analysis made by the National Council of Women, in Great Britain, of the courses elected by grammar-school boys and girls showed the girls were nearly three times as likely as boys to choose biology. And boys were four times as likely to choose chemistry.

David McClelland suggests that women not only have a keener interest in people but a keener interest in the interrelations between people. He cites evidence that women tend to look longer into the faces of people than men do and are more concerned about the feelings involved in interpersonal relationships.[13]

This greater fascination of the female with human relationships may account for a trend in TV's Wild West shows. Ad-man Robert Eck explained in 1967 how the TV shows had been redesigned to attract the darling of sponsors, the housewife. The straight shoot-'em-up show is being overhauled. He explained, "The trouble with the authentic Western is that its appeal is restricted to grown men and small boys; so a bastard form has begun to replace it, the sagebrush soap opera: Marshal Dillon, of *Gunsmoke,* is Dodge City's resident sociologist," and Ben Cartwright, the patriarch of *Bonanza,* he said, is a kindly, wise, old father in chaps. Eck observed, "Underneath the outward semblance of the violent morality play that men and boys find relieving and pleasurable, the sagebrush soap opera presents the emotionally manipulative, self-conscious interplay of communal and family personalities women enjoy."[14]

Women appear to be more expert in estimating how people will react to a situation. Sociologist J. Richard Udry found that when men and women were asked to fill out a personality inventory in the way they thought their spouse or engaged partner would fill it out, the women were substantially more accurate than the men in guessing how the partner would respond.[15]

Differences in the special contributions of partners in making a marriage work. Anthropologists and sociologists have argued how sex-typed the two principal family roles, as defined by sociologists Talcott Parsons and Robert Bales, are. The concept of these two authorities, as noted, is that in small groups such as the famliy there is usually one person who is better at achieving goals and coping with the outside world ("the instrumental leader"), and one who is skilled at cooperation, conciliation, and making people feel good within the group ("the expressive leader"). Parsons and Bales believed that in most marriages the husband is the instrumental leader, the wife the expressive leader. In recently reexamining all the evidence, sociologist Udry said that despite seeming contradictions, "In the great preponderance of known societies, men have generally played instrumental and women expressive roles."[16]

Husbands seem especially skilled at analysis, manipulation of physical forms, and intense concentration toward a goal, and tend to be weak on the interpersonal end of the married partnership. McClelland states:

"To be fair, one should point out that men are just not weak on the interdependence dimension; they are often deaf, dumb, and blind to what is going on around them because they are so busy assertively concentrating on a task."[17]

In her study of blue-collar marriages Mirra Komarovsky noted, "Confronted with a marriage conflict, a greater proportion of the husbands than of the wives withdraw, either physically or psychologically, by such means as walking out of the house . . . or by silence."[18]

Differences in natural skills. One widely admired woman who feels we might have a better world if we accepted the fact that each sex has different gifts that should be enhanced is Margaret Mead. She believes that men, for example, will tend to have that razor-edge of extra gift that makes the difference in such fields as instrumental music, the physical sciences, and mathematics. And she feels that women have a special superiority in the human sciences that call for intuition.[19] Louise Bates Ames, of the Gesell Institute of Child Development, also believes females tend to be unusually strong in roles requiring intuitive skill.

Another skill in which women seem clearly to excel is verbal fluency. This has shown up in a variety of psychological tests. Leona Tyler, psychologist at the University of Oregon, who is an authority on human differences, states, "From infancy to adulthood, females express themselves in words more readily and skillfully than males."

The scholastic-aptitude tests for entrance into many U.S. colleges measure primarily two aptitudes: verbal or language skill and mathematical reasoning. About two-thirds of women score higher on the verbal tests than they do on the mathematical reasoning tests. In contrast, about two-thirds of all males taking these tests score higher on mathematical reasoning than they do on the verbal tests. On the average, males outscore females in the math section; females outscore males in the verbal section.[20]

Men also score higher in solving mazes or puzzle boxes, or in assembling objects. In one widely used measure, the Mechanical Comprehension Test, it developed that females failed to excel males in every one of the 60 items. On the other hand, women came out far ahead on aptitude tests involving deft, swift hand and finger movement.[21] Women also have a clear advantage in tasks requiring quick perception of details, as in clerical work.

Two other areas where women show vastly more competence than men are in nurture or care of others and social concern. This may annoy some women who view nurture as a stereotyped female role. Psychoanalyst Bruno Bettelheim has concluded that women have a special genius for nurturing, humanizing, and preserving. These skills are desperately needed in the new, dehumanizing environment into which we are moving. McClelland suggests that in view of the findings on aptitudes, it is not surprising that the large majority of social workers, nurses, and teachers are female. A survey by the National Opinion Research Center has shown that when women face a choice of graduate study, no more than 1 in 10 has chosen physics, pharmacology, or business administration, while in great numbers they have gone into the humanities, social work, education, or the health-preserving fields. (Perhaps social pressures are at work, but at some universities in Argentina about 90 percent of the students in psychology, sociology, and the humanities are women, while less than 1 percent of engineering students are women.)

Bruno Bettelheim was interested to find, in his study of the kibbutzim of Israel, that, although in the early days men and women drew the same jobs, today women are much more conspicuously at work in child care, teaching, nursing, and food preparation. He found these changes were brought about by the women themselves.

That most alienated, conversation-smashing, sex-equalizing segment of young America, the hippie movement, evolved patterns of communal life that proved surprisingly traditional in terms of who contributes what. In my talk with a longtime hippie female who had spent time on a communal farm in California, she explained, "I have run a chain saw; but it is easier for chicks to cook, clean, and mend because they know how to do it."

Differences in concern for a stable, predictable environment. On the Cattell 16 Personality Factor Test women shine most sensationally over men in "sensitivity," and men shine most sensationally over women in having an "experimenting" nature.[22] It is often the wife's misgivings about experimental courses the husband wishes to take that strain marital bonds. On the other hand women, we've noted, have a genius for preserving. A healthy society undoubtedly needs both experimenters and preservers. At any rate, in politics women tend strongly to be on the preserving side. The Norwegian sociologist Harriet Holter has noted that throughout Scandinavia women have strengthened the conservative political element in most of the countries.

In 1965 when the conservative General Charles de Gaulle of France was fighting for his political life, he appealed on the eve of the election to "every French woman and every French man" to assure the continuity of his regime. He knew his primary source of strength by listing women first. They did not let him down. An analysis of the vote showed that de Gaulle got only 40 percent of the male vote but 53 percent of the female vote. The French author, André Maurois, offered this comment on the voting habits of French women, "Many vote consistently for General de Gaulle. They like to feel that a strong father-figure is watching over them, and because they are more closely bound to the children they have borne, they dread war and revolution more than men do. . . ."

In the U.S.A. Jessie Bernard noted in her study of academic women that female professors tend to stay out of areas which are "politically liberal and unconventional."

Perhaps women's concern for stability also helps account for the fact that they are the more faithful churchgoers. They are more concerned about the welfare of others. They are more moralistic. Harriet Holter comments, "Women have traditionally been more interested in religion, morality, and personal relations." (Women also are more concerned about doing what is proper, whether it is in dress or observing etiquette.)

Differences in sensory perception. Women generally have a greater acuity of smell than men.[23] Thus it is possible that when, in the TV ad, a husband hugs his wife who has just sudsed herself with Safeguard soap and murmurs, "Mmmm, you smell nice and fresh," the person actually doing most of the smelling (and the person being addressed by the message) is the wife, not the husband. It seems probable, too, that the recent phenomenon in which males have been persuaded to spend hundreds of millions of dollars on scents is more the result of feminine suggestion or interested notice than their own inclination.

Males and females also seem to differ in the kind of visual configurations that appeal to them. Men prefer simple solid-line designs; women prefer figures that are incomplete, less defined, more complex. Quite possibly the New York department store Lord & Taylor is drawing upon this insight in the signature it uses in ads aimed at women. Instead of using highly legible block type, the words "Lord & Taylor" are in a florid handwriting that a male is just barely able to decipher. Cartoonist Charles Saxon, who tries to keep posted on the latest trends in male and female grooming, as a part of his work, advised me: "For the most part, male fashion drawings are specific and literal, while drawings for females are so sketchy and impressionistic that my supposedly trained eye often can't decipher what the clothes really are like, but Nancy [his wife] always knows."

Differences in the speeds at which males and females mature. During the first 14 years of life, girls mature far more rapidly than boys. In the early grades, most educators now agree, the girls are about 6 months ahead of the boys. Researchers at the Gesell Institute of Child Development in New Haven matched 33 boys and 33 girls in the early grades on the basis of age, IQ, and family background. Each year, for 3 years, the Institute gave them a battery of tests. The investigators concluded, "For all tests . . . at nearly every age, the responses of girls were superior to those of boys."[24]

Girls mature more rapidly not only mentally, but physically. Their bones harden sooner, they walk sooner, they develop their permanent teeth sooner. And by the age of 13 they are on average about three-fourths of an inch taller than boys the same age. At this age they are both physically and mentally nearly a year ahead of boys, which is one reason why, when they start considering male dates, they focus on boys 1 to 3 years older than themselves. To them, most of the boys their age are still just kids.

At puberty, boys show a spurt in both physical and mental development and start narrowing the male-female gap. But still by senior high school, possibly as much for reasons of temperament as intelligence, the girls are still getting the better grades. It is only in college that a parity develops, with boys forging ahead in some special areas.

On the television show *General Electric College Bowl*, all-girl teams are occasionally pitted against all-men teams. I have a report on 29 such encounters. The girls won 12 and lost 17, but in more than a dozen of the contests they were up against male teams who were doing repeat appearances and so had the advantage of on-the-air experience. Also, in this particular type of mental combat, aggressiveness counts, and males, we've seen, tend to be the more aggressive. Teams go through "buzzer drills" before they appear. Being first to hit the buzzer requires not only brains, but aggressiveness and precision. When Pembroke, a women's college, was invited to appear, a group of Brown University men volunteered to give them practice. One man, in recalling how they beat the girls, attributed their success purely to being more aggressive in hitting the buzzer.

The results of male-female clashes on *College Bowl* have been so inconclusive regarding mental ability that an official would offer only this generalization: "Girls are prettier on television."

In assessing various ways in which males differ from females one always comes up against the critical question: how much are the differences due to biology, how much to social conditioning? In short, can a society seeking few differentiations by sex view the proven differences as modifiable, either by conditioning or chemistry?

It is interesting that some of the more ardent champions of the notion that male and female roles should be viewed as relatively immutable have been psychoanalysts, psychiatrists, and some psychologists. Experts holding this view contend that it shows up in contour of body, pitch of voice, and so forth. Freud said that "anatomy is destiny." Psychologist Theodor Reik has revealed that in one of Freud's last unfinished papers he pondered the duality of the sexes as the great enigma and concluded that any clarification "belongs obviously as a whole to biology." Reik concurs.

Erik Erikson, lecturer in psychiatry, is inclined to the same view, at least to the extent that anatomy influences personality configurations. He contends, "The modalities of woman's commitment and involvement, for better *and* for worse, also reflect the ground plan of her body." Louise Bates Ames, of the Gesell Institute, feels that sex differences in the *rate* of development, at least, must be viewed largely as biological.

Possible support for the biological concept is available in observations of man's closest relatives, monkeys and apes. At least some of the male-female differences they display could hardly be socially conditioned. At any rate, psychologists have reported that infant male chimpanzees are far more aggressive and less well-behaved than female chimpanzees, that female chimpanzees are more willing to learn to dress and undress themselves, and, indeed, that they show more indication of enjoying the wearing of clothes. The young females are more deft in the use of their hands, just as human females are. Harry F. Harlow, psychologist at the University of Wisconsin, who has been experimenting with monkeys for many years, states, "Females are innately blessed with better manners; in particular, little girl monkeys do not threaten little boy monkeys." Males initiate play behavior far more than females and are more inclined to rough-and-tumble play. And Harlow adds, "I am convinced that these data have an almost total generality to man."[25]

Others, however, would agree with Alice Rossi, who contends, "By far the majority of the differences between the sexes which have been noted in social research are socially rather than physiologically determined." Alfred Adler, one of Freud's early disciples who broke away, leaned to this concept that the social order determines masculine and feminine behavior.

Undoubtedly, we strive for appropriate behavior as a way to get ahead or win approval. A great many fathers are distressed by any sign that their young sons are sissies. Girls, to a lesser extent and at a later date, may be disapproved of by kinfolk if they exhibit tomboy behavior. Mirra Komarovsky in collecting the reminiscences of 73 college girls found that 30 mentioned instances where they felt keen social disapproval because they were not behaving according to the stereotype of femininity. They felt pressure to be more quiet, neat, conforming, gentle, and emotionally demonstrative.

While there are a few human societies in which women seem to act as we expect men to act and a few where men act as we expect women to act—as Margaret Mead has reported—societies in general have tended to evolve patterns close to the male-female stereotypes. Anthropologist George Murdock found in his analysis of more than 100 cultures that men almost always handled metal-working, weapon-making, pursuit of sea mammals, hunting; women almost always handled cooking, grinding grain, gathering herbs and seeds. Virtually all cultures train boys to be aggressive and girls to be skilled in interdependent relationships. (We should bear in mind, however, that a maiden in a jungle tribe has considerably fewer options in life than a career girl with her own unsupervised New York apartment.)

Scientists are finding that some presumably innate sex characteristics can be modified by chemistry or upbringing. Some fascinating research has been taking place with monkeys at the Oregon Regional Primate Research Center in Reproductive Physiology and Behavior at Beaverton. When female monkeys still carrying a child are injected with testosterone propionate at a certain phase of pregnancy, any female child born of the mother not only has some visible sex characteristics of male monkeys but will, when she grows up, start behaving in characteristically male ways, such as indulging in rough-and-tumble play. Investigators speculate that the injections actually modified the neural tissues that determine sexual behavior.[26]

John Money, medical psychologist at Johns Hopkins University, reports an investigation of two human child hermaphrodites with identical anatomical defects. One was arbitrarily assigned to be a boy. The other was assigned to be a girl. Both were able, over the years, to maintain their psycho-sexual identity, thanks to the fact that their parents raised them respectively as a son and a daughter. To help fix their identities they underwent some surgery and, at puberty, were assisted with hormone injections.[27]

Psychologists are discovering that girls can, by the way they are reared, be conditioned to have many of the personality characteristics of boys and boys the characteristics of girls. It has been found, for example, that one kind of treatment by the mother will have opposite effects upon a son and daughter.[28] Let us assume the mother is hostile to both of them. In such a situation the girl is likely to develop into an assertive, masculine-type personality, and the boy is likely to become withdrawn, shy, and nonaggressive. If the mother instead is warm and protective, the girl is likely to be shy and demure, the boy outgoing and assertive.

Eleanor E. Maccoby, Stanford University psychologist, has been puzzled by the fact that although girls are getting equal educational opportunities, they are not achieving intellectual parity with the men from the same classes in which they were educated. She has concluded that for a girl to be good at analytical thinking—which is essential to outstanding scientific achievement—she has to be given a good deal of independence during her early life. It will help, in fact, if at some point she was something of a tomboy.[29]

Maccoby suggests that qualities of assertiveness, independence, and striving, which appear to go with a capacity for good analytical thinking, are in conflict with the conventional image of appropriate female behavior. Thus, in many cases, the girls who do develop fine analytic minds pay a price in anxiety, which damages their capacity for creative thinking in too many cases. She asks, "Could we not accept and encourage the active, dominant, independent qualities of the intellectual girl without labeling her as masculine, and encourage her in whatever aspects of femininity are compatible with an analytical quality of mind?"

While Maccoby and her colleagues found that early independence in children fostered analytical thinking, they also noted that the mothers who are highly supportive when their children face problems and who keep offering suggestions tend to create girls who are high in verbal skills but low in analytical skills.

The sum of the evidence would seem to indicate that much that we consider to be male and female in personality patterns has a biological basis, but that the way children are reared also has much to do with shaping personality. Furthermore, behavior traditionally assumed to be masculine or feminine can be modified by the use of hormones and other chemicals in early life.

But by and large, the fact remains that most of the young males and females that come into our school systems are quite different in terms of rates of learning . . . in terms of behavioral patterns . . . in terms of special talents they are likely to develop. Furthermore, many of these differences do have a biological basis.

The question therefore arises whether our present methods of education are really designed to bring out the greatest talents of children and produce superior male and female citizens for the future. Are children of both sexes hurt at some stages by the present headlong trend toward coeducation, from nursery school through graduate school? Are they being hurt by the general assumption of educators that male and female students have reasonably identical interests, needs, and rates of growth? And are they hurt by the general assumption that both male and female students progress best with female teachers in the early grades, with increasing proportions of male teachers as they move through high school into college?

Or, to use Margaret Mead's challenging question: "In educating women like men, have we done something disastrous to both men and women alike . . . ?"

Virtually all of the public schools of the U.S.A. in their equalitarian idealism have proceeded upon the similarity-based assumption that learning is sexless. In 1962, finally, a respected college educator charged in the NEA *Journal* of the National Education Association, "We do not consciously reject the matter of sex as something that might influence learning; rather it seems we have not even seriously considered it."[30]

In elementary schooling, as things stand, there is little recognition that the girls will be moving ahead faster or that they will approach learning tasks differently from boys. When young boys reach school age and come from their homes (where they have usually had vastly more exposure to Mother than to Father), they find themselves overwhelmingly in a female environment. The original thinking may have been that such tender youngsters needed teachers who were really substitute mothers gifted in nurture. Some educators now are arguing that it is important to get young boys exposed to male teachers, but this has become difficult. Status has become involved. Many male teachers now have it fixed in their minds that they would lose status with their peers if they took over traditionally feminine teaching roles. Patricia Cayo Sexton, educational sociologist at New York University, offers this scathing analysis of the current approach to educating young boys and girls by suffusing them in femininity:

"The problem is not just that the teachers are too often women. It is that the school is too much a woman's world governed by women's rules and standards. The school code is that of propriety, obedience, decorum, cleanliness, silence, physical and, too often, mental passivity. . . . Unfortunately, the masculine virtues are usually diametrically opposite to the school's female ones. The masculine stress is on aggressiveness in all things. . . . It is on action and movement . . . independence . . . speaking out rather than keeping quiet. . . ."[31]

In such an environment girls, with their superior maturity and perception of interpersonal relations, tend to be the more eager students. Leona Tyler comments, "Docility and submissiveness, usually considered feminine traits, enable girls to make a better impression on teachers than boys do. Inevitably this will show up on report cards, and in places other than the deportment column." She adds that such traits would tend to prevent their possessors from assuming leadership roles in the outer world.

In this feminized environment, boys tend to get off to a bad start. They are unruly, disruptive, and uncomfortable. Teachers often complain that boys are difficult to manage, without realizing they have on average higher metabolism than girls, which propels them into higher levels of activity. The results in Patricia Sexton's words are, "In vastly disproportionate numbers, boys are the maladjusted, the low achievers, the truants, the delinquents, the inattentive, the rebellious." She notes that the national delinquency rates are 5 times higher among boys than girls. Perhaps, however, we are seeing a change caused by the new enchantment with uninhibited behavior among both sexes. At the end of 1966, the U.S. Children's Bureau reported that delinquency rates among girls had been soaring considerably faster than the already high rate of boys.

The champions of equality urge that the solution lies in starting, at the elementary-school level, to wipe out male and female "stereotypes" and moving toward a more androgynous concept of sex roles. Alice Rossi, for example, suggests, "If boys and girls took child care, nursing, cooking, shop and craft classes together, they would have an opportunity to acquire comparable skills and pave the way for true parental substitutability as adults."

This puts her emphatically at odds with Benjamin Spock, who proposes, "Since girls have a different temperament to start with, and since they are going to spend their crucial years being wives and mothers, they should be brought up and educated in such a way . . . that they will take the deepest satisfaction in these roles."

As for boys, Patricia Sexton proposes that we make the early education of boys "active, exploratory, problem-solving, adventurous and aggressive." Others are urging that we move emphatically to get more male teachers into the elementary schools and more female teachers into the high schools and colleges.

Despite the present rush to coeducation, I feel a strong case can be made for having boys and girls in separate classes within the same school systems at certain critical grade levels. They could still share the same homerooms and assemblies. The grades where such separation seems especially important are the first 3, and the junior-high-school years—when the sexes are becoming so erotically conscious of each other that it is often difficult for them to concentrate on studies, and when both physically and scholastically the girls are more mature. Some would argue that the social importance of boys and girls being together overrides any shortcomings of the present patterns. I feel that, ideally, the schools should work out a blend that would provide the advantages of both mixing and separating.

There are some signs that this view may receive attention. A report in the NEA *Journal* a few years ago tentatively suggested that there might be some basis for separating the sexes at the junior-high-school level.

An official of SIECUS, in suggesting how to improve sex education, made this observation: "I'd like to see experiments in separating sexes during the 3 years of junior high school. It should be just at this level. This is the age when girls take over social decision-making and outstrip the boys in this regard. . . . This is the age when they are just being pushed into the dating situation when the boys are not ready. Only at the senior-high level should the boys and girls come back together again— after thorough sex education that will help them understand the differences in male and female sexual responses."

A pertinent experiment occurred in the Broome Junior High School in Rockville, Maryland, where all-boy and all-girl classes were set up for English and history. The courses were taught by teachers who simultaneously had mixed classes in the same subject. All 4 teachers involved in the experiments concluded that in the classes grouped by sex they had fewer behavior problems. The students were reported to be more relaxed and the classroom discussions less inhibited.[32]

If the world of education is to reflect physiological reality, the entering age for boys into first grade should be raised so that, as long as there are mixed classes, they will be a half-year older than the girls in the same classes. This might reduce some of the humiliation of boys at the outset of their educational experience. A suggestion for such a change was made to the American Association of School Administrators in 1959 after a study of about 30,000 school children in Tulsa, Okla.

At the college level, the president of Wellesley College has proposed that the world would be happier if girls in general were younger than boys at the time of college entrance. She was convinced that such girls would be more likely to stay on to graduation. They would also be more likely to date undergraduate men who were at the same stage of educational development. They would be more likely to have advanced study or practical job experience before starting their marriage-motherhood service years.

Bringing about a separation by sexes admittedly runs squarely counter to present school policies and student desires. In our College Survey we asked students to indicate what they thought of the idea of separating males and females, at least by classes, at some period between the ages of 14 and 20. The idea found little favor among either males or females (less than 15 percent). And the responses were much the same in the International Sample, with the least support of all coming from Norwegians.

In their amplifying comments, students indicated they were thinking of the survey's question primarily in terms of college. They felt that socially the coed situation was more real and reduced tensions. A number of males indicated they were not particularly eager to have girls in their classes, but they did like the idea of having them around. As for the girls, two reasons why they thought it beneficial to have men in their classrooms were:

• Girls think too much alike and thus their discussions are limited. Boys provide a different viewpoint.

• Males more often initiate discussions, which would be beneficial.

As for the social aspect, here are two feminine comments. A coed at the Rocky Mountain state university said, "If you see each other only on weekends there is an awful lot of pressure." When I asked my own daughter, attending a woman's college, if she wanted to transfer to a coed school, she responded, "Are you kidding? . . . The weekends are enough!"

Some observers suggest that girls at coed schools tend to spend so much time looking and acting sexy that their studies suffer. The contrasting argument is that where separated, their studies suffer because of so much preoccupation with sexual fantasy. As for the male viewpoint, a bitter comment was offered by the president of Kumamoto University, in southern Japan, who was seeking to curtail enrollment of girls even though they score high in entrance exams. He said that too many of the women regarded a college diploma as a bride's accessory and that their presence was reducing the proportion of students who might become serious researchers and scholars.

This same point came up in a lively editorial debate staged between two leading professors at Wesleyan University where proposals were seriously being considered to reintroduce coed education. (It has been all-male for 60 years.) The professor making the pro-coed case contended:

• Mixed classes are livelier and more interesting. The difference and variety make the intellectual give-and-take productive.

• If a liberal education is to prepare students to live with a wide variety of human beings, it is perverse to leave out half the population: women.

• With women in classes, there would be less tendency for men to regard women merely as sex objects.

The anti-coed professor made these three principal points:

• Mixed classes are not as responsive and stimulating as claimed. Women frequently hold back comments or questions until after class.

• Men tend to be less preoccupied with the other sex than women are.

• The introduction of women would reduce the number of real scholars turned out, at least in his own field of English. Wesleyan rates very high in the percentage of graduates taking Ph.D.s in English. He cited figures showing that at coed colleges, students electing to become English majors tend, rather overwhelmingly, to be women, with English becoming "a girl's major." He then noted that girls have a greater tendency to drop out of college without a degree (often for marriage).

Students at Wesleyan tended to support strongly the idea of bringing women to the college, primarily on social grounds. One said, "I think it is bad for the school, but good for me." Another remarked that it would be nice to have a friendly conversation with a girl without having to seduce her or spend a whole weekend with her.[33] The argument was ended in May,

1968, when Wesleyan's president announced that the school would start going coed and would work toward achieving an "optimum balance" of 2 women to 3 men.

Underlying most such arguments is the more basic question of what colleges are supposed to accomplish. We have noted evidence that half of all U.S. students go to college primarily for fun or social reasons or to size up possible mates. This seems to be a distortion of an expensive social institution. Should we not start developing less expensive institutions where young males and females with such orientation can get together and not overcrowd the classrooms and get in the way of students seriously embarked upon academic pursuits?

Finally, what attitude should our society take toward the traditional differences in male and female roles and the trend of the past quarter-century to minimize differences?

In our College Survey we sought to probe the attitudes of students by asking a double question. The first part was:

Do you support the idea that the individual in society functions best if male and female roles in life remain essentially different even though equal?   YES ___ NO ___

Those social observers professing to see a strong trend toward the elimination of differences in sex roles in the future can find little support from these students, probable leaders in shaping the future. In the United States, both male and female students overwhelmingly supported the different-though-equal concept. More than four-fifths answered "Yes." The reverse side of the question was:

Or do you feel that progress lies in the direction of minimizing sex role differences in life as far as anatomically feasible?
     YES ___ NO ___

For both U.S. men and girls this was supported again by less than a fifth of the students. Canadians concurred. When the U.S. girls who responded were divided on the basis of whether they indicated, elsewhere, that they had serious career plans, those who did have career plans were twice as likely to favor minimizing sex roles (22 percent) as those who were uncertain whether they wanted a career or not (11 percent).

In Europe there was a dramatic drop in the proportion agreeing to the different-though-equal concept. About two-thirds of the English students answered "Yes." A bare majority of male and female German students did; and slightly less than a majority of male and female Norwegian students did. Here are a few comments by U.S. students:

• A male at the state college in the Southwest: "Polarization of sex roles lends more variety and excitement to life, whereas minimizing sex role differences resembles more the lethargic, automated life portrayed in George Orwell's *1984*."

• A girl at the state university in California: "I want the opportunity to compete in all ways equally, but I don't want to win very often."

• A French girl who received a questionnaire in our aborted distribution there: "It is necessary for the woman to remain feminine for society to retain its equilibrium."

• An Ivy League male: "What concerns me is the nagging suspicion that such minimizing of roles would damage or radically reorient meaningful 'I-Thou' relationships between man and wife and thereby weaken family structure."

In general, women indicated they felt strongly they should have equal opportunity to perform jobs within their physical competence but seemed content that women's and men's roles in life be viewed as essentially different.

Some of the traditional extremes in sex-role expectations obviously are no longer functional. We do not need the authoritative husband and the dutiful wife. And there is a need for the males and females to divide the world's *interesting* work more fairly. There is also the need to be more fully aware of, and to recognize, the skills, traits, and potentialities that are possessed equally by fortunate human beings of both sexes.

But it now seems to me that a good many observers and enthusiasts have gotten themselves into untenable positions in equating similarity with equality. There should be recognition that different kinds of people can be equal—and that sexual nature is a major source of differentness.

Even assuming that, in the future, we do develop techniques to modify what seem to be essentially male and female traits, we should hope that such efforts be kept to a modest level. Humans by their masculinity and femininity have a capacity to make fundamental contributions that should be respected rather than blurred. The French sociologist P. Chombart de

Lauwe, writing in *The International Social Sciences Journal,* states, correctly I think, "The real equality of the sexes can be insured only by the creation of social structures and institutions which enable women to fully enjoy the same rights as men while remaining true to their own nature."

Psychologist Eleanore B. Luckey, in commenting on the Erik Erikson concept of the female as oriented to inner space, suggests the female may be designed not only physically but *mentally* to receive the male and carry the child. She explains, "By this I mean that she has qualities of special depth and understanding that equip her for creating . . . for nurturing, for healing—in short, for loving." She notes that women who speak of their greatest satisfaction and fulfillment usually recount those moments when they have extended themselves in some *loving* gesture. The most satisfying trait for men, she suggests, is *strength,* particularly moral strength, and today's woman still wants it in her man. Luckey believes Western societies will be best equipped to meet the challenges of the future if both sexes develop in particular those qualities which they are uniquely able to express, and in a new and appropriate manner.

We are humans with common aspirations and emotions first, but I suggest there are hazards in pressing for similarities in the nature of males and females, and gains to be had by cherishing masculinity and femininity. Here are what seem to be 4 good reasons for this personal viewpoint:

• Children need parents as models whose behavior is consistently sex-typed if they are to grow up confident in their own psycho-sexual identity.

• The complexity of our society and the potentials for catastrophe require the exceptional talents associated with the most constructive aspects of both masculinity and femininity. We need man's special genius for analytical thinking and creative innovation to achieve a livable environment for the long run. And we need woman's special genius for harmonizing, conserving, and loving if we are to survive in, let alone enjoy, the world we hope to build.

• The masculinity of men and the femininity of women produce an enjoyable tension that is absent in one-sex groups. Marriage sociologist David Mace commented, "There is a richness in the interplay between the sexes that could be lost if distinctiveness is removed from the roles of the two sexes.

The pattern of male and female equilibrium leads to a creative balance. It is lost if we go too far either way." His wife, Vera, who was participating in the discussion, expressed in different words the same viewpoint.

• The world is happier when each sex can enjoy the special competence and attractiveness of the other. In the outside world it is true that some women now can do just about anything that men can do; but it still makes sense if most of them gravitate to areas most likely to lead them to feel they are fulfilling their greatest potentialities and using their greatest natural skills. I applaud the girls who succeed in physics or engineering if they have a natural talent for those disciplines but at the same time recognize that far fewer females than males do have such natural talent. And in the home it seems true more today than ever before that a partnership between a man and woman makes sense only if each partner brings to the partnership distinctive qualities and talents that please and delight the other. Otherwise, why bother to formalize a friendship with wedlock? Many of these qualities that delight are likely to be sex-linked.

The world will be more ugly and less charming if each of the two sexes cannot enjoy the special attractiveness of the other. If both sexes persist in trying to look alike and act alike, there would be a loss of enchantment in both camps, a loss of gallantry, for example, among men and a loss of appreciativeness among women.

In short, human fulfillment of our potentialities would seem to lie in the direction of working for a world in which males and females are equal as people and complementary as sexual beings.

CHAPTER 22

On Widening the Life Choices of Women

"To be young and feminine at 16 is no achievement. To be a respected person at 60 is." Rosemary Park, as president of Barnard College.

If we accept the capacities and flexibilities of the female nature and the fact that we are in a rapidly changing world, what are the implications to women in shaping their lives? Sociologist David Mace points out that women today have greater opportunities to be *persons* than ever before in human history. But the opportunities are often lost because of all the uncertainties, guilt, and frustration modern women feel.

If they mark time while waiting to get the marriage thing settled, they not only suffer inadequacy feelings, but may be undermining their long-term potential. Those who become "just housewives" often gain the impression their contribution is not appreciated, even when they have an appreciative husband and delightful children. The mothers who do work tend, in surprising numbers, to feel guilty even though they may seem to have a fine arrangement.

Psychologist David McClelland suggests that women like being women for the most part, but they wish it didn't seem to mean they had to be so "unsuccessful." And Margaret Mead points out that the woman who clerks in a five-and-dime store or sews buttons in a factory may, in our society, feel more like a person than the homemaker because her paycheck and fixed hours give her a clearly defined productive status.

The housewife suffers the kind of frustration that the corporate personnel manager complains about: there are few ways he can prove with measurable precision how well he is doing.

The first thing we need to start recognizing is that females vary immensely in their capacity for, and enjoyment of, careers, nurture, and glamour. In late 1964 a professor of obstetrics and gynecology at Baylor University, Erwin O. Strassman, created a tempest by suggesting in *The International Journal of Fertility* that the better the brain of a woman, the smaller her breasts tended to be; and the bigger the breasts, the lower the IQ. He suggested there might be an antagonism between a woman's brain and her reproductive system. His study was based on 717 infertile women, a high proportion of them slim and bright.

As I started thinking of women of outstanding intellectual achievement, several of them mothers, I became wary of the doctor's thesis. Some of these outstanding women were squat, some were big-bosomed, some had broad shoulders. I queried Charles M. McLane, authority on infertility at Cornell Medical College. He advised, "I have been very interested in the problem of infertility for well over 30 years, and I have not been impressed by that fact that smart people with small breasts don't get pregnant and stupid people with large breasts do. I have delivered women who resembled boys more than girls, and I have had the most lovely-looking feminine creatures who cannot get pregnant."

Whatever the merits of Strassman's views on pregnancy-prone females, his stress on the varieties of females and their capacities does deserve our reflection. Women do vary vastly in shapes, in reproductive capacity, in mental capacity, in the enjoyment of maternity, in their ambitions, in their energy output, and in their capacity for affection. Yet most little girls grow up with the impression that a first major challenge in their lives is to prove their power to be attractive to males and then, at some later time, to become good mothers. The former may offer negative preparation for the latter.

There should be greater understanding that many women do gain a tremendous emotional thrill out of giving birth. Some enjoy a considerable real expansion of sensory perception and sense of well-being while carrying a child. For others pregnancy is a wretched time, and mothering small children proves to be more exasperating than enchanting.

One young mother who has a good job and a motherly full-time housekeeper—whom she pays $3500 a year out of her own salary—says she feels guilty about two-thirds of the time because she doesn't spend more time with her children. But on reflection she added: "Tending to the children—as I do on weekends—during the baby years is a lot of hard work and for many offers surprisingly little satisfaction. Spending a day with them in a city apartment for me can be nerve-wracking. I know that, much as I love them, I am not able to take the wear and tear of small children as well as others can, and for the protection of the nerves of myself and my family it is probably better that I am away at least part of the day." And a lovely mother-career woman in Sweden said, "Every Monday morning I feel at peace in coming to my desk. No one is screaming at me here."

I received another glimpse of the variety of ways women feel fulfillment in a remark made by own wife, Virginia, who is an income-earning artist by trade. One early afternoon as she was completing a frustrating 4-hour session at her easel, she began wiping her brushes and said with a sigh, "Well, I've got to go to work."

"Isn't this work?" I inquired.

"No. Work is doing what I don't like to do, such as what I have to do right now—straighten up the house, get the laundry together, and shop."

Millions of other wives, on the other hand, would feel more creative in putting their houses in order and planning the shopping for their families than in trying to slap paint interestingly on a canvas.

The point is that women today do have an unprecedented variety of options for finding fulfillment. Our society is so diversified that feminism and femininity can coexist. Despite all the allegations that males and females will soon be working together as colleagues, only about half of the young women responding to our College Survey (all in the last half of their college undergraduate training) indicated that they were seriously planning a career—and about half said they were not. Both groups are exercising modern options.

When we talk of women's options, we should also remember—though our society is inclined not to—that women have an option not to marry at all, or to wait to marry until after they are well established in careers. In our society, the option of choosing to be choosy about marrying is reasonable and increasingly feasible. Such a course may provide not only more gratification for some than plunging into marriage would, but may be socially beneficial. With the population pressures building up, we need women who can be creative with their brains as well as their wombs, or who can be creative both ways.

In this connection, a surprising paper was presented at the 1967 annual meeting of the National Council on Family Relations by Luther G. Baker, Jr., of Central Washington State College.[1] He had compared the social and personal adjustment, through standardized tests, of 38 women still single with those of 38 women who indicated they were happily married. Both groups involved older professional and business career women working in an urban area. I say "surprising" because he had hypothesized that the never-marrieds would fall significantly below the marrieds in their sense of fulfillment and their adjustment to life. That fits our image of the single woman as a failure, a deserter from the marriage process. In fact, there was very little difference between the two groups in their adjustment scores. Both groups scored well above normal, and the best explanation was that the women in both groups were engaged in significant employment that was intrinsically satisfying to them. He decided this was a far better indicator of adjustment than whether they were married. Baker interviewed a number of the never-marrieds. Sexual intimacy was no problem for them. Most had simply eliminated overt sexuality from their lives. Few felt that singleness was as big a problem as their families and friends had tried to make it.

Alice Rossi in a study of 3500 female college graduates, out of school 3 years, divided them into 3 groups: the homemakers . . . the traditional careerists in fields where women long have been strong, such as teaching . . . and "the pioneers" in fields long overwhelmingly masculine, such as the natural sciences, engineering, and architecture. She found that almost all the homemaker-type young women were married within 3 years out of school . . . two-thirds of the traditional careerists had married . . . and half the pioneers had married.

Perhaps in our focus on career women in recent years we haven't sufficiently appreciated, too, those women who elect to put their prime emphasis upon becoming good homemakers. Some countries are starting to correct this. Norway is guaranteeing a 4-week annual holiday for housewives. A state court in Bavaria, Germany, came through with a decision that was highly gratifying to the German hausfrau. It set a fair insurance compensation in case the housewife was so injured in the line of duty that she could not work. It ruled her work worth 14,160 marks, or about $3500 a year. This was somewhat higher than the average male wage-earner in West Germany was receiving for a year's work.

Book publishers are discovering that the main buyer of books for the home is the wife. Presumably she is reading more, and sharing insights and creative experiences gained from the reading with her family and helping them to become better informed citizens. The thoughtful, well-informed, emotionally mature mother tends to raise children who will be thoughtful, well-informed, and emotionally mature. Benjamin Spock, the child specialist, feels that more girls planning their lives should realize that the good mother is not just feeding her child pablum, but also helping to shape the child's character, ideals, and destiny.

In future decades, it is probable that the woman who demonstrates an outstanding capacity to be a good mother will have an opportunity to develop a full or part-time career in being a professional mother. This startling possibility arises out of the studies of animal behavior indicating that there is a critical period—the time of "imprinting"—when the recently born individual is exceptionally impressionable in terms of the formation of behavior patterns. Psychologist Eleanore Luckey, of the University of Connecticut, suggests that the discoveries being made regarding imprinting may create a whole new system of child-rearing and family life. She speculates:

"Suppose we do discover that some time between the 126th day and the 194th day of the infant's life the imprinting takes place that determines the individual's IQ, his thresholds of emotional response and tolerance, and his reaction time. This might well occasion a whole restructuring of the family pattern—and a whole new profession for our most talented and intellectual women, that of professional mother-imprinters."[2] She suggests that if such outstanding women, trained in imprinting, were available for the critical months to assist the child's natural mother, great strides could be achieved in reducing neuroticism and mental retardation and in developing strong children for the future.

Women, whether married or not, are finding they can be creative in ways in addition to childbearing. Social investigator Alice Lake reports that while women used to dabble in charity with luncheons and fund-raising, they are now starting increasingly to work directly with the sick, the poor, the children who need mothering. They befriend the mentally ill, perform electrocardiagrams in heart clinics, and help teach illiterate adults, on relief, how to read. She reported that 110 cities now have volunteer bureaus to assist community service agencies.[3]

Married women who work often explain to friends they do it to get extra money for the family. But an often stronger motive is a zest for challenge and yearning for fulfillment. I have seen a young mother in Connecticut change before my eyes within a year after she began selling houses. She developed more sparkle and self-assurance, and it didn't come entirely from the fact that she had added $11,000 to the family's income. (Her husband earns about $20,000-$25,000.)

When a wife contemplates the possibility of working, 3 questions in particular are likely to perplex her. What will be the likely impact upon the husband . . . the marriage . . . the children? Until fairly recently, the prevaling opinion was that the impact in all 3 cases was likely to be disastrous.

Let us look at some of the best recent thinking on all 3 situations.

The impact on the husband when the wife works. Today husbands who have wives who are working, or are active in outside affairs, generally like the arrangement or at least tolerate it. F. Ivan Nye, sociologist of Washington State University, who has investigated this situation as thoroughly as any behaviorist, advises that he found there were more husbands who like the idea that their wives are working than there were husbands who like the idea that their wives are *not* working.

Emily Mudd and her counseling associates at the University of Pennsylvania had the opportunity a few years ago to study outstanding families from every state in the union. The families had been screened and chosen by informed observers in their states. Each family had been judged to be outstandingly successful as a functioning family. I had the interesting experience of working for a week under Dr. Mudd's direction in the assessment-interviewing of some of these families. They were gathered together for a national conference in Florida.

Later a number of the families were studied in greater depth in follow-up studies by Dr. Mudd and her associates, who related all their findings to other studies.[4] She and her colleagues reached this conclusion relevant to our present discussion:

"In our successfully functioning families, the percentage of wives working is above the national average, the husband approves of the arrangement, and the wife derives considerable satisfaction from her work."

Sociologist Mirra Komarovsky in her study of blue-collar marriages, where attitudes are more traditional, found that working-class males still tend to think the wife's place is "in the home" (even though vast numbers of them are now working). But she added that they at least have moved a great distance from traditional hostility and can discuss the subject calmly. She cited one young husband with 10 years of schooling who explained, "If a wife works, she keeps up with things, meets more people, and has something interesting to talk about."[5]

Some of the greatest resistance among husbands to the idea of their wives working is found among men whose wives have not worked. Strong resistance also appears in U.S. areas where people aren't accustomed to seeing wives work. In the community where there are visibly many other married wives working, the husband of the working wife will feel more at ease.

Still another situation where the husband may well be uneasy occurs if he is a rising manager in a large corporation in a middle-sized city where the company has a good deal of scrutiny over his life. The company may have a known aversion to the wives of its managers working, since it may seem undignified, or (they feel) detract from her capacity to fit into the Wife Set, or to maintain a well-ordered home for the manager to retreat to at night.

The typical husband is least likely to be happy about his wife working:

• If she is making more money or achieving greater recognition than he is.

• If she clearly considers her career more important than her marriage. (This is not commonly the case. Most wives work, at least in the beginning, to add to the family income.)

• If he surmises that her working is causing her to be more dominant in her relations with him. Sociologist Lois Hoffman, of the University of Michigan, who has made several studies of the working wife, has found no support for the idea that working wives have any greater need for power than those who do not work.

The effect of the wife's employment upon her marriage. One difficulty in trying to draw conclusions here is that the total sample of working wives is staked on the side of unhappy marriages to start with. If a wife becomes dissatisfied with her marriage and surmises that it may break up, she is more likely than the average to seek a job as a hedge against the future. Also, as a generalization, it seems that working mothers at least tend to be somewhat less satisfied with life.[6] (But working wives also tend to be smarter than nonworking wives and, since they are working, may be more inclined to acknowledge dissatisfaction to a surveyer than would women staying at home.) Another study indicates that, while it is true working wives tend as a group to be more unsatisfied than non-working wives, there is little traceable relation between the fact the wife is working and any increase or decrease in marital satisfaction.[7]

One of the more thorough studies of employed mothers was that by Ivan Nye in which data was collected from 1993 mothers in 3 State of Washington towns about a decade ago. His data suggest that there is more quarreling and disagreement between the husbands and wives in such marriages. On the other hand, he noted that there might be a counterbalancing, because the employed mothers were better satisfied with their communities and with their daily work.[8]

The impact of a working mother on her children. This is the area where working mothers have felt most guilt; and this guilt, until recently, was encouraged both by society's conviction that such impact was harmful and by the views of social scientists. In summarizing the various major studies a few years ago Lois Hoffman stated, "Until recently the general view was that maternal employment had a great many effects on a child—all of them bad."[9]

Sixteen years ago the English child psychiatrist John Bowlby reviewed the literature on the children of working mothers for the World Health Organization and came up with an ominous picture of the effect of maternal separation.[10] Shortly thereafter, U.S. sociologist James H. S. Bossard presented a similarly gloomy view.[11]

Some of the early experiments involved raising children antiseptically, on much the same scientific principles as rearing laboratory animals, and produced horrendous results that were attributed to lack of personal love.[12] A number of the psychiatrists encouraging the ominous viewpoint regarding maternal deprivation quite possibly were influenced by their theoretical framework. They have usually attached very great importance to the emotional feelings of the small child toward his mother.

At any rate, by 1960, we had developed what sociologist Peter Rossi has called the "fire department ideology of child-rearing." The mother should be available to her children 10 hours a day on the chance that the child might need or want her help for 1 of those 10 hours.

What was little noted in some of the early reports of deleterious effects was that the studies were frequently based on situations where children were separated from parents months or weeks at a time, or where they were institutionalized in understaffed orphanages.

More recently investigators of mother-child relations have recorded—first with obvious surprise—that the picture was not nearly as black as pictured. There has been some recent evidence, for example, that the impact of a working mother is different upon daughters than upon sons (the daughters become more self-reliant, the sons more withdrawn). Some see this as evidence that sons are demoralized by feeling their father has lost status. Psychologist Eleanor Maccoby, however, suggests that daughters may seem somewhat less respectful to their fathers if their mothers work. This may be due to the father's being unstable, which may have caused the mothers to work in the first place.[13] Behaviorist Lois Hoffman, after assessing studies about personality changes in daughters, concluded that the findings were suggestive but not statistically significant.[14] For older children, the fact of the mother working is seen by some investigators in quite positive beneficial terms. A study by the National Institute of Mental Health indicated that adolescent daughters tend to be under firmer control by their working mothers than are adolescent daughters of mothers not working.

Nye and Hoffman both have concluded that it is no longer appropriate to make any sweeping statements about harm to children when mothers work. Nye advised me, "Children are fairly tough. There is a wide range where they are not hurt." And Hoffman stated a few years ago, "None of the studies done thus far has found meaningful differences between children of working mothers in general and children of nonworking mothers."[15] She points to a number of studies indicating that *part-time* employment, at least, can have a positive effect on an adolescent.

It is only when we get down to specific kinds of situations involving working mothers that we start seeing clear-cut differences in the impact of working mothers on their children. For example:

• One of the worst situations seems to be where the mother works sporadically. Warnings have come from 3 countries on this kind of situation. In the United States, Sheldon and Eleanor Glueck, of Harvard, found in their famous study of factors differentiating delinquent from nondelinquent boys that when the mother was working regularly, there was little to distinguish delinquents from nondelinquents. The Gluecks found, however, that the delinquent group did contain a notably larger proportion whose mothers worked sporadically. Studies from England and Norway make the same point. Norwegian psychologist Aase Gruda Skard concluded after a study of maternal deprivation:

"For some women the best thing is to go out to work, for others it is better to stay in the home. But it seems important that the mother have a permanent arrangement."

The mother working sporadically apparently gets into trouble because she is less likely to have regular arrangements for the children. Also, such a mother probably is more moody to start with. A rapidly growing industry in the U.S.A. provides industry with temporary help, primarily women. There are now nearly 500 temporary-help firms obtaining jobs for more than a million persons. This may be helpful to industry but is dubious as an opportunity for the young mother unless the job offers a clear possibility of developing into regular employment.

• Adverse effects upon children if mothers work are more likely to be felt in families at lower socio-economic levels than with families at higher levels. This has been noted by Ivan Nye. At the higher levels there is less probability that the working mother will be making more money than the father, and a greater chance that a large part of her motivation is that she enjoys the work and is not working from necessity.

• Harmful effects are least likely to occur if the father and the children approve in general of the idea that the mother is working. If the children are rather proud of the specific work the mother is doing, that is a strong plus factor.

• Age of the child seems to be a factor, though this is far from settled. Hoffman reports, "Although there is no research evidence for this, most psychologists feel that the child needs his mother at home during most of the first 5 years of life." The National Council of Women of Great Britain supplied me with a statement in which that group expressed opposition to the mother leaving the home "until the children are older and while in school." This was a 1960 statement and on the margin was a handwritten note saying, "Our views have modified on this." They had modified because of later research and the growing demand for women in the British labor market. The new view was that if the mother is a responsible woman, she should have freedom of choice in this matter and should be careful to arrange, if she does work, to have reliable and skillful care for the children in her absence.

Louise Bates Ames, of the Gesell Institute of Child Development, advises that some children in the difficult ages of 2½ and again 3½ just seem to go to pieces if their mothers are "away from home too much."

For what it is worth, college women today—judging by the responses to our College Survey—are quite conservative in their still untested ideas about when mothers of children should take jobs or resume careers. We asked:

Some observers contend that a wife who is really interested in a career should resume her career as soon as any children born are past the nursing stage. Do you think this is—
A GOOD IDEA ___ A POOR IDEA ___
IT ALL DEPENDS UPON CIRCUMSTANCES ___.

Those U.S. college women and men with firm opinions were about four times as likely to check "poor idea" as to check "good idea." However, a strong majority of both girls and men checked "It all depends upon circumstances." University students in Norway and England were considerably more liberal in thinking it was a good idea for mothers to resume their careers after the nursing stage. In both countries, girls were five times as likely as U.S. girls to check "Good idea."

Some investigators take issue with those arguing that mothers should wait until their children are ready for school and and would agree with Alice Rossi that the rule should be: The younger the better. Eleanor E. Maccoby states that if the mother's daily departure is begun in the child's infancy, rather than after the child has become accustomed to a single caretaker, the child's adjustment seems to be easier.[16]

Norwegian psychologist Aase G. Skard, after years of observing children, notes that during the first several months a baby is not particularly aware of the identity of its mother, but only of warmth and mothering and voices and having things to suck. Skard adds, "From the age of 5 to 7 months it will be important for the child that one particular adult return again and again. The child needs real personal contact. From around 6 to 7 months or so, the baby evidently will become tied to the one or more adults who take care of it, and this process is a quick process, like imprinting in the animal young ones. When the children have more adults around, as for example, in the Israeli kibbutzim or in societies where all grown women care for and act as mothers for all babies, it seems as if each child has one main person to whom it is more tied than to the others. But in addition to this one, the child may also be tied to other adults without damage to his personality." Then Skard makes this point: "For some children, it seems to be better if their mothers have always been employed, since the actual transition from having a domestic mother to a working mother is the most difficult for them."[17]

• If the mother works, the impact upon children will vary tremendously depending upon the quality of child care that is substituted.

• Another crucial variant is whether the mother enjoys her work or not. Skard makes the point that when you compare children of working and nonworking mothers, on the whole, these investigations show few differences, and then adds, "But greater differences are found if the mothers are grouped another way, namely in one group, those who love their outside work and those who love their domestic work; and in a different group, those who are discontented with staying at home and those who are discontented in their outside work. More well-adjusted, happy children are found in the first group than in the second."

• Finally, in assessing impact, one must know how the mothers and children spend their time when they *do* have time together. Marion Radke Yarrow, of the National Institute of Mental Health, states, "Strangely enough, research indicates that employed women are frequently together with their children more than women who remain at home and that the working mothers strive harder to participate in activities in which the children are currently interested."[18]

Whether a wife has children or not, some types of jobs are more congenial than others. It often seems to help greatly if the woman has some flexibility in her daily work pattern. In New York a number of talented wives edit books for publication. They can do this at home and set their own pace. Freelance magazine writers have much the same freedom, as do women who run their own public relations or other small firms. In Sweden, a great many of the female doctors are psychiatrists. In addition to the natural knack women have for assessing feelings and relationships, they like psychiatry because of the flexibility. Psychiatrists are rarely on call.

Feminists tend to scorn fellow-women willing to settle for part-time jobs, while observers such as Ivan Nye report finding that the best jobs for mothers are those that are half- or three-quarter-time jobs with good flexible hours. He finds you have a real problem, in the U.S.A., when the mother has young school-age children and doesn't get home until 6 o'clock at night.

One of the best sources of information for stimulating part-time jobs or voluntary activity for educated younger mothers is a guide to part-time opportunities issued by the Radcliffe Institute for Independent Study.[19] Here is a listing of some of the part-time jobs that women reported to the Institute they had obtained:

Writing and editing copy for local suburban newspaper.

Manuscript reader for juvenile book publisher.

Public relations director of a private school.

Secretary to a town planning committee.

Interviewing mothers in a maternity hospital for research project.

English tutor for foreign students.

Hospital admitting officer.

Psychological research assistant.

Librarian in private day school library.

Interviewer for "Cost of Living Index," U.S. Department of Labor.

Research for psychiatrist working with juvenile delinquents.

Editor of a subject index of psychological abstracts.

Laboratory technician in hospital.

Many such jobs obviously provide training that would permit a woman to move on to fuller employment if she desired.

In today's many-faceted society, opportunities for part-time work are plentiful for the woman with imagination, even if she does not have a college diploma. She can have an upholstery service, repair chinaware, do catering, sew, sell houses, be a travel agent, have a home mimeograph service or a sitter service, or run a home nursery, or do home-to-home selling.[20]

Women who have a strong aspiration to achieve outstanding success in creative or leadership fields need, in their planning, to minimize the time they will withdraw completely from their outside work to devote themselves to motherhood service. They can be seriously handicapped if they withdraw 5 or 10 years while they are in their late twenties or early thirties. Alice Rossi in warning about the effect of such withdrawals points to psychological studies showing that for both women and men the peak of their creative activities tends to be in the late twenties and early thirties for the sciences, and the late thirties for fields such as music and philosophy. And a drive toward a leadership role, such as in striving to become a school administrator, is handicapped by a prolonged withdrawal at any age. The process of management training is broken.

If young mothers in large numbers are to have a real opportunity to participate more fully, and without strain and anxiety, in the world of careers, then in the coming years a number of social arrangements to facilitate this seem strongly indicated. There will be need, for example, for:

• A great expansion of child-care centers. In 1962 there were licensed day-care facilities in the U.S.A. for only 1 working mother in 16 with children under the age of 6.[21] An analysis made in 1958 of day-care arrangements showed that only 2 percent of the children of working mothers were getting any group care away from home. Eight percent were getting no care whatever and presumably were "key children" left to run the streets with house keys around their necks. And 11 percent were left at home with "relatives under the age of 18." One state that has pioneered in state support for child-care centers is California, which has several hundred child-care centers now serving more than 27,000 children a year.

A survey of more than 2000 companies (made by the National Office Management Association) showed that 86 percent of them employed women, holding a great variety of jobs, who had preschool children. Yet U.S. companies have been doing virtually nothing to provide day nurseries for working mothers. Their attitude seems to be one of non-involvement. Their only concern is that the mother gets to work quite regularly. The anguish she may go through to arrange it is not their concern. One reason for hesitancy may be the cost of good child care. For full-time working mothers, the cost of caring for a child in a day-care center is about $20 a week. It is probably unrealistic to expect U.S. employers to agree to provide all this cost, so that there will need to be contributions from the mothers and perhaps from the state and federal governments. A number of European countries have gone considerably further in providing child-care centers than the affluent U.S.A. has.

• Maternity holidays or allowances. Most European countries are far ahead of the United States in assuring women that they can leave their jobs for a few months before they have their babies and return to their jobs a few months afterward at full or part pay. In the U.S.A., the woman not only is rarely paid a maternity allowance, but has to be fearful that she will lose her job if she stops to have a child.

• Revision of school practices to accommodate the older children of working mothers. Again some European countries have done more to modify school arrangements and school sessions so that children of working mothers can use libraries for study, and playgrounds for supervised play, until late afternoon. A strong resentment reported by some children is having to come home to an empty house.

• Tax deductions of the working mother's expenses in arranging child care. Any humane society should permit the mother to deduct at least half of her costs as a reasonable business expense.

• Shorter work schedules. We can assume that as organizations begin competing for the qualified women, they will create jobs that can be handled in 5 or 6 hours a day, especially since the general employment trend for both sexes is likely to be in that direction anyway. And professional graduate schools training young mothers, it is hoped, will start making available to them programs permitting a slower than average pace.

The young woman following a multi-phase plan for her life with some of it devoted to motherhood should plan how she will withdraw and re-enter the vocational world with a minimum loss of competence in her field. If she is a lawyer, she can keep up to date by working part-time doing research for lawyers. If she is a doctor, she can work part-time as a manuscript reader for a medical journal. And she can now find, thanks to urbanization, that there is probably a college within 15 miles of her home where she can take a couple of courses a year to maintain her competence. The University of Minnesota has a fine continuing-education program specifically geared to married women hoping to re-enter the vocational world. There are other good programs at Sarah Lawrence, Barnard, Rutgers, Syracuse, and the University of Pennsylvania, to mention just a few. Most are geared primarily to women with some college education, but others, such as the University of Minnesota, also are specifically offering advisory and coordinating services to women with high-school educations. The Minnesota Plan is aimed at all "rusty ladies."

The evidence we have seen that so many college students, particularly girls, are going to college largely for social reasons raises the question whether a 2-year liberal arts course might better fit the needs of the girls who are not interested in careers or are uncertain what they want. (We have noted that this includes about half of all the women responding to our College Survey.) In the survey we asked all the male and female students—who were all in their third or fourth year of college—this question:

Do you think a 4-year college education is generally as essential for the personal fulfillment and life satisfaction of girls as it is for men of comparable intelligence?

DEFINITELY YES ___   PROBABLY YES ___
PROBABLY NO ___   DEFINITELY NO ___

In the United States, the girls were more than twice as likely to say "Definitely yes" as the male students were. But when we totaled the "Definitely yes" and the "Probably yes" responses, it developed that a solid majority of both male and female students thought the 4-year college education for girls was either definitely or probably as essential for girls as for men. Solid majorities were also registered in all the international samples, with the Norwegians again being most emphatically affirmative.

One persuasive reason why women need approximately the same amount of education as their future husbands is the evidence reported by Blood and Wolfe in their study of Detroit wives. They reported, "Educational differences interfere with companionship more consistently than age differences. Even a one or two year difference in education creates a marked decline in satisfaction."[22] (Many of their wives had only high-school educations or less. In such cases a 2-year difference in education might loom larger than among collegians.)

Perhaps a more compelling reason why young women should get all the education they can, even though they are not presently planning careers, is that they will be the primary educators of any children resulting from their union in marriage. The words and thoughts the mothers use will be shaping the minds of the children. The head of a Catholic college for women in Iowa made the familiar observation, "You educate a man and you educate him for a job. You educate a woman and you educate a family." The president of a college in Florida offered this variant: "You educate a man and you educate a person. You educate a woman and you educate a family." Women also will have perhaps the major influence in shaping the cultural content of tomorrow's society, since they not only educate the children of the future, but are likely to be the members of their families most in contact with the world of books, the arts, and the theater.

Whatever the young woman today undertakes—whether it is a full-fledged career with a minimum of interruption, a multi-phased program for her life, or a life primarily of domesticity, at least until her later years—she might well bear in mind as a goal this fine comment by Morton Hunt, a student of women. He states:

"When woman envisions herself as a whole person and harmoniously combines all the roles needful to her in modern life, she has the best chance of being enduringly feminine in a civilized, sophisticated sense, functioning well as a homemaker and as a mother to her children, proving a good mistress and a friend to her husband, and being not only a valuable asset to her society, but a reasonably happy, fulfilled, and self-approving human being."[23]

CHAPTER 23

Some Man-Sized Challenges for Males of the Future

"Men are going to have to quit whining. It is not fair of them to use their usual manipulative tricks to maintain their position of superiority. From now on they've got to be really better if they want us to recognize that they are better." LuJean Cole, head of the Student Center, Simpson College.

In the future, men cannot continue to dismiss women—by using their "For Men Only" signs, or as artist Richard Lindner does, by depicting females as monstrous, ridiculous floosie-ogres with ballooned breasts and buttocks. They must relate to women in terms of the altered world in which both sexes will be functioning. Males haven't lost their importance, but they certainly have less basis than in the past for self-importance.

A number of observers have been offering the male disquieting if not alarming predictions about the ways he is going to have to overhaul his identity. Some sociologists are telling him that there must be more "interpenetration" of roles by the sexes. And a number would agree with social critic Myron Brenton, who talks of the "invisible straitjacket" that still keeps man tied into antiquated patriarchal notions of what he must do and be to prove himself a man.[1]

Actually it may turn out that the male is considerably more resilient than he has been depicted. Perhaps he has been in a straitjacket in his attitudes toward appropriate roles for women. But he has recently been responding to the "New Woman," with her interest in companionship and careers, more tolerantly than might have been dreamed conceivable a quarter-century ago. This resilience is appearing not only in the U.S.A., but in Europe and in Japan. Munich psychiatrist Hans Luxenburger commented to me that in his once patri-archial country "Men have absorbed the new role of women surprisingly well. The men today just don't want a hausfrau, and men don't feel that women are losing their femininity by working."

The new mood is consistent with reality, since the need for emphatic sex-typing has become less apparent. There is rather a need for more perceptiveness in our definition of what is essentially feminine and what is essentially masculine.

Males are finding they can do some things they didn't know they could do, such as competently tending babies. We should follow with interest, rather than with distaste, the evolution of role changes first dramatized by the male hippies and mods who have experimented flamboyantly with making a funda-mental break from the traditional male identity. They not only broke out of the male straitjacket in grooming and in their scorn for the virile look but, in their peculiar way, many have tried hard to practice gentleness.

At the same time, however, we should be wondering how far we can go in redefining a man's identity without doing something damaging to him and to society. Brenton contends, "If a male is real—if he is fundamentally secure in his man-hood—women do not threaten him; nor does he need to con-firm his masculinity at their expense." This seems a fair state-ment, but it also raises the question how the male becomes secure in his manhood in the first place. David Mace suggests that much of the difficulty and confusion in male-female rela-tionships in the Western world is due to the fact that we have been undermining the authority of the man in the family. When we undermine him, we hurt everybody else, as well. He explained, "The wife cannot function in her feminine role if her husband's masculine role is taken from him. . . . If the husband can no longer play his part as leader and initiator, the wife is paralyzed in her responsive function. She may re-taliate by developing resentful, hostile attitudes and try to tear him down."[2] This concept, I believe, should be one of the key elements in shaping the male role of the future.

J. R. Napier, of the Unit of Primatology and Human Evo-lution at the Royal Free Hospital School of Medicine in London, advised me there is evidence among our fossil ancestors of considerably more sexual differentiation in prehistoric days than there is today. The excessive maleness of Stone Age man, he suggests, was a device of natural selection to guarantee the safety of the tribe, and excessive femininity was maintained in the same way. The female was the means by which man could perpetuate his tribe. Men today are selected by women less for their brawn than for their brains, and women by men more for their fitness for companionship, and for creating a gratifying home environment, than for their potential fecundity. Social selection already is tending toward the brainy, rather than muscular, man and to the capable, well-educated, not necessarily fecund, female.

While Napier expects that over the centuries secondary sex differences will become reduced, he envisions a world in which men will be facing some very formidable male-type challenges, though different from those of the caveman. He predicts:

"The environment of the future will be increasingly man-made and man-controlled. Instead of the natural jungle we have the concrete jungle where movement is mechanical and even the climate can be artificially moderated. Man, in other words, is beginning to learn how to control his physical environment."

Men can gladly accept the help of enterprising, ingenious females in coping with such formidable new environmental challenges, but given the nature and interests of most females, there is little possibility that the male's preeminent role in modifying the physical aspects of the modern physical environment will be seriously challenged in the lifetime of anyone now living. He rightly should see this as a sphere where he can and should make the primary contribution.

It might be profitable to look at the man of the future in terms of 4 of his principal life roles.

Men of the future as breadwinners and outside leaders

The changing nature of the work world has unquestionably made it more difficult for tens of millions of males to feel they are affirming their manliness to any conspicuous degree on the job. And bureaucratic organizations employing them should take this into account in developing future job descriptions and provide more opportunities for individual responsibility, initiative, and creativity. They should also arrange tapering-off periods for men of advancing age rather than have arbitrary, ever-earlier retirement deadlines which assault the male's sense of worth.

We have the incongruity that much of industry is infatuated, almost obsessively, with assessing its managers on the basis of traditional he-man traits. Yet at the same time, they are sending their leader to special schools to acquire skills of interpersonal insight and group integration, which are skills that come more naturally to females. Tens of thousands of aspiring young managers in the past 2 decades have been screened by psychological testers who require them to wrestle with testing tools purporting to measure their masculinity-femininity components. A common practice of managements has been to knock out any male candidate whose test responses did not put him emphatically on the masculine side of the personality profile chart. The developers of the various M-F tests have had widely varying, often ludicrous, concepts of how to measure modern masculinity. Some have assumed that any evidence of interest in art, music, or other cultural forms suggests femininity. Often the same companies being guided by these M-F tests have been sending promising managers to "sensitivity training schools" located throughout the country. Many of these schools are designed to help the company's overly thing-minded, hard-boiled, insensitive male managers acquire better insights about human behavior and better skills in interpersonal relations. The corporations belatedly have been discovering that the typical corporation-reared male in line for high office is often weak on skills crucial to his effectiveness as a people-leader—such as having insight and group-integrating expressiveness. Hopefully, the companies will start realizing the ideal leader does not have to be a jut-jawed, hairy-chested, 6′ 2″ specimen with a booming voice. Rather the good modern leader needs a blend of such masculine virtues as assertiveness, even-handedness, and analytical thinking along with traits at which females are good, too, such as articulateness, personal warmth, and perceptiveness.

Meanwhile males should understand that there are many hundreds of occupational categories where they have solidly based advantages or superiority because of their maleness. Men are more likely to have a special knack for innovation . . . for leadership . . . for abstract thinking . . . for being objective in dealing with people in tense situations . . . for having a capacity for sustained drive . . . for having a talent in manipulating the natural world to meet mankind's needs and desires. And there are still a good many categories where strength and physical endurance and mechanical ingenuity count.

They might also bear in mind the evidence that women still look to men for guidance on important matters—though this may eventually change somewhat—and still usually like the man to take charge.

Elihu Katz and Paul F. Lazarsfeld, social psychologists at Columbia, made a study of how 800 women form their opinions.[3] Women were asked, "Do you know anyone around here who keeps up with the news and whom you can trust to let you know what is really going on?"

The investigators reported, "Whether women are married, single, or separated they apparently look to men for competence in public matters." They reported that two-thirds of the persons whom these women identified as most influential in their understanding of general affairs were men. Also two-thirds of the women who had changed their opinions attributed the change to men. As a footnote, the investigators made this interesting comment, "It was found that while wives frequently referred to discussions with their husbands, the latter rarely returned the compliment. The husbands apparently did not feel that they were 'discussing' politics with their wives. Rather they were telling their wives what politics was all about."

One of the findings of the social scientists studying student culture at Vassar College stated that when the girls described the qualities of an ideal husband, the majority were quite explicit in their preference for the man who would assume the more important role, and especially make the majority of decisions, outside the home.[4]

Males of the future as lovers of women

Just as the male can no longer automatically assume that his role in the occupational world will proclaim his sexual identity, he can no longer depend only upon his sexual prowess for such identity. Mary Calderone of SIECUS puts it this way: "Our boys should not grow up having the idea that the way the man demonstrates his ability to be a man is only in bed." With the new sexualization of the female and liberation from her old ideas of dutifulness and restraint—along with the liberation and possibly enhanced sensual feelings produced by the pill—males can no longer assume they will be so clearly the primary actors in intimate encounters as husband or lover as in the past. Alice Rossi in her advocacy of sex equality makes this comment as a footnote about intimate acts: "If the view of the sex act presupposes a dominant male actor and a passive female subject, then it is indeed the case that full sex equality would probably be the death knell of this traditional sexual relationship."[5] While she insists that men and women should approach sexual intimacy as essentially equal partners, she agrees they should complement each other sexually; and she makes this important point: "Sexually men and women do, after all, each lack what the other has and wishes for completion of the self. . . ."

Psychologist Abraham Maslow, of Brandeis University, in his study of people who achieve a high degree of fulfillment in life comments that fully healthy people make no sharp differentiation between the roles of the two sexes in sexual play. The men were so assured of their maleness and the females of their femaleness, he found, that they did not assume the female was passive and the male active whether in sex or love or anything else. He explained, "They could be both active and passive lovers . . . kissing and being kissed . . . being above or below in the sex act . . . these were all found in both sexes."[6] Still, men generally tend to be the more assertive partners. Both the male and female will find that in the climactic phase, if the male is in a position for easily effecting a maximum union of the bodies, the experience will usually be more joyous for both than any self-conscious effort at side-by-side embracing as proof of an equalitarian relationship. Such an approach is also more likely to contribute to the woman's deep-seated need to feel desired.

The future of males as husbands

I have found no evidence that in the future husbands will be, by and large, dominated by their wives—or that wives have any interest in achieving a dominant role. The great majority of women can still see contentment in life only if they have some sort of an enduring relationship with a man. And the studies by Robert Blood, Jr., and Donald Wolfe of several hundred wives in the Detroit area produced strong evidence that women have little to gain and much to lose when they assume a dominant position in the household. These investigators state:

"We will find throughout this study . . . dissatisfaction associated with wife-dominance. This is not, however, simply a reflection of breaking social rules. Rather, the circumstances which lead to the wife's dominance involve corresponding inadequacies or incompetencies on the husband's part. An inadequate husband is by definition unable to make a satisfactory marriage partner, so the dominant wife is not exultant over her 'victory' but exercises power regretfully by default . . ."[7]

Other evidence suggests that wife dominance is dysfunctional to a good marriage relationship and that wives in wife-dominated families are less likely to indicate marital satisfaction than are wives in either husband-dominant or equalitarian families.[8]

The male of the future as father

In recent decades so much attention has been focused upon the quality of mother-child relationships that one might get the impression the father is a sort of fringe character like the male lion. In many cases, as noted, the U.S. father is peripheral. But mounting evidence indicates this is an unnatural, inadequate situation, one likely to be crippling to the development of the children and to produce a family that rarely senses genuine love.

In 1965 Daniel P. Moynihan, now Harvard-Massachusetts Institute of Technology urbanologist, wrote a government report entitled "The Negro Family: The Case of National Action." In this much-argued report, he examined the matriarchal pattern so prevalent in Negro homes. Often in such homes there is only one visible parent present, the mother. Or, if the father is visible, he has frequently been demoralized by our society. Moynihan reported that in homes where the father disappears, the IQ of the children on average drops 7 points.

Some estimates indicate that nearly half of all Negro families are headed by a woman, if you count those where there has never been a father present.[9a] The father-absent pattern so common in Negro homes can, in large part, be traced to slavery, when it was illegal for Negro males to take on any contract, including marriage. More recently the pattern has been encouraged by welfare regulations that have permitted payments to mothers of dependent children only if there was no father visible to the welfare inspectors. Thus the phenomenon of dusk-till-dawn husbands. In many cities, too, Negro women have many more job opportunities than do Negro men. These are a few of the host of environmental factors that have undercut the pride and authority of many Negro males. Students on the honor rolls of essentially Negro high schools were found in one analysis to be overwhelmingly female. At least until quite recently, the majority of Negroes with college degrees were female. And Negro females have clearly outperformed males in obtaining what federal officials call "significant white collar jobs."

One of the more noteworthy studies on the impact of absent fathers upon children was conducted by Per Olav Tiller of the Institute for Social Research, in Oslo, a decade ago. Tiller compared the children of seamen who had to be away from home for long periods with children whose fathers were regularly home at night. In the homes where the father was away a good deal, a larger proportion of the children showed a high degree of dependence and tended to idealize the father. Subsequently two American investigators analyzed his data to see if the impact of the absent father was different upon the son than upon the daughter.[9b] The investigators found that boys had much more difficulty than girls in adjusting to young people their own age if their father was off at sea much of the time. They found that more boys showed immaturity where the father was absent than did those where the father was present, and that boys where the father was absent tended to react to their insecure masculine identification by compensatory displays of masculinity.

In early 1968 a professor of social welfare at the University of California, Los Angeles, reported she had been unable to find much difference in attitudes and concepts between boys when father was absent and when father was present. But she noted the boys in both groups were of low socio-economic status and suggested that in such homes even if the father was present, he didn't seem a warm or close figure.

At about the same time, however, two psychologists at St. Louis University reported finding, by the use of a novel probing technique, that children in father-absent homes were clearly more dependent than when the father was present.[9e] On the usual pencil-and-paper tests to probe "masculinity" they had found few differences. But when they put the boys in a darkened room and asked each one to adjust a luminous rod to an upright position when it was in a luminous tilted frame, differences between the matched groups stood out. The boys from father-absent homes had less success because they were more influenced by the tilted frame. To many psychologists this suggests deep-seated passivity. On the other hand, the boys from father-present homes had much more success in ignoring the tilted frame and getting the rod upright. To the investigators this suggested they were "field-independent" and thus more analytic and aggressive: in short, more masculine.

Interestingly, half the boys in both groups were Negro, and they tended on the average to reveal more passivity than same-group whites. The investigators surmised that the general features of their Negro subculture tend to demasculinize boys from a very early age, whether fathers are home or not.

A few years ago, sociologist Judson T. Landis, of the University of California, Berkeley, concluded from responses made by 3000 U.S. college students that their feelings toward their fathers when they were adolescents were much better indicators of whether a happy marriage existed than were their feelings toward their mothers. It seems that both boys and girls tend to feel close to their mothers, whether the husband-wife relationship is a happy one or not. She is their main contact; but if the youngsters don't feel close to the father, it is an excellent sign that the marriage is in trouble.[10]

There is also specific evidence now that a competent father, firm but warm, is crucial to the development of young men and women secure in their sexual identity. For example:

• Since the father seems to have considerably more interest than the mother in wanting his children to have firmly fixed sexual identities, he exerts a stronger influence in the general sex-typing of both sons and daughters.[11]

• A crucial part of the socialization of children is that they learn to accept restraints upon their behavior. It is still the father who is most likely to impose these restraints, if they are imposed.[12]

• In the early years, both male and female children tend to develop a deep dependency upon the mother; and the father is better qualified than the mother to pry the children loose from this dependency so that they can grow up and accept their responsibilities as adults. In confronting this difficult task of loosening dependency feelings, the weak, ineffectual father is more of a threat to the family as a system than is the weak, ineffectual mother.[13] Sociologist J. Richard Udry explains the vital importance of this prying loose process in these words:

'The easiest thing for the young boy to do is to remain in his 'feminine' role. The mother has some real emotional benefits in retaining the old relationship with the boy. As long as he is still 'feminine' he is docile and easy to handle. He is also the dependent partner in a relationship which is very satisfying to mothers and, consequently, not easy to give up. If the mother yields to these temptations and encourages the boy to remain in his role of dependency, then the father becomes the main source of pressure for role disruption and independence."[14] Udry suggests that this transition may explain why young males experience more anxiety than do young females concerning the problem of achieving the proper sex-typed personality.

• A warm, strong but not domineering father appears to be crucial to the optimum development of his sons in the world outside, and the absence of such a father can be devastating. High academic motivation is most likely to be found in boys from equalitarian families where the father is strong and bold enough to allow the children freedom for independent decision-making.[15]

If the son is to develop a normal masculine personality, he must become firmly fixed in his masculine identification in his early years. And according to one study, the particular type of techniques the father uses with the son is far less significant than the degree of *importance* the father plays in the boy's life.[16]

There is an abundance of evidence that, if boys are to develop into males with secure sexual identities, they need to see what masculinity is like; and the best possible situation is for the father to provide the model.

Juvenile delinquency among boys is particularly common in families where there is no visible father, or a demoralized father. And if a son is reared in a family where the father is absent or demoralized, there is a far greater than average chance that he will become a homosexual. Such a situation also usually requires a mother who is excessively smothering in her handling of the child. But the role of the father, according to several authorities on homosexuality, frequently is critical, since homosexuality is so frequently associated with a fatherless home or its equivalent of an absent or neglectful father—or a home where the mother is dominant and the father ineffectual.[17]

• The need of a daughter for a strong, warm father. Psychiatrist Robert Odenwald stated that a girl needs such a strong, warm father if she is to have some early understanding of what it is like to love and be loved by a man.[18]

While the experts are not wholly in agreement, a number of respected figures report that a high proportion of girls who become pregnant out of wedlock come from broken homes where they haven't had the benefit of a strong, affectionate father. One who is impressed by this pattern is Leontine Young, now head of the Child Service Association, Newark, who made an often-cited study of 350 unmarried mothers and concluded, "With monotonous regularity, one hears from girl after girl . . . of a family which has been shadowed by the possessiveness and unhealthy tyranny of one of the parents . . . the great majority of unmarried mothers come from homes dominated by the mother . . . [who] both envies and despises her husband and she generally marries a passive man who cannot or will not oppose her domination of the family."[19]

Another supporter of this view is Henry M. Graham, executive director of the Family Service Association, Indianapolis, who advised me that practically all of the girls in a study he made of unwed mothers had poor relationships with their fathers. In one case, the girl had deliberately become pregnant because of an intense hatred of her father, who was a community leader but, according to her, a tyrant inside the home.

In short, one of our great social needs in building a promising generation for the future is an increase of fathers who are strong, affectionate—and close to their children.

We will see in the coming years considerably more thinking about the norms that modern society has set for masculinity. At present, both the experts and the public at large are divided. Many social scientists stick to the idea that even with the radical changes in the work world, the best situation still is one where the male is the instrumental leader (the outside man who gets things done), while the feminine partner is the expressive leader who makes the family members feel pretty good about themselves. Other observers argue that the times call for a somewhat greater blending of roles.

We should recognize that there is some logic in both sides of the argument without hotly contesting either position. Here are a few guidelines that strike me as useful to keep in mind as we move toward a new definition of masculinity.

• It remains important that males develop ways of growing up that help them know they are male and not have to worry about it . . . that they be confident in their maleness. We need to recognize that the male, in growing up, has a harder time achieving his sexual identity. Our best insurance for developing self-assured males in the future is to focus on the development of the boy in the first several years of his life to make sure that his image of maleness is firmly fixed. That image, once rooted and solidly derived from the model that he sees in his father, cannot be easily modified by the changing conditions of later life.[20] His essential maleness will be a source of content not only to himself but to his wife and children.

• We should recognize that it is more important for males to be recognized as masculine than it is for females to be recognized as feminine. Crusading females in their quest for justice and equality often neglect to make a distinction still important to males: that you can have both equality and distinctiveness.

Males are deluding themselves when they imagine they are really at bay in the face of onslaughts on their positions by some females. Most females want strength in their men and are unhappy when they don't find it. Two of the most perceptive women in the intellectual battle over sex roles—anthropologist Margaret Mead and psychiatric consultant Edna Rostow—both stress the hazard of homogenizing the sexes.[21] Mead suggests the world might lose more by sacrificing sex differences than it would lose by concentrating the exercise of feminine talents primarily to certain ways of life. She believes it would be of doubtful value to bring talented women into traditional male fields if it only served to frighten the males, unsex the women, and cause men to abandon the field or change the quality of the contribution they make. And Rostow states, "The man has to be a man in order to help them [women] to be women." She suggested it may be that women are afraid of their own strength, afraid it will lead them to become henpecking wives who would tend to select dependent men or reduce the ones they marry to acquiescent, withdrawn figures.

• Social arrangements should be developed to help all men by the time they are 20 to be essentially self-supporting. This is the period when they most need to feel they are moving into manhood. We have seen the prospects that young men in the future will be expected to stay longer and longer in colleges and that this may be undermining their selfhood at a critical period, if they remain essentially dependent upon their parents for financial help. Perhaps it may be possible—when the draft is not hanging over their heads—to encourage young men to work between high school and college to develop a sense of self-sufficiency and assemble some resources. Considerably more could be done to make available work-study programs, loans and scholarships in college—and even salaries for outstanding students—and schools should emphasize some study-tracks specifically designed for students who want a relatively light schedule so that they can hold down part-time jobs while they study. The goal should be to assure that no talented young man need feel dependent upon his parents after the age of 20—nor have to start his career (and marriage) with a staggering debt incurred in college. In our College Survey we asked:

Some observers are urging that we develop social arrangements to enable all young people to be financially independent by the age of 21 regardless of whether they pursue a higher education. Do you think this would help produce a stronger society? YES ___ NO ___
MAYBE, BUT IMPRACTICAL ___.

Slightly less than a third of either the males or females gave an unqualified "Yes" to this question. Somewhat less than another third said, "Maybe, but impractical." The largest response was "No," possibly suggesting some ambiguities about the clamor of many students for independence. The response of students in international samples may not be comparable, because a number of European countries already assure talented students that most of the cost of a university education will not fall upon the student or his parents, especially if they do not have high incomes. In any case, German and Canadian students were even less attracted by the idea than American students, whereas about half of both the Norwegian and English students said "Yes" in approving such social arrangements.

In the comments of U.S. students it was clear that while the idea of independence appealed to them, they seemed to feel that institutional support was just as bad as parental support. If the question had contained reference to self-help arrangements being made more common, the "Yes" responses would undoubtedly have been higher.

The least support came from students in the Midwest, where, as we have seen, there seem to be more conservative attitudes on most of the questions that were asked. Some seemed to think it would have to involve some kind of socialistic or socialized arrangements. My own feeling is that the goal of social arrangements that would encourage independence and self-reliance of young adults, especially males, is important despite the wary responses of students to the question as it was worded.

Another area of social concern should be that of the very rapid job obsolescence of technological skills as it may affect male self-confidence. Much needs to be done in the coming decade to develop the concept of continuing education so that enterprising younger males can feel confident that they will always have skills in demand.

• Males should not be frightened by talented females who do have the good fortune to have bold, inquiring, analytical minds and have serious career aspirations. In the present period we have seen a substantial diminution—but far from a full one—in such fright and in increased casual acceptance of female colleagues if they are qualified. Males should understand that there probably will never be, in their lifetime, more than a small percentage of talented women who will be particularly interested in careers requiring aggressive striving. And they should develop a relaxed appreciation that while few women will want to wear the pants in a family, an increasing number of bright girls will want to be active, enthusiastic, and successful in community affairs and in the world of work without losing their feminine identification. Our image makers (mostly male) in motion pictures, television, and fiction can and should stop stereotyping the girl with aspirations as one with horn-rimmed glasses, big flat shoes, and hair tightly drawn back in a bun.

• At the same time, there is a need for our males to get masculinity in perspective and to realize the great variety of possibilities of behavior males, secure in their sexual identity, can engage in. We don't all have to be James Bonds, or Marshal Dillons, or Joe Namaths.

Psychiatrist Frederick A. Weiss suggests it is important that we understand that a healthy masculinity can combine strength and tenderness. In recent times, that concept has been replaced, perhaps as a compensatory response, by the image of an aggressive super-male whose rashness is glorified as masculine. Weiss states, "We are in need of an image of man in which sensitivity and creativity are no longer seen as lessening masculinity."

Further thoughts on how males and females may become more secure in their sexual identity will be considered in the next chapter.

III. Possible Norms for Coping Agreeably with Our Sexuality

CHAPTER 24

The Sexual Feelings of Males and Females

"Sexuality is not a separate compartment of human life; it is a radiance pervading every human relationship, but assuming a particular intensity at certain points." Alan W. Watts, religious philosopher.

Perhaps a first requirement for developing norms for coping agreeably with our sexuality is to understand better what is involved with persons of both sexes. The action of a male and a female in responding to their physical attraction for each other can have any of several meanings. For some couples, the action that leads to an excited union of the two bodies carries little more meaning than a gratifying spell of pelvic sneezing. To some feminine participants the act of union is a gracious servicing of a husband, or of a friend they hope to know better. For other males—and now increasingly for females—the act is a diverting bit of playful athletics.

Abraham Maslow in developing his famous hierarchy of primary human needs pointed out that the first need must be satisfied before the next is felt as having urgency. The "love needs" come third in his list. His needs, in order, are physiological needs, safety needs, love needs, esteem needs, self-actualization (or fulfillment) needs. For some, coital intimacy may be classified as a purely physiological need, but ordinarily sexual behavior comes under the need for love and affection. Maslow further points out that our love needs involve not only receiving, but giving, love.[1] Under the right circumstances, he adds, physical union is one of the paths to transcendent experience. A coed in the West responding to our college checklist seemed to agree. She commented, "The act of making love is a special and beautiful thing if handled properly."

Psychoanalyst Rollo May has speculated that the sexual union of a man and woman has a number of special rewards that can be of considerable importance to the participants. These include:

• The enrichment and fulfillment of personality that comes from the expansion of one's awareness of one's feelings and those of another person.

• The tenderness that comes from the fact that two persons overcome their separateness and isolation.

• The act of giving often is sensed as essential to one's own full pleasure.

• At the climactic phase the lovers may be united not only with themselves but with nature.

• Sexual love can provide a meaningful way to help attain personal identity.

California philosopher and religious thinker Alan Watts has made the most fascinating exploration of the meaning of sexuality I have encountered.[2] Watts sees sexuality as a special mode of the total intercourse of Man and Nature. He thinks religious celibates have been mistaken in assuming that the highest spiritual life demands the renunciation of sexuality— as if the knowledge of God were an alternative to the knowledge of woman.

In Watts's view this most intimate of relationships can become a major sphere of spiritual insight and growth. He sees in the lovers' removal of clothing a taking off of the personal mask; and he finds the climactic phase of union, if it comes spontaneously, one of a bursting in upon us of peace. In such a contemplative surrender of the partners, the sense of identity can become particularly intense. It is not a deed but a gift, and when the experience bursts in upon fully open feelings, there is not simply a release of physical tension but, to use his words, "an explosion whose outermost sparks are the stars."

In the beginning, young males and females often have different motivations in tentatively undertaking sexual play. Mary Calderone, executive director of SIECUS, offers this neat distinction between the motivations of a boy and of a girl: "We can say the girl plays at sex, for which she is not ready, because fundamentally what she wants is love; and the boy plays at love, for which he is not ready, because what he wants is sex."

A coed in the Rocky Mountain area who acknowledged she was promiscuous for a time explained, "I can only speak for myself, but it wasn't my sex drive that usually placed me between those sheets. It was my tremendous fear of rejection."

Michael Schofield in reporting the reactions of British teenagers to first coitus found that a third of the boys and two-thirds of the girls were disenchanted. And half of the girls even after they had had repeated experiences still didn't particularly enjoy it except "sometimes." They liked it because it seemed to please the boys.[3]

At the college level, however, the Institute for Sex Research has recently found that among coeds reporting on their first premarital coital experience there has been, in the 2 decades (approximately) since the Kinsey group did its interviewing, a substantial increase in those who characterized the experience as enjoyable. Whereas earlier, less than half of the young women indicated enjoyment, by 1967 about two-thirds were indicating enjoyment. It was surmised that a reduction in guilt feelings and an increase in sexual equality might help account for the change.

In a French survey, most of the women who were interviewed about the first time they had ever experienced intercourse stated that it had definitely been a disappointment. It was only gradually that sensuality was awakened and gave rise to pleasure. One said, "I felt absolutely nothing, but I was so happy to belong to him."[4]

A U.S. study of the sexual behavior of high-school students revealed that for both boys and girls those *least likely* to involve themselves in promiscuous sex behavior were those who felt most secure in their sexual identity.[5] Many youths seem to be experimenting in coitus to calm their anxieties about their sexual identity.

Any effort to understand the distinctive sensations experienced by males and females when they are subjected to sexual stimulation leads us into physiology and psychology. There is still a good deal of argument, but here are a few of the relevant findings that are widely accepted.

During the first few months of life, the male fetus and female fetus are indistinguishable. Both have a sex gland and a genital tubercle that seem identical. As the unborn baby's body develops, the sex gland becomes the ovary in the female and becomes the testis in the male; and the genital tubercle becomes the clitoris in the female and the penis in the male.

In some way, the sexual responsiveness of both the male and the female seems to be related to hormones, though the relationship is far from clear. The so-called female hormone is estrogen and the male hormone is androgen. I say "so-called" because both hormones exist in about equal amounts in pre-adolescent boys and girls. After puberty, girls show a marked increase in their estrogen level and the boys an increase in their androgen level.[6] The so-called female hormone, however, apparently has little effect upon sexual desire. The male hormone androgen is much more clearly related to sexual desire in both males *and* females. John Money, medical psychologist at Johns Hopkins, reports that there is considerable evidence that androgen is the libido hormone for both men and women. It influences the intensity or urgency of sexual desire. He points out that when males are given estrogen, they usually report a loss of sexual desire and potency. On the other hand, when normal women are given androgen treatments, their libidinal intensity frequently is increased, sometimes to unfamiliarly high levels.[7] Money relates that a typist of one of his manuscripts disclosed that young men about town who wished to "make" their young female friends were spiking the girls' martinis with the male hormone testosterone (a form of androgen) one week in advance.

One thing that perplexed researcher Alfred Kinsey and his associates was that even androgen levels did not clearly and closely correlate with what they had discovered to be the frequencies of sexual activity in the sexes. He and his colleagues became greatly interested by the fact that the presence of compounds called 17-ketosteroids showed rather striking correlations with the level of sexual response in both the male and the female, and were found in considerably higher quantities in the male than in the female from the age of 13 on.[8] Some of the 17-ketosteroids are androgens, the so-called male hormone.

The areas of the human body on which caresses are most likely to arouse erotic feelings (the erogenous zones) are those rich in nerve endings. They are pretty much the same in males and females. The mouth is nearly as often a source of sexual arousal as the genitalia. Some of the other erogenous zones are the nape of the neck, the throat, the palms of the hand, the tips of the fingers, the thin skin on the inner surface of the thighs. The breasts of both the male and female are somewhat more sensitive than other parts of the body, but American males greatly overestimate the importance of the female breast as an area to be caressed if they wish or hope that she will become erotically aroused.[9]

The Kinsey investigators were impressed that males seemed vastly more affected by psychologic stimuli as a source of arousal than females. Erotic pictures, erotic talk, and erotic thoughts were considerably more likely to generate sexual arousal in males than in females.[10] Females who become aroused apparently are aroused primarily by caressing (and endearing words).

Kinsey noted that despite all the lusty magazines produced for male readers revealing the female figure, he could find almost no comparable magazines of male nudes produced for female readers. Those magazines that do appear showing male nudes are produced, he concluded, primarily for males with a special interest in looking at male nudes. His group was also impressed with the fact that of the thousands of unpublished amateur documents containing erotic material it examined over a 15-year period, only 3 had been written by females. Since Kinsey's group made their observations, we have seen a new phenomenon—possibly reflecting a new assertiveness, if not eroticism, in females—of young ladies writing successful novels built largely on boudoir scenes. But in any case, the Kinsey investigators noted that three-quarters of the males who were exposed to "portrayals of sexual action" became erotically aroused; whereas only a third of the females, so exposed, reported any notable feelings of arousal.[11]

Caressing, however, is another matter. Kinsey and his associates related, "Females appear to be as capable as males of being aroused by tactile stimuli; they appear as capable as males of responding to the point of orgasm. Their responses are not slower than those of the average male if there is a sufficiently continuous tactile stimulation."[12]

Other investigators have placed similar stress upon the important role of touch to the woman. Phyllis and Eberhard Kronhausen, sexual researchers, have contended that women need the feeling of being touched. The French observer

Simone de Beauvoir suggests that to a woman sexual pleasure is a kind of magic spell demanding abandon. She explains that "if words or movements oppose the magic of caresses, the spell is broken."[13] And in 1965, John Money, in summarizing some of the known facts about human sex behavior, stated, "Men appear to be more responsive to the visual and narrative erotic stimuli and images, women to be more dependent on touch."[14]

Virtually all the evidence available suggests that the sex drive (but not necessarily the capacity to respond sexually) is more keenly felt by males than females, at least until well into adulthood. In 1959, Indiana University sociologist Clifford Kirkpatrick summed up the evidence by stating, "In our culture, at least, males on the average have an earlier, a more intense, more uniform, more genital, more rhythmic, more continuous, and more promiscuous sex drive than females."[15]

Kinsey found that contemporary males, by the time of marriage, had experienced about 7 times as many orgasms as females. The famous Kinsey chart on total "outlets" or orgasms per week, regardless of stimulus, for *single* males and females showed that the average for the females never rose above once every two weeks from age 13 through age 60. For the single males, the average soared up at the age of 13 to nearly 2½ per week and then declined over the decades until by age 60 the rate of the single male was about the same as that of the single female. A number of investigators have been told by unmarried women who had never experienced coitus that one of the main reasons was simple lack of desire for it.

One biological factor that may make the young male's sex drive more intense than the female's (though this is argued) is the build-up in the male of seminal fluid and the regularity of its discharge one way or another. There is no comparable regularity of outlet among females.

There is persuasive evidence that among females, orgasm is likely to be a learned experience. The Kinsey finding that after marriage female orgasms showed a sixfold increase strongly suggests that learning takes place in the marriage bed. A good many adolescent girls do experience orgasm, even multiple orgasm, and the number may be increasing. But family specialist Frank Shuttleworth, of New York City, concluded in 1959, after a review of available data, that in general the development of female sexuality is a slow and gradual process of learning to respond erotically—and of learning to respond with an orgasm.[16]

It also appears that sex desire in women, at least until well after marriage, tends to be well diffused throughout the body, whereas it is localized in the male. The all-pervasive sensuality that has been characteristic in women was caught, perhaps intuitively, by author John O'Hara when he had a girl say during intercourse, "I am all around you."

With both sexes there is a very great range in the degree of sexual desire or drive or tension from individual to individual; and it is wrong to assume that most males find their desires difficult to handle. There is for males, after all, the ever available outlet of nocturnal emission. Family specialist Lester Kirkendall has found in counseling boys who complained of frequent sexual tension that they seemed commonly to be the type who experienced much *general* frustration and tension in their lives. On the other hand, strong, virile boys who were self-accepting and persons of achievement rarely mentioned difficulty in handling sexual drives.

Among females, it has been found that the same kind of women who enjoy eating are also more likely to enjoy sex. At the annual meeting of the Eastern Psychological Association in 1967, Seymour Fisher and Howard Osofsky, of the State University of New York in Syracuse, reported a year-long study of 42 women in their late twenties, most of them wives. They found an almost dramatic positive correlation between sexual responsiveness and a general positive attitude toward food and eating. The women who enjoyed sexual activity also tended to be physically active people.

There appear to be very great differences by sex in the ages when sexual arousal is first likely to be felt. Several studies have indicated that for males the median age for first arousal is before the age of 8, whereas for females it is closer to the age of 16. Preadolescent males by the age of 12 are likely to be having vastly more experience with sexual arousal than are preadolescent females at the same age. The Kinsey investigators found that the peak in outlets for boys occurred in the late teens, for women in the late twenties. And this high rate in the late twenties seemed to involve almost entirely married women, with the pace presumably set, at least at first, by the husband. In 1966 sociologist Jessie Bernard offered this analysis of the sexuality of teen-age girls: "Most young women in their teens, although suffused with sexuality, are not driven by strong genital urges. If they had their way, most would not feel compelled to seek genital sex relations. Since most are married by their early twenties, premarital virginity is no handicap for them. They want caresses, tenderness, sexual appreciation; they want the interested attention of men; the relations they want are playful, meaningful, but biologically superficial."[17]

The head of sex education in Swedish schools, Gosta Rodhe, put it this way: "Girls are not at all eager to start intercourse at an early age. I think it's a matter of biology but it also might be due somewhat to culture. The girls are more interested in the total social relationship than the specific sexual experience."

A large majority of lower-class Negro girls have experienced intercourse by their mid-teens. Many U.S. whites would conclude that these girls happily accept premarital coitus since many are closer in centuries to the Natural Man state. Sociologist Lee Rainwater, who has studied lower-class sexual behavior extensively, rejects as a myth the "natural man" explanation. He finds that such girls, despite the indicated high incidence, are dealing with boys who are highly competitive among themselves for sexual triumphs, and tend to be extremely exploitive in their attitude toward the girls. In 1968 he explained, "Negro girls who do engage in sexual relations in response to the strong lines of the boys who 'rap to' them often do not seem to find any particular gratification in sexual relations, but rather engage in sex as a test and symbol of their maturity and their ability to be in the swim of things. Over time, a certain proportion of these girls do develop their own appreciation of sexual relations, and engage in them out of desire as well as intrinsic reasons."

Much that we have been reporting might seem, at first glance, to conflict with the findings reported in 1966 by William H. Masters and Virginia E. Johnson in their now celebrated study. They found that in the laboratory setting males were responsible for 65 percent of the failures to achieve orgasm in the photographed encounters. Perhaps the apparent conflict is not as significant as it first seems. All the participants performing before the Masters-Johnson cameras were coitally experienced men and women, many of them married, and virtually all were at least in their twenties or thirties. We might also surmise that most of the women who would volunteer for this project were confident of their capacity to respond to stimulation—especially continuous tactile stimulation—with orgasm. Thus the findings were largely anticipated by the Kinsey findings cited earlier. (See Note 12 of this chapter.) As for the males' higher rate of failure in coitus while on camera, this might readily be explained by the pressures of performance in attaining and maintaining tumescence while the cameras were running.

Winston Ehrmann, in his massive study of dating behavior of college students, felt that his single most important finding was that the female's sexual expression is primarily and profoundly related to being in love and to going steady. He concluded that the female, unlike the male, seems to need love to release the more direct genital aspects of erotic behavior.[18]

Tying sexual expression with romanticism, of course, has its hazards, too. Girls may rationalize that they are in love to justify going to bed with male after male.

All of the above evidence about the male and female sexual responsiveness offers the strong implication that we will have a more harmonious society if boys better understand the sexual nature of girls.

Mary Calderone, of SIECUS, suggests that every boy if he contemplates making serious advances to a girl should ask himself whether this girl is ready for this kind of sexual awakening. Wallace Fulton, former president of SIECUS, has had many dozens of sessions with teenagers where sex differences have been freely discussed. He recalls:

"At our meetings teen-age girls would turn to the boys and say, 'You see, you see why I can't do it.' I've heard that frequently. Boys can't believe girls are not as pantingly hot as the boy is. When he begins to understand the physiological differences, he begins to understand the girl."

And there would seem also to be some implications in all this for girls who in our society are besieged in the communications media to look and act sexually provocative from age 12 on. While the girl may be pleasantly fascinated and exhilarated by being touched by a boy, she may unwittingly be exciting him to the point where his sex drive is uncomfortably stimulated.

In speaking with girls, Mary Calderone sometimes challenges them to consider what their impact is upon boys when they swish their cute little hips inside their cute tight little dresses. Girls concede that they often have done this and admit they didn't realize they might be provoking boys to the point where it might be bothersome.

Males and females, whether married or not, will have a more enjoyable relationship, too, if they take a relaxed view of the simultaneous orgasm. Sometimes it happens, sometimes it doesn't. And sometimes one partner experiences the orgasm some seconds or moments after the other. One of the more interesting comments encountered in this connection was made by a working-class wife, as reported by sociologist Mirra Komarovsky. The woman was asked if her sexual relations with her husband often left her feeling disappointed. She said, "Well, even if I don't work up to going off like a factory whistle, it's still almost always nice."

It is in these areas of helping young people understand their own sexuality and the sexuality of people of the other sex that a well-conceived sex education program can make a major contribution, though a well-conceived program will embrace the totality of male-female relationships. Most sex education still comes to youngsters from their age-peers and consequently is likely to be weak on these points. Often the young pick up their working knowledge of sexuality rather rapidly during a wrestling bout in the back seat of an automobile, or from wisecracks—often fantasy-loaded—heard in locker rooms.

Although sex education is now much in the news, it has prehistoric roots. In many primitive societies, when both boys and girls reach puberty, an older member of the tribe gives them a thorough briefing on passion arousal and conception. In Samoa, Margaret Mead reports, as young males and females become ready, the girls are chosen for first love affairs by older boys who have been initiated into full sex experience by older girls.[19] Until quite recently, at least, a somewhat comparable procedure has been followed fairly widely in France. Laurence Wylie, Harvard professor of the French civilization, relates, "A traditional means has evolved in France for the indoctrination of young people in the expression of their sexual feelings. The adolescent boy receives the experience and training from an older woman and then, in turn, initiates the girl—supposedly his virgin wife—in the art he has learned."[20]

This procedure has been depicted in French movies and in the novels of such writers as Colette. Recent depictions, as by Françoise Sagan, however, suggest the situation may have changed. Sagan has depicted older men seducing quite young girls.

The question that inevitably is raised by adults, whenever there are proposals to introduce sex education, is whether the giving of such information may stimulate sex experimentation and tacitly seem to give permission to such experiments. I suspect that the advocates of sex education, imbued with the clear worthiness of their cause, too readily deny that this can happen. Going still further, some argue that such education will promote restraint and more decisions to wait until marriage. The truth seems to be that, if sex education is judged simply by the increase or decrease of incidence of premarital coitus, the evidence is still too fragmentary to reach any firm conclusion. An official of SIECUS has stressed: "Sex education is not disaster insurance."

Perhaps premarital pregnancy, however, may be reduced. In Washington, D.C., two schools were considering introducing a sex education program. One finally refused, and the other accepted the program. At the school accepting it, the high rate of illegitimate births was cut in the first year. At the other, with no program, the rate of illegitimacy continued to rise.[21] While this was a small study, the evidence is certainly worth noting. Whether premarital coitus was reduced would be more difficult to determine.

Some suggest that if knowledge about conception-control techniques encouraged sex relations, we would logically see a much higher rate of premarital coitus among college students than among high-school drop-outs, since collegians are assumed to be generally more knowledgeable. The evidence points to a much higher incidence among the drop-outs. But there may well be other factors involved, such as social conditioning and a greater self-discipline among collegians that enables them to delay gratification.

On the other side, we have the evidence in the studies at the "people's colleges" in Sweden, by Georg Karlsson, that during the recent period when sex education had been compulsory in Swedish schools there was a quite considerable increase in reported premarital coitus by students. But again, we should be cautious about jumping to conclusions because accompanying the compulsory sex education was a general growth in acceptance by the Swedish people of premarital coitus. Also the actual effective implementation at various schools of the national program appears to have been spotty.

A study of sex education programs in Minnesota high schools indicated that principals of 9 out of 10 schools reported having some kind of family-life education. It is probable that many of the so-called sex education programs were simply discussions of hygiene, or reproduction, or were so moralistic in tone that the students ignored them. But, in any case, it may be noteworthy that two-thirds of the marriages between high-school students at these schools involved girls who were pregnant before marriage.[22]

Two authorities at the Institute for Sex Research—at least one a strong advocate of sex education—have recently stated, "few people take seriously the assumption that sex education will lower rates of illegitimacy, venereal disease, or promiscuity. . . ."[23] Another authoritative statement comes from Michael Schofield, who studied the sex habits of more than 1000 English teenagers. He states, "Sex education did not seem to prevent premarital intercourse or to encourage it. The experienced boys, like the other boys, wished they had been told more about sex at school and by their parents."[24]

Whether sex education has the effect of increasing or decreasing sexual experimentation—or has no effect either way —probably depends upon the specific program and the competence of the people handling it. In any case, we are on more solid ground if the major goal of sex education is not to affect the *quantity* of sexual encounters among youngsters, but rather to affect the *quality* of the attitudes the younger people have toward sexuality as they move toward adulthood.

Another argument centers on who should be entrusted to handle the sex education of young people.

The traditional argument is that it is best left to the parents. In actuality, some but not all parents can handle the "plumbing" aspects of sex education by helping them understand physiology, and all can, in the rearing of children, inculcate important life values. However, it may be excruciatingly awkward for them to offer their adolescents plausible guidance on specific behavior unless they are prepared (as so many Scandinavian parents are) to assume their children will become involved in premarital intercourse. Another awkwardness is that, in such talks with their children, the parents find they must present a sense of their own sexuality to the children and admit to themselves the sexual nature of their children.[26]

It used to be fashionable to suggest that youngsters get their sex education by having a heart-to-heart talk with the family doctor. This has been unsatisfactory, at least until recently, because beyond giving information on hygiene and contraception, doctors have usually been beyond their depth in discussing sexuality and interpersonal relationships. Many doctors are surprisingly shy and inhibited about sexual behavior. The situation is improving now, as more than 30 medical schools are developing programs to help medical students understand the emotional aspects of sexuality—and to be comfortable in discussing them. As recently as 1965, only 3 medical schools had such programs!

Some have held that ministers are best prepared to handle sex education, since they can offer guidance on ideals and moral values. But often their counsel has consisted of a rationale for restraint until marriage, and many of today's young accept such counsel with reservations. A more important difficulty is that perhaps half of all adolescents—and that half includes most of the youngsters likely to experiment—are not active enough in church affairs to come under effective guidance. It should be noted, however, that the clergymen are changing quite dramatically from the old attitude that sex is nasty to offering youngsters information and thoughts that stress the positive aspects of human sexuality.

Schools would seem to be the most logical place for a fully integrated program of sex education to be attempted; and in the past few years, there has been an enormous increase in the introduction of sex education into both public and private schools. The National Association of Independent Schools has encouraged all its members to introduce sex education. A number of public schools as widely separated as Anaheim, Calif., and Evanston and Downers Grove, Ill., have sex education programs that are broad and thorough and are handled by competent, relaxed personnel. Some start right in kindergarten. The good schools have teachers who are comfortable handling the subject, and they call a uterus a uterus instead of "Mommy's tummy."

On the other hand, many school courses are still handled as "hygiene," or biology, or health talks by the school doctor and tend to put human sexuality into a constricted, physiological setting. Also many teachers expected to handle the instruction in the schools feel even more uncomfortable than most doctors and parents in talking about sex with youngsters. But still the situation has vastly improved since I was in high school. The only sex education officially presented at my school was a sex-segregated talk by a doctor who spent most of the half-hour describing the "two beasts lurking in the halls" of our school. Those beasts, it turned out, were syphilis and gonorrhea.

A new forthrightness in course content and in available educational materials has recently become apparent. This should help win the interest and confidence of a generation that believes strongly in the motto, "Tell it like it is." It also should help those handling counseling and education to be relaxed in discussing human sexuality. A dramatic example of the trend is evident in the pioneering course Family Studies 100 being offered in 1968 at the University of Minnesota by the veteran marriage counselor Gerhard Neubeck. The course title is "Human Sexual Behavior," and Neubeck offers a forthright discussion of the subject. The course is for upperclass and graduate students who are preparing for careers where they will be involved professionally with sexual matters. There has been a long waiting list for the Fall course. Another example of the new tell-it-like-it-is approach is a book addressed to boys entitled *Boys and Sex* that has become available to schools (and the general public). It is by marriage counselor Wardell Pomeroy, a long-time colleague of Alfred Kinsey. The book is so honest and realistic that many elders hearing about it have been startled. One important point that Pomeroy makes is, "Penises and vaginas can't love each other; only people can do that."

Sex education of the broadest sort is badly needed. My impression is that sex education is most effective—whether handled by teachers, parents, ministers, doctors, or respected older young people—if those doing the teaching have been made both comfortable and strong in insights by special college training or attending special short courses such as the one held at the University of Connecticut during the summer of 1967 for teachers, clergymen, and anyone else interested. By

1968 the number of universities sponsoring summer workshops rose to 40. The emphasis should be as much on attitudes as on knowledge. Eleanore B. Luckey, who organized the Connecticut course, believes that "Sexual maturity rather than sexual normality may be the better goal for sex education." It helps, too, if the schools can receive some guidance in setting up their programs by independent organizations specializing in sex education such as the Sex Information and Education Council of the U.S. (SIECUS), whose executive director, Mary S. Calderone, is a person of considerable insight. She is a dynamic, straight-speaking grandmother and a Quaker who was formerly medical director of the Planned Parenthood Federation of America. The national board of SIECUS represents all significant views and positions on appropriate sex behavior and includes representatives from the major faiths and all pertinent academic disciplines.

Although SIECUS has been in existence only since the mid-1960s, it has received hundreds of requests for speakers and for setting up programs. It considers its primary role that of cross-fertilization of ideas and of being a clearing house, and acting in a consultative capacity for other organizations. After one session that Mary Calderone had with a group of high-school youngsters, a 10th grade boy commented, "I never before realized there was more to sex than just doing it."

It is my impression that any good program of education about male-female intimacy, whoever handles it, should include these 4 objectives:

• It should help the young person understand his sex organs and his sex feelings and the organs and feelings of persons of the other sex.

• It should help boys and girls understand the role that sexuality is probably going to play in enriching their lives through relationships with at least one particular person of the other sex.

• It should help young people understand how married people now are learning to have only wanted children and the marvel of that new possibility.

• It should help young people become aware of the possible consequences of sexual acts engaged in before marriage. They should be provided with enough insights about values to help them in their personal decision-making.

We will explore this last point in the next two chapters.

CHAPTER 25

Should Sex Freedom Now Be Left to Individual Choice?

"If two people desire to have intimate sexual relations then they should be very careful and obtain the proper contraceptives, but there is no reason why they should restrain themselves." From editorial in campus newspaper, *The Gazette*, The University of Western Ontario.

Young people in the U.S.A. and a number of other Western countries have been more and more insistently asserting their right to express their sexuality in whatever way they choose, as long as nobody is hurt. It is a part of the very widespread feeling that they are entitled to independence in their personal lives, and that permissiveness is the only reasonable norm if two persons wish discreetly to express their individuality through sexual acts. As indicated, this was a viewpoint that students frequently offered in their amplifying comments to our College Survey. And social critic John Keats, after visiting several dozen campuses, came away with the conclusion: "Nearly all students and most faculty members today believe that sexual intercourse is not subject to moral judgment."

One noon in 1965, when I entered the Student Union of the University of California in Los Angeles, an attractive girl behind a table offered me a leaflet being distributed. It was entitled "Legalize Homogenitalism." It asserted the moral right of individuals to engage in an imaginatively wide variety of sexual acts, many of them illegal, and stated as its first contention: "Where there is no victim, every act is morally right."

John Gagnon of the Institute for Sex Research, who is no

conservative on sexual matters, states that any kind of liberation of the sexual instinct carries with it an enormous responsibility.

A number of noted researchers and academicians have cited evidence and viewpoints sharply in conflict on this issue of whether it is now time that Western societies move to a clearly more permissive attitude toward individual sex behavior.

A number of the more enthusiastic advocates of sex freedom today draw their arguments from the evidence of anthropologists and historians of societies where sexual activity seems relatively uninhibited. They cite, for example, the evidence of the cross-cultural studies by anthropologists George Murdock and William Stephens. Nearly three-quarters of the societies in Murdock's large sample permit premarital coitus. Stephens, in his smaller analysis of 39 societies, found premarital intercourse permitted in more than half of them.[1]

Hundreds of thousands of college students have read, with fascination, anthropologist Margaret Mead's account of the sex life of the Samoans in the South Seas.[2] She found the Samoans treating sexual intimacy as a delightful way to pass the time. There was a preoccupation with sex, with suggestive dancing and salacious songs. Mead stated that the Samoans she encountered rated romantic fidelity in terms of days or weeks at most and were inclined to scoff at tales of lifelong devotion. They viewed the Christian attitude toward virginity with complete skepticism, although the wooing of a virgin was considered more zestful and challenging. She reported, "Premarital affairs and extramarital affairs were conducted with enough lightness not to threaten the reliable sex relationships between married couples." The expectation of virginity was not imposed upon all girls but rather confined to a ceremonial princess of the village. She was usually required to show evidence of the blood of virginity at marriage. However, she might, if necessary, use chicken blood.

There is anthropological evidence that for some primitive societies coitus is the equivalent of the concert, the novel, the TV show, and the Saturday evening binge. Some observers contend that a case can be made for treating sexual enjoyment at the level of ballroom dancing. A turn-of-the-century gymnast using the pseudonym of Weckerle worked out, with the aid of gymnastic mats and horizontal bars, 531 postural variants for achieving healthy sexual pleasure. He contended,

"Too much sex never wore out anyone, except a weakling who is out of training."

In the United States, one of the most articulate advocates of all-out sensuality as a way of life is the classics professor at the University of Rochester, Norman O. Brown, whose books, *Love's Body* and *Life Against Death,* are favorites of many college undergraduates. Brown advocates a rebellion against all the restraining values that Western societies have developed, and proposes a return to a Dionysian world of sensuality and a return to innocence with an emphasis upon uninhibited expression of sexuality.

Probably the most famous American advocate of sex freedom is psychologist Albert Ellis, cited earlier. In his widely read book, *Sex Without Guilt,* he makes a bow to objectivity by listing 17 disadvantages in allowing premarital intercourse and then lists 17 advantages.[3] One soon perceives where his enthusiasm lies, because in evaluating each of the 17 disadvantages, he scoffs or shows that each is outdated (such as hazard of pregnancy), or is a dubious proposition. He is not impressed, for example, by the listed disadvantages of "guilt and anxiety." Today, he argues, many people are becoming anxious and disturbed because they are *not* copulating before marriage. As for the alleged "horrors" of sex without love he states, "Sex without love, moreover, is hardly a heinous crime, and appears to be quite delightful and to add immeasurably to the lives of literally millions of individuals."

When he takes up the 17 advantages of premarital coitus, his assessments become clearly more enthusiastic. He lists such advantages or gains as:

- Sexual release.
- Psychosexual release.
- Sexual competence.
- Ego enhancement.
- Adventure and experience.
- Improved marital selection.
- Heterosexual democratization.
- Decrease in jealousy.
- De-emphasis on pornography. (The Swedish experience would not support him here.)
- Sex is fun.

Some of the advocates of sex freedom include freedom for extramarital, as well as premarital, intimacy. There is less anthropological support here. Murdock found that four-fifths of his societies had rules against adultery, and Stephens found almost as high a proportion. Some advocates of sex freedom, however, suggest that the new mode of life in Western society —with the pill, with the sexualization of females, and with the considerable mobility of couples—makes extramarital affairs acceptable and even desirable. Ellis, in his listing of pros and cons of premarital sex, dismisses the argument that it would produce an increase in subsequent adultery by more or less asking, so what? He states, "There is some evidence that adultery may aid, save, and stabilize a marriage rather than disrupt it and lead to its dissolution." He contends that if married men and women would stop viewing each other as exclusive property, there would be a great decrease in violent jealousy.

Ohio State sociologist John Cuber, in reporting his findings regarding adultery among the hundreds of successful Americans whose marriages he studied, said triangles were not necessarily destructive to marriage. "As a matter of fact," he explained, "both for cases in which the spouse knew about the affair and where the affair was secret, we can document with a long list instances in which spousal relationships remain at least as good qualitatively as within the average pair without adultery."[4]

Some conservatives argue that the United States is headed for a fall comparable to the decline of Rome because of the growing preoccupation with sex. It is true that in imperial Rome there was, at times, a widespread acceptance of nonmarital sexuality, at least for males. Dean Robert Fitch, of the Pacific School of Religion, is one who has contended that the decline of Rome coincided with a breakdown in sexual morality. But psychologist and sexologist Isadore Rubin good-naturedly scoffs at the certitude of those pointing to a Roman parallel in moral decline. He cites a theory, now being discussed by some geneticists, that the decline of Rome might well be attributed in large part to the fact that the elite upper classes ate food cooked in expensive lead pots, whereas the lower classes had to use cheaper crockery. Under this theory, the elite of Rome were gradually brought down by lead poisoning, not sexual license.

But let us look at some of the more noteworthy contentions that sex freedom is indeed hazardous, and that sexual restraint may promote the best functioning of both society and the individual. Some greatly respected figures in sociology, anthropology, history, sexology, family counseling, and psychiatry have, by their statements or research, raised cautionary questions. Since sexual permissiveness is so clearly in the ascendancy today, especially among younger people, we shall look at these views and findings with some thoroughness.

Stephens, in his cross-cultural studies, offered evidence suggesting there might be a connection between the fact that the majority of primitive tribes are sexually permissive and their primitiveness. He states, "Primitive tribes tend to have greater sexual freedom than do 'civilized' communities. . . . People in kingdoms tend to have tighter sex restrictions. . . . Kingdoms, in contrast to tribes, seem to have less in the way or orgiastic ceremonials, drunkenness, and laughter and singing. . . ."[5]

The anthropologist who explored this possible connection most thoroughly was J. D. Unwin, a scholar at Oxford and Cambridge who wrote a massive book in 1934, called *Sex and Culture*. David Mace, who did his doctoral work at Cambridge under the same professor who had guided Unwin in his research, recalls Unwin as a brilliant young man who died prematurely. Unwin's book appears to be almost forgotten in the United States and England. It is out of print. I finally found a copy at an American university, and I was apparently the volume's first reader, since the pages were uncut.

Unwin conducted a massive investigation of the sex regulations characterizing 80 uncivilized societies and also a number of historically advanced societies such as the Sumerians, the Babylonians, the Hellenes, the Romans, the Moors, the Anglo-Saxons, and the English. He investigated sex regulations covering both premarital virginity and postmarital fidelity. For the primitive societies, he tried to assess the degree to which they had advanced toward thoughtfulness. And the civilized societies he measured in terms of "expansive social energy," as displayed in the Roman conquest of Carthage, and the "productive energy" displayed in the way the Athenians built the Acropolis and the Moors invented algebra.

The aim of his study was to test the conjecture of analytical psychologists of his time that if social regulations forbid direct satisfaction of the sexual impulse, the inhibition causes an expression in another way. The conjecture was that the placing of a compulsory check upon sexual impulses, by limiting opportunity, tends to produce thought, reflection, and energy.

His conclusions had startling implications. He concluded, for example, that the amount of cultural ascent of the 80 primitive societies closely paralleled the amount of limitation they placed upon nonmarital sexual opportunity. And he concluded that virtually all the civilized societies—such as the Babylonians, the Athenians, the Romans, the Anglo-Saxons, and the English—"started their historical careers in a state of absolute monogamy."[6]

The one exception where a polygamous society displayed great productive energy, he found, was the Moors.

In speaking of the vigorous societies that built civilizations he said that in each case the compulsory continence arising from the adoption of absolute monogamy (and premarital chastity) produced great social energy. "The group within the society which suffered the greatest continence displayed the greatest energy, and dominated the society. When absolute monogamy was preserved only for a short time, the energy was only expansive, but when the rigorous tradition was inherited by a number of generations the energy became productive."[7] His findings led him to make this provocative comment:

"Any human society is free to choose either to display great energy or to enjoy sexual freedom; the evidence is that it cannot do both for more than one generation."[8]

In referring to the fall of Rome, he stated that the Teutons who overran the Western Roman Empire possessed, in regard to sexual regulations, the same monogamous ideas that the Romans had once possessed and later discarded.

In the Unwin view, it would be hazardous for us to try now to assess the impact of the permissive sex behavior spreading in many Western societies today. He stated, "The full effect of an extension or limitation of sexual opportunity, whether in the whole society or in one of the social strata of the society, is not revealed for at least three generations after its adoption" (or roughly a century).

David Mace suggests that expansive energy—in contrast to the more civilized productive energy—can be something of a nuisance in the world today when expansiveness threatens general annihilation. Mace says he was influenced in his own thinking, to some degree, by Unwin's thesis. Regarding the Unwin study as a scientific investigation, Mace has made this comment, "His work was flamboyant on a colossal scale. . . . I think there is something fundamentally sound about his general position. . . . But I recognize that his scientific method does not have the precision which the rigid disciplines of today call for. He is really throwing out a fascinating hypothesis, and supporting it with a rather disordered mass of evidence."

I invited an anthropologist greatly respected for his studies of a variety of human cultures to give me, confidentially, his frank evaluation of Unwin's contribution. In his letter of reply he stated, "I regard Unwin's study as a useful one, even though I do not agree with some of his major conclusions. It is occasionally quoted today, although I do not believe it is generally regarded as especially authoritative."

We asked students in our College Survey:

What do you think of the thesis of the late anthropologist J. D. Unwin? He concluded after studying about 90 societies that the frustration of quite strict sexual regulations has produced the social energy which in turn has been directly associated with Man's greatest advances upward toward rationality, thoughtful speculation and higher civilization.

MAY WELL BE TRUE ___ DON'T KNOW ___
DOUBT ___ PURE NONSENSE ___.

In both the U.S. and international samples there was never more than a third of the male or female students who checked "May well be true." The amplifying comments of students were almost entirely skeptical. Either they felt he had put too much emphasis upon sexual frustration or they felt that rationality and thoughtful speculation were not the only hallmarks of higher civilization. The student who made an analysis for me of all the comments reported, "These students seem to look on Unwin's theory as one that is based on a preromantic theory that civilization should be based on rationalization, that man's id must be repressed. These students cannot accept this. They are in a sense romantics, they believe that civilization cannot be formed by the ego alone, they believe that the id must be allowed to function, they are strong believers in the emotions and the fullness of life."

Let us then turn to some other scholars who have offered strongly cautionary evidence about the hazards of sexual permissiveness.

In 1965 Arnold J. Toynbee, the British historian who has spent much of his life studying the civilizations of man, advised me, "I myself believe, on the historical evidence, that the later we can postpone the age of sexual consciousness, the better able we are to educate ourselves. As I see it, this feature in the mores of the Western people has been one of the causes of their comparative success during the last centuries." I had gotten in touch with him because earlier he had expressed public concern about some of the trends relating to sexual behavior in Western society in recent decades.[9] He had stated:

"While we are lowering the age of sexual awareness, we are prolonging the length of education. How can the young be expected to give their minds to study during these sex-haunted years. . . . I admire the 19th century West's success in postponing the age of sexual awakening, sexual experience, and sexual infatuation far beyond the age of physical puberty. You may tell me that this is against nature; but to be human consists precisely of transcending nature—in overcoming the biological limitations that we have inherited from our prehuman ancestors."

The sex researcher Alfred Kinsey was dispassionate in his viewpoint toward sex behavior and tended to scoff at moralistic positions regarding sex; but it should be noted that he and his associates did report a fact that might be interpreted as relevant to Toynbee's concern about early sex experiences (although Kinsey might have quarreled with Toynbee's use of the phrase "sexual awakening"). Kinsey and his associates found that the educational level that a male achieves shows a marked correlation with the pattern of his sex behavior. (It was less evident for females.) The males who had gone on to college, in the Kinsey group, had depended mainly on masturbation and considerably less on coitus for their premarital "outlets"; whereas males who had not gone beyond grade school reported 5 times as much premarital coitus as the college males.[10] This pattern becomes evident in prospective college students while they are still in their mid-teens.

A long-esteemed sociologist, Carle C. Zimmerman, while at Harvard in the 1940s, traced the development of the family in the Western world and concluded that crises in the family tended to coincide with convulsions or crises of the civilizations of the same time. He focused, in particular, on 3 periods of crisis: the Greece of about 300 B.C., the Rome of about 300 A.D., and the Western world of about 1910–1945. He concluded that in each of these 3 periods—lead pots or not—the family showed many of the same symptoms of crisis as an institution. Some of these identical evidences of crisis, in his view, were: Youth in revolt, a high degree of sensualism in public life, and a high rate of marital disruption. More recently, in March, 1968, Boston anthropologist Theodore N. Ferdinand wrote in *The Annals* of The American Academy of Political and Social Sciences about the analogy of ancient Rome and present-day America. He observed that in both cases, "The harsh ascetic standards of the founding period were crumbling in favor of an opportunistic code in which the future and its obligations were gladly sacrificed for the pleasures of the moment." (It might be noted also that anthropologist Charles Winick has contended that the final centuries of power of both ancient Greece and Rome were characterized by a widespread blurring of sex roles.)

A noted colleague of Zimmerman's at Harvard in the mid-century period, who also became known for his dim view of sexual permissiveness, was Pitirim Sorokin. Sociologist Sorokin paid high tribute to J. D. Unwin and accepted the Unwin thesis that the pattern of sexual behavior in a culture decisively influences the culture's progress or regress, and that great cultures are most likely to flourish where there is a strong emphasis upon premarital chastity and postmarital fidelity. Sorokin went on to contend that "excessive sexual activity, particularly when it is illicit, has markedly deleterious effects."[11]

The notion that a draining of seminal fluid in males brings some weakening of the individual body has long been widely held. Some American Indians on the nights before battle were admonished not to sleep with their wives. Russian athletes before recent Olympic games were required to lead sexually Spartan lives for some weeks. And David and Vera Mace have reported that throughout the entire Eastern world, they found the view tenaciously—if erroneously—held that loss of seminal fluid meant the loss of a man's strength and vitality.[12]

Mace feels that Sorokin went too far in accepting the idea of the physically delibilitating effect of "excess." (If it were true, one might expect unmarried adult males to be healthier than married adult males, which is not supported.)

It is apparently true that for the male the immediate after-effect of the discharge of seminal fluid is frequently a feeling of fatigue, but it is temporary. After discussing this matter with medical sexologists, Mace concluded, "The sexual apparatus, like most other bodily organs or groups of organs, has its own built-in safeguards against over-use that might result in damage. Repeated use of the sexual function, both in men and in women, simply leads to fatigue and a consequent cessation of operating faculty. This creates the need for rest, which soon leads to the complete recovery of functional capacity."[13]

Warren R. Johnson, health educator at the University of Maryland, tested 14 married male former athletes for strength and endurance the morning after they had engaged in coitus. The testing was done on a hand dynometer. These same males performed the same tests at the same time of day six days after they had last experienced coitus. Johnson found no significant differences in the results of the two tests.

David Mace does agree with Sorokin, however, that excessive preoccupation with sex can lead to moral and spiritual degeneration.

There have been some contentions by presumably perceptive people that a high level of sexual activity, married or unmarried, affects creativity (if not physical energy). To author Ernest Hemingway is attributed, by his biographer A. E. Hotchner, the saying "If you make love while you are jamming on a novel, you are in danger of leaving the best part of it in bed." And author Albert Camus in his *Notebooks* stated that sex may not be immoral but it is unproductive and that one can indulge so long as he does not want to produce.

John Cuber and Peggy Harroff in their study of the sex lives of highly successful Americans were impressed that sexual activity seemed to play a relatively insignificant role in the lives of a great many of them. They speculated that there might be something to the concept of sexual sublimation. They explained, "Many of these career-dominated people had channeled almost the whole of their energies into success aspirations."[14]

Some of the most provocative suggestions about the hazards of a hyper-active sexual life have come from noted psychiatrists and psychologists. Here we can start with Sigmund Freud, who, as noted, has been often cited for his theory that neurosis frequently arises from the damming up of the sexual instinct. But elsewhere, Freud was emphatic in stressing the role that sexual restraint has played in the development of civilized societies (much as Unwin suggested). In his *New Introductory Lectures on Psychoanalysis* Freud stated, "We believe that civilization has been built up by sacrifices in gratification of the primitive impulses, and that it is to a great extent forever being recreated as each individual repeats the sacrifice of his instinctual pleasures for the common good. The sexual are amongst the most important of the instinctual forces thus utilized; they are in this way sublimated, that is to say, their energy is turned aside from its sexual goal and diverted toward other ends, no longer sexual and socially more valuable."

Harvard psychologist Henry A. Murray seemed to accept much the same concept of sublimation. In referring to it, he has stated that the sexual instinct is involved in many of the greatest accomplishments of the imagination. Psychologist Oscar Sternbach, of New York, points out that a correct reading of Freud would show that the road to emotional health is not in giving way to one's instincts, but rather in developing the ability to curb them. A few years ago Sternbach revealed to an audience, at the Child Study Association of America, an incident in Freud's life that illuminates the controversy about where Freud stood regarding sexual abstinence. It seems that in one of Freud's lectures to medical students at Vienna University, during the question period, a student asked bluntly:

"Professor, since according to your theory sexual abstinence can bring about anxiety neurosis, would you care to tell us students whether we should or should not abstain from sexual activities?"

Freud seemed taken aback for a moment but then said firmly, "It is my opinion that you should abstain." And then he added quickly, "But not without protest."[15]

Sternbach contends that the crux of the misreading of Freud has rested in the fact that the sexual impulses are essentially infantile. He explained, "This aspect of Freud's theory, namely the stress of the sexual and emotional infantilism behind a neurosis, has never been popularized I am afraid.

And yet in the end it is the most important aspect for therapy and for education. While many educators and parents still stress 'don't frustrate' the stress should be on 'don't infantilize' so that your child learns to bear frustration." Sternbach charged that our consumeristic society has promoted such infantilism. He said that to live by the infantile pleasure principle is no longer publicly chastised as a pathogenic tendency. Instead, he said, it is almost directly praised as a necessary moving force of our economic basis of living, as necessary for the continuation of an affluent society.

The question we set out to explore in this chapter is whether the trend toward sex freedom should be encouraged or should be a matter of social concern. In seeking an answer—beyond what we choose to believe regarding the pros and cons just examined—it seems pertinent to ask 3 questions:

I. What is the impact of a sexually permissive atmosphere upon the society involved?

Unwin, at the least, should make us wary of accepting the popular argument that we can safely be permissive because primitive tribes are. We have to consider what is appropriate to our cultural stage of development. Psychologist O. Hobart Mowrer of the University of Illinois had an interesting comment on the recent fascination of college students with the carefree sexuality of some South Sea Islanders, particularly the Samoans. He explained, "The people of Samoa don't need that *second* decade to acquire their culture and technology." Advanced societies, he felt, do require that their young people devote the second decade of their lives largely to the discipline of learning. He suggested that people who think the South Sea Islanders have the idyllic life should take a close look at the ethnic groups of Hawaii. The native Hawaiians are Polynesians and have much the same approach to life as the Samoans. They tend to be carefree. And, although they were there first on the islands, they're now close to being at the bottom of the totem pole in economic status. Others, such as Orientals, disciplined themselves for long-term advances. The descendants of Chinese coolies imported as plantation labor have, on the average, moved far ahead of the Polynesians socially and economically. Mowrer says the traditional carefree Polynesian style of life is "okay for a stone age technology in a favorable environment."

There is evidence that in advanced societies the sex patterns (on the strict-to-permissive continuum) tend to reflect the broader goals of the society. Historian Arthur Schlesinger, Jr., has pointed out that we think of the Puritans as being prudes. They were, he says, about many things, but not about sex. Hawthorne's prim, moralistic Puritans, he points out, were really more out of the 19th than the 17th century. It was in the 19th century that women were put on a pedestal, and men and women had to visit the art gallery in Philadelphia in separate groups so that they wouldn't be embarrassed by exposure to the classical statues, which often were partially draped. Schlesinger theorizes, "Men absorbed in building a new land in the wilderness had little time or energy left for the cultivation of romantic passions. And, as the nation grew, they seemed to have even less time. By the early part of the 19th century, the making of money had become an obsessive masculine goal." He contends that the males became preoccupied, the females cool.[16]

Sociologist Jessie Bernard, commenting on the same era, suggests, "The Victorian consensus was a suitable one for an age that required a vast investment of human energy in the creation of capital. It gave men the prerogative of determining when and how often they would have sex relations; it put them in a dominant sexual position; it freed them from having to concern themselves about pleasing women. They could concentrate on the important masculine things like work, making money, building factories, expanding markets, creating empires, and the like."[17] While there was a considerable amount of nonmarital coitus in Victorian times, as in all other times, there was an ascetic ideal. Perhaps it is the prevailing *ideal* as much as actual behavior patterns that affects a society's performance.

Much the same motivation as in America's Victorian times may have been behind the Soviet reversal to a strong emphasis upon strict morality to the point of prudery in the 1930s. On the other hand, in assessing the considerable sex freedom in modern Sweden it may be relevant to note that it has been some centuries since Sweden was an expansionist or warring country. Nor has it been weighed down by problems of holding an empire together. Possibly it is relevant here to note that the leaders of a number of the emerging nationalistic countries of Africa have become quite prudish about nudity. Some are even campaigning against above-the-knee skirts.

But what about the startling change of public morality in England, where until the last decade the idealized norm, at least in the middle and upper classes, was restraint and propriety? Quite suddenly, in historic terms, everything seemed to change. There has been a bursting of inhibitions, which seems to have been reflected in the high levels, relatively, of sexual activity and permissive opinions of the English students sampled in our College Survey. (This high level conceivably could be explained partly by the inherent difficulties in trying to get a representative sample of English students from a single university.) But there was the national mood at the time of our sampling that may be pertinent. In the same month that we were sampling there, in 1966, the English political commentator, Henry Fairlie, commented upon the swinging, switched-on, blooming, uninhibited style of life then rocking London. He suggested that Britain, because of its loss of role in the world, had turned inward to enjoy every "ingenuity of indulgence." But he added, hopefully, that there were signs that the more intelligent among the young were seeking a return to some kind of reticence.[18]

It has been frequently asserted that individual guilt and repression are hard on a person. While this may be true, they are not invariably bad for a society. The accumulated wisdom of mankind suggests that rules are needed, even though they create repression for some members, if they are observed, and create guilt for some when they are violated. Mowrer states:

"This whole emphasis today on the individual doing what he or she thinks is right can only lead to moral anarchy. Every known society has a set of regulations for patterning and controlling sexual behavior. A society can't exist that is chaotic."

We certainly have little social need today for extreme asceticism, but it seems reasonable to wonder if widespread promiscuity does indeed promote unstable or ineffectual societies. Until we have better evidence than we do today that it does not, we should view with caution those who advise us to leave any sexual regulation up to each individual. We might bear in mind Unwin's warning that it takes 3 generations for the effect of a significant change in sexual rules to be reflected in the society's social energy.

At the very least, it seems plausible that any society that is preoccupied with play—sexual or otherwise—to the point that it neglects social well-being for the long term is not likely to be a forward-moving society.

2. What is the impact of sex freedom upon the individual?

Here by "freedom" we will confine comment to the types of premarital coitus that are not related to serious courtship. On the positive side, it seems reasonable to claim, as Ellis does, a number of personal benefits. For example, casual premarital sexual encounters, if successful, can be fun for some . . . they can reduce tensions . . . they can produce a sense of accomplishment, of adventure . . . they can make males feel grown up . . . they can improve one's sophistication as a connoisseur of bed partners . . . they can give a young person a sense of independence . . . they can provide girls with proof of sexual equality.

The contention that premarital experience necessarily has the negative effect of creating emotional upset and guilt has not been convincingly supported. Sociologist Harold T. Christensen's findings suggest that it depends upon the environment. In his analysis of contrasting student groups, he found that premarital coital experience had pronounced negative effects of upset and guilt among the group who largely came from environments where there was a strong religious condemnation of the sinfulness of premarital sex. This was in the Intermountain region where Mormonism, in particular, is strong. However, the negative effects were considerably less noticeable among Danish students, even though they had reported a much higher level of sexual experience. In the Danish environment there was considerably less likelihood of social condemnation of premarital coitus.

While an episode of sexual encounter may produce a sensation of adventure, there is no evidence that young people who have such experiences are enjoying life any more than those who do not. This view has been advanced by Dana L. Farnsworth, head of student health services at Harvard. And in 1967, the American Psychiatric Association was advised by psychiatrist Seymour Halleck, of the University of Wisconsin:

"Students who are psychiatric patients are likely to be promiscuous. Many of these patients both male and female can be described as alienated. . . . While the alienated student seems to be leading a stimulating sex life, he frequently complains that it is unsatisfying and meaningless."

The impact of such episodes can be disastrous, of course, if unwanted pregnancy, or venereal disease, or expulsion for breaking rules occurs. But perhaps these hazards are risks that enhance the sense of adventure. So let us look at the more intangible, unfortunate side effects that seem often to occur when varied, casual, sex experiences are sought. We'll put them in terms of losses.

• There is often a loss of capacity to grow and to love in the fullest sense. David Mace suggests that some very bad reasons for keeping an emphasis upon chastity have been advanced, but that at the core of human culture there is one good, sound reason that we ignore at our peril. He explained, "That is the question of individual growth to maturity . . . the integration of sexuality with our capacity to love."

This loss of capacity to grow was emphasized by Paul A. Walters, Jr., Harvard psychiatrist, in addressing the 1964 annual meeting of the American Orthopsychiatric Association. He stated, "The sexual impulse of the adolescent [girl] seems to be somewhat like that of the hysteric, i.e. diffused and unfocused and consisting primarily of vague longings for fusion with the love object. If because of poor impulse control and lack of self-esteem sexual gratification assumes a major role and intercourse does occur . . . lack of selectivity continues. These girls are never able to emancipate themselves from the infantile ties with their mothers."

• There is often a loss of capacity for intensity of feeling. When longing disappears, tenderness usually does, too. Adolescence is a time of enormously heightened sensitivity that can be thrilling to experience. This sensitivity is frequently eroded, if not destroyed, by promiscuity and is frequently enhanced by sexual restraint. The great love affairs of history have typically involved people who were willing to struggle and to wait and to long, as Jacob waited for Rachel for 14 years, according to the Biblical version. Psychiatrist Ralph R. Greenson suggests that waiting and enduring make the loved person more precious. He states, "The cool set is accustomed to quick and easy gratifications. Instant warmth and instant sex make for puny love, cool sex."[19]

• There is often a loss of sense of integrity by those no longer bothered by guilt. Chastity may have lost much of its magic for young people, but fidelity and commitment have not. They talk a great deal about both. The concepts of fidelity and commitment are difficult to integrate with sex freedom.

Additionally, for girls there may be 2 other losses worth noting:

• The loss of mystery. A girl tends to reveal considerably more about her sensual nature in a sexual encounter than the male does. When, on the Yugoslav freighter, I saw teen-age girls in their bikinis rolling about the decks with boys, often a different boy each day, I saw a Scottish woman shake her head in puzzlement. In our discussion she said, "Those girls. I don't think it is good for them. I don't see how they can gain from it." When I asked her to amplify, she explained that with all this exposure of their bodies and sexual response, "They will have less to reveal of themselves to the boy they really want to marry for life." (Some, however, insist that the modern female prizes openness above mystery.)

• The probable loss of some feminine traits that have long fascinated males. A disquieting question was raised by writer Cynthia Seton in 1965 when she wondered what would happen if the constellation of traits traditionally associated with virginity, such as delicacy, personal pride, self-discipline, grace, tenderness, restraint, went down the drain along with chastity as the idealized mode of behavior for girls.[20] (A female social scientist reading this paragraph offered this dissent: "These are factors that women have used in the exploitation of men. Let us be done with them!")

3. What is the likely impact of sex freedom upon the relationship between the man and the woman, especially after they marry?

Can young people today comfortably marry each other in the knowledge or on the assumption that the partner has had premarital sexual experiences with one or more other persons? We have seen in our College Survey that about half the U.S. students felt it possible for a person to have numerous affairs and still bring an enduring commitment to the person married. Perhaps many were impelled to this response by the fact that they had already experienced those "numerous affairs" and might be reluctant to consider that they may have lost the capacity for a deep, enduring emotional commitment. Or possibly, after numerous affairs, they recognized in themselves the ability still to be deeply committed. And we have seen in the College Survey that while the majority of U.S. girls said they would not be seriously troubled by such knowledge about a partner, more than two-thirds of the men said they would be troubled, at least somewhat.

Their response suggests that most men have not emotionally accepted the concept of sex freedom for girls that they might consider as mates. If this is so, a couple's relationship, where such feelings were involved, could be in for some trouble during courtship or after marriage.

There have been a number of studies of the impact of premarital sex experience upon a marriage relationship. There seems to be a general acceptance among investigators that the girl who has premarital coitus before marriage is substantially more likely at some point to become unfaithful after marriage. Psychologist Gerhard Neubeck states, "The more conservative you were before marriage the more likely you are to be after marriage."

Another way to assess the impact of sexual experience before marriage is to note whether it seems to affect the sexual adjustment of the couple after they marry. Here the preponderance of evidence is that the premarital experience promotes somewhat better sexual adjustment during the first phase of marriage. But some of the studies make little distinction between the girl who has experienced coitus only with her fiancé shortly before marriage and the girl who has quite a history of sleeping around.

The studies by Lewis Terman, by the Kinsey group, and by the Burgess-Wallin group all indicate that women who have had intercourse frequently before marriage were more likely to experience orgasm in intercourse with their husbands in the first year or so of marriage.

A later study of Eugene Kanin and David Howard puts a somewhat different light on the experienced woman's apparently better record of achieving a good physical relationship after marriage. They asked approximately 170 wives about their honeymoons and then asked them simply to rate whether the sexual relationship was "very satisfying," "satisfying," "not satisfying," or "very unsatisfying." They found that while the sexually experienced brides had a clear edge in terms of satisfaction on the wedding night, by the end of 2 weeks the difference was not remarkable. And the great majority of wives in both groups were contented with the sexual aspect of their relationship with their new husbands. Seventy-six percent of the wives with no premarital coital experience reported finding intercourse either "very satisfying" or "satisfying," while 92 percent of the brides with premarital coital experience checked either "very satisfying" or "satisfying." The investigators were puzzled by the fact that more of the experienced than the inexperienced brides mentioned having sexual difficulties during this honeymoon phase. They finally concluded it might be explained by the fact that they had higher expectations. The investigators were even more startled to find that *all* 14 of the women who stated that events of the honeymoon phase had created long-term difficulties for their marriages were women who had engaged in premarital intercourse. Four of them, for example, indicated that wedding-night confessions of prior sexual experiences were still plaguing their marriages.[21]

Still another way to assess the impact of premarital sex experience is to note what effect it seems to have, if any, upon the couple's *general* marriage happiness. Here a quite different picture emerges than when you simply look at the couple's sexual adjustment. As sociologist Robert Bell put it: "Factors that make for good sexual adjustment may have little to do with overall marital adjustment." Some of the other factors that come quickly to mind are emotional maturity, loyalty, and affection.

A number of studies indicate that people who have intimate sexual encounters with a variety of partners before marriage are substantially less likely to end up happily married. Psychologist Lewis Terman found, in analyzing the happiness scores of married couples, that the happiness of those couples who had entered marriage as virgins was about the same as that of couples whose only premarital coital experience was with each other. In contrast, he found that the happiness scores declined rather sharply if one of the partners had experienced intercourse with someone other than the partner. Burgess and Wallin agreed and suggested that perhaps what was operating here was that the kind of people who engage in premarital intercourse may have less aptitude for successful marital adjustment. (Both of these studies, it should be emphasized, were based on samplings made before 1950.)

Another more recent study that may be relevant was made by psychologist William R. Reevy. In preparing a doctoral dissertation at Penn State University, he compared the sex experience of 139 girls who had scored high or low on an inventory used for predicting marital happiness. The girls averaged about 20½ years of age. The girls who had experienced intercourse were about twice as likely to score low on the inventory as the girls who had not.[22]

To summarize, in looking at the evidence regarding the impact on *society* of an environment where a good deal of sex freedom and changing of partners is permitted or encouraged, I come away more impressed by the cautionary views of Toynbee, Unwin, Freud, and Sternbach than by those calling for still greater permissiveness and naturalism. The evidence regarding the impact on the *individual* is mixed and inconclusive, but again suggests caution. And the small amount of evidence available regarding the impact of premarital sexual experimentation upon *marriages* quite clearly suggests caution.

In short, the case for sexual freedom as it is commonly understood—where every male and every female is free to behave sexually as he or she sees fit, as long as no one is hurt—seems to be a dubious goal. This, of course, does not necessarily mean that in our new kind of world we should strive to reinforce the traditional norm under which the bride and groom have been expected to confront each other as virgins. We will explore that and other possible patterns in the coming chapter.

CHAPTER 26

What Sex Standard Is Appropriate Today?

"It is doubtful that any society can get along, and serve its individual members in the best way, without standards and patterns regarding sex that are more or less generally accepted." Nevitt Sanford, Director of the Institute for the Study of Human Problems, Stanford University.

As the morals, or lack of them, among college students became a matter of considerable public controversy, the present provost of Columbia University offered his students some challenging thoughts in a campus publication.[1] David Truman stated, "The difficult task for youth of discovering who one really is becomes additionally formidable if the limits on permissible behavior are themselves unreliable or unknown. . . . The predictability of limits on behavior is essential in itself."

Rebellion against such limits, he added, is of course to be expected, but the rebellion must be against boundaries that are known. Some young collegians, not knowing what is expected of them, rationalize a demand for license by a specious moral relativism. The dean then made this further important point, "the college cannot effectively urge restraints that the adult world outside does not support."

What restraints will the adult world and society in general support, if any? The lessons of history suggest that codes of behavior are not worth the papyrus they are written upon unless reinforced by general disapproval of violators and the punishment or ostracism of persistent or flagrant violators.

Historian Max Lerner suggests that realistic codes must be based on the values that set our life goals. He expects that as we begin to shape a new set of values in American society

397

the shaping of a new set of codes, a new set of moral standards will follow.

Some observers contend that there can be enduring values despite rapid social change. Others say the only kind of moral code that makes sense (has a chance of functioning) is a pragmatic morality based on whatever the existing situation is, as established by research on the prevailing patterns.

I incline to the view that we need an agreed code of behavior that fits the needs of the greatest number in our era, even though it may not currently be in vogue. This may be a somewhat idealistic goal, but then the U.S. Bill of Rights set goals that were more idealistic than accepted at the time, and to some extent they still are.

It is not enough to dismiss a code simply because there will be some backsliders. There always will be. Author William Faulkner stated, "I think that man tries to be better than he thinks he will be. I think that that is his immortality. . . ."

It is inevitable that we will have some kicking over the traces—just as we will always have some adults complaining that the current young are unworthy to accept the torch. Psychologist Richard DeBold, of Wesleyan University, says, "I doubt that there's ever going to be a generation that will give up visiting doom upon the young. This in essence is the nature of the old-young business."

But still there should be a standard that the young and old can respect even while some are violating it. The official code calls for chastity of all males and females until marriage. It is not generally respected by the younger generation, and is not even respected by a great many family specialists, who have been giving more thought to our sex behavior than anyone else. In 1963 Jessie Bernard noted that "There was a time when those arguing for premarital virginity could be assured of a comfortable margin of support in the group [National Council on Family Relations]. This is no longer always true. Especially the younger members no longer accept this code."

If we reject the concept of sex freedom and also question the viability of the official code inherited from Victorian days, what is the most attractive alternative? Ideally any code that is adopted would, above all, meet 5 tests:

1.　It should contribute to individual fulfillment, integrity, dignity, and emotional well-being.

2. It should contribute to the strength and stability of our society.

3. It should promote not only companionship between the young males and females before marriage but, more importantly, enduring companionship among those males and females who do marry.

4. It should ease the present dangerous gulf between the generations.

5. It should assure that only children wanted by both parents are brought into the world.

Is there a reasonable code regarding physical intimacy before marriage that will meet these objectives for young people of the Western world? I believe a code that would win majority respect is possible and it should consist of 3 elements. I will start with the element that would have the widest support from family specialists.

The elements of a good relationship

There is virtually complete agreement among family specialists that any exploitation in the male-female relationship should be deplored. Neither the female nor the male should be left, after any kind of physical encounter, feeling that she or he has somehow been taken advantage of, or deceived. Society should deplore a relationship where there is any lack of truthfulness or any indiscretion that will cause embarrassment to the partner.

Lester Kirkendall found, in his interviewing of 200 college men who had experienced intercourse, that a substantial number bragged to their male peers of their exploits in order to win prestige. Kirkendall cited one young man who recalled his thoughts in these terms, "This is what I have been wanting—to get into her. Now I have. I'll really have something to tell the boys."

Some professional students of sex behavior contend that the element of *fair play* is the principal and perhaps the only element that should be in a modern sex code. Psychologist Albert Ellis, the ardent advocate of premarital sex as fun, would deplore any exploitation. The British psychiatrist and researcher on sex, Eustace Chesser, asks, "Yet say neither suffers remorse and no third party is injured, wherein lies the harm or the immorality?"[2]

Sociologist Ira Reiss, in his study of premarital sexual standards in America, focuses a great deal of his attention on what he calls "permissiveness with affection," and suggests this may well become a key norm. He predicts, "I believe Americans will increasingly move . . . to full acceptance of permissiveness with affection."[3]

In our mobile society it is quite plausible that a girl, during the 10-year period starting with her puberty, will have a feeling of affection for a least one or two dozen males; so that if society accepts a sex code based upon permissiveness with affection, it must also accept the possibility that modern young females may have coital experiences with a substantial number of males.

At a symposium on sexual morality at Wesleyan University, a professor of philosophy, in making a distinction between what he called "sex neat" and "sex with a history," explained that "sex neat" was the casual, impersonal kind of relationship that shrinks the soul. On the other hand, he said that "sex with a history" requires that you become involved with the other person, know that person well, have something else in the relationship besides sex, and be willing to accept all consequences. He left the students with the impression that this kind of sexual intimacy might be all right. A group of students, in discussing his remarks afterwards, felt that one difficulty was how to keep sex from overwhelming the relationship. As one student said, "That is really the problem."

The investigator who has probably done most to propose a sex code that would put the primary test upon the depth of the relationship is Lester Kirkendall, of Oregon State University. After exploring the callousness of the attitudes of so many of the young college males in talking about their sexual relations with girls, he was deeply impressed with those males who reported their relations involved respect, warmth, and protection. This led him to develop a proposed code that put the stress almost entirely upon the quality of the relationship. This concept impressed a number of colleagues and has been widely accepted among college students. Kirkendall was probably responsible for the fact that the word "relationship" has become a big word among collegians. As he saw it, premarital sexual intercourse was not an act that was good or bad, or right or wrong, in itself. The act—or prospect of it—should be judged on how it affects the interpersonal relationships of the 2 persons involved. This focus upon the *quality* of a relationship was an important contribution to current thought. He stated, "Morally, our first concern should be for the development of effective interpersonal relationships. . . . Whenever a decision or a choice is to be made concerning behavior, the moral decision will be the one which works towards the creation of trust, confidence, and integrity in relationships. It should increase the capacity of the individuals to cooperate and enhance the sense of self respect in the individual. Acts which create distrust, suspicion, and misunderstanding, which build barriers and destroy integrity, are immoral."[4]

(In some of his later elaborations of his thoughts he has mentioned, also, that such factors as motivation, maturity, ability to communicate, and sense of commitment color any interpersonal relationship. But his focus has remained primarily on the quality of the relationship as the crucial factor, and that is the element that has reached the consciousness of so many collegians.)

The several proposals for a code, which we have just examined—those which put the emphasis upon fair play, affection, and other qualities in the relationship—are good as far as they go. But they seem to have certain deficiencies, when left to stand alone, as a basis for society to judge specific behavior.

The main difficulties of any code based upon the tenor of the relationship between the 2 people are:

• Such a code leaves the judgment of what is morally appropriate to the 2 people who find themselves approaching the point of sexual intercourse. Most of the advocates of a code based upon relationships make no allowance for social assessment of the act. I believe the individual, while cherishing freedom of personal action, needs to recognize that there may be a legitimate social interest in the way he behaves.

Nor do they take into account the competence of the 2 young persons, in a moment of sexual excitement, to reach a sensible decision about whether their relationship really does involve such things as trust, loyalty, and integrity. Family specialist Paul H. Landis, in assessing the Kirkendall moral philosophy said, "This thesis, were it to become accepted social policy, poses a difficult problem in social control. . . . And in moral codes taboo acts must be condemned regardless of advantages gained by certain individuals or groups who violate them. As a basis for social control, Kirkendall's proposal must be classed with the Robin Hood theory of theft. . . . When the individual is authorized to decide whether or not violation will be advantageous, the moral code vanishes."[6]

• The "relationship" approach ignores the fact that sexual acts may reasonably concern more persons than the 2 actors involved. Society is involved; the life of a conceived child may become involved; and the feelings of the parents of the 2 actors may become involved.

• The "relationship" approach focuses upon the immediate situation and offers little attention to possible long-term ill effects of these acts upon the relationship of the 2 people involved or to possible long-term ill effects on the relationship that the 2 persons involved may develop with other partners in later years.

• The "relationship" approach makes no allowance for the possibility that restraint in itself may be socially desirable in young people who hope to become effective citizens in the modern world (as Arnold Toynbee, J. D. Unwin, O. H. Mowrer, and others suggest).

• Also, the advocates of the "relationship" approach rarely take into account the factor of maturity. Adolescents and overgrown children, as well as young adults, presumably are invited to evaluate the quality of their relationships before embarking upon intimacies. Family specialist Thomas Poffenberger, in criticizing the relationshp approach, cited a high-school teacher who told him that the "relationship" concept had been a great help to her. She explained, "Now I have an answer; I just tell the girls and boys that they have to consider both sides of the question; will sexual intercourse strengthen or weaken their relationship?"[6]

At a seminar in 1966, chaired by Kirkendall, family specialist Richard Hey of the University of Minnesota stated, "Kirkendall does not come to terms with considerations of age and level of maturity of the persons involved."[7]

The element of maturity

Any moral code that has a chance of functioning should recognize that what may be appropriate for adults or young adults may not be appropriate for youngsters. The youngsters are not likely to have an adequate understanding of their own motivations, urges, and impulses or those of persons they confront of the other sex. Mary Calderone argues that sexual experience should be viewed as a privilege reserved for persons who have reached a certain emotional and chronological maturity. She notes that we set ages for legal majority, for voting, for driver's licenses; so why are we so afraid, she asks, to state forthrightly, "While you are still in high school you are just plain too young in every way to make the mature judgments and decisions that this important step requires."

The Harvard authority on human development, Erik Erikson, has defined 8 stages in the healthy emotional growth of man that, hopefully, occurs from infancy to mature age. Success at each stage is based upon the successful integration of the earlier stages. If an individual develops successfully, then he moves through the 8 stages in this order: from trust, to autonomy, to initiative, to industry, to identity, to intimacy, to generativity, to integrity. During adolescence, on this scale, the individual is primarily fighting to shape his identity in a contest wth forces that would create identity diffusion. Erikson points out that when a youth is maturing in his physical capacity for procreation, he is as yet unable to love in that binding manner that only 2 identities can offer each other. But, when this youth emerges from his identity-forming stage successfully and becomes a young adult, he is eager and willing to fuse his identity with that of others. "He is ready for intimacy, that is, the capacity to commit himself to concrete affiliations and partnerships and to develop the ethical strength to abide by such commitments. . . ."[8]

A further point might be made that adolescents by their natures frequently seek escape from restraint and from responsible behavior as goals in themselves. Psychologist and management consultant Robert McMurry, of Chicago, made some comments about emotional maturity that are relevant to the problems of young people experimenting with intimacy. At a conference in New York with personnel directors, he was advising them how to identify young men and women with leadership potential. He stressed emotional maturity as crucial and explained that all of us start out in life being utterly immature emotionally, and as we grow older, if we are lucky, we shed our childish immaturities and achieve emotional maturity. Then he wrote on the blackboard 9 traits common to people who have not yet outgrown the emotional immaturity they knew as children. Those traits were: Selfishness . . . pleasure-mindedness . . . disregard for consequences . . . lack of self-discipline . . . show-off tendencies . . . destructiveness . . . refusal to accept responsibility . . . wishful thinking . . . and dependency. At least the first 8 of these traits are commonly present as motivating factors in the sexual experimentation of unsupervised adolescents.

Granted that some adolescents are more emotionally mature than others, no moral code could survive that depended upon individual adolescents assessing the level of their own emotional maturity. A code has a better chance if the expected level of maturity is visible to all. It seems reasonable to me that society insist that sexual intercourse be out-of-bounds for unmarried high-school-age teenagers. And for those going on to college, it should be out-of-bounds for teen-age freshmen. The freshman year seems to be the year when late adolescents transplanted to a new environment and freed from parental supervision are particularly likely to take up promiscuous behavior to prove how grown-up or appealing they are.

In our College Survey, the collegians themselves recognized that premarital coitus was considerably less reasonable for adolescents than for legal adults. Rather overwhelmingly, both the male and the female students agreed that under the age of 18 coitus would not be acceptable unless the couple was married. And a substantial majority of female students felt that unmarried coitus was unacceptable under the age of 21. On the other hand, only a minority of both men and women students felt that after the age of 21 coitus should be reserved for marriage.

Two final possible reasons why society in general should declare premarital coitus out-of-bounds for most unmarried adolescents are: (1) coitus is a form of play that can best be appreciated by people who are adults, or close to it, and (2) our increasing life span makes it seem sensible that youths and adults alike recognize that certain recreations be reserved for adults. Why should we encourage youngsters to try to experience the ultimate in sensual exhilaration while they are still in the first quarter of their life span?

The element of commitment

The ideal of chastity until the full commitment of the wedding ceremony is admirable, particularly for the girl. Some may argue that the sense of commitment that is felt when two virginal people have intercourse immediately after their wedding may more than wipe out the disadvantage inherent in the fact that they are bumbling, perhaps fearful, and probably encountering difficulty in suddenly releasing themselves in one night from long-maintained inhibitions.

While some will maintain this ideal, I feel it should be a personal decision and not be a part of the normative code defining what is acceptable and unacceptable.

A good argument can be made that a marriage is off to a more promising start if the full sexual encounter is out of the way before the marriage ceremony. In that case the bride and groom are not plagued by the anxiety that something may happen in one critical night that may give them a sense of success or failure. A girl at the Protestant university in our College Survey said she and her fiancé would be married in a matter of months, upon graduation. She had recently lost her virginity with him, and she said, "I am glad that I will not have to make that adjustment after marriage."

Perhaps an equally compelling reason to suggest that virginity at marriage should not be a part of the code of acceptability today is that it could not assuredly command majority support in the foreseeable future.

Still, I feel that any code of acceptability must contain an element of commitment. As an act of revelation, bodily union is important enough to be reserved for the courtship process— and not be acceptable as a form of play between attractive new acquaintances or even good friends.

Furthermore, any code that includes an element of commitment would be far easier for society to implement, and so would have a greater chance of surviving. A commitment adds an ingredient to a relationship that can readily be assessed by friends, relatives, and neighbors.

So what should the stage of commitment be? Certainly it is not sufficient to extend the privilege of coitus to any couple going "steady" because in some girls' minds steadiness is achieved by a second date. And the mere fact of pinning should not be sufficient among college girls, because many girls collect pins for status reasons.

On the other hand I would not go along with those who suggest that the commitment must be an official and binding one—with the ring, the picture in the paper, and the notice to parents (so that reneging on marriage becomes virtually impossible). There may be sound reasons why a man and a girl who feel they are engaged should change their minds in the final exploration process. In any case, a good many do. Furthermore, official engagements with rings and newspaper announcements are becoming considerably less common in the United States for all except the affluent or ambitious. (Marriage announcements are another matter.)

But all serious courtships reach a stage where the man and girl agree they want to marry at a propitious time. They reveal their desire to do so to their best friends. Usually, too, they convey to their parents that they are making long-term plans that involve one another. This then in my view is the stage of commitment where society should agree that they should feel free to experiment in physical union if they want to. Social control would be exercised at least by the requirement that the friends they both respect most know that an intention to marry exists. And the intent is usually apparent to neighbors and parents.

To sum up, under the code I have described, society would disapprove of sexual intercourse between unmarried young people unless three elements are present:

1. That a deep friendship based upon substantial acquaintance exists between the man and the girl.

2. That both are out of high school; and if college is planned, that they have completed the first year of college if they are still teenagers.

3. That they hope to marry, and their best friends know of the hope.

It should be recognized that such a code will be tolerable in the long run only if effective techniques of conception control are available to unmarried couples who have achieved this readiness to experiment.

Despite all the rebelling and talk of privitism among young people today, I believe that some such code of acceptability would be appreciated by them. Sociologist David Riesman has

suggested that permissiveness, liberating in its earlier install-
ments, has created unanticipated problems and that many
young people feel a need for "some permission to resist
permissiveness."

While such uneasiness about permissiveness exists among
the younger generation it will probably take at least half a
decade for any code of acceptability to win broad acceptance.
Explanations of what is acceptable would need to begin with
the younger teenagers. The widespread mood of privitism of
college-age youths was summed up bluntly by the president of
Cornell University when he said, "Students today want no
restrictions." That, however, may be too sweeping a generalization. We asked our college sample of juniors and seniors
this question:

*Some observers contend that younger people, especially those
under 21, would welcome more definite guidelines and limits
from society on what may reasonably be regarded as appropriate in male-female intimacy. What do you think?*

YES ___   NOT NEEDED ___

DOUBT IF FEASIBLE ___

Approximately half of the U.S. females agreed with this
thought, and a third of the males did. Only about a quarter of
the students checked "not needed." For both males and females a substantially larger proportion of the respondents
who were *not* coitally experienced were in favor of such guidelines and limits than were that substantial proportion who
were already experienced. In the International Sample, Canadian males and females were roughly in accord with the U.S.
students. In England and Norway less than a fifth of the males
would welcome such guidelines, and about a fourth of the
English girls and a third of the Norwegian girls would welcome such guidelines and limits.

The college students who made an analysis for me of the
students' amplifying comments said regarding this question,
"There seems to be a great reluctance on the part of both
sexes to thrust their beliefs on anyone else. They feel a person's sexual morals should be left up to himself, and that
therefore one should not to try to direct anyone else." The
students were not strongly against "loose" guidelines, but they
didn't want set rules.

In our College Survey the students were also asked as a second part this question:

If you feel there is a need for more clearly defined standards, who under modern conditions should have the main responsibility for setting them?

The possible alternatives listed were "Youthful peers" (same-age associates), "Parents," "Schools," "Churches," "Adults."

About two-thirds of the U.S. students responded to this question, or 878 students. Males and females were almost in complete agreement on who should have the main responsibility for setting more clearly defined standards. Their approximate responses:

Parents	40%	Schools	6%
Adults	29%	Churches	5%
Youthful Peers	20%		

Possibly "schools" and "churches" were in such low favor because the words may have had connotations of rules and moral concern.

A sampling of adults might not produce the same percentages for the 5 possible standards-setters, but it is interesting that the responses of our students do not reflect the strong anti-adult bias presumed to exist in the younger generation today. We will take up the 5 possible standards-setters in the order that the students ranked them:

What parents might do

We have seen the difficulties parents have today in being credible life models to the young generation. Some parents have quietly abdicated. On the other hand a girl, still a virgin, at one of the women's colleges in the Northeast wrote on her comment sheet, "I am very fortunate. My parents have trusted me yet have also let me know what they expect. We can talk to each other and I don't feel the need to go out and raise hell just for the sake of raising it."

After youngsters reach their mid-teens there is only a certain amount that most parents can offer in terms of specific admonition or advice in American society without feeling awkward. Much more important is whether or not the parents, throughout the youngster's life, have taught, by precept, the importance of such traits as personal integrity, pride, concern for others, responsibility, dignity, fidelity, self-respect, and tenderness. And the good parents also have been encouraging the youngsters to exercise self-discipline from an early age. Attitudes toward sex are simply one aspect of all this character training.

The parents can also serve by helping their youngsters stand up to peer group pressures by discouraging steady dating in the early teens, by discouraging commercial and social pressures on the daughters to prove they are glamorous—and social pressures on sons to prove they are virile by demonstrating they are sexually experienced.

What adults in general can do

"Adult" is an elusive category, but I will suggest a few areas where adults in general—as distinct from parents, educators, and clergymen—can play a role.

• Concerned adults of enlightenment and a capacity for leadership should be working to develop a normative sex code that young people will respect.

• They can work to secure an environment of living in which the young will not be inundated with sensual stimuli designed to make them feel inadequate if they are not behaving as voluptuously as many of the stars of contemporary films do.

The various states use their power to regulate the age when children can drive automobiles or purchase liquor, so why should they not have commissions classify films as suitable or not suitable for viewing by children? *The New York Times* in deploring the harm that can be done to the immature mind by arousing emotions that the young people are not yet capable of managing noted that a rating system would escape the objection of censorship. It would leave adults free to choose their own films, while giving them an opportunity to protect their young.

• Adults can establish a dialogue between the generations by providing forums where people of all ages can contribute thoughts on their hopes and ideals regarding male-female relationships.

• Adults might well take a less admiring view of an economic system that glorifies instant gratification of whims and desires.

• And they can work for a society in which cordial, meaningful relationships between people are esteemed above the marvels of technology. Kirkendall in talking with me about the future prospects of sexuality suggested, "As we keep building toward a more dehumanized society we can expect to see a lot more casual sexuality. If, however, we are able to keep warmth and human closeness in our culture, premarital sex has a better chance of being carried out in the context of responsible affection and less of it will seem to be needed."

What youthful peer groups can do

Sociologist Ira Reiss states that because adults have continued to stress traditional values while ignoring the emergence of new modes of behavior, "Our young people are devising a sexual code of their own making."

The crucial question is whether in the name of freedom we are abandoning the young to a new tyranny, that of their own peers. Some suggest that the peer groups, in the zest of their new influence, have been adopting many of the shabbier habits of adult society. Certainly one hazard here is that the young people are much more liberal about what they are willing to allow members of their peer group to do in terms of sex behavior than they are in their own personal codes.[9] It is almost impossible to get them to condemn promiscuous behavior by members of their own group unless it becomes embarrassingly visible. Many of the present peer-group codes can and do generate pressures that force some girls and young men to go further in their sex behavior than they feel ready to go.

So the question is: Can they seriously be depended upon to play any serious role in the development of a plausible code of sexual behavior? I believe that they can; although, as Winston Ehrmann, authority on youth behavior, points out, this is virtually a unique expectation in the history of a culture. He adds optimistically that our American youth culture in this century, with almost no help from a succession of parental generations, developed or invented new social devices for coping with their new environment. He suggests as innovations of recent decades largely produced by youth culture—in response to changing conditions—dating, petting, going steady, and early marriage.[10] And he suggests some of these innovations have met with considerable success.

While our younger individuals may seem reluctant to regulate the sexual behavior of their associates by recognizing anything except completely permissive standards, they are showing in other ways a very considerable interest in setting standards and improving the conditions of their existence. This is evident in the great growth of demands for a voice in matters close to their concern in colleges. They are demanding better library hours, better professors, better school facilities, the right to govern themselves and to set up their own rules of discipline. At some schools they now have their own chapel service. One of the interesting changes in the pattern of lecture and concert series that many colleges conduct is that increasingly the series have passed from being under the control of faculty committees to being under the control of student committees. Some have budgets of $100,000 or more to administer, and most seem to do it conscientiously and responsibly.

One of the more fruitful kinds of interchanges among students that take place at many colleges is the discussion of male-female relationships in small groups where both upperclassmen and lowerclassmen participate. The former, it is my observation, are more likely to counsel prudence than license —and are more likely to be listened to than older adults. Having somewhat older young adults close enough in age to be regarded as respected peers in such discussions can help the younger students understand the social-sexual life around them and sense uncouth behavior.

What colleges can do

Since our college students in their comments indicated they were thinking almost entirely about colleges as the "schools" supplying "more definite guidelines and limits" we will focus here primarily on colleges as a good case in point. They are much more likely than public schools to be expected by society to be responsible for student behavior outside the class-room, and to act to some degree *in loco parentis*.

The colleges in general have evaded the issue of stating what they believe is a reasonable standard for students in regard to sex behavior. Instead, they have either vaguely stated that they expect everyone to be a gentleman/lady and scholar, or else they have published detailed police-type rules specifying how many dates per week a girl may have. Some also are prone to specify the punishment for each minute that a female is late in arriving back at her dormitory.[11]

In the mid-1960s a number of college officials and educational consultants began taking a strongly permissive view toward what the colleges' attitudes should be. John T. Rule, who was dean of students at M.I.T. until 1961, is a good example. He has argued, "Many adolescents consciously seek critical life experiences that they believe will test out and confirm their adulthood. The college years are a period of reaching for sexual maturity, for a personal identity which includes sexuality."[12]

It was his concept that most of the educational process takes place outside the classroom and that various kinds of interaction between students are valuable in developing character and personality. He was one of the principal consultants to the "Committee on the College Student" for The Group for the Advancement of Psychiatry, which published its report on sex and the college student in 1965. The statement from the report that often made the headlines was: "Sexual activity privately practiced with appropriate attention to the sensitivities of other people should not be the direct concern of the administration [of a college]."[13] This was under its "Guidelines for college policy toward sexuality." But in the same guidelines the committee report stated:

"It is desirable for the college to make explicit its attitude toward sex on the campus. . . . In the final analysis, the college cannot control the sexual behavior of students, but college officials can be clear and explicit about their own and the college's expectation of acceptable behavior on the campus. For example, if the institution disapproves of sexual intercourse in the dormitory and is not prepared to tolerate self-regulation of sexual behavior of students, it should be prepared to state explicitly that the college does not consider the dormitories an appropriate place for intercourse, that any students who had thought otherwise were mistaken, and that such activity will not be condoned."[14]

This is not explicitly contradictory to the committee's earlier statement that sex activity is not the direct concern of the administration, since it confines its admonition to defining what is acceptable sex behavior "on the campus." Thus it seems to take a narrow view of the college's role in helping students know what is considered to be appropriate behavior (since at many schools it is often only a few yards from the campus to a bordering motel or to off-campus student apartments).

Others suggest that the college has the responsibility of stating its attitude toward sex in broader, less geographically oriented terms. In the early 1960s, during the uproar that developed at Harvard because men were so freely interpreting the permissive environment then prevailing there that many were engaging in intercourse in their dormitories between classes, some of the university's officials began issuing cautionary statements. Graham Blaine, Jr., psychologist on the staff of the Harvard Health Services, argued that college authorities have an obligation to take a clear stand upon premarital sexual experiences. He said, "When, by our silence, we give students the impression that we are actually in favor of such experiences, we push them into situations which they are often not ready to handle."[15]

A year later, Dana L. Farnsworth, director of the Harvard Health Services, stated, "Even though the colleges are not 'in loco parentis' to their students in the literal sense, they do have a responsibility to encourage them to adopt reasonable standards of behavior. . . . Standards of morality and how they are determined and transmitted from one generation to another are proper and necessary subjects for continuing discussion between students and faculty members."[16] And David Truman, as Dean of Columbia College, stated:

"The college cannot, in my judgment, avoid the responsibility of defining behavioral limits. The chief reason for this is that a college must be concerned about the level and source of student anxiety, since a deeply troubled young man is unlikely to be a good student. And at least a portion of this student anxiety derives from the uncertainty of moral standards. . . ." He suggested that students could help in the setting of standards but said that ultimately, "the responsibility for setting moral limits for college students must remain with the college's faculty and officials. . . ."[17]

One of the major mistakes that most colleges make is to assume that, since students are big enough to come to college, they are now all mature. In a great many colleges, if not most, the social controls are essentially the same for male and female freshmen who may be 17 or 18 as they are for male and female upperclassmen, even though the great bulk of freshmen are still adolescents and virtually all the seniors are legal adults. An important transition has occurred in the student's capacity for self-regulation that most schools do not sufficiently recognize.

In early 1968 the journal *Medical Aspects of Human Sensuality* asked 5 college physicians, "Should teenagers be given the pill?" Two were gynecologists, 3 were heads of the college health service. Their response: One "Yes" (Harvard). Three "No" (Temple University, Smith College, Marquette University). The fifth hedged by saying it all depends on circumstances (Indiana University). The Temple physician, in saying essentially "No," commented, "If they [college physicians] prescribe contraceptive pills, the students can only assume that the college itself is being permissive."

It seems to me, too, that colleges have a responsibility to provide places of privacy where students and their dates can talk and perhaps neck a bit if they wish without being exposed to general scrutiny, as in the entry lounge, and yet not have to get on a bed, which is not only likely but often literally necessary if they retire to talk in a student bedroom. A coed at the state university in the East in complaining about the lack of privacy at that campus said, "There is just no place to go for conversation and a few hugs and kisses. In the dormitory lounge, even holding hands is frowned upon. That leaves a car, where the conversation part quickly declines."

We asked our College Survey sample:

At your school do you feel that lack of opportunity for privacy is a real problem in developing a deep, meaningful relationship with someone of the opposite sex?
                          YES ___   NOT REALLY ___

About a third of the men and women felt such a lack, with

students at the Midwestern schools most emphatically saying "Yes."

At the U.S. schools the male and female collegians while wanting closeness seemed a little uneasy about too much closeness in actual living arrangements. In our College Survey we also asked this question:

> *At several Scandinavian universities men and women live in the same dormitories in private rooms or with roommates of the same sex but without any separation of sexes by floors, wings, etc. Do you think this concept might well be introduced onto coeducational campuses here?* YES ___ NO ___
> NOT PRACTICAL ___ SOUNDS DANGEROUS ___

In the United States only a fourth of the females and only a third of the males liked the idea enough to respond "Yes." Both males and females who had experienced coitus were substantially more inclined to say "Yes" than those who had not. In the International Sample male and female students in both England and Germany were considerably more enthusiastic about the idea, approximately 6 out of 10 saying "Yes."

Those who seemed to like the idea contended that it simply represented a real-life situation they would be encountering in the outside world and so they might as well get used to it. On the other hand, some pointed out that they would have a hard time studying, knowing there was a bunch of girls (or boys) down the hall. Members of both sexes, although the girls were more emphatic, felt that the pressure to look good all the time would be very uncomfortable and would draw them away from their studying. Also girls worried that they couldn't walk around in their curlers; and the boys worried that they couldn't slop around the halls in their underwear.

What the churches can do

It took the Christian churches about 15 centuries to break loose from the concept that there was something inevitably sinful about sexuality, that it might also involve feelings of tenderness, joy, and love. The position until quite recently of all major Christian church groups was that coitus must be reserved for marriage. The new explosion of scientific knowledge about the universe and about human behavior, along with rapid social change, has unsettled many of the old certitudes—and the means of assuring respect for them.

The British Council of Churches considered a report in 1966 to modify somewhat its traditional position that sexual intercourse must be confined to marriage, and finally tabled the proposal for the time being. A publication stating the view on sexuality of a group of Quakers in England suggested that love affairs involving coitus are "not necessarily or invariably destructive. We do not, however, encourage anyone to think that it would be 'perfectly all right' to make love with a charming friend who equally desires the experience."[18]

In the United States there has been a great deal of discussion by theologians, especially at the divinity schools, of the concept of "situation ethics," which puts the emphasis in sexual decision-making upon the context and the circumstances. People must search their consciences to decide the proper way to behave in each situation. One leading advocate of the "situation-ethics" approach, Joseph Fletcher of the Episcopal Theological School in Cambridge, Mass., has stated, "Even a transient sex liaison, if it has the elements of caring, of tenderness and selfless concern, is better than a mechanical, egocentric exercise of conjugal 'rights' between two uncaring or antagonistic marriage partners."[19]

This is reminiscent of the Kirkendall viewpoint putting the focus on the quality of the relationship.

Critics of the morality that would judge each situation on its merits are asking whether young people must go into every situation where sexual arousal may occur and on the spot weigh all the ethical and moral elements of the situation. Dedicated believers in situation ethics would usually have well-thought-out ethical positions to guide behavior. But in any case the critics ask if it wouldn't be preferable to have some commonly held standards that help instant decision-making. William H. Genné, director of the Commission on Marriage and Family Life of the National Council of Churches of Christ in the U.S.A., has cited contentions that there is a parallel with rules that keep traffic moving on the right even when certain emergency vehicles, such as ambulances, may run red lights when the situation requires.[20] Without our commonly agreed-upon traffic laws, traffic would be an enormously worse problem.

Hopefully church leaders of the future will from their great perspective on man search their insights and evolve a moral standard for young people that will fall between the traditional rigid morality and the elusive morality of "situation ethics."

While the schools, churches, parents, the adult world, and young peer groups grope for an agreed position on sexual morality, it seems increasingly imperative that individual young people, if only as an interim solution, work at developing internalized controls. These would regulate the kinds of behavior that have been largely controlled in the past by external sanctions, or church-inspired conscience, or fear of pregnancy or disease. Whatever develops, internalized controls seem to be increasingly needed in the world of both today and tomorrow. An official at Southern Methodist University advised me, "There is the parallel of buildings in the earlier centuries that used to be held up by external props. Now they are held together with internal steel bonds."

While I strongly doubt that internalized controls alone, in each individual, can fully meet the needs of modern society, they can be of enormous help, especially in view of the present unsettled situation. If we encourage teenagers, for example, to understand the importance of developing a personal moral code, they will at least be better able to resist pressures of conformity that may be coming from their own peer-group associates.

Helping young people have a better understanding of themselves and their sexuality and their motivations can make them more resistant to spur-of-the-moment rationalizations.

In the college surveying and in my interviewing I have come across evidence that a good many young people are indeed thoughtful about physical intimacy in the absence of clear-cut, generally agreed standards.

I learned of one girl and young man who have developed a system where they have agreed to take turns applying the brakes.

A girl attending an urban university in the Midwest said that she and her present boy friend had experienced intercourse. She analyzed the situation by saying, "We were victims of romantic environment, naiveté, curiosity and plenty of unplanned hours. Our relationship deeply troubled both of us." They talked with 2 adults they respected. She added, "Through their help and trust and our determination we have been able to minimize our sexual relationship to affectionate rather than passionate petting about the waist. We are much happier in achieving our goal and have greatly gained confidence in ourselves and in each other."

A male student leader at the University of Arizona in talking about his friends who were "making out" sexually offered what I thought was a particularly interesting comment. He said:

"To me it is a matter of pride. We are dealing with the essence of life. If you make it as easy to get as candy, what good is it?"

IV. On Improving the Prospects for Sound Marriages

CHAPTER 27

Looking Toward the 21st Century

"Even with our higher divorce rate, the actual number of years that husbands and wives now stay married on an average exceeds that of some generations ago. This prolonged duration of married life has very important practical consequences." Alva Myrdal, Swedish sociologist and diplomat.

Most of the rules regulating marriages and their dissolution were made in eras when the bride and groom could look forward to fewer than half the number of years together that the couples marrying in the next few years can anticipate. For that reason alone, entering into wedlock calls for a new high level of prudence. There is now obviously a greater chance the partners will outgrow each other, lose interest, or become restless. In the past quarter-century, instead of greater prudence, however, we have seen a considerable increase in imprudent embarkations upon marriage.

Wives in the future surely will spend an increasing proportion of their married life as equal partners of the husband free of the "motherhood-service role," and so will have more options for the outlet of their surplus energy. They can no longer view marriage as a haven where they will be looked after by a husband in return for traditional services rendered.

Instead, more than ever before, women will have not only the opportunity but the expectation to push out for themselves and function as autonomous individuals who happen to have marriage partners. Marriages will apparently continue to be brittle for some time. Families in the immediate future will be expected to be highly mobile, and ever smaller in size.

While, as noted, the traditional economic functions of marriage have shrunk, there are 2 particularly compelling reasons looming why people will be marrying in the coming decade despite the relatively free availability of unmarried sexual partners:

- The warm, all-embracing companionship that in marriage can endure through the confusion, mobility, and rapid social change of our times.
- The opportunity to obtain immortality and personal growth for married individuals who perpetuate themselves through reproduction as they help mold personalities of their children and proudly induct them into the larger community.

This opportunity is so profoundly desired by most adult humans who are capable of reproduction that childlessness by choice would seem to be almost as difficult to popularize on any large scale as singleness by choice. Both would probably require intensive, prolonged social conditioning.

The institution of marriage is obviously in need of modifications to fit the modern needs. Author Jerome Weidman made an important point in his book *Your Daughter Iris* when he wrote of today's marriages: "Human beings do not obtain permanent possession of each other when they marry. All they obtain is the right to work at the job of holding on to each other." In pressing for modification of marriage as an institution we should seek above all to assure that the 2 functions of marriage just stated be fulfilled.

A variety of predictions and proposals are being heard today as to how the male-female liaison will or should evolve in the next few decades to meet the changing conditions of modern life. Here, for example, are 8 possible patterns of marriage or near-marriage that are being discussed:

1. *Serial mating.* Sometimes it is called serial monogamy, sometimes serial polygamy, sometimes consecutive polygamy. But the basic idea is pretty much the same for all. It would assume a turnover of partners over the 50-odd years that a man and a woman can expect to live after they first consider marriage. Swedish sociologist Joachim Israel suggested that 4 or 5 marriages might be about par for a lifetime. The mood behind such proposals was summed up by a New York model when she said, "Why lie to yourself? We know we're not going to love one man all our lives." Among others, a psychologist-social worker in California, Virginia Star, has advocated the

adoption of renewable marriage contracts. She suggests the contract lapse unless renewed every 5 years.

2. *Unstructured cohabitation.* These are the prolonged affairs without any assumption of permanence or responsibility. Such so-called unstructured liaisons—long popular in the lower classes—have been springing up in many of the larger universities in the off-campus housing. A psychiatrist at the University of California in Berkeley has suggested these liaisons may be the shape of the future. He said, "Stable, open non-marital relationships are pushing the border of what society is going to face in 10 years."[1]

A man's magazine in the mid-1960s presented some unconventional views of a woman who had been involved in a national controversy. During the presentation, she was asked, "How many lovers have you had, if you don't mind our asking?"

She responded, "You've got a helluva nerve, but I really don't mind. I've had five, if you count my marriage as an affair . . . five affairs, all of them really wing-dings."

3. *Mutual polygamy.* At a conference of marriage specialists in 1966 one expert from a Midwestern university speculated, "If we are moving into a new pattern where we are not claiming that marriage can do all the things that have been assumed, we may be moving into a kind of situation where there will be more than one partner. A compartmentalizing." Each partner in any particular marriage might have several mates, each chosen for a special purpose—for example, economic, recreational, procreational. A more informal variant of this would be "flexible monogamy," which in the view of Phyllis and Eberhard Kronhausen would frankly allow "for variety, friendships, and even sexual experiences with other individuals, if these are desired."[2]

4. *Single-parent marriages by intent.* These, on the Swedish model, would be the females—and occasional males—who yearn for parenthood without the burdens of wedlock.

5. *Specialists in parenthood.* Anthropologist Margaret Mead, in looking a few decades ahead, suggests the time may come when pressures to keep the birth rate low will produce a social style "in which parenthood would be limited to a smaller number of families whose principal function would be child-rearing; the rest of the population would be free to function—for the first time in history—as individuals."[3]

6. *Communal living.* In such a situation, several adult females and several adult males might live together in the same large dwelling and consider themselves an enlarged communal family, much as the hippies and other unconventional family groups have already been doing for some time.

7. *Legalized polygamy for senior citizens.* This is a form of polygamy that enables a man to have several wives at the same time. It has been advanced as a way to ease the demographic problem created by the fact that after the age of 60 there are increasingly more females than males in the population. One such proposal was advanced in the magazine *Geriatrics* by Dr. Victor Kassel, of Salt Lake City (the Mormon capital). The idea was taken seriously enough to be debated and unofficially turned down by the National Council of the Aging. A widow in South Carolina gave one feminine viewpoint when she said, "I am lonesome—but not that lonesome!"

8. *A variety of liaison patterns functioning in society simultaneously.* David Mace suggests we are moving toward a 3-layer cake type of society as far as male-female liaisons are concerned. He speculated that there may be a coexistence of several patterns. One pattern, as he sees it, will be that a proportion of the people will settle for sex freedom. They will not marry, but will drift into liaisons of long and short terms. There will be no attempt to punish or suppress such persons. He suggested that the second layer of this cake would involve somewhat more structuring, with a number of people choosing to go in and out of marriage and probably having several marriages in a lifetime, as in the common Hollywood pattern. Probably in this second layer there will be an attitude of freedom regarding extramarital sex while the couples are married. He suggested that in the third layer of the cake will be those who accept the concept of exclusive monogamy, preceded in at least some cases by premarital chastity.

Moral standards aside, one complication of most of the 8 possible patterns cited above is that they do not allow sufficiently for the intense desire that most women have for a secure arrangement—or at least women have had this intense desire until very recent times. They have had greater difficulty accepting fluid arrangements, especially after they pass the age of 30, than males.

An even bigger complication is that while most of these

arrangements might seem attractive in terms of providing the companionship so important to male-female partnerships today, they do not come to terms with the second crucial ingredient of modern marriages: a partnership where there is a sound environment for reaching for immortality through the rearing of children. Thus most should be rejected from serious consideration as socially unfeasible—at least for people interested in having children (and we suspect that those who don't will remain a small minority). Some of these patterns, of course, might seem more attractive after the child-rearing phase has passed.

But whatever hope we have for the future lies in the quality —not the quantity—of the children our homes produce. The highest-quality children, we now know, are *wanted* children who have both mothers and fathers as visible models, two parents who offer them affection, a sense of security, stability, and family unity. In the future we should settle for nothing less. It is the one-parent homes, the broken homes, parental abdication, and inadequate parental models that account for much of our social distress today: delinquency, deviance, dope, and divorce.

Any effort to modernize our marriages should start with a reorganization of our present haphazard system of launching marriage partnerships in the first place—partnerships that are supposed to last for the lifetime of the partners. Presently, as noted, nearly half the marriages that are launched disintegrate in one way or another.

The nominal entrance requirements into marriage that prevail in most parts of the U.S.A. were adequate for a rural society where marriages were very much under the scrutiny of the families and the church. The families and the church were almost certain to prevent impetuous and foolish ventures into the state of matrimony.

Those social safeguards have largely withered away in our mobile, secular society, and we are left only with the requirements to obtain a license. These are not much more difficult to obtain in most states than a license for a dog or for fishing (and often easier to obtain than a driver's license). There is not a state in the Union that requires as much as a week's wait from the moment of application to the uttering of "I do." Twenty of the states require no wait whatever. There seems to be a feeling that it would be an impingement upon personal freedom to ask infatuated youths to wait out a brief period of reflection before entering into presumed lifetime partnerships. Yet many of these same states that perfunctorily issue marriage licenses to any couple who will pay a few dollars for a license have elaborate regulations and painful waiting periods when the same couple tries to dissolve the marriage, which may have been undertaken on a binge or as a lark.

Millions of people could be saved from years of distress—and government agencies could save hundreds of millions of dollars a year in funds for combating delinquency and emotional distress—by requiring a more prudent approach to marriage. Our goal should be to encourage the formation of solid marriages based upon tested friendships in the first place. These can offer the greatest long-term sense of pride and exhilaration. As it is today, the only gainers in areas where the rate of marital breakup is especially high are the lawyers.

When people are taking on a partnership that is expected to last a half-century, it seems fatuous that they think of marriage at all until they have known each other as good friends for at least half a year. Sociologists Ernest Burgess and Paul Wallin in their study of young married couples found that an engagement of at least 9 months was necessary to assure an average probability of success in marriage.[4] I wouldn't go so far as 2 Soviet sociologists who, after a study of divorced couples in Leningrad, recommended that engaged couples be required to wait 18 months before they marry, to assure better unions.

I do feel, however, that state laws should be changed to require a 1-month period of reflection between the time that a marriage license is applied for and the time it is issued. It would seem prudent to review the state laws on the age when teenagers can marry, especially in view of the longer expectation of education. There are now 9 states where girls 13, 14, and 15 years old can marry with parental consent, and there is no state where the girl has to be over 16. There should be better social mechanics for handling the pregnancy of young adolescent girls, such as humanitarian abortion, so that they do not feel impelled to plunge into marriage before the condition becomes visible to save their families from disgrace.

We could achieve an improvement in the quality of marriages, too, if the states dignified the process of applying for a marriage license by having the couple—instead of standing at a counter petitioning a bored clerk—enter a chamber where a person professionally qualified in interpersonal relations could serve them (and dignify the process). Such a person could upon request advise them on appropriate housing, or birth-control arrangements, or respond to any questions on the mind of either prospective partner then or at any time during the 1-month reflection period.

Society should also work to establish seminars of a few hours where any prospective bride and groom could, if they wished, obtain information about marriage. These seminars might well be sponsored by local colleges. Couples would be presented with the kinds of problems that would inevitably confront them after they marry. A good prototype of this approach is the marriage-induction seminar that's been held for several years at Duke University by Ethel Nash, former president of the American Association of Marriage Counselors. During the weekend seminar there are 2-hour sessions attended by about a dozen couples who have declared they will be marrying within a few months. There is role-playing, discussion about contraception, discussion about marriage behavior, etc. When an engaged person tells how much he or she loves children, Mrs. Nash suggests the couple borrow the most obnoxious ones in their neighborhood and take care of them for a day. And if 2 engaged persons say they have never had an angry word, Mrs. Nash suggests, "Well, then why don't you start? A good way to do this is to have a joint bank account in which you agree you won't spend anything without the approval of the partner." A number have done this. And some who have never had arguments find that when Christmas approaches and the question of gift spending comes up, they do indeed have some heated words.

Once a couple has said "I do," what is the best way for society to regard the institution of marriage in our rapidly changing society? What arrangement would meet the test of providing optimum companionship for the greatest number of people and optimum stability for the greatest number of children that may be born from these marriages?

In the past few years there has been more discussion of the need to revamp the institution of marriage than at any time since the 1920s. It was then that Judge Ben B. Lindsey, of Denver, proposed his concept of "companionate" or "trial" marriages that could be dissolved by mutual consent if there were no children. He had been inspired to make the proposal by seeing so much evidence of sick marriages that resulted in juvenile delinquency in his courts. The national uproar caused him to lose his judicial bench, and he was denounced from thousands of pulpits. Today a number of theologians have been speculating that some kind of "trial" or probationary marriage might make sense after all.[5]

Two decades ago, anthropologist Margaret Mead was observing that no known society had ever invented a form of marriage strong enough to stick that did not contain the till-death-do-us-part assumption. (Most human contracts provide for termination after a specified number of years.) More recently Mead has been suggesting arrangements to permit the easier dissolution of "individual" type marriages if no children are involved.

Any proposal to modify marriage as a lifelong commitment has inherent shortcomings, as could be seen in some of the 8 concepts for modification listed earlier. But on the other hand, an arrangement might be feasible where the advantages to both the individual couples and to society might outweigh the shortcomings.

My own conclusion is that the first 2 years of marriage—which are the hardest—should be viewed by society as a confirmation period. At the end of the 2-year period, the marriage papers would become final and the couple would be awarded a certificate of confirmation if they want to continue the marriage. If, however, as the end of the 2-year period approaches, one or both of them wish to dissolve the marriage, it can be done by a formal request for the dissolution by one or both parties 2 months before the confirmation period is up. No dissolution would be permitted until this 2-year period is completed, without specific proof of extraordinary hardship.

Under such an arrangement the young husband and wife would have the option to make the union indeed a permanent one. This early-option period would greatly reduce the number of couples who stay married simply because they do not know how, decently, to undo a mistake they have made, or who can't afford the legal and travel expenses of a divorce. It would also release those of a restless nature who could probably never sustain a viable marriage, anyhow.

If the couple proceeds with the marriage after the confirmation period, society should reasonably consider them well married and expect them to make a go of it. And I imagine the overwhelming proportion of them would.

All couples getting married should have access, at the time they apply for a marriage license, to booklets prepared by various national associations concerned with stable marriages that indicate some of the challenges posed by marriage. Some of these booklets undoubtedly would stress that all couples getting married should get to know each other in their new roles as married companions for at least a few months before adding another dimension to their relationship by the conception of children. If, during the 2-year confirmation period, the couple conceive a child (when effective conception-control techniques are available to them and when, hopefully, legal abortions will be available on humane grounds) society can assume the child was wanted. Thus the birth of any child should be taken by society as confirmation that the couple plan a lifetime union. The certificate of confirmation would automatically be issued to them upon the birth of their child.

We have noted that a child's chances of achieving emotional maturity are vastly enhanced if it has parents of both sexes present as good models. No marriage, of course, should be indissoluble. After the 2-year confirmation period has passed, society should have 2 sets of divorce proceedings. One would be for marriages where there are children, and the procedure would be quite stiff in its requirements, with an administrative hearing 2 months after a filing for divorce. No decree should become final for at least a year. The other type of divorce would be for couples where no children are involved. This procedure should be relatively mild, with a 2-month waiting period before an administrative hearing and another month before the decree is issued. These procedures are discussed in detail later in this chapter.

It would be erroneous to refer to the proposed confirmation period as a "trial" marriage. A trial marriage is a highly tentative thing, little more than unstructured cohabitation. The month of reflection here proposed before the marriage begins would assure an earnestness of intent that is so widely lacking in marriages today. And the concept of confirmation assumes that when the couple marry, they are in earnest and hope it will continue. The chance to withdraw in 2 years will simply dissolve, easily and relatively painlessly, those unions that would have little chance of succeeding in any case.

The most serious criticism that could be made of the confirmation approach, I believe, is the fact now widely accepted by marriage specialists that the expectation that a marriage will continue is in itself a factor that contributes to the success of the marriage. Burgess and Wallin were impressed, in their study of hundreds of married couples, with the fact that "the determination of husband and wife to make a success of the marriage increases their motivation to adapt." And they found that this expectation that for better or for worse their marriage would continue was a strong stabilizing and reinforcing factor.

The factor of expectation as a strengthening force is a major reason why I would reject the proposals of such people as Mervyn Cadwallader, sociologist at San Jose State College, that a marriage contract be viewed as a flexible contract with periodic options to renew. I don't think there should be periodic options to renew, because of the unsettling effect it would have in terms of promoting uncertainty and anxiety over the years and weakening the cohesive force inherent in the expectation that the marriage will continue. Furthermore, as we have seen, a great many people are attracted to marriage by the sense of security that it offers.

Since, however, we are talking about a contract that is going to last 50 years or more, it does seem prudent that the pair have a chance to take a second look at the situation after a couple of years. This gives them a chance to assure themselves that they want to proceed for the additional 48 or more years that they may live. Forcing people to continue what they already perceive to be a mistake would certainly create more social instability and individual misery than letting them gracefully dissolve the union after 2 years without recrimination.

If there is a decision to dissolve after 2 years, there should be an automatic splitting of cash, real estate, and other resources on hand, and each would go his own way; there would be no question of alimony. It might prove useful to refer to such individuals as withdrawees rather than as divorcees.

Any realistic reform of the framework by which people enter and leave marriage would also alter the present assumption in the United States about divorce, namely, that someone has failed and the failure must be attested to by the aggrieved party in public court. The truth, of course, is that it usually takes two to fumble a marriage. Marriages typically fail for such reasons as poor communication, incompatibility, or too much difference in the socio-economic background of the couple. In Scandinavian countries and in Russia, obtaining a divorce is no easy matter, but it is handled sanely without the humiliation or pretense of an adversary proceeding.

All couples married more than 2 years who seek divorce should have the opportunity to discuss the ailing marriage, if they wish, with a qualified marriage counselor attached to the court where the application is to be filed. The aim would not necessarily be to save the marriage, but rather to help the man and wife understand their situation, understand how deep or superficial their rift really is. And if after the assessment the couple agree that divorce is the best answer, the counselor will advise them on ways to proceed with the least pain. If there are children, the counseling should be compulsory, and the primary concern would be to work out a future arrangement most helpful to children caught in such a situation. This again would not necessarily mean that the more probable proposal would be for the husband and wife to stay together. A number of studies have indicated that we may do more damage to a child—or at least as much—by keeping him in a household battleground where the marriage is ostensibly still intact than to let one of the parents, usually the mother, raise the child in a home presumably more free of strife.[6] The chances are better than even that the mother will remarry and acquire a new father-model for the child.

A modern concept of marriage would also recognize that alimony payments are archaic, where there is no child, and deepen the couple's hostility. The laws that remain in effect calling for alimony payments should be reexamined. In some states this is now being done. Customarily, U.S. courts award the wife at least one-third of the husband's annual earnings.[7] With the growing equality and economic competence of women, when a couple split, there should be a sharing of resources and the only additional payments, if there are not children, should be for the husband to make payments for the first year of their separation while the wife is rearranging her life. This should be handled as a lump-sum settlement. With the explosive growth of credit institutions seeking customers it seems reasonable that there should be a credit institution that would supply divorce loans. The divorced husband would make his regular payment to the bank rather than to the wife and thus avoid all the bad feelings arising from such payments, especially when they are late. If there are children, payments by the husband to the loan agency should be spread out over the years that each child is under 18 and the wife has not remarried. Most husbands would not resent this. Writer Alexander Eliot, who wrote a forceful plea for the abolition of alimony, made this eloquent point: "Although alimony has become a kind of extortion, child support remains a privilege. One can be an ex-husband but never an ex-father."[8]

A modern approach to constructing a viable framework for marriage would also set as a social objective the concept that only *wanted children* would be brought into this world. This should be feasible within a decade. It is the mistakes, the unwanted children, that create so much of our social agony. We should be heartened that most of the major churches are moving toward acceptance of decent and humane means of birth control, and within a decade, it is hoped, all will be in favor. Already the vast majority of all U.S. families are using family-planning techniques. Within this period, hopefully, the avalanche of changes starting finally to be made in state abortion laws will have wiped out the more punitive and inflexible prohibitions that have been driving millions of women to seek illegal abortions. Harriet Pilpel, authority on laws relating to abortion and other sexual matters, argues that most of the present state laws are unconstitutional because they deny "a woman's right to life, liberty and the pursuit of happiness."

Undoubtedly, at first, changes in the laws will relax the provisions regarding danger to health. But I would hope that within a decade a legal abortion will be available to any woman who applies to a doctor or a clinic for one. With one qualification I would agree with sociologist Alice Rossi, who recently contended, "Any woman, whether married or not, should be able to secure a safe abortion, upon her own request, at a reasonable fee, in a licensed hospital by a licensed and competent physician." But just as we should provide a period of reflection before marriage, it would be appropriate to require a week of reflection, if medically feasible, on the part of the woman after she applies for an abortion and has talked with a physician, to make sure she becomes totally aware of the consequences of the proposed action and still wants to proceed.

At the same time I would hope that we develop social mechanics to discourage any woman from having a child unless she is married and unless both she and the father want the baby. It would seem to me that the medical profession has a responsibility to encourage this development. The doctors now have ample evidence from their own psychiatrists that the genesis of sexual deviance and delinquency is fostered where there is either no father or a hostile father. Gynecologists and obstetricians should develop a code justifying the conditions under which they will accept a pregnant mother as a regular patient and encourage her to proceed to full-term pregnancy. They should be satisfied on two counts: that the parents are married and that both affirm they want the child to be born. The gynecologist who is not satisfied on these counts should be free to recommend, while he treats her temporarily, that the mother consult a free family-service agency before he accepts her as a regular patient. At the agency the counseling would include a discussion of the hazards to a child when its parents are not married and eager to have the child, a discussion of how much the mother really wants to proceed with having the child, and if she does not, the possible remedy of abortion which, hopefully, will, within a few years, be legally available in such situations in many states.

A second approach in developing a society in which only wanted children will be born will be through sex education courses that help young people understand the terrible damage anyone does to a child by bringing it into the world unwanted or outside the protective framework of an intact marriage.

As for the various proposals that we become more flexible and tolerant in our attitude toward marital infidelity, they all seem to be quite unhealthy, socially at least. There seems to be little to say for such arrangements beyond the fact that it is human for some people to slip, inevitable that some people will be promiscuous whether married or not, and inevitable that some people bored with ailing or burned-out marriages—or distressed by inadequacy feelings—will seek release or reassurance elsewhere.

The argument often heard that extramarital affairs can save

marriages might be restated as follows: Faltering marriages can be made temporarily tolerable by extramarital affairs. It is impressive that much of the evidence about the healing qualities of extramarital affairs comes from therapists who have heard about such healings from people upset enough to be their patients.

The attitude that extramarital affairs are just good fun represents a short-range, insensitive view of what is involved. First of all, there is the breaking of a personal contract. In the few instances where the other partner knows and shrugs it off, the contract has in effect lapsed and not been fully terminated because of bothersome legal requirements. Extramarital affairs, if widely tolerated, would threaten the family especially during the child-rearing phase, and this in turn would threaten society. If we accept the highly suggestive evidence of anthropologists, we can assume that in permitting monogamy to be optional we might well be undermining the advance of Western civilization.

The arrangement I have suggested for a 2-year confirmation period should greatly reduce the amount of, and tolerance of, marital infidelity. If couples proceed with their marriages after the 2-year confirmation period, we could expect to have far fewer people who could rationalize infidelity on the ground of being trapped in unfortunate wedlock. And more important, we would have considerably stronger emotional bonds than we have today between the husbands and wives in the marriages that do continue.

CHAPTER 28

Some Final Thoughts on Creating Enjoyable Unions in Any Century

---

"Marriage under the best of circumstances is something of a gamble." Morris Ploscowe, authority on laws relating to marriage.

A somewhat different version of this same admonition has been offered by psychiatrist Peter L. Giovacchini, of the University of Illinois, who stated, "A long-established marriage does not necessarily mean a well-established marriage." Gerald Sanctuary, head of the Guidance Council of Great Britain, is intrigued by the fact that in New Zealand marriage counseling is largely financed by a state lottery. He also notes that at a leading marriage counseling center in Finland, the counselors wear white hospital coats while counseling battling spouses.

The hazards of a dull or worrisome marriage can, of course, be greatly reduced by choosing thoughtfully in the first place. Traits that are delightful and charming in a boy friend may be onerous in a husband. The enchanting whimsicality of a bride may prove to be the exasperating instability of a wife.

In the absence of much guidance from parents or community, most modern young males and females interested in marriage must try to evolve a rationale to justify their choice of a future mate. Behavioral scientists have sought to develop theories to account for the people we end up with, and some offer guidelines for the choosing. But much of this theorizing is still controversial. Quite probably the varieties of human personality and human circumstance may continue to confound efforts to produce any single all-embracing theory to systematize our mate selection. And there is always the element of love, which can be based upon mature or immature considerations, but in any case is an elusive element to scale or to include in any theory.

But we do have glimmers of why, for example, men and women do become strongly attracted to each other. Some are hardly reassuring. Giovacchini, for example, has been impressed with the number of wives with alcoholics for husbands who keep complaining about their sorry lots in being trapped in life with irresponsible husbands. Yet after the husband's death, he notes, such a wife often plunges back into marriage with another alcoholic. There are emotionally immature males and females who will be attracted to almost any mates who will accept them as children and protect them as children.

One theory that had wide backing at mid-century was that males wanted someone with the personality configurations of Mom, and females wanted someone with the personality of Daddy. In 1959 a study of 170 students at the University of Wisconsin offered some support for the first half of this proposition, but found little to support the second half.[1]

In contemplating the possible traits to look for in a mate there are two quite different kinds to bear in mind. In one category are the traits that seem to be important to the success of just about any marriage; and in the other are the traits believed to be at work in producing the *fit* of the specific union in question. More seems to be acepted about the former than about the latter. We will consider them separately, starting with the latter.

Theories for getting the best "fit" in traits and characteristics between possible mates have been advanced—and critics have sought to shoot them down—for at least three decades. Here are a few of the theories about achieving such fits that seem particularly worth noting.

Homogamy. This is sometimes called "assortive mating," or more simply "likes marry likes." In the 1940s some psychologists developed polar scales on which two people could measure themselves to see how much alike they were on traits assumed to be important. The ideally mated couple was presumed to be the couple where the waves profiling the male roughly corresponded to the waves profiling the female. As recently as 1963 an investigator summed up current theories of marital compatibility by saying, "It is generally considered to be important to pick a mate who shares one's interests and who appears to be as 'alike' one as possible."[2] And at a national meeting of marriage counselors in 1965 a University of Massachusetts sociologist contended that homogamous marriages (likes attract) are less likely to produce strain than heterogeneous marriages (opposites attract).

If you measure marital success by lack of strain, quite probably homogamy offers a promising fit, but homogamy may also make for a dull marriage. A marriage can be so stable that a partner could scream from boredom.

A better case for homogamy can be made if you confine the matching to the ideas the male and female have about what is important in life and to their similarities in social and economic background than if you try to include a matching of personality traits. The males and females who come from much the same kind of home and social setting apparently have a substantially better chance on average of being compatible. Two investigators who studied 88 student marriages at a Midwestern university claimed that they found "no homogamous tendencies whatever" among the couples who met and married while on the campus. But they may have missed a major point: there would presumably be a considerable amount of built-in socio-economic homogamy among such students to start with.

Sociologist Marvin B. Sussman found in a study of 195 parents and their children that it was common for the parents to use a variety of persuasions and subtle threats to assure that their offspring married within their own social class.[3]

One factor that has weakened the tendency of people to marry persons of the same social background is that girls, with considerable support from their mothers, have traditionally tried to marry upward socially. A girl's status in life has depended far more upon whom she married than did her husband's status. But if girls marry too far upward, they may find themselves with males whose whole value-system conditioning and outlook on life are so alien that compatibility may be difficult to maintain.

Another factor weakening the likelihood that social homogamy will control the choice of mate is that with the extreme mobility of our times, and the loss of parental influence, young people are marrying more freely across ethnic, religious, color, and social class lines. And there is less social disapproval of such marriages than ever before in this century.

Similar backgrounds, however, can contribute to dullness, just as too similar personalities can. David Mace says, "Sometimes I feel that people who marry from very different backgrounds have much more depth in their marriages. When they are alike they are not stimulated by creativity and growth." He acknowledged that marriages of people from substantially different backgrounds are harder to maintain, but they can be very creative.

There is very little argument, however, that similarity of "interests" as an aspect of homogamy does help bring a man and woman into a serious relationship and can create bonds that make for a more companionable marriage.

It was popular for a while to assert that people who were attracted into marriage tended to be people who have much the same attitudes toward the world around them. This may however have been overstated. The theory of alikeness of attitudes was impressively challenged by an investigator who looked into the scores that married mates had made on a standard survey of attitudes conducted when the two were in high school together years earlier, and before they had become interested in each other. The finding was that any similarities of attitude in their precourtship days were not impressive. It was theorized that the seeming similarities of attitudes that are often found in engaged or married couples develop as they have a chance to interact with each other for a year or so.[4]

On the other hand, similarity of values—strong feelings about right and wrong ways for their world to function—do seem important in promoting a promising fit.[5]

Another factor somewhat related to homogamy that seems important to successful mating is what investigators at Uppsala University in Sweden call sharing the same "symbolic environment." The two people need to speak the same emotional language so that they don't have to keep correcting misunderstandings and explaining themselves.[6]

Complementary personality needs. There is little scientific support for the true opposite of homogamy, the "opposites attract" notion of heterogamy. There has been, however, a great deal of interest and controversy in the past dozen years over one special form of heterogamy. This is the theory that when people fall seriously in love, they may be seeking to complete themselves by uniting with a person whose traits complement their own felt needs.

This concept was most fully developed in the late 1950s, and in recent refinements, by Robert F. Winch, sociologist at Northwestern University.[7] Winch and his associates spent several years studying the psychodynamics of mate selection with special attention upon a study in considerable depth of 25 recently married couples.

Winch concluded that homogamy does indeed play a very great part in the early stages of courtship. The "field of eligibles" from which we choose people for serious courtship tends to consist of people who have much the same socio-economic backgrounds as we do ourselves. We have been exposed more to them. But from this field of eligibles, Winch concluded, we tend to choose the person whose personality gives us the greatest promise of providing us with the maximum gratification of needs we feel. Such a person gives us a sense of fulfillment that comes when we unite with a companion of the other sex whose emotional makeup at some important points complements our own. For example, they may have what we sense as a need, whether it be a desire for someone to take care of us or a desire for strength, vividness, or steadiness.

Winch found evidence that the young husbands and wives studied often were markedly different in complementary ways. Some of the partners exhibited a compelling need to protect and nurture someone, whereas their partners in marriage might indicate a need to be protected and nurtured. In one of the marriages his group studied, the girl was markedly assertive, and she had married a young man who had long been dominated by his mother and was glad to have a partner who would take charge. More recently he has also been impressed by the fact that a person who lacks a sense of achievement may be particularly attracted to a person strong in achievement. Winch found marriages where one partner was markedly outgoing, while the other was aloof. There were cases where one partner had a vivid personality, while the other had a personality notably lacking in color. And he found couples where one was shy, while the other was relatively uninhibited.

The concept that in choosing a partner we seek someone who will satisfy, at least in some way, some of our felt needs has been noted by a number of observers in addition to Winch.

Burgess and Wallin in their study of recently engaged couples stated, "Satisfying the needs of the person was mentioned perhaps more than any other single factor as one of the bases of love." As an example they cited this as an excerpt from an interview with a young husband: "She has a certain stability that I need. I'm restless and flighty. I feel that she has a steadying, calming influence."[8]

Peter Giovacchini tells of a number of studies indicating that "the neuroses of husband and wife complement each other and indicate that there is a dovetailing of conflictual and defensive patterns."[9]

When we consider what the male-female relationship is all about in terms of mutual attraction, a complementing element seems inherent. Alice Rossi comments, "Sexually men and women do after all each lack what the other has and wishes for completeness of the self." And David Mace has stated that "in the past equality of men and women was suppressed in favor of their complementarity." He added, "Today we are suppressing their complementarity in favor of their equality."

Still, when some other investigators sought in their own testing to verify the theory of complementary needs, some reported little luck.[10] One problem apparently was uncertainty about the formulation of human needs, and another was that Winch had used interviewing techniques in assessment, whereas most of the later investigators were using a pencil-and-paper testing inventory designed to identify personality traits. Sociologist J. Richard Udry in wrestling with the complementary-need approach concluded there were traits present in each partner that were deeply satisfying to the other but that these traits were not necessarily opposite sides of the coin.[11]

In June, 1962, *The American Sociological Review* carried a report that put still another light on the complementary-need theory.[12] Alan C. Kerckhoff of Duke University and Keith E. Davis of Princeton University in testing factors that might be causing young couples to be attracted to each other decided to retest them after their courtship had progressed for a half-year. Something quite interesting seemed to emerge. They had been able to find little evidence that the complementing of needs had been a factor in bringing couples together in the early stages of friendship. But they found that complementing of needs quite clearly evident among those whose courtship had progressed another 6 months. From their findings they developed the concept that a series of at least 3 "filtering factors" operates in mate selection. During the first stage, what was most apparent was that the couples were indeed very homogamous with respect to social background factors. At the second stage, there was considerable evidence that the couple's degree of consensus on values was important in determining whether they progressed into serious courtship. It was only at the third stage, when the man and girl now knew each other extremely well, with their masks down, that the complementarity factor moved in as a significant dynamic factor in their relationship.

In all the arguments there does seem to be an agreement that couples who finally marry are seeking fulfillment of some kind of personal need. The needs in some cases may be what the partners sense that they lack in themselves, and in other cases they have been attracted by similarity of values, interests, or socio-economic background. Or all these factors may be at work.

The bargain concept of mating. This is sometimes called the summation theory. It has been advanced by Swedish sociologists, particularly Gunnar Boalt.[13] His concept is that those who marry are likely to have attributes that, although quite different, when they are added up present a picture in which a fair bargain is struck between the two. He suggests, "Beauty can compensate for lack of education, intelligence make up for a less attractive exterior, wealth for lack of intelligence, and so forth. . . . In other words, despite certain differences, husband and wife will prove to be very much on a par if all the circumstances are taken into consideration." The young bride with little or no income, he suggested, can compensate social distance more easily if she is much younger than her prospective husband.

Boalt readily concedes difficulties in testing his theories because there are so many variables that go to make up a bargain. It might, however, be noted that in the United States at about the same time, a report in a psychiatric journal advanced a theory of marriage based on the "bargain concept."[14]

Using the "bargain" concept, one might conclude that if at a wedding the relatives of both the bride and groom feel vaguely that their representative isn't getting as good a spouse as he or she deserves, then the two partners involved have indeed probably achieved a fair bargain!

The role that sex drive plays in promoting or hindering progress in courtship emerged interestingly in a study made by psychologist Bernard I. Murstein at Connecticut College. He assembled 99 couples who were seriously contemplating marriage and gave them a series of tests, and later repeated the tests to see how the various factors correlated with courtship progress. He found only modest evidence of correlation for most of the factors. However, there was a fairly clear tendency for courtships to progress when the couples had similar mental health profiles. . . . where they were similar in the degree of their physical attractiveness . . . where they shared ideas on the ideal role they felt a spouse should play in marriage. And most interesting was the finding that a *low* overall sex drive in the man "tended to be strongly associated with courtship progress."

In searching for explanations for this finding, Murstein suggested, "A strong sex drive in the male presumably makes it necessary for him to be less finicky about the fit of his personality relationship with his fiancée. . . . There is considerable support for the belief that difficulty in the control of sex drive is associated with poor personality fit and some possibility that high sexuality is also associated with poor personality fit."[15] A female behavioral scientist, in commenting to me on Murstein's thesis, said, "Practically any of us females could tell you why it is so. When the male sex drive is low the female—who has in our culture been taught to beware the exploitive male—will *trust* him more, will reveal more, communicate more—i.e., the courtship is better."

If further research develops the fact that low sex drive in the male is associated with courtship progress, then girls will have a reason—or additional reason—to be wary of the males who seem especially eager to move their relationship to a bed. Murstein noted that if men had a low sex drive and the women they were courting had a high orgiastic capacity, there would be "less discrepancy in the sex control problems." And he added that a lessened discrepancy too would more likely be in accord with courtship progress.

Now let us turn to the traits that are not required in the

specific "fit" of two individuals but are believed to be associated with highly effective, enjoyable marriages of all kinds.

Some clues came out of the study supervised by Emily Mudd (in which I participated briefly) of the 100 American families from 50 states who had been chosen by community leaders and family specialists as being outstandingly successful families. Mudd and her associates, Howard Mitchell and Sara Taubin, analyzed the results of the interviewing and testing, and they conducted several dozen retests of couples before issuing their final report.[16] While their focus was upon the total family, they gained a number of impressions about successful husbands and wives.

Comparisons were made by the Mudd group of the responses provided by these successfully functioning husbands and wives with those of matched couples who were so much in conflict that they had sought professional counseling.

A principal finding was that the highly successful couples seemed to have their share of woes, tragedies, headaches—but they seemed better able to cope with them. For both groups—the successful couples and the conflicting couples—the problems causing disagreement could be listed in approximate descending order. What was noteworthy was that in virtually all the 22 different kinds of areas of disagreement the couples in conflict were about four times as likely to mention any particular item as the successful couples were. For example, on the matter of sex adjustment as a problem, it was mentioned by 80 percent of the conflicting couples and only 20 percent of the highly successful couples.

Disagreements about the wife's working showed up as a problem with 40 percent for the conflicting couples but with less than 10 percent of the successful couples. More than a third of the wives in the successful marriages were working, and overwhelmingly their husbands approved of their working.

The investigators concluded that the successful couples were couples who had learned early how to handle their problems. About 20 percent of them acknowledged that during arguments they did get pretty angry at times. But they almost never threw things or slammed doors or slapped their partners or taunted one another meanly or threatened to leave the home. Most frequently, their responses indicated, they tried to discuss the problems fair-mindedly with their partners, and many were able to criticize themselves while criticizing their partners.

In these successful marriages there seemed to be elements of both the traditional and the new equalitarian relationship. The husbands were described as being masterful but flexible; and the wives were described as devoted, but striving and equal. The wives, even more than the husbands, thought the husbands should have the main say-so. (I will note some of the other findings of the Mudd group in the section that follows.)

In the course of my 4-year exploration of male-female relationships I have come across a number of lists of general traits believed by marriage specialists to be important to success in marriage and have noted some observations of my own. What follows is my own impression of 7 traits that seem particularly likely to enhance the enjoyment of *any* marriage. Note that I put the emphasis upon *enjoyment*, not adjustment. The 7 might also be viewed as contributing to an enduring sense of love. (I should stress that many enjoyable marriages do not have all 7 traits in evidence. And I am skeptical that there is such a thing as a perfect marriage.)

A few of these 7 cannot be assessed fully until the partners have had their feet in the fire of marriage for a while. But most are traits that any perceptive young woman or young man can at least roughly gauge in a prospective mate if there has been an active courtship stage of several months. Here they are:

I. A large capacity for affection

I put this first because more and more in our turbulent era the giving and receiving of affection is what marriage is mainly about. A longing of love may bring partners to the altar, but affection will be the cement that will help them enjoy their marriage more and more, year after year, as they have more shared experiences. Psychologist Ernest van den Haag has stated—perceptively, I believe—that affection differs from love as fulfillment differs from desire. If both partners are affectionate, reveal their affection by thoughtful acts, and enjoy each other as persons for reasons other than erotic stimulation, they can and probably will remain best friends throughout their lives.

2. Emotional maturity

Marriage counselor Evelyn Duvall states that an emotionally mature personality is the best dowry you can bring to a marriage. Another noted counselor, Walter R. Stokes, trained in psychiatry, states, "It so happens that marriage is the chief proving ground of emotional maturity. . . . It is in marriage that the symptoms of emotional immaturity and neurosis most strikingly appear." When some young couples find themselves confronting the perplexities of marital interaction, one or both may start showing some of the classic symptoms of emotional immaturity we noted earlier, such as selfishness, lack of self-discipline, wishful thinking, refusal to accept responsibility, or preoccupation with pleasurable stimulation. People with these traits may seem gay companions at college house parties but are pretty hard to take in the day-to-day interaction and cooperation that married couples need to experience if they are to enjoy a long-haul marriage.

3. The capacity to communicate effectively and appealingly each other's thoughts and feelings

Inability to communicate these is a leading cause of the misunderstandings and suspicions that lead to marital misery. In choosing a partner it is crucial that the two know each other well enough to confirm that they really enjoy talking with each other on a substantial variety of subjects, are open in discussing problems that bother them, and are comfortable being together during long periods of silence.

Years before Mudd made her study of outstanding families, she told me that behind most of the specific complaints about marriage difficulties is a more common difficulty: that of poor communication between the two partners. In marriage-counseling sessions it often becomes clear that one partner has only the haziest notion of how the other feels about a specific situation. When the 100 outstandingly successful families were invited by the Mudd group to rank, in order of importance, the characteristics they considered vital to a successfully functioning family, they ranked near the top the ability to be sensitive to the needs of the other and the ability to communicate a wide range of emotions and feelings. These

100 outstanding couples were compared with the conflicting couples, through questionnaires, on how accurately they could predict their partners' feelings in various phases of physical lovemaking. It turned out that the successful couples were twelve times more accurate in understanding what was going on in the feelings and thoughts of the partner than were the couples involved in marital conflict.

Psychologists have been discovering that this factor of perception may be of considerably more importance than was formerly realized in courtship or marital success. Distortions of perception tend to create trouble. It is no help for a wife to be a trusting person if her husband perceives her to be a highly skeptical person, or if she herself perceives herself mistakenly to be highly skeptical. At the 1965 annual meeting of the American Association of Marriage Counselors, Eleanore B. Luckey reported a study on personality characteristics and marital interaction. She had drawn from several hundred people tested on their marital happiness 41 couples who scored highest on the marital happiness scales and 70 who had scored lowest. Couples in both groups completed an interpersonal checklist designed to assess their *concept* of themselves, of their spouses, of their ideal spouses, etc. Here were some of her more interesting findings:

• Couples high in satisfaction tended to agree with each other more in describing the kind of person each partner is.

• Satisfaction in marriages was related significantly to the degree to which the husband's self-concept harmonized with the concept held of him by his wife. (Agreement in perceiving the wife seemed less important.)

• In the low-satisfaction marriages the husbands felt the wives were more managerial than they were themselves; yet these same wives thought of themselves as being very self-effacing, timid, and so forth.

Incidentally, the old idea that in the successful marriage the husband is strong while the wife presents an appearance of ineffectiveness was not supported in the Luckey study. She stated, "Both the husband and the wife in the successful marriage see the wife as being quite a capable gal!"

Sociologist Gordon Shipman, of Wisconsin State University, Stevens Point, found in a study of speech thresholds and voice tolerance among married couples that it is important that the prospective partners expose themselves to each other's verbal patterns for some months before marriage. They need to do this to be sure their verbal dialogue in marriage does not become a source of unrecognized strain. He found that in general among the married the woman is more apt to have a low threshold of talk (i.e., more apt to talk readily at every opportunity) than the man. He found that among unhappy couples there were extreme differences in proneness to talk. Also happily married couples are more likely to involve a female partner who has a well-modulated voice. Women whose voices become strident when angry are more likely to be classed as unhappy wives. (Perhaps the anger contributed to the stridency.) Shipman concluded that because women have a greater range of vocal expression, "the female voice has greater potentiality for good or evil. It also suggests that the emotional tensions of women find release by way of the speech apparatus more often than do those of men. . . . It augurs ill for a marriage when husbands become silent . . . on the other hand it augurs well for a marriage when equalitarian patterns prevail and when good communication is present." [17]

4. A zest for life

The marriage that is enjoyable—and not just well-adjusted —is one where the two people are busy with their various challenging enterprises and find doing things together makes their activities more delightful than doing them alone or with someone else. This would even involve fixing a screen door together. Such couples have their private jokes and areas of good-natured chiding. They seek new experiences together— rather than the adulterer's way of seeking new experience as an escape from a partner.

5. The capacity to handle tensions constructively

This means keeping the tensions in proportion and at times even enjoying the process of discharging the tensions.

Marriage specialists still are far from agreement on the function of constructive conflict in marriage. Some contend they have found a correlation between marriage happiness and lack of conflict. My feeling is that some of the marriage textbooks put too much stress on a neat ongoing adjustment and too little on the enjoyment of living zestfully and fully with each other. In one marriage where the husband and wife had separated the wife confided to me that she and her husband had never in 8 years, even in the final disruption, raised their voices to each other or had an argument. There are other couples who say they love a good fight and the fun of making up afterward. Some psychiatrists suggest that such fighting plays an important role in restoring to the married couple the sense of longing that contributes to romantic love.

The anxiety generated by the tension and suspense creates a longing in the partners to rush back into each other's arms, and they usually do.

The marriage where the partners never raise their voices in anger is probably unrealistically based. The pioneering sociologist William Graham Sumner described marriage as an experiment in antagonistic cooperation in which two people seek in various ways to create unity out of diversity.

It may well be that the expression of feelings, including angry feelings, has become more functional in today's marriage than it was in the marriages of half a century ago. Sociologists Talcott Parsons and Robert Bales have suggested that in modern marriages "tension management" has taken on greater importance. They point out that as the Western family becomes less task-oriented—and is concerned more with achieving an optimum emotional arrangement for affection, security, companionship, and personal growth—tension management provides more gratification for the partners.[18] Young couples today, as we have seen in the research of Reuben Hill, who compared 3 generations, are more open in expressing grievances than were married couples a half-century ago. But they are also more adept at winding up their arguments with consensus and affection.

6. A playful approach to sex

All the emphasis upon the mechanics of the sexual encounter gives young people a formidable image of what goes on between a man and a woman who have a fine total relationship in which occasional tender romps are a part. It is difficult to imagine that the couples, married or unmarried, who brought themselves to orgasm before the cameras of William Masters and Virginia Johnson dallied, joked, laughed, reminisced, conveyed their feelings of tenderness or their feelings of exuberance. They had a job to do, and the tape was running out.

Psychologist Abraham Maslow, in describing the love relationship of healthy people living life to the full, suggests that to them the sexual encounters are not just a serious business of reproducing the species or reduction of tension, or even the occasional attainment of ecstasy. He states rather that the sex life of these fulfilled people at times might be "compared to the games of children and puppies." Frequently it is cheerful, humorous, and playful.[19]

7. The capacity to accept fully the other person with full knowledge of his shortcomings

There can be no reservations. Despite everything, there must always be respect. It is only in such an environment that the two people dare let down their defenses and truly be themselves, which is a requirement for contentment and for a sense of completeness in marriage. Of the 100 couples in the Mudd study one of them nicely summed up what a good marriage meant by saying, "Home means you can expose your weaknesses without shame, can brag a little without fear of misunderstanding, and can make mistakes without being ridiculed."[20]

Love in its most gratifying sense means the full acceptance of the other person. Philosophers and theologians sometimes refer to this kind of love as *agape*. Theologian Helmut Thielicke reasons that *agape* becomes creative because "the other person knows that he is being addressed and respected at the core of his being. . . . It is not neo-Romanticism to dare to say that one can tell by looking at many older married folks that they have been much loved. Qualities have been released within them, 'loved out of them.' "[21]

If you fully accept the other person as he is, knowing his shortcomings, you will also be far more inclined to trust him. People who are trusted show a very high level of reciprocation of trust. And mutual trust is at the heart of marital success. Eleanore Luckey has found in her studies that one of the big differences between couples high in marital satisfaction and those low in it is that those who are high in satisfaction—far more than those who are low—are more trustful in their attitudes toward their partners.

Here are a few last thoughts about the relationship of men and women who marry. While roles in marriage should be equal, the often-cited ideal of similarity of roles in a sexually undifferentiated companionate-type male-female relationship has serious shortcomings of dullness and inefficiency for both partners. These shortcomings, I hope, will frustrate the attainment of the ideal on any wide-scale basis in the future.

Sociologists Robert O. Blood and Donald M. Wolfe, in their long study of husbands and wives, concluded, "Where young couples find companionship in doing the dishes together, middle-aged couples come to take each other for granted sufficiently so that they can appreciate each other's work at separate tasks. No longer is it necessary to work together to prove their love. Love has been tested and accepted. Now they can express their love through each other's separate contribution to a complementary whole."[22]

A clear differentiation of roles in marriage seems most productive, too, when we look at the impact of the husband and wife upon their children. Sociologist Murray A. Straus, of the University of Minnesota, tested the impact of various types of parental relationships and power distribution on 287 high-school boys in Wisconsin. How did the various patterns affect their grades, their ambitions, and anxiety, their admiration or rejection of their parents?

The best overall parental pattern, he found, was that where there was equalitarianism between the husband and wife, but also a clear differentiation in their roles in the home.[23]

Young couples will be greatly assisted in enjoying their transition into marriage if they can make the transition in a congenial, stimulating locale. Their marriages will be strengthened if both can have a sense of participation in a genuine community. For many this sense of participation will be possible only if their society comes to terms with conditions currently making such a sense of community difficult for many couples to attain. I refer to the difficulties in establishing a home offering fulfillment and contentment where there is urban sprawl, clutter, garishness, and sameness. There are similar difficulties when one or both partners must work in a giant, depersonalized bureaucracy demanding highly mobile personnel.

An easing of the impact of such conditions on the individuals involved must be achieved if we are to have a congenial environment in which males and females in love can experience their encounters, tribulations, and delights.

We can expect that close to nine-tenths of the unmarried young men and women now entering the third decade of their lives will become married before their third decade has ended.

Those who marry and are lucky will succeed in achieving two patterns of life above all. Both partners will gain a sense of personal fulfillment as they do the very best they are capable of doing as *individual* men and women. And second, the two partners will achieve something close to a sense of completeness. They will develop a male-female unity. What one partner experiences will often be experienced almost as vividly by the other. Out of the completing and unifying they will create the next generation.

Participating in this process of fulfilling, unifying, and re-creating remains, for most of us, still the ultimate of attainment in this or any century.

APPENDIXES

Appendix to Chapter 9

(This is an amplification of studies summarized in Chapter 9. The numbers in parentheses identify the various studies as listed and described in the Reference Notes for this Chapter 9.)

CIRCUMSTANTIAL FACTS REGARDING INCIDENCE OF PREMARITAL COITUS IN THE UNITED STATES

Illegitimacy

• From 1940 to 1963 the rate of illegitimacy tripled. It rose from 7.1 per 1000 unmarried females of childbearing age to 22.5. (See Reference Note 1 for Chapter 9.)

• The rate at which illegitimate births have occurred in the white population has increased more rapidly in recent years than in the nonwhite population. (Note 2). . . . Nonwhites contribute a majority of all illegitimate births, 58% in 1963, according to the estimates of the Public Health Service. (1). . . . Vincent reports, however, that in 1957 nonwhites accounted for 65%. (3). . . . From 1960 to 1965 the illegitimacy rate for white women increased 26% while the rate for nonwhites showed a slight drop, according to the National Center for Health Statistics in 1968.

• Whether illegitimacy is measured by number, ratio, or rate, it was the females under 20 who had the smallest percentage increases in illegitimacy during the 20-year period of 1938-1957, according to Vincent. (4)

Abortion

• At least as many unmarried women abort their babies as become unwed mothers. Ira L. Reiss stated in 1966 that "It is estimated that each year almost 300,000 brides are pregnant when married, that an equal number of single girls have abortions, and that an equal number become unwed mothers." (5)

Premarital Pregnancy

• On the basis of his interviewing in the 1940s, Alfred Kinsey concluded that 10% of all females become pregnant before marriage. (6) In contrast, in 1966 staff officials of the Connecticut State Department of Health estimated that 17% of the girls of that state then in their teens would become pregnant out of wedlock *before* their 20th birthdays, and the national rate is estimated to be about the same, or perhaps a little higher. (8)

• In their study of high-school girls in Nebraska, Moss and Gingles found that 31% of those who married while still in high school acknowledged they were pregnant when they married. (7) A study by Lee Burchinal in Iowa indicated that 57% of the high-school marriages there involved pregnant brides. (6)

Venereal Disease

Between 1956 and 1960, venereal disease among adolescents in the U.S.A. increased by 130%, according to Celia Deschin. (9) And between 1960 and 1965, it increased another 200%, according to the American Medical Association. (10) Thus, in a decade it more than tripled.

DENMARK—CIRCUMSTANTIAL FACTS

Kirsten Auken (34) reported that 50% of the girls who had married, in her study, were pregnant at the time of marriage.

SWEDEN

Birgitta Linnér (36B) reports that in Sweden "more than 40% of all first born babies are conceived before the wedding takes place."

ENGLAND

Hartley (38) reports that, in the 25 years ending in 1962, the rate of illegitimacy in England and Wales tripled, from 5.8 to 18.9.

DIRECT EVIDENCE INDICATING INCIDENCE OF PREMARITAL INTIMACY

(As revealed in surveys of behavior and attitudes)

Two of the early studies are particularly helpful, since they made breakdowns of respondents by the decade of their births. Those are the Terman and Kinsey studies. (13, 17, 18) For readier comprehension, we have taken the liberty of translating decade-of-birth to the decade when the respondents over 20 were

20 years old (and consequently near the peak of any premarital sex activity).

Kinsey, it should be noted, evidently changed his view about the persistence of a society's sex behavior between the time he and his associates wrote the male book and, later, the female book. Perhaps this was because there was less evidence of change by decades among males than among females. At any rate, he did not break the males down by decade of birth, but simply divided them into "older generation" and "younger generation," based roughly on whether they were at the peak of any premarital sex activity before or after 1925. That, perhaps, was an unfortunate split point because it tended to blur the substantial changes that took place in premarital sex patterns during the turbulent decade of the 1920s. He corrected this in the female book by using decades of birth. But in the earlier male book, he expressed doubt that any considerable change in sex behavior could be expected "within a generation or two." Two generations span more than half a century.

REGARDING THE GENERAL POPULATION—U.S.A.
(Samples drawn from a broad segment)

EVIDENCE OF PREMARITAL COITUS (ALL FIGURES ARE FOR CUMULATIVE INCIDENCE)

The Situation Before 1920

• Davis found (11, p. 20) that among married *women* who mostly were in their courtship phase just before World War I, the incidence by *time of marriage* was 7%.

• Terman found (13) that among *men* and *women* who had their 20th birthdays beween 1910 and 1919, the coital rates by *time of marriage* were:

For males ....58%   For females 26%

About two-thirds of the experienced wives in this age group indicated that all of their coital experience had been with the men they later married. Of the men in his sample who reached the age of 20 before 1910, fewer than one-third of those with experience said they had had any of the experience with the women they subsequently married!

• Kinsey (17, p. 339) found that of women who reached their 20th birthdays before the 1920s, 8% had experienced premarital coitus *by the age of 20,* and 14% were experienced *by the age of 25.*

Decade of the 1920s

• Terman (13) found for his subjects who had their 20th birthdays between 1920 and 1929 the incidence *by marriage* was:

For *males* ....67%   For *females* 49%

By now, two-thirds of his males had at least some of their experience with their brides-to-be.

• Kinsey (17, p. 339) found that of *women* who reached their 20th birthdays during this decade, 18% had now experienced coitus *by the age of* 20, and 36% had experienced coitus *by the age of* 25.

Kinsey's "older generation" *males* (in their sexual prime between 1910 and 1925) showed extraordinary differences based on education. (18, pp. 395–404) Of those males who eventually went to college, 9% had experienced coitus *by the age of* 15; and 39% had *by the age of* 20. In contrast, those males with only a grade-school education showed this experience for the same ages:

By age 15................34%   By age 20 ....82%

Decade of the 1930s

• Kinsey's "younger generation" *males* (in their sexual prime roughly between 1925 and 1945) showed not only a small, but a consistent, rise in coital experience by various age levels, but still showed very great differences by educational level. Of these younger males who ultimately went to college, those with coital experience were:

By age 15 .... 9%   By age 20 ....45%

The experience for those with only a grade-school education was:

By age 15 ....51%   By age 20 ....87%

As for Kinsey's findings on *females* who had their 20th birthdays during the decade of the 1930s (17, p. 339), their coital experience by *specific ages* was as follows:

By age of 20 ....23%   By age of 25 ....39%

• Terman's controversial findings, for the very few subjects in his sample who had their 20th birthdays in the decade of the

1930s, showed a coital incidence *by marriage* of 86% for the males and 68% for the females.

Regarding the male experience, it should be noted that 4 out of 5 had at least some of their experience with their future brides, whereas in the "Before 1910" group, he found less than 1 in 3 so indicating. As for the high Terman female score in this decade, it should be noted that his sample here was very small, between 60 and 75 individuals. This may have led Terman to his famous speculation that patterns were changing with such "extraordinary rapidity" that "intercourse with future spouse before marriage will become universal by 1950 or 1955"—meaning among people born between those years. (18, p. 556)

• The 666 married couples of the Burgess and Wallin study (20) were questioned between 1936 and 1946. Thus, while the book itself appeared in the 1950s, it was reflecting premarital behavior that occurred largely, if not primarily, in the 1930s. Their coital rates by the time of marriage (pages 164, 330):

For males ....68%   For females 47%

Decade of the 1940s

• Kinsey (17, p. 339) found that for women who reached their 20th birthdays during the 1940s, the coital (premarital) rates by age were:

By age 20 ....21%   By age 25 ....37%

Regarding Kinsey's total female sample born in all decades covered, he found:

1. "Nearly 50% of the females in our sample had had coitus before they married" (p. 286). But of college women who married, 60% had experienced coitus by marriage (p. 293). (Perhaps it was because of later age of marrying.)

2. But of all females who had married at a *given* age, approximately the same percentage experienced coitus irrespective of educational level. (This is quite different from his male picture.)

3. Of married females with premarital experience (p. 292), 46% had confined coitus to their fiancés.

4. For his *total* female sample, born in all decades, the percentages by age (p. 286) were as follows:

By age 20 ....20%   By age 22 ....30%
By age 21 ....25%   By age 25 ....37%

• M. P. Warner (19) found that of 402 brides who sought medical consultation those who had already experienced coitus were 42%.

Decade of the 1960s

The survey for *Seventeen* magazine of 1166 U.S. teen-age girls in its Consumer Panel (32X) indicated that about 15% had experienced coitus. The age range was wide: from 13 to 19 years. About 25% of those girls in the 18–19-year group reported they had experienced coitus.

EVIDENCE OF PREMARITAL PETTING IN GENERAL POPULATION

Definitions of petting vary. Our own is the fondling of parts of the body normally covered by clothing. Kinsey's apparently was considerably broader. But he did have, by decade of birth, figures on "premarital petting to orgasm."

His figures on this for women (17, p. 275) show the following pattern for 25-year-old women who reached their 20th birthdays during the decade indicated:

Before 1920	...........15%	The 1930s	...............34%
The 1920s	.... 30%	The 1940s	...............43%

In 1967, in *Seventeen* magazine's survey of 1166 teen-age girls, 71% of the 18–19-year-old girls reported they had engaged in some form of petting (not necessarily to orgasm).

FOREIGN SURVEYS REGARDING PREMARITAL COITUS
WITHIN GENERAL POPULATION

FRANCE

• The *French Institute of Public Opinion,* in a sampling made during the 1950s (41, p. 109) asked of women: "Did you give yourself to your husband before you were married, as many girls do nowadays?"

The answer of 30% of the married women was yes.

Of those married women between ages 21 and 24, 37% said yes.

Of the married women between ages 45 and 49, 15% said yes.

GERMANY

• The *Divo Institute* made a survey in 1950 asking people whether they had had "intimate relations with" persons of the opposite sex before marriage.

The *yes* responses: 70% of women, 89% of men.

(This study is cited by William J. Goode, *World Revolution and Family Patterns.* New York: The Free Press, 1963.)

• L. von Friedeburg reported in 1950 that 69% of 517 German females had experienced premarital coitus. (17, p. 287)

The German figures seem rather spectacularly higher than the French figures.

ENGLAND

• The Chesser group (39) made a decade-of-birth analysis in the manner of Kinsey and Terman. Here is the incidence of premarital coitus (p. 311) reported by women who were married:

Women who reached the age of 20 before 1924 ....19%
Women who were 20 in the 1924–34 period 36%
Women who were age 20 in the 1934–44 period ... 39%
Women who were age 20 in the 1944–54 period 43%

• Schofield found (40), in his group's random interviewing of 1873 teen-age boys and girls in the 15–19-year-old range earlier in this decade, that the following percentages had experienced premarital coitus by the age of 18 (p. 247):

Boys ....34%   Girls 17%

And by the age of 19 (p. 42) the cumulative incidence had reached:

For boys ....37%   For girls 23%

The majority of experienced girls had had experience with more than one partner.

SWEDEN

• In the city of Örebro, investigators Hans Linderoth and Bengt Rundberg have recently completed a study of the sex habits of 497 school students who averaged slightly less than 18 years of age. They found 57% of the boys and 46% of the girls had experienced intercourse. (364, p. 19) This latter figure would suggest that as of a few years ago about twice as many 18-year-old Swedish girls had been experiencing intercourse as indicated for same-age U.S. girls. (32X)

• Gustav Jonsson reported in 1951, on the basis of sampling a small group of approximately 180 married women, that 80% had experienced premarital intercourse. (37X)

DENMARK

•Kirsten Auken (33) reports that of the 183 married, divorced, or separated women she randomly sampled in Danish hospitals, about 97% had experienced premarital coitus. This sampling took place in the 1944–47 period. Of all the married and single women she sampled, however, about 70% had serious relationships (married, engaged, or "walking out") with the men with whom they experienced first coitus.

EAST GERMANY

• Professor Rolf Borrmann of Leipzig University interviewed 900 young people and found that by age 20, 78% of the girls and 83.5% of the young men had had premarital sexual relations (source, *The New York Times*, February 26, 1967).

ITALY

• Gabriella Parca, an anthropologist-journalist who is a member of the Center for Cultural Anthropology at the University of Rome, interviewed 1018 men in Italy between ages 20 and 50 and reported her findings in her book *The Sultans*, published in 1966. She found:

—75% condemn or have reservations about any woman who has premarital coitus.
—75% of the men reported they themselves had consorted with prostitutes. In short, a classic picture of the double standard.

REGARDING THE PREMARITAL INTIMACY OF COLLEGE STUDENTS
(As revealed in surveys of individual respondents)

These surveys of the behavior and attitudes of college-educated individuals while they were virtually all still in their undergraduate years in college provide a good focus for decade-by-decade comparison.

INCIDENCE OF PREMARITAL COITUS—U.S. STUDENTS

All percentages shown are for the cumulative incidence while the students were college undergraduates, unless otherwise specified.

The 1930s
• Bromley and Britten (15) found from their combined questionnaire-and-interview sampling of 1364 college students that

The incidence was:

For male students .... about 50%

For female students .... about 25%

The median age of first coitus for males was 17, for females 18.

The 1940s

• The Kinsey studies fortunately presented findings both by age level and by level of education. Thus, for example, they provide information on college-educated males and females when they were 20, 21, and 22 years old. (17, p. 94 and 18, p. 550) (It should be noted that while virtually all of the informants were interviewed in the 1940s, some were in college before 1940.) The results:

	MALES	FEMALES
20-year-olds	44%	20%
21-year-olds	49%	27% (approx.)
22-year-olds	54%	31% (approx.)

• Porterfield and Salley (16) in their highly conservative sample that included many ministerial students:

Cumulative incidence while still in college:

Male .... 32%   Female 9%

In general, for both male and female students, non-churchgoers were twice as likely to have experienced coitus as were churchgoers.

The 1950s

• Although Landis states (21) that he surveyed 3000 students in 11 colleges on a broad range on subjects, he covers only the sex behavior of females in his published reports. His figure (p. 172) for girls, 9 to 12%.

Students familiar with the moralistic tone of his textbook conceivably might be reluctant to state even on his anonymous questionnaires that they had been involved in "disregarding . . . standards concerning sex conduct." All respondents were in family sociology courses.

• Ehrmann (22) likewise surveyed students from all 4 years of undergraduate life, but confined his survey to 1 southern university (Florida). His findings regarding "Lifetime behavior" of 841 students on his AB Schedule (p. 56).

Cumulative incidence while still in college:

Male .... 65%   Female 13%

He expressed surprise (p. 95) that the coitus rate of his females varied little from the youngest to oldest groups.

• Freedman (26) found in his study of 49 Vassar girls in the class of 1958 that the percentage who experienced coitus before graduation was 22%.

Freedman entitled his report, you may recall, "Sexual Behavior of American College Women." And near the end, he stated that the data he presented were consistent with the findings of other studies which he said are "almost unanimous" in finding the incidence of non-virginity among college women to be "25% or lower." The other studies he specifically cited were Ehrmann and Kinsey.

• Bell and Blumberg (23) found the incidence of coitus for females, but not males, varied depending upon the degree of involvement. For example, for 3 kinds:

Cumulative incidence while still in college:

	MALES	FEMALES
Dating Relationship	46%	10%
A Going Steady Relationship	40%	15%
An Engaged Relationship	46%	31%

And they found some intriguing differences of behavior, especially among Catholic students, based on degree of commitment.

	MALES	FEMALES
Dating Relationship, Catholics	64%	8%
Engaged Relationship, Catholics	33%	56%

They state that most of their Catholic students were of Italian background. At any rate, among the Catholics we see the double standard most clearly. The male's experience becomes less as commitment deepens, while the Catholic female's experience rate soars dramatically with commitment.

• Kanin and Howard (24) sampled only wives of students residing in 3 housing units on a Midwestern university campus. Mean years spent in college by the wives was 2.5. The percentage of the females who had experienced premarital coitus with spouse was 43%.

The coital rate for lower-class females was twice as high as that for either middle- or upper-class females.

The authors concluded that premarital intercourse is "most characteristic of couples where the male is of a higher class." Presumably, the lesser-status wife feels a desire to compensate by extending sexual favors.

• Kirkendall (27) reported that 19% of his 200 college men who had experienced coitus had, at some time or another, patronized prostitutes. Of those who had patronized prostitutes, at least 88% had done it as a group activity (p. 26).

The 1960s

• The Freemans (30) report that the 800 college *senior* women they studied revealed that the percentage who had experienced coitus was 55%.

In analyzing their data the Freemans conclude further that "college women have had coitus in the following percentages:

freshmen	15 to 20%
sophomores	30 to 35%
juniors	40 to 45%
seniors	50 to 60%
graduate students	60 to 70%"

Average age of first coitus of experienced seniors was 18, or "4.5 years after the average first date and 2 years after the first petting." The girls in their noncoital group had, on the other hand, not begun petting until age 18. From this they conclude: "There is thus a nearly mathematical formula, with age at dating, age at petting, number of dates, and number of men determining the likelihood of premarital intercourse." However, they indicate any formula would have to allow also for educational plans. Presumably college girls, they suggest, are "the ones who avoided marriage or pregnancy in high school." And they add: "Similarly, our survey proves that those senior women who plan to go on to graduate school have fewer fiancés and are less sexually involved." In short, girls, they suggest, pace their sexual behavior according to how far away they perceive marriage to be!

• In 1967, considerable newspaper and other attention was given to statements by 2 psychiatrists writing or speaking to national medical audiences who both cited a study made of 300 women students at the University of Winsconsin. They cited it to support their opinion that sex behavior had changed very little in recent decades. The study, made in early 1965, by Schmitt and

Grinder, (28) indicated the following percentage of sexually experienced: 22%.

What was generally overlooked was that this "survey" had been quite incidental to a study of the students' knowledge of contraception. (There was only one brief sentence in the authors' report mentioning coital experience.) And more to the point, it was generally overlooked that nearly half of the questionnaires (46%) were distributed to freshmen, many of them entering freshmen.

FOREIGN STUDIES OF PREMARITAL COITUS
AMONG COLLEGE-LEVEL STUDENTS

DENMARK

• Christensen and Carpenter (25A) found in their comparison of university students at 2 U.S. universities and 1 in Denmark during the late 1950s the following levels of response on premarital coitus:

Cumulative incidence while in college:

	MALES	FEMALES
Danish university	64%	60%
U.S. Midwestern university	51%	21%
Intermountain univ. (U.S.— Mormon influence strong)	39%	9%

Both the Danish men and girls who had experienced coitus had the experience first about 1½ years later than the experienced Americans.

Of the females who had experienced coitus, those recalling having "pleasant" feelings on the day after first experience showed this variation: Danish—73% pleasant; Midwestern—34% pleasant; Intermountain—14% pleasant.

Christensen and Carpenter also note that a larger percentage of Danish men had experienced first coitus with a steady girl friend or a fiancée than American men.

SWEDEN

• Evidence indicating a swift, emphatic change taking place in the sex habits of young college-oriented Swedes emerges from 2 studies supervised by Georg Karlsson of the Sociologist Institute in Uppsala. In 1960 he made a study of the sex habits of students at several "Peoples' Colleges" or "Folk High Schools" (roughly comparable to community colleges in the U.S.A.). (37) The incidence of coitus reported was:

Male .... 72%   Female 40%

Five years later he repeated his study at several Peoples' Colleges (36A, p. 19) and found the following higher figures:

Male .... 81%   Female 65%

The increase for the girls over the 5 years is particularly sharp, more than 60%.

• In 1958 the Sociological Institute at Uppsala University translated a Swedish version of the Christensen-Carpenter questionnaire and distributed it to 117 of the university's sociology students. (37) The incidence of coitus reported by these university students was:

Male .... 65%   Female 45%

Karlsson and his associates also found from their studies that for both males and females the experienced university students, who usually faced a longer haul of education, had their first coital experience at least a year later, on the average, than students at the Peoples' Colleges.

COLLEGIATE ATTITUDES TOWARD PREMARITAL COITUS

1950s

• Ehrmann (22) reported that 53% of his male students (Southern) wanted to marry a virgin—although 65% of Ehrmann's male students were not themselves virgins (p. 237).

• Landis (21, p. 175) found among his students 52% opposed premarital coitus for both male and female; and only 20% favored it for both.

In Denmark, Christensen and Carpenter (25B) found that 43% of the male students and 34% of the female students found premarital coitus acceptable on casual dates if there was mutual desire. American students at a Midwestern university found such coitus acceptable only by 17% of the male students and 3% of the female students. This was during the late 1950s.

1960s

• Columbia College yearbook (29), *The Columbian*, 1964, reports that of 540 senior men 83% believed in premarital intercourse. But some noted it was vaguely put. One asked, "For me or my sister?"

• Freeman's female seniors (30) responded with these percentages for premarital coitus:

All right if engaged	64%
All right if in love	58%
All right if there is no exploitation	40%

• Reiss (32) found a vast difference between adult and student attitudes on what is acceptable. Full premarital sexual relations are acceptable, he reported, in these ways:

	ADULT SAMPLE % FINDING COITUS ACCEPTABLE		STUDENT SAMPLE % FINDING COITUS ACCEPTABLE	
	FOR MALES	FOR FEMALES	FOR MALES	FOR FEMALES
If engaged	19	17	52	44
If strong affection	16	12	37	27
No affection	12	7	21	11

His "student" sample includes students from a white and a Negro high school in Virginia, a white and a Negro college in Virginia, and a white college in New York State with liberal rules. A comparison of responses by students at the white Virginia college and students at the Negro college indicates the total "student" response above was substantially liberalized by responses from the Negro schools and the white New York colleges. Here is how students at the white and Negro colleges in Virginia responded on the same items. The figures show the percentage finding coitus acceptable under the indicated condition.

	WHITE VIRGINIA COLLEGE		NEGRO VIRGINIA COLLEGE	
	FOR MALES	FOR FEMALES	FOR MALES	FOR FEMALES
If engaged	32%	22%	72%	54%
If strong affection	21%	9%	50%	34%

EVIDENCE RELATING TO THE POSSIBILITY THAT SIGNIFICANT
REGIONAL PATTERNS AND VARIATIONS BY SCHOOL MAY EXIST
REGARDING PREMARITAL INTIMACY

Aubrey Wendling, sociologist at San Diego State College, told us he thought an important aspect of premarital sex behavior in the U.S.A. today is the regional differences. And he added, "Certainly in this region [Southern California] there is a widespread impression at least that there is a greater incidence of promiscuousness than in the rest of the country."

Specific evidence of regional differences is fragmentary but strongly suggestive, most of it from studies of collegians. Here is the most specific information we have encountered of variations by region or school.

Ira Reiss seems impressed with differences from school to school. In #32 he shows a striking difference between sex standards considered appropriate for both males and females at 2 schools in the East (1 in New York, 1 in Virginia). He compared his total sample, of males and females combined, at a "white Virginia college" (small liberal arts) with the comparable responses at a "white New York college believed to contain a highly permissive group of students." Results in views on when full sexual relations are acceptable:

	VIRGINIA COLLEGE		PERMISSIVE N.Y. COLLEGE	
	FOR MALES	FOR FEMALES	FOR MALES	FOR FEMALES
If in love	31%	16%	77%	72%

In talking with me, Reiss indicated that coital experience for females at the very permissive college (in New York) might run as high as 65%, whereas coital experience for girls at the other school (in Virginia) might be as low as 5%.

Reiss, in his recent book *The Social Context of Premarital Sexual Permissiveness,* reporting on his extensive studies, ranked the U.S. regions by the proportion of adults giving "highly permissive" responses in a national sampling. Here is the ranking on high permissiveness:

Northeast	19%
West	17%
North Central	14%
South	11%

• The Freemans (30) seem impressed with the fact that there are some noteworthy regional variations, but feel there are also strong similarities by regions.

They suggest geography is a factor both *from* (where the girls came from) and *to* (where they went to school). They offer these impressions:

Re sex behavior: "The East and West are most liberal; the South [except Florida and Texas] most conservative. The Midwest is median." Also, girls in the East and South are more likely to sleep with a boy without intercourse, they reported.

• Gael Greene in her talks with small groups of girls in many parts of the country (31, p. 10) reported that she had gotten as a major impression the fact that the sexual mores on college campuses varied considerably by location and type of school. She said, "It seems clear from my own research that geography [California hedonism, Southern fundamentalism, Texas automobilism], location [how far to the nearest metropolis, the most accessible boys' college, the quickest source of alcohol] and type of institution [Big Ten, country club, church-run, Brahmin deb, community college] does influence the sexual climate, the atmosphere of freedom or repression, and the pressures under which sexual decisions are made."

• At the teen-age level, *Seventeen* magazine's survey of 1166 girls in the general population (32X) found regional differences that were considered worth noting: "More girls from the West . . . reported having intercourse, with the Southerners second, Easterners third, and girls from the North Central area last."

• Ehrmann, in his 1959 report (22) on premarital dating behavior, reported on only 1 Southern university. He said that "it seems reasonable to assume that it is representative both of this and other comparable student bodies in most, but certainly not all, respects. *That there are, no doubt, differences among college groups according to geographic origin and social origin is not questioned. . . .*" (Italics supplied.)

• And by 1963, in writing in the January, 1963, issue of *The Journal* of the National Association of Women Deans and Counselors he stated:

"Bromley and Britten called attention to some large variations of campus to campus groups." He related that Bromley and Britten found the premarital coital rate at 1 of the more conservative women's colleges at only 18% whereas it was 36% at a woman's college with a reputation for liberal views.

APPENDIXES TO CHAPTER 10

Appendix A to Chapter 10

INFORMATION SHEETS ATTACHED TO EACH CHECK-
LIST DISTRIBUTED AT U.S. COLLEGES

Thank you for examining this. Approximately 100 unmarried older students on your campus are receiving this informal checklist of attitudes and behavior regarding male-female relationships. A good many hundred other students in schools across the country and abroad are receiving the same checklist.

This survey is one aspect of a larger investigation I am making, over a period of several years, of the possible impact of social change on individual attitudes and behavior patterns. The findings will ultimately be summarized in a book of social comment I expect to prepare.

Arrangements for assuring your anonymity are described in "Regarding Protective Procedures" on the following page.

The questionnaire can be entirely completed with simple check marks. Attached is a stamped envelope addressed to me. If you are agreeable to checking all or part of the checklist, after you finish put it in the envelope and drop it in the nearest mailbox. If you check nothing at all I would be grateful if you would still mail the blank form back so that I can assuredly tabulate it as a decline.

I have attached separately a sheet for any amplifying comments. These could be valuable to me. Just type or jot your comment by item number.

In seeking your views in this anonymous survey I make one strong plea. Please respond to items only where you feel absolutely comfortable and candid in doing so.

(signed Vance Packard)

Regarding Protective Procedures

The President of the Russell Sage Foundation recently set forth 3 conditions he felt should ideally be met in any research into individual attitudes and behavior to assure that each individual's private personality is respected. The 3 conditions—some of which, he conceded, can at times not be fully met—were anonymity, confidentiality, and consent.

This project is designed to meet all 3 of these conditions absolutely. Consent is inherent in the volunteer nature of the survey. To assure anonymity and confidentiality, I have designed a triangular form of inquiry. I have asked one or more young adults on your campus who, I am assured, are responsible and conscientious to distribute the approximately 100 survey forms as randomly as feasible. The questionnaire can be completed by simple checkmarks.

Students distributing the forms are instructed to make no record whatever of the identity, when known to them, of recipients of the form. You mail the form directly to me. If you make any written comments on the "Sheet For Amplifying Comments" and for any reason wish to isolate them when you mail the main checklist, just send the comment sheet to me in a separate envelope.

All forms that I receive will be secure in my files for a number of years.

No codes are involved beyond the stamping you see ————————————————————. And that is the extent that anyone will be identified in any report I make public.

I would appreciate it if you, in turn, would keep the contents of this inquiry reasonably confidential; and of course bear in mind that none of it is for publication.

Appendix B to Chapter 10

INSTRUCTION TO CHECKLIST DISTRIBUTORS ON U.S. CAMPUSES

The student managing distribution at each college or university was directed to seek as representative a sample as feasible; and possible procedures were discussed. In addition, each manager was given the following mimeographed instruction sheet:

Procedures for Distribution

— Distribute only to undergraduate juniors and seniors.
— Distribute to assure a full spectrum of personality types in the sample, not just extroverts, etc. The best approach is to go room-to-room in dormitories, fraternities, etc. And stop at every room.
— Other possible distribution points are student lounges, cafeterias, etc., where students relax. Make certain you approach all juniors of your sex, not just friends, etc.
— Try to distribute on an individual basis. Avoid groups of more than two persons.
— Do not distribute outdoors. Distribute only in student territory, not in the more clearly academic territory such as classroom buildings.
— In approaching each individual simply say something along these lines: "Vance Packard, the author (etc.) is making a survey on many campuses of the attitudes and experiences of older college students. Would you care to look at his checklist when you have a few minutes and see if you would be interested in completing all or part of it."

– Leave checklists only with students who indicate a willingness to give the questionnaire a serious inspection.

– If they seek more detailed information about the checklist, you can indicate the checklist has questions about "career plans, marriage, dating, things like that." Or let them look at it. Such a general approach is essential so that your sample of persons accepting the checklist for more careful inspection represents a good variety of personality types and not just the more worldly, outspoken ones.

APPENDIXES TO CHAPTER II

Appendix A to Chapter II

The "yes" responses of students in the East and the Midwest to the question "Do you feel that ideally it is still true that a man and a girl who marry should have their first full sexual experience together?" were:

	MIDWESTERN STUDENTS	EASTERN STUDENTS
Male	66%	39%
Female	73%	40%

Appendix B to Chapter II

Here are the responses to the question whether students would be troubled to marry a person with premarital coital experience with someone else:

	U.S. MALES	U.S. FEMALES
No	30%	61%
Some, but not seriously	53%	30%
Yes, seriously	17%	9%

Appendix C to Chapter II

The order in which male and female students checked "No" (that they would not be troubled by the idea of marrying someone with previous premarital experience) was as follows:

MALES	"NO"	FEMALES	"NO"
East	38%	East	71%
South	36%	West	68%
West	28%	South	67%
Midwest	21%	Midwest	34%

(Note: Figures here and elsewhere in regional analysis are based on an averaging of school percentages.)

Appendix D to Chapter 11

TABLE 1. Age Level and Type of Relationship that U.S. College Males Viewed as Appropriate for Considering Coitus

	AGE LEVEL			
TYPE OF RELATIONSHIP	14–17	18–20	21–23	24 & OVER
Only if married	67.6	33.5	23.4	18.9
Officially Engaged	10.7	14.8	15.0	13.9
Tentatively Engaged	06.7	15.5	16.1	11.5
Going Steady	08.5	20.5	19.0	18.1
Good Friends	02.1	08.1	14.3	13.9
Casually Attracted	04.4	07.6	12.2	23.7
	100%	100%	100%	100%
Number of respondents	(469)	(540)	(566)	(501)

TABLE 2. Age Level and Type of Relationship that U.S. College Females Viewed as Appropriate for Considering Coitus

	AGE LEVEL			
TYPE OF RELATIONSHIP	14–17	18–20	21–23	24 & OVER
Only if married	86.5	58.6	46.0	38.3
Officially Engaged	07.7	16.7	19.2	17.4
Tentatively Engaged	02.1	11.7	15.4	14.0
Going Steady	02.5	09.7	13.6	19.2
Good Friends	00.8	01.2	03.2	06.1
Casually Attracted	00.4	02.1	02.6	05.0
	100%	100%	100%	100%
Number of respondents	(530)	(580)	(624)	(557)

Appendix E to Chapter 11

Here is an averaging of collegiate scores among female students *upholding* the reasonableness of waiting until marriage to experience coitus for individuals in the 21–23-year-old group, by types of school:

	ONLY IF MARRIED
An averaging of 7 private institutions	36%
An averaging of 10 public institutions	47%
An averaging of 2 church-related institutions	82%

And for the males the pattern is similar, though less emphatic:

An averaging of 7 private institutions	20%
An averaging of 10 public institutions	23%
An averaging of 2 church-related institutions	53%

Appendix F to Chapter 11

Below are the contrasting responses of career and non-career-oriented girls in insisting that any coitus between people in the 21–23-year-old group be confined to marriage:

Career-oriented girls	40%
Girls not oriented to careers	56%

Appendix G to Chapter 11

Females at 4 universities abroad showed the following percentage of approval of premarital coitus as appropriate if the individuals involved not only had a relationship of love, protectiveness, loyalty, and trust, but also were chronologically and emotionally mature.

Girls at Canadian university	68%
Girls at Norwegian university	78%
Girls at German university	83%
Girls at English university	86%

APPENDIXES TO CHAPTER 12

Appendix A for Chapter 12

Here are the regional percentages for males and females of premarital coital incidence if the 2 schools listed at the high extreme and low extreme are eliminated. (This is based on an averaging of school percentages.)

FOR MALES		FOR FEMALES	
The South	69%	The East	49%
The East	64%	The West	48%
The West	62%	The South	32%
The Midwest	51%	The Midwest	31%

Appendix B for Chapter 12

An averaging of the reported coitus of student samples grouped by type of institution yielded these percentages:

MALES

Public institutions	63%
Private institutions	60%
Church-related institutions	38%

FEMALES

Private institutions	49%
Public institutions	42%
Church-related institutions	12%

Appendix C for Chapter 12

Types of Sexual Behavior for U.S. College Total Sample by
Percentage of Subjects' Age and Sex

SEXUAL BEHAVIOR	AGE									
	19		20		21		22		23	
	M	F	M	F	M	F	M	F	M	F
Light embrace	100.0	100.0	100.0	98.3	97.5	98.6	97.8	96.7	98.6	100.0
Casual kissing	100.0	100.0	97.5	96.6	95.3	98.2	97.8	93.3	97.2	100.0
Deep kissing	97.4	94.1	97.5	97.1	95.3	97.7	95.6	98.3	93.0	100.0
Horiz. embrace	89.5	85.3	90.4	79.4	89.4	83.1	93.4	88.3	87.3	100.0
Petting breast, outside	94.7	70.6	90.4	75.4	89.8	81.3	89.0	83.3	87.3	62.5
Petting breast, inside	78.9	61.8	81.8	65.1	82.2	70.6	87.9	71.7	87.3	75.0
Petting below, female	76.3	55.9	80.8	61.7	80.8	60.7	82.4	61.7	84.5	62.5
Petting below, both	57.9	55.9	58.6	58.9	61.4	56.2	70.3	63.5	74.6	87.5
Nude embrace	59.5	50.0	60.6	45.7	66.5	51.8	71.4	48.3	74.6	82.5
Coitus	47.4	36.4	51.0	40.6	56.8	42.5	69.2	40.0	78.9	75.0
One-night affair	23.7	5.9	23.7	7.4	26.8	8.2	44.0	6.7	45.1	12.5
Involvement in whipping-spank. (males)	10.5	8.8	7.1	4.0	8.5	3.7	9.9	5.0	8.5	12.5
Pay-as-you-go	0.0	—	4.5	—	2.9	—	3.2	—	12.5	—
N=	(38)	(34)	(198)	(175)	(236)	(219)	(91)	(60)	(71)	(8)

The above analysis by age was based by necessity on a somewhat abbreviated sample of all the U.S. males and females who provided information about behavior. Nearly 200 females and more than 100 males failed to circle their ages. The place for checking age was at the very end of the checklist, after a brief section addressed to males only, which probably accounts in large part for the omissions.

Appendix D for Chapter 12

TABLE 1. International University Sample by Percentage of Males Who Reported Experiencing Specified Sexual Behavior

TYPE OF SEXUAL BEHAVIOR	CANADA	ENGLAND	GERMANY	NORWAY	U.S.A.
Light embracing or fond holding of hands	98.9	93.5	93.8	93.7	98.6
Casual goodnight kissing	97.7	93.5	78.6	86.1	96.7
Deep kissing	97.7	91.9	91.1	96.2	96.0
Horizontal embrace with some petting, but not undressed	92.0	85.4	68.8	93.6	89.9
Petting of girl's breast area from outside her clothing	93.2	87.0	80.4	83.5	89.9
Petting of girl's breast area without clothes intervening	92.0	82.8	69.6	83.5	83.4
Petting below the waist of the girl under her clothing	85.2	84.6	70.5	83.5	81.1
Petting below the waist of both man and girl, under clothing	64.8	68.3	52.7	55.1	62.9
Nude embrace	69.3	70.5	50.0	69.6	65.6
Coitus	56.8	74.8	54.5	66.7	58.2
One-night affair involving coitus; didn't date person again	21.6	43.1	17.0	32.9	29.9
Whipping or spanking before petting or other intimacy	5.7	17.1	.9	5.1	8.2
Sex on pay-as-you-go basis	4.5	13.8	9.8	2.5	4.2
N=	(88)	(123)	(112)	(79)	(644)

TABLE 2. International University Sample by Percentage of Females Who Reported Experiencing Specified Sexual Behavior

TYPE OF SEXUAL BEHAVIOR	CANADA	ENGLAND	GERMANY	NORWAY	U.S.A.
Light embracing or fond holding of hands	96.5	91.9	94.8	89.3	97.5
Casual goodnight kissing	91.8	93.0	74.0	75.0	96.8
Deep kissing	91.8	93.0	90.6	89.3	96.5
Horizontal embrace with some petting, but not undressed	81.2	79.1	77.1	75.0	83.5
Petting of girl's breast area from outside her clothing	78.8	82.6	76.0	64.3	78.3
Petting of girl's breast area without clothes intervening	64.7	70.9	66.7	58.9	67.8
Petting below the waist of the girl under her clothing	64.7	70.9	63.5	53.6	61.2
Petting below the waist of both man and girl, under clothing	50.6	61.6	56.3	42.9	57.8
Nude embrace	47.6	64.0	62.1	51.8	49.6
Coitus	35.3	62.8	59.4	53.6	43.2
One-night affair involving coitus; didn't date person again	5.9	33.7	4.2	12.5	7.2
Whipping or spanking before petting or other intimacy	5.9	17.4	1.0	7.1	4.5
N=	(85)	(86)	(96)	(56)	(688)

Appendix E for Chapter 12

The reported coital experience of the 3 special groups we sampled for comparative purposes is as follows:

The California beach group

Males	about 85%
Fémales	about 40%

U.S. Army enlisted men .... about 85%

Recently married wives living in campus
housing, reporting their premarital coital
experience *with fiancé only* .... about 50%

All the above samples involved fewer than 60 individuals; and
the California and Army samples involved a low rate of return.

(Note: Figures here and elsewhere in regional analysis are
based on an averaging of school percentages.)

REFERENCE NOTES

REFERENCE NOTES

CHAPTER 1

1. Wilbert Moore, *Social Change* (New Jersey: Prentice-Hall, Inc., 1963), p. 2.

2. Gregory Pincus, *The Control of Fertility* (New York: Academic Press, 1965), p. 299.

3. "Rising Tide of the 17-year-olds," Population Reference Bureau, Sept. 7, 1964.

4. Michael Schofield in collaboration with John Bynner, Patricia Lewis and Peter Massie, *The Sexual Behavior of Young People* (London: Longmans, Green & Co., Ltd., 1965), p. 254.

CHAPTER 2

1. Margaret Mead, *Male and Female* (originally published by William Morrow & Co., Inc., New York, 1949; page citations here from Mentor Books edition, 7th printing, 1964), p. 216.

2. William Goode, *World Revolution and Family Patterns* (New York: Free Press of Glencoe, 1963), p. 80.

3. Robert R. Bell and Jack V. Buerkle, "Mother and Daughter Attitudes to Premarital Sexual Behavior," *Marriage and Family Living*, Nov., 1961.

4. Ernest Burgess and Paul Wallin with Gladys Shultz, *Courtship, Engagement and Marriage* (Philadelphia: J. B. Lippincott Co., 1953), p. 102.

5. Grace and Fred Hechinger, *Teen-Age Tyranny* (New York: William Morrow & Co., 1963), p. 132.

6. Michael Schofield, *op. cit.* (Ch. 1, Note 4), pp. 224–256.

7. Clay Brittain, "Adolescent Choices and Parent-Peer Cross-Pressures," *American Sociological Review*, June, 1963.

8. *Deuteronomy*, 22:20–22.

9. Jack Shepherd, "'Are You a Teen-Ager?' 'Yeah, I'm Afraid So'," *Look*, Sept. 20, 1966.

10. Henry M. Graham, "Marriage in Today's Culture" (Lec-

ture in course, Psychiatry for the General Practitioner and Non-Psychiatric Specialist, Indiana University School of Medicine, 1962 and 1963).

11. Alfred C. Kinsey, Wardell B. Pomeroy, Clyde E. Martin, Paul H. Gebhard, *The Sexual Behavior of the Human Female* (Philadelphia and London: W. B. Saunders Co., 1953), pp. 304–307; Ernest Burgess and Paul Wallin, *op. cit.* (above, Note 4), p. 337; and Winston Ehrmann, *Premarital Dating Behavior* (originally published by Henry Holt & Co., New York, 1959; page citations here from Bantam Book edition, 1960), pp. 115–116.

12. O. Hobart Mowrer, "Science, Sex and Values," *Personnel and Guidance Journal*, Apr., 1964.

13. News report, *The Knickerbocker News*, Albany, N.Y., Dec. 6, 1963.

14. *The Journal* of the National Association of Women Deans and Counselors, Jan., 1963.

15. Committee on the College Student of the Group for the Advancement of Psychiatry, Report #60, *Sex and the College Student* (New York: Mental Health Materials Center, Inc., 1965), p. 16.

CHAPTER 3

1. Winston Ehrmann, *op. cit.* (Ch. 2, Note 11), pp. 102, 152, 167.

CHAPTER 4

1. Sanford Brown, "May I Ask You a Few Questions About Love?" Elmo Roper Survey of 1000 Americans, *Saturday Evening Post*, Dec. 31, 1966.

2. George P. Murdock, *Social Structure* (New York: The Macmillan Co., 1949), p. 265.

3. David and Vera Mace, *Marriage East and West* (New York: Dolphin Books, Doubleday & Co., Inc., 1959), p. 43.

4. Alan W. Watts, *Nature, Man and Woman* (New York: Pantheon Books, Inc., 1958), p. 156.

5. Ira Reiss, *Premarital Sexual Standards in America* (New York: Free Press of Glencoe, 1960), p. 132.

6. It is true that a great many French women have a sparkle and a capacity for affection that is greatly appealing to many males. And it is also true that after marriage, French males have a long proneness for establishing outside liaisons. But a number of French men and women expressed amazement at their reputa-

tion abroad. Recently, a leading French magazine presented to the French a long, wide-eyed account of the sex freedom found in Swden. A French university student (male) commented to us that he wished his countrymen would adopt the Swedish approach to sex education. The University of Paris information agency tried to conduct a national survey of the sex life of French students. Although the researchers were students themselves, they found it difficult to get their subjects to talk frankly about sex behavior or attitudes. They concluded the students were so naïve about contraception techniques that "One would think themselves in the Middle Ages." The survey discovered that virginity before marriage was considered desirable by the majority of the students questioned, and most of the males expressed the desire to marry a virgin.

Mme. Rose Vincent, editor of one of the nation's leading women's magazines, *Femme Pratique,* told me, "As far as we know, our young are much less free than Scandinavians." She said that since World War II there had been a tendency to permit a girl to have a physical relationship with the man she was about to marry, as a first step toward marriage, but that, throughout France, any other kind of experience for a girl was still considered to be wrong. Mme. Vincent, in talking of her problems in editing a French magazine, said, "I still don't talk about sex as a question between husbands and wives in the magazine. This is very difficult. It hasn't been done very much." She said that an article was then under preparation, but that its publication would be quite unusual.

7. Cross Currents, *Sexuality and the Modern World* (New York: Cross Currents Corp., Spring, 1964), in presentation by Marie Gregoire, p. 259.

8. Leslie Farber, "I'm Sorry, Dear," *Commentary,* Nov., 1964.

9. Harold T. Christensen, "Scandinavian and American Sex Norms: Some Comparisons, with Sociological Implications," *Journal of Social Issues,* Apr., 1966. See also his chapter "The Intrusion of Values" in *Handbook of Marriage and the Family,* edited by Christensen (Chicago: Rand McNally & Co., 1964).

10. Isadore Rubin, "Transition in Sex Values—Implications for the Education of Adolescents," *Journal of Marriage and the Family,* May, 1965.

11. Eustace Chesser, *Unmarried Love* (New York: David McKay Co., 1965), p. 37.

12. A. S. Neill, "Sex Attitudes," in *The Family and the Sexual Revolution,* edited by Edwin Schur (Bloomington, Ind.: Indiana University Press, 1964), pp. 169–182.

CHAPTER 5

1. Helen Lawrenson, ". . . Androgyne, You're a Funny Valentine," *Esquire*, Mar., 1965.
2. Geoffrey Gorer, "Man Has No Killer Instinct," *The New York Times Magazine*, Nov. 27, 1966.

CHAPTER 6

1. Carl N. Degler, "Revolution Without Ideology: The Changing Place of Women in America," from *The Woman in America*, edited by Robert J. Lifton (Boston: Houghton Mifflin Co., 1965), pp. 193–210.
2. Doris Stevens, "Jail for Freedom," Appendix 5 (New York: Boni & Liveright, 1920).
3. Nevitt Sanford, *Self and Society:* Social Change and Individual Development (New York: Atherton Press, 1966), pp. 257–258.
4. Betty Friedan, *The Feminine Mystique* (New York: W. W. Norton & Co., 1963; 4th Dell printing, 1964, cited here), p. 148.
5. Morton Hunt, *Her Infinite Variety:* The American Woman as Lover, Mate, and Rival (New York: Harper & Row, 1962), p. 4.
6. Paul Landis, *Making the Most of Marriage* (New York: Appleton-Century-Crofts, 1965), p. 104.
7. Edna Rostow, for a good amplification see her chapter "Conflict and Accommodation" in *The Woman in America, op. cit.* (Note 1, above).
8. Vivian Cadden, "How Women See Themselves," *Redbook*, May, 1965.
9. Edna Rostow, "The Best of Both Worlds: Feminism and Femininity," *Yale Review*, Spring, 1962.
10. Jessie Bernard, *Academic Women* (University Park, Pa.: Pennsylvania State University Press, 1964), p. 198.

CHAPTER 7

1. Based on a statement by Mary Dublin Keyserling to a symposium in New York City, Oct. 6, 1966, sponsored by Kelly Services and *Ladies' Home Journal*.
2. "Background Facts on Women Workers in the United States," Women's Bureau, U.S. Department of Labor, Sept., 1965.
3. Carl N. Degler, *op. cit.* (Ch. 6, Note 1).

4. Eli Ginzberg, "Life Styles of Educated Women," *New York Herald Tribune*, Feb. 27, 1966.

5. *The New York Times*, Nov. 21, 1966, "More Ex-Coeds Retaining Jobs Despite Marriage and Children," citing a survey by the Women's Bureau, U.S. Department of Labor.

6. *Op. cit.* (Note 2 of this chapter).

7. Jessie Bernard, *op. cit.* (Ch. 6, Note 10), pp. 189–191.

8. Richard H. Bolt, "The Present Situation of Women Scientists and Engineers in Industry and Government," Symposium on American Women in Science and Engineering at the Massachusetts Institute of Technology, Oct. 23, 1964.

9. "God—Male or Female?" *Newsweek*, July 12, 1965.

10. Doris and Howard Hunter, "Neither Male nor Female," *The Christian Century*, Apr. 28, 1965.

11. "Are Women Executives People?" *Harvard Business Review*, July-Aug., 1965.

12. Donald Michael, *The Next Generation* (New York: Random House, 1963), p. 137.

13. Nancy Seear, Veronica Roberts, and John Brock, *A Career for Women in Industry?* (London: Oliver & Boyd, Ltd., 1964), p. 90.

14. Vance Packard, *The Pyramid Climbers* (New York: McGraw-Hill, 1962). See Chapter 13.

15. National Education Association paper, "Wanted—More Women in Educational Leadership," The National Council of Administrative Women in Education, 1965.

16. "Call Her Mister," *Time*, Aug. 27, 1965.

17. Walter Goodman, "Women's Prejudices Against Women," *Redbook*, Feb., 1965.

18. "The Gripes of Rath: Laid Off Men Holler as Women Get Jobs," *The Wall Street Journal*, Sept. 22, 1966.

CHAPTER 8

1. Emily Mudd, Howard Mitchell, and Sara Taubin, *Success in Family Living* (New York: Association Press, 1965), p. 64.

2. David Mace, "The Identity Crisis of Men and Women in Contemporary Culture," speech at Earlham College, Apr. 8, 1965.

3. Gabriella Parca, "The Crime of Honor," *Atlas*, Feb., 1965.

4. Bruno Bettelheim, *Symbolic Wounds* (New York: The Free Press of Glencoe, Inc., 1954). See Chapter "The Men-Women."

5. Charles W. Ferguson, *The Male Attitude* (Boston: Little, Brown & Co., 1966), pp. 14, 15.

6. Helen M. Hacker, "The New Burdens of Masculinity," *Marriage and Family Living*, Aug., 1957.

7. Max Gunther, "The TV Plot to Slander Manhood," *True*, Oct., 1965.

8. Craig McGregor, *Profile of Australia* (London: Hodder and Stoughton, Ltd., 1966), pp. 60–61.

9. Ned Polsky, "Poolrooms: End of the Male Sanctuary," *Trans-Action*, Mar., 1967.

10. Frederick A. Weiss, in discussion on "The Meaning of Homosexual Trends in Therapy," *The American Journal of Psychoanalysis*, Vol. XXIV, 1, 1963.

11. Irving Bieber, "Speaking Frankly on a Once Taboo Subject," *The New York Times Magazine*, Aug. 23, 1964.

12. Harry Gershman, *op. cit.* (Note 10, above).

13. "The Homosexual in America," *Time*, Jan. 21, 1966.

CHAPTER 9

*STUDIES OF ATTITUDES AND BEHAVIOR REGARDING
PREMARITAL INTIMACY SINCE THE END OF
WORLD WAR I*

CIRCUMSTANTIAL EVIDENCE CONCERNING U.S. CITIZENS

1. Public Health Service, "Vital Statistics of the United States 1963: Volume 1—Natality," U.S. Dept. of Health, Education and Welfare, 1964.

2. Frank R. Locke, "The Challenge of Change" *Obstetrics and Gynecology*, Sept., 1964.

3. Clark E. Vincent, "Illegitimacy in the United States," from *Sex Ways—In Fact and Faith*, edited by Evelyn and Sylvanus Duvall (New York: Association Press, 1961).

4. Clark E. Vincent, "Teen-Age Unwed Mothers in American Society," *Journal of Social Issues*, Apr., 1966.

5. Ira L. Reiss, "The Sexual Renaissance in America," *Journal of Social Issues*, Apr., 1966.

6. Harold T. Christensen, "Pregnant Brides—Record Linkage Studies," in *Sex Ways—In Fact and Faith*, edited by Evelyn and Sylvanus Duvall (New York: Association Press, 1961).

7. J. Joel Moss and Ruby Gingles, "The Relationship of Personality to the Incidence of Early Marriage," *Marriage and Family Living*, Nov., 1959.

8. Ruth and Edward Brecher, "Every Sixth Teen-Age Girl in Connecticut—", *The New York Times Magazine*, May 29, 1966.

9. Celia S. Deschin, "Teenagers and Venereal Disease," *Children,* July–Aug., 1962.

10. Walter Sullivan, "A.M.A. Opens A Drive On V.D., Now 'Epidemic' In Some Cities," *The New York Times,* Sept. 2, 1965.

DIRECT EVIDENCE, FROM INDIVIDUAL RESPONSES TO QUESTIONNAIRES AND INTERVIEWS REGARDING BEHAVIOR AND ATTITUDES—THE U.S.A.

THE 1920s—INVESTIGATORS WHO DID THEIR SAMPLINGS IN THIS DECADE

11. Katherine Bement Davis, *Factors in the Sex Life of Twenty-two Hundred Women* (New York: Harper & Bros., 1929). This pioneering study is particularly important, since it measured courtship behavior before World War I. Conducted in 1923–25 with women who were then in their late thirties. Total sample: 2200. Sampling method: a mailing to about 10,000 women, mostly college graduates.

12. G. V. Hamilton, *A Research in Marriage* (New York: Albert and Charles Boni, 1929). He made his much smaller study from 1924 to 1926, of 100 married men and 100 married women, virtually all patients in therapy. Sampling method: interviews.

THE 1930s—INVESTIGATORS WHO DID THEIR SAMPLINGS IN THAT DECADE

13. Lewis M. Terman, *Psychological Factors in Marital Happiness* (New York: McGraw-Hill Book Co., 1938). Study of primary concern here was of 792 married couples, who in groups filled out a long questionnaire. Mostly college level.

14. H. Cantril & Mildred Strunk (eds.) *Public Opinion, 1935–1946* (Princeton, N.J.: Princeton University Press, 1951). Public Opinion poll methods.

15. Dorothy D. Bromley and Florence H. Britten, *Youth and Sex: A Study of 1300 College Students* (New York: Harper & Bros., 1938). Sample: 1364 college students (772 F and 592 M), average age 20. Sampling method: 5,000 questionnaires distributed on about 39 campuses, by students paid a dime for each one distributed. This brought 1088 of the responses in envelopes addressed to the survey director, or a 20 percent return.

IN THAT DECADE

THE 1940s—INVESTIGATORS WHO DID THEIR SAMPLINGS PRIMARILY

16. Austin L. Porterfield and H. Ellison Salley, "Current Folkways of Sexual Behavior," *The American Journal of Sociology,*

Nov., 1946. Sample: 613 subjects (285 M and 328 F). Mostly college students. Half of men ministerial students. Many of women student nurses. Method: questionnaires.

17. Alfred C. Kinsey, Wardell B. Pomeroy, Clyde E. Martin, Paul H. Gebhard, *Sexual Behavior in the Human Female* (Philadelphia and London: W. B. Saunders Company, 1953). Total sample: 5940 case histories of white females, plus other information sources. Sampling method: direct interview by trained men of volunteers drawn from a great variety of cohesive groups. Most interviewing done in the 1940s, ended in 1949.

18. Alfred C. Kinsey, Wardell B. Pomeroy and Clyde E. Martin, *Sexual Behavior in the Human Male* (Philadelphia and London: W. B. Saunders Co., 1948). Total sample: 5300 case histories of men, plus other informants. Method: same as with female. The major sampling of males took place in the 1943–46 period.

19. M. P. Warner, *Medical Woman's Journal*, vol. 50 (1943), p. 295, on brides seeking medical consultation; 402 brides.

20. Ernest Burgess, Paul Wallin, *Courtship, Engagement & Marriage* (Philadelphia: J. B. Lippincott Co., 1953). Data collected on 666 married couples and 226 engaged couples between 1936 and 1946.

THE 1950s—INVESTIGATORS WHO DID THEIR SAMPLINGS PRIMARILY
IN THAT DECADE

21. Judson T. Landis and Mary G. Landis, *Building a Successful Marriage*, Fourth Edition (Englewood Cliffs, N.J.: Prentice-Hall, Inc., 1963), in chapter on Premarital Sexual Relations. Especially, p. 172. Sample: 3000 students in family sociology courses. Data collected between 1952 and 1955 at 11 U.S. colleges: 9 were in California or the Midwest; the other 2 were in Louisiana and New York. Method: anonymous questionnaires in which students gave background, dating history, etc. Only female responses regarding sexual behavior were reported.

22. Winston Ehrmann, *Premarital Dating Behavior* (New York: Henry Holt & Co., 1959), Bantam Edition, 1960. (Note: latter used for page references.) The main sampling by questionnaire was done from 1947 to 1950. Sample: 1157 students at the University of Florida. Usable questionnaires were obtained from 841 students (576 M and 265 F). Later a partial schedule tried on an additional 137 students (71 M, 66 F). Girls used tended to be in lower 2 college classes. Males averaged 2 years older than females. Sampling method: students in Marriage & the Family classes invited to fill out schedules. Only 2 refused. When a group com-

pleted filling out schedules, a sheet was passed around on which students recorded their names for his files. Name was not related to schedule.

23. Robert Bell and Leonard Blumberg, "Courtship Intimacy and Religious Background," *Marriage and Family Living,* Nov., 1959. Student sample at one university.

24. Eugene J. Kanin and David H. Howard, "Postmarital Consequences of Premarital Sex Adjustments," *American Sociological Review,* Oct., 1958. Sample: 177 married women, living in 3 housing units on a Midwestern university campus. Method: questionnaire.

25A. Harold T. Christensen and George R. Carpenter, "Value-Behavior Discrepancies Regarding Premarital Coitus in Three Western Cultures," *American Sociological Review,* Feb., 1962.

25B. Harold T. Christensen and George R. Carpenter, "Timing Patterns in the Development of Sexual Intimacy: An Attitudinal Report on Three Modern Western Societies," *Marriage and Family Living,* Feb., 1962. Both describe aspects of *the only survey we know* (25) *that attempted to make cross-national comparisons.* The sampling was done around 1958, by questionnaire. The sample: 758 students at 2 universities in the U.S.A. (1 in the Midwest and the other a Mormon culture university in Rocky Mt. region) and 1 university in Denmark. The Danish sample contained 149 males, 86 females. A Swedish version of the Christensen-Carpenter questionnaire was administered separately in 1958 to a smaller group of Swedish students, 117 sociology students at Uppsala University. The findings of this Swedish sampling are referred to by Georg Karlsson and his associates at Uppsala in their study of Swedish "peoples' colleges" (See Note 37).

26. Mervin B. Freedman, "The Sexual Behavior of American College Women," *The Merrill-Palmer Quarterly,* Jan., 1965. This article has been widely quoted as proof there has been little change in the behavior of U.S. women students in recent decades. Though it appeared in 1965, it was based on a study of 49 Vassar graduates of the Class of 1958. Sampling method: It began as a random sample of 80 freshmen women. They were interviewed during their college careers about many aspects of their lives. Twenty-nine of the subjects left Vassar before graduation (some because of marriage); 2 declined to cooperate after the first year. This left a sample of 49 graduating seniors.

27. Lester Kirkendall, *Premarital Intercourse and Interpersonal Relationships* (New York: The Julian Press, Inc., 1961). Sampling method: interviews with 200 college-level men between 17

and 28, average age 20.7, who had experienced premarital coitus. Contains description of the circumstances. Sampling was done in the late 1950s.

THE 1960s—INVESTIGATORS WHO HAVE DONE THEIR SAMPLINGS PRIMARILY IN THIS DECADE

28. Sue S. Schmitt and Robert E. Grinder, "Coeds and Contraceptive Information," *Journal of Marriage and the Family*, Nov., 1966. Survey of 304 college women, 60% in freshman and sophomore class and 46% were beginning freshmen, in 1965.

29. *The Columbian.* Columbia College yearbook, 1964. Questionnaire to 660 graduating seniors; 540 responded.

30. Harrop A. and Ruth S. Freeman, "Senior College Women: Their Sexual Standards and Activity—Part II. Dating: Petting-Coital Practices," *The Journal,* The National Association of Women Deans and Counselors, Spring, 1966. The sampling methods: a mixture of interviewing and questionnaire responses in the 1963-65 period; 400 senior college women were interviewed (some of whom had sought counseling); 400 other senior women responded to questionnaires. They came from, or were attending, schools in various parts of the U.S.A.

31. Gael Greene, *Sex and the College Girl* (New York: Delacorte Press, 1964). Not intended as a survey, but rather to develop impressions and insights. Sample: 614 students, primarily coeds at 102 U.S. colleges and universities throughout the country. Sampling method: Mainly, students were interviewed in small informal group settings.

32. Ira L. Reiss, "The Scaling of Premarital Sexual Permissiveness," *Journal of Marriage and the Family*, May, 1964. His concern was with attitudes rather than behavior. There were 2 main groups sampled: (1) 903 high-school and college students, mostly from Virginia schools. Four of the schools were in Virginia: 2 white and 2 Negro. Also a college in New York state was used. It was known to have "a highly permissive group of students." Sampling of the students was either random or on an entire school population basis. (2) 1515 adults responded to the same questionnaire items but in interviews conducted by the National Opinion Research Center. This was also a probability-type sample.

32X. Alice Lake, "Teen-Agers and Sex: A Student Report," *Seventeen*, July, 1967. Survey based on approximately 1500 responses from questionnaires sent to members of *Seventeen*'s Consumer Panel. The age of the girls responding ranged from 13 to 19, with the median age around 16½ years.

SOME FOREIGN SURVEYS AND REPORTS

DENMARK

33. Kirsten Auken, "Unge Kvinders Sexuelle Adfaerd" (with an English summary), 1953. Interviews and questionnaire sampling of 315 women chosen randomly. Survey conducted 1944–47.

34. Kirsten Auken, "A Sequential Study of 300 Younger Families in Copenhagen," 1963. Eighth International Seminar in Family Research, Oslo, Norway.

NORWAY

35. William Simenson and Gilbert Geis, "Courtship Patterns of Norwegian and American University Students," *Marriage and Family Living,* Nov., 1956.

SWEDEN

36A. Birgitta Linnér, *Sex and Society in Sweden* (New York: Pantheon Books, 1967). Includes summaries of several recent Swedish studies.

36B. Birgitta Linnér, "Society and Sex in Sweden" (booklet), 1965, published by The Swedish Institute, Box 3306, Stockholm 3, Sweden.

37. George Karlsson, Siiri Karlsson, and Karin Busch, "Sexual Habits and Attitudes of Swedish Folk High School Students," Research Report No. XV, Department of Sociology, Uppsala University, Uppsala, Sweden. The Folk High School—or peoples' college—in Sweden is comparable to U.S. community colleges. Sample: students from 6 folk high schools representing different geographical regions. In 1960, they filled out questionnaires.

37X. Gustav Jonsson, "Sexualvanor hos Svensk Ungdom," in SOU, 1951.

ENGLAND

38. Shirley M. Hartley, "The Amazing Rise of Illegitimacy in Great Britain," *Social Forces,* June, 1966.

39. Eustace Chesser, *The Sexual, Marital and Family Relationships of the English Woman* (England: Hutchinson's Medical Publications, Ltd., 1956). Describes responses of 6500 women, married and single, to questionnaires distributed through offices of physicians.

40. Michael Schofield, in collaboration with John Bynner, Patricia Lewis, and Peter Massie, *The Sexual Behavior of Young People* (London: Longmans, Green & Co. Ltd., 1965). Survey made by the Central Council for Health Education, with a grant

from the Nuffield Foundation. Interviews with a random sample of 1873 teenagers. The "younger group" was age 15–17 and the "older group" 17–19. Average age of males and females was 17.

FRANCE

41. French Institute of Public Opinion, *Patterns of Love and Sex* (New York: Crown Publishers, Inc., 1960). Sample: 90 women. Based on depth interviews in the 1950s with French women of various ages both married and unmarried, and with 10 adolescent girls.

CHAPTER 10

1. In the sampling at the German university, it was decided to attempt a true random distribution by mailing checklists to students whose names were chosen on a fully random basis. We surmised (incorrectly) that a mailed distribution would produce a comparatively low rate of response. Also we had no way of identifying those 12% of the students at the university who were married and so ineligible to respond to the checklist. For these 2 reasons we mailed out 450 checklists, approximately 400 of them presumably going to unmarried students eligible to participate in the survey.

Also it should be noted that our German distributors, in preparing a German-language version of the checklist, altered the wording of a few of the questions to the point that it was judged inadvisable to tabulate them in making any cross-cultural comparisons. That explains why no German response is reported on a few of the questions.

2. The mean age of students responding in the U.S.A. was 20.7 for females and 20.9 for males. In the foreign samples, the highest mean age was at the Norwegian university, where both males and females averaged slightly over 21½ years of age. The youngest national sample was that from the English university, where the mean age of both males and females was 20.6 years.

3. Also, at 3 of the U.S. campuses sampled exploratory rechecks were made. A full recheck was made at the state university in the South Central region where the rate of return had been the lowest for any U.S. school. In the second check made by a different distributor, the return rate was still low (42%), but a few points higher than the original return of 37%. At the Catholic university and at the state university in the Rocky Mountain area rechecks were made only of girls, since at both places the distributor reports had indicated they may not, in their first distribution, have

achieved a proportional representation as between dormitory students and girls living off campus. Unless otherwise specified, the U.S. College Sample includes only response to the original distribution.

4. In fact, while it may bother some methodologists, we advised each student responding to the checklist to respond only to questions where he felt comfortable doing so. As it turned out, this suggestion did not create much of a problem in terms of data analysis, because the overwhelming majority of students who responded at all sent us responses to every question. However, since a few did elect to skip some items, our percentages will be based on the actual number of persons responding to that particular question.

5. Also tabulated were 2 other samples that will not be used in any analysis except for possible occasional references, since they are the inadequate samples involving responses from 43 U.S. Army enlisted personnel and 41 young Californians encountered near that state's beaches.

6. See Note 1 of this chapter. The 62% response listed assumes that approximately 400 unmarried Germans eligible to respond received mailed copies of the checklist. Altogether, 450 checklists were mailed out, and of these there were responses from 253 as of April 1967, or 56.2%.

7. The unusually high rate of response from students at the English university can perhaps be partly explained by a technicality. That was the one school in the U.S. and international samples where the respondents, after they had completed the checklist, did not mail the checklist directly to the author. There was a deadline imposed by the availability of computer time for analyzing the English returns, and so the distributors advised each student accepting the checklist for inspection that if he did complete it, he should put the checklist in an attached envelope, seal it, and return the sealed envelope to the distributor at an agreed place. The sealed envelopes that were returned to the distributors were all placed, still sealed, in a large box and shipped by air mail to the author.

8. Nevitt Sanford, "Morals on the Campus," *NEA Journal,* Apr., 1965.

9. Winston Ehrmann, "Some Knowns and Unknowns in Research into Human Sex Behavior," *Marriage and Family Living,* Feb., 1957.

10. Henry Fairlie, "Britain Seems Willing—," *The New York Times Magazine,* June 12, 1966.

11. D. W. Brogan, "The English Sickness," *Harper's,* June, 1967.

CHAPTER 12

1. Checklist item E-1 was presented to students in these words:

Please check on the following list those types of encounter you have happened to have. The list covers some of the various possible forms of premarital intimacy with the opposite sex that some people experience.

—Light embracing or fond holding of hands
—Deep kissing
—Casual goodnight kissing
—Petting below the waist of the girl, under her clothing
—Petting of girl's breast area from outside her clothing
—Coitus
—Horizontal embrace with some petting, but not undressed
—Petting below the waist of both man and girl, under clothing
—Involvement in whipping or spanking before petting or other intimacy
—Petting of girl's breast area without clothes intervening
—Nude embrace
—Engaged in one-night affair involving coitus and did not date person again
—Have not involved myself in any of the above types of encounter
—(For male respondents only) Have experienced sex on a pay-as-you-go basis.

2. In the German checklist, statement 3 was reworded to read: "Most are satisfied with necking." And 51% of the German girls checked that.

CHAPTER 13

1. James K. Skipper, Jr., and Gilbert Nass, "Dating Behavior: A Framework for Analysis and an Illustration," *Journal of Marriage and the Family,* Nov., 1966.

2. William Kloman, "My Mother Said I Should Give It a Try," *The Saturday Evening Post,* Oct. 8, 1966.

3. Terry Galanoy, "Apartment Houses for Singles: Love with a Lease," *Cosmopolitan,* June, 1966.

4. Janet Abu-lughod and Lucy Amin, "Egyptian Marriage Advertisements: Microcosm of a Changing Society," *Marriage and Family Living,* May, 1961.

5. "Courtship by Computer," *Newsweek,* Mar. 29, 1965.

6. Richard Peterson, "Some Biographical and Attitudinal Char-

acteristics of Entering College Freshmen," *ETS Research Bulletin,* Dec., 1964.

7. Elizabeth Douvan and Carol Kaye, "Motivational Factors in College Entrance," *The American College,* edited by Nevitt Sanford (New York: John Wiley and Sons, Inc., 1962), p. 207.

8. Robert Coombs and William Kenkel, "Sex Differences in Dating Aspirations and Satisfaction with Computer-Selected Partners," *Journal of Marriage and the Family,* Feb., 1966.

CHAPTER 14

1. Ralph Linton, *The Study of Man* (New York: Appleton-Century, 1936), p. 175.

2. Margaret Mead, *op. cit.* (Ch. 2, Note 1), p. 146.

3. French Institute of Public Opinion, *Patterns of Sex and Love: A Study of the French Woman and Her Morals* (New York: Crown Publishers, 1960), p. 122.

4. Robert O. Blood, Jr., and Donald M. Wolfe, *Husbands and Wives* (New York: Free Press of Glencoe, 1960), p. 149.

5. H. Schelsky, "Changing Family Structures Under Conditions of Social and Economic Development," Publications on Social Change, 1958, pp. 7–8.

6. Evelyn Duvall, "Adolescent Love as a Reflection of Teenagers' Search for Identity," *Journal of Marriage and the Family,* May, 1964.

7. Ernest Burgess and Paul Wallin, *op. cit.* (Ch. 2, Note 4), p. 70.

8. Sandford Brown, *op. cit.* (Ch. 4, Note 1).

9. David and Vera Mace, *op. cit.* (Ch. 4, Note 3), pp. 132 and 311.

10. William Goode, "The Theoretical Importance of Love," *American Sociological Review,* Feb., 1959.

11. Clark W. Blackburn, "The Psychological Attitudes of Young Couples and the Harmony of the Couple." Speech to International Family Conference, Rome, July 6, 1965.

12. Robert Parke, Jr., and Paul C. Glick, "Prospective Changes in Marriage and the Family," *Journal of Marriage and the Family,* May, 1967.

14. J. Joel Moss, "Teenage Marriage: Cross-National Trends and Sociological Factors in the Decision of When to Marry," *Acta Sociologica,* Vol. 8, 1964.

15. Marvin Sussman and Lee Burchinal, "Parental Aid to Married Students: Implications for Family Functioning," *Marriage and Family Living,* Nov., 1962.

16. Wayne Anderson and Sander Latts, "High School Marriages and School Policies in Minnesota," *Journal of Marriage and the Family*, May, 1965.

17. Peter R. Kann, "I Do, I Do; Justices in Las Vegas Get Rich Marrying Day and Night," *The Wall Street Journal*, February 27, 1967.

18. Gerhard Neubeck, "The Decision to Marry While in College," *Acta Sociologica*, Vol. 8, 1964.

19. Victor Christopherson, Joseph Vandiver, and Marie Krueger, "The Married College Student, 1959," *Marriage and Family Living*, May, 1960.

CHAPTER 15

1. Clark Blackburn, *op. cit.* (Ch. 14, Note 11).

2. *The Ladies Book* (Philadelphia: L. A. Godey and Company, 1832), 4:228.

3. David Heer, "Husband and Wife Perceptions of Family Power Structure," *Marriage and Family Living*, Feb., 1962.

4. Eleanore B. Luckey, "Marital Satisfaction and Personality Correlates of Spouse," *Journal of Marriage and the Family*, May, 1964.

5. Robert O. Blood, Jr., and Donald M. Wolfe, *op. cit.* (Ch. 14, Note 4), p. 11.

6. For an elaboration of Waller's concepts see: Willard Waller, *The Family*, revised by Reuben Hill (New York: Dryden Press, 1951), especially pp. 190–192.

7. Harriet Pilpel, symposium in New York City, Oct. 6, 1966, sponsored by Kelly Services and *Ladies' Home Journal*.

8. Robert O. Blood, Jr., and Robert L. Hamblin, "The Effects of the Wife's Employment on the Family Power Structure," *Social Forces*, May, 1958.

9. Robert O. Blood, Jr., and Donald M. Wolfe, *op. cit.* (Ch. 14, Note 4), p. 52.

10. Mirra Komarovsky with the collaboration of Jane Philips, *Blue-Collar Marriage* (New York: Random House, 1962), p. 222.

11. Nicholas Babchuk and Alan Bates, "The Primary Relations of Middle-Class Couples: A Study in Male Dominance," *American Sociological Review*, June, 1963.

12. See William F. Kenkel, "Dominance, Persistence, Self-Confidence and Spousal Roles in Decision Making," *Journal of Social Psychology*, 1961, pp. 349–58; and William F. Kenkel, "Husband-Wife Interaction in Decision Making and Decision Choices," *ibid.*, pp. 255–62.

13. Robert O. Blood, Jr., "The Measurement and Bases of Family Power: A Rejoinder," *Marriage and Family Living*, Nov., 1963.

14. David Heer, "The Measurement and Bases of Family Power: An Overview," *Marriage and Family Living*, May, 1963.

15. Robert O. Blood, Jr., and Donald M. Wolfe, *op. cit.* (Ch. 14, Note 4), p. 23.

16. Charles E. Bowerman and Glen H. Elder, Jr., "Variations in Adolescent Perception of Family Power Structure," *American Sociological Review*, Aug., 1964; and Theodore Johannis, Jr., and James Rollins, "Teenager Perception of Family Decision Making," *The Coordinator*, No. 7, 1959.

17. Pierre Fougeyrollas, "Prédominance du Mari ou de la Femme dans le Ménage," *Population, Revue Trimestrielle*, 6, 1951. (Paris: Institut National D'Etudes Démographiques), pp. 83–102.

18. David Heer, "Dominance and the Working Wife," *Journal of Social Forces*, May, 1958.

19. Robert O. Blood, Jr., and Donald M. Wolfe, *op. cit.* (Ch. 14, Note 4), p. 42.

20. Hyman Rodman, "Marital Power in France, Greece, Yugoslavia and the United States: A Cross-National Discussion," *Journal of Marriage and the Family*, May, 1967.

21. Reuben Hill, "The American Family of the Future," *Journal of Marriage and the Family*, Feb., 1964.

CHAPTER 16

1. Mervyn Cadwallader, "Marriage As A Wretched Institution," *Atlantic*, November, 1966.

2. "Private Report on the Housing Market," Home Facts Research, Inc., Darien, Connecticut, July and August, 1966.

3. Lee Rainwater, "Social Status Differences in the Family Relationships of German Men," *Marriage and Family Living*, February, 1962.

4. Mirra Komarovsky, *op. cit.* (Ch. 15, Note 10), p. 140.

5. John Cuber and Peggy Harroff, *The Significant Americans: A Study of Sexual Behavior Among the Affluent* (New York: Appleton-Century-Crofts, 1965). See especially pp. 43–58, 106, 145.

6. Helena Z. Lopata, "The Secondary Features of a Primary Relationship," *Human Organization*, Summer, 1965.

7. Marya Mannes, "I, Mary, Take Thee, John, as . . . What?" *The New York Times Magazine*, Nov. 14, 1965.

CHAPTER 17

1. John Blazer, "Married Virgins—A Study of Unconsummated Marriages," *Journal of Marriage and the Family*, May, 1964.

2. Alfred Kinsey *et al.*, *Sexual Behavior of the Human Female*, *op. cit.* (Ch. 2, Note 11), p. 397.

3. Robert R. Bell, *Premarital Sex in a Changing Society*. (Englewood Cliffs, N.J.: Prentice-Hall, Inc., 1966), pp. 136–137.

4. French Institute of Public Opinion, *op. cit.* (Ch. 14, Note 3). See Table 18.

5. Paul Montgomery, "Contraceptive Use Noted," *The New York Times*, May 1, 1966.

6. Morton Hunt, *op. cit.* (Ch. 6, Note 5), p. 114.

7. Kinsey, *et al.*, *op. cit.* (Note 2, above), pp. 375, 408.

8. William H. Masters and Virginia E. Johnson, *Human Sexual Response* (Boston: Little, Brown & Co., 1966), pp. 301–302.

9. Cuber and Harroff, *op. cit.* (Ch. 16, Note 5), p. 174.

10. Robert R. Bell, *op. cit.* (Note 3, above), p. 137.

11. Paul Wallin and Alexander Clark, "Culture Norms in Husbands' and Wives' Report of Their Marital Partners' Preferred Frequency of Coitus in Relation to Their Own," *Sociometry*, 21, Sept., 1958.

12. Robert R. Bell, "Some Emerging Sexual Expectations Among Women," *Medical Aspects of Human Sexuality*, Oct., 1967.

13. Alexander Clark and Paul Wallin, "Women's Sexual Responsiveness and the Duration and Quality of Their Marriages," *American Journal of Sociology*, Sept., 1965.

CHAPTER 18

1. Griselda Rowntree, "Some Aspects of Marriage Breakdown in Britain During the Last Thirty Years," *Population Studies*, Nov. 1964.

2. "Roundup of Current Research." A report based on studies by Jessie Bernard of Pennsylvania State University and J. Richard Udry of the University of North Carolina, *Trans-Action*, Apr., 1967.

3. Kinsey *et al.*, *op. cit.* (Ch. 2, Note 11), pp. 417 and 437.

4. June Callwood, "Infidelity," *Ladies' Home Journal*, Apr., 1965.

5. French Institute of Public Opinion, *op. cit.* (Ch. 14, Note 3), p. 185.

6. Paul and Emily Avery, "Some Notes on Wife Swapping,"

Sex in America, edited by Henry Grunwald (New York: Bantam Books, 1964), pp. 248–254.

7. Gerhard Neubeck and Vera Schletzer, "A Study of Extra-Marital Relationships," *Marriage and Family Living,* Aug., 1962.

8. Morton Hunt, *op. cit.* (Ch. 6, Note 5), pp. 139–140.

CHAPTER 19

1. Paul Montgomery, *op. cit.* (Ch. 17, Note 5).

2. Richard D. Lyons, "Birth Control Found As An Aid To Adjustment in Marriage," *The New York Times,* June 20, 1967. See also Somers H. Sturgis, "Oral Contraceptives and Their Effect on Sex Behavior," *Medical Aspects of Human Sexuality,* Jan., 1968.

3. Ernest Pawel, "Sex Under Socialism," *Commentary,* Sept., 1965.

4. David Mace, "Sorokin's Theories on Sex and Society," *American Sociological Forum,* 1963.

5. Ernest Pawel, *op. cit.* (Note 3, above).

6. For an amplification of Kharchev's findings about changes in Soviet attitudes toward marriage and the prevailing one see A. G. Kharchev, "Marriage and the Family in the USSR" (Moscow: Mysl Socio-Economic Publishing House, 1964).

7. David Mace, "The Employed Mother in the U.S.S.R.," *Marriage and Family Living,* Nov., 1961.

8. Gunnar Boalt, *Family and Marriage* (New York: David McKay Co., 1965), pp. 11–14.

9. Bruno Bettelheim, "Does Communal Education Work? The Case for the Kibbutz" in *The Family and The Sexual Revolution,* edited by Edwin Schur, *op. cit.* (Ch. 4, Note 12).

10. See Albert Rabin's "Kibbutz Children—Research Findings to Date," in *Children,* Sept.-Oct., 1958.

11. Howard Halpern, "Alienation from Parenthood in the Kibbutz and America," *Marriage and Family Living,* Feb., 1962.

12. William Goode, *op. cit.* (Ch. 2, Note 2), pp. 24–25.

CHAPTER 20

1. Lars Gustafsson, *The Public Dialogue in Sweden* (Stockholm: P. A. Norstedt and Söners Förlag, 1964), p. 95.

2. Two studies which offer a comparison of Danish and Swedish premarital coital experience of females about 2 decades ago are: Kirsten Auken, "Unge Kvinders Sexuell Adfaerd," 1953 (see Ch. 5, Note 33); and Gustav Jonsson, "Sexualvanor hos Svensk Ungdom," in SOU, 1951 (see Ch. 9, Note 37X).

3. Harriet Holter, "Scandinavia," from a manuscript on "Women in the Western World."

4. *Ibid.*

5. See Appendix to Chapter 9 of this book for further details.

6. Birgitta Linnér, *Sex and Society in Sweden* (New York: Pantheon Books, 1967), p. 20.

7. Lester Kirkendall, "Issues and Goals in Sex Education," Forty-second Annual Conference of Child Study Association of America, Mar. 7, 1966.

8. Birgitta Linnér, *op. cit.* (Note 6, above), p. 2.

9. Robert Moskin, "Sweden's New Battle Over Sex," *Look*, Nov. 15, 1966.

10. "Sweden Is Casual on Pornography," *The New York Times*, Nov. 5, 1967.

11. Gustav Jonsson and Anna-Lisa Kalvesten, "*222 Stockholmspojkar*" (Stockholm: Almquist & Wirksen, 1964).

12. Birgitta Linnér, "Sexual Morality and Sexual Reality—The Scandinavian Approach," before the annual meeting of the American Orthopsychiatric Association, Spring, 1965.

13. Birgitta Linnér, "Society and Sex in Sweden," The Swedish Institute, 1965.

CHAPTER 21

1. J. Richard Udry, *The Social Context of Marriage* (Philadephia: J. B. Lippincott Co., 1966), pp. 35–36.

2. Phyllis McGinley, "Wives and the Moonlight Adventure," *Ladies' Home Journal*, Aug., 1964.

3. Alice Rossi, *op. cit.* (Ch. 6, Note 1), pp. 98–143. (Originally in *Daedalus*, Spring, 1964.)

4. Leonard Carmichael, "Are the Sexes Really Equal?" *Science Digest*, Oct., 1957.

5. Robert Bierstedt, *The Social Order* (New York: McGraw-Hill Book Co., Inc., 1957), p. 313.

6. David McClelland, "Wanted: A New Self-Image For Women" in *The Woman in America*, edited by Robert J. Lifton (Boston: Houghton Mifflin Co., 1965), p. 174.

7. Leona Tyler, *The Psychology of Human Differences* (New York: Appleton-Century-Crofts, 1965), p. 258.

8. Jean Macfarlane, Lucile Allen, and Marjorie Honzik, *Behavior Problems of Normal Children* (Los Angeles, Calif.: University of California Press, 1962), pp. 105 and 146.

9. Benjamin Spock, "Are We Minimizing the Differences Between the Sexes?" *Redbook*, Mar., 1964.

10. Erik Erikson, "Inner and Outer Space: Reflections on Womanhood," *op. cit.* (Ch. 6, Note 1), pp. 1–27; and Marjorie Honzik, "Sex Differences in the Occurrence of Materials in the Play Constructions of Preadolescents," *Child Development,* Mar., 1951.

11. Evlyn Goodenough Pitcher, "Male and Female," *Atlantic Monthly,* Mar., 1963; and Evelyn Wiltshire Goodenough, "Interest in Persons as an Aspect of Sex Difference in the Early Years," *Genetic Psychology Monographs,* 1957, #55.

12. Jessie Bernard, *op. cit.* (Ch. 6, Note 10), p. 82.

13. David McClelland, *op. cit.* (Note 6, above), pp. 176-178.

14. Robert Eck, "The Real Masters of Television," *Harper's,* Mar., 1967.

15. J. Richard Udry, "Complementarity in Mate Selection: A Perceptual Approach," *Marriage and Family Living,* Aug., 1963.

16. J. Richard Udry, *op. cit.* (Note 1, above), p. 30; and Talcott Parsons and Robert Bales, *Family, Socialization and Interaction Process* (New York: The Free Press of Glencoe, 1955), in collaboration with James Olds, Morris Zelditch, Jr., and Philip E. Slater. See especially Ch. 6.

17. David McClelland, *op. cit.* (Note 6, above), p. 177.

18. Mirra Komarovsky, *op. cit.* (Ch. 15, Note 10), p. 193.

19. Margaret Mead, *op. cit.* (Ch. 2, Note 1), p. 283.

20. Eleanor E. Maccoby in *The Potential of Woman,* edited by Seymour Farber and Roger Wilson (New York: McGraw-Hill Book Co., Inc., 1963), p. 28. (Third symposium on "Man and Civilization," Jan., 1963, University of California Medical Center.) See also David McClelland, *op. cit.* (Note 6, above), p. 179.

21. Leona Tyler, *op. cit.* (Note 7, above), p. 246.

22. J. Richard Udry, *op. cit.* (Note 1, above), p. 36.

23. John Money, "Psychosexual Differentiation" in *Sex Research—New Developments,* edited by John Money (New York: Holt, Rinehart and Winston, 1965), p. 16.

24. Louise Ames and Frances Ilg, "Sex Differences in Test Performance of Matched Girl-Boy Pairs in the Five-to-Nine-Year-Old Age Range," *Journal of Genetic Psychology,* 1964, #104.

25. Harry F. Harlow, "The Heterosexual Affectional System in Monkeys," *The American Psychologist,* No. 17, 1962.

26. William Young, Robert Goy, and Charles Phoenix, "Hormones and Sexual Behavior," *op. cit.* (Note 23, above), pp. 176–191. Also see "Monkey Business," *Newsweek,* Nov. 15, 1965.

27. John Money, *op. cit.* (Note 23, above), pp. 10–11.

28. See David McClelland, *op. cit.* (Note 6, above), p. 182, for description of studies by J. Kagan and H. A. Moss.

29. Eleanor E. Maccoby, "Women's Intellect," *op. cit.* (Note 20, above), pp. 24–38.

30. Walter Waetjen, "Is Learning Sexless?" *The NEA Journal*, May, 1962.

31. Patricia Sexton, "Schools Are Emasculating Our Boys," *Saturday Review*, June 19, 1965.

32. Lester David, "Girls and Boys Together?" *This Week*, May 9, 1965, citing a report published by the National Education Association.

33. "Women at Wesleyan?" *Wesleyan Alumnus*, Feb., 1967.

CHAPTER 22

1. Luther G. Baker, "The Personal and Social Adjustment of the Never-Married **Woman.**" **P**aper presented at the meeting of the National Council on Family Relations, San Francisco, Aug., 1967.

2. Eleanore Braun Luckey, *Journal of Home Economics,* Nov., 1965.

3. Alice Lake, "The Empty Days," *McCall's*, Sept., 1965.

4. Emily Mudd, *op. cit.* (Ch. 8, Note 1).

5. Mirra Komarovsky, *op. cit.* (Ch. 15, Note 10), p. 62.

6. Jack E. Rossman and David P. Campbell, for an analysis of why wives work, *Personnel & Guidance Journal*, June, 1965.

7. Bethel Paris and Eleanore B. Luckey, "A Longitudinal Study in Marital Satisfaction," *Sociology and Social Research*, Jan., 1966.

8. F. Ivan Nye, in *The Employed Mother in America*, edited by F. Ivan Nye and Lois Hoffman (Chicago: Rand McNally & Co., 1963), p. 272.

9. Lois Hoffman, "Effects on Children," *ibid.*, p. 210.

10. John Bowlby, "Maternal Care and Mental Health," Geneva, Switzerland, World Health Organization Monograph Series No. 2, 1951.

11. James H. S. Bossard, *The Sociology of Child Development* (New York: Harper & Bros., 1954), pp. 282–286.

12. Robert Odenwald, *The Disappearing Sexes* (New York: Random House, 1965), p. 14.

13. Eleanor E. Maccoby, "Children and Working Mothers," from *Children*, May-June, 1958.

14. Lois Hoffman, *op. cit.* (Note 8, above), p. 202.

15. Lois Hoffman, *ibid.*, p. 191.

16. Eleanor E. Maccoby, *op. cit.* (Note 13, above).

17. Aase G. Skard, "Maternal Deprivation: The Research and

Its Implications," *Journal of Marriage and the Family,* Aug., 1965.

18. Marian Radke Yarrow, "Maternal Employment and Child Rearing," *Children,* Vol. 8, 1961.

19. Martha S. White (ed.), "The Next Step: A Guide to Part-Time Opportunities in Greater Boston for the Educated Woman." Radcliffe Institute for Independent Study, 78 Mount Auburn St., Cambridge, Mass. $1.50.

20. See Ruth Lembeck's *380 Part-Time Jobs for Women* (New York: Dell Publishing Co., 1968).

21. "Working Mothers and Day Care Service in the United States," *Facts About Children,* Children's Bureau of the U.S. Department of Health, Education and Welfare, 1962.

22. Robert O. Blood, Jr., *op. cit.* (Ch. 14, Note 4), p. 164.

23. Morton Hunt, *op. cit.* (Ch. 6, Note 5), pp. 292-293.

CHAPTER 23

1. Myron Brenton, *The American Male* (New York: Coward-McCann, Inc., 1966), p. 13.

2. David and Vera Mace, *op. cit.* (Ch. 4, Note 3), pp. 328-330.

3. Elihu Katz and Paul F. Lazarsfeld, *Personal Influence.* A Report of the Bureau of Applied Social Research, Columbia University (The Free Press of Glencoe, 1955; The Free Press Paperback, 1964), pp. 140–160 in latter.

4. John H. Bushnell, "Student Culture at Vassar," *The American College, op. cit.* (Ch. 13, Note 7), p. 509.

5. Alice Rossi, "Equality Between the Sexes: An Immodest Proposal," *op. cit.* (Ch. 6, Note 1), p. 139.

6. A. H. Maslow, "Love in Self-Actualizing People," in *Sexual Behavior and Personality Characteristics,* edited by Manfred De-Martino (New York: Citadel Press, 1963), p. 152.

7. Robert O. Blood, Jr., and Donald M. Wolfe, *op. cit.* (Ch. 14, Note 4, p. 45.

8. Lois Hoffman, "Effects of the Employment of Mothers on Parental Power Relations and the Division of Household Tasks," *Marriage and Family Living,* Feb., 1960. (Especially its Note 14.)

9A. Richard H. Rovere, "Letter From Washington," *The New Yorker,* Sept. 11, 1965. See also his "Letter From Washington" of June 18, 1966, for a further discussion of the Moynihan Report.

9B. D. B. Lynn and W. L. Sawrey, "The Effects of Father Absence on Norwegian Boys and Girls," *Journal of Abnormal and Social Psychology,* 59 (1959), pp. 258–262.

9C. Allan G. Barclay and D. R. Cusumano, "Testing Masculinity in Boys Without Fathers," *Trans-Action,* Dec., 1967.

10. Judson T. Landis, "A Re-examination of the Role of the Father as an Index of Family Integration," *Marriage and Family Living,* May, 1962.

11. Evelyn W. Goodenough, "Interest in Persons as an Aspect of Sex Difference in the Early Years," *Genetic Psychology Monographs,* 1957.

12. G. M. Carstairs, *This Island Now* (Harmondworth, England: Penguin Books, Hogarth Press, 1962), p. 46.

13. Morris Zelditch, Jr., *op. cit.* (Ch. 21, second reference in Note 16), p. 315.

14. J. Richard Udry, *op. cit.* (Ch. 21, Note 1), pp. 68–69.

15. Charles Bowerman and Chris Elder, Jr., *op. cit.* (Ch. 15, Note 16).

16. Paul Mussen and Luther Distler, "Masculinity, Identification and Father-Son Relationships," *Journal of Abnormal and Social Psychology,* 59 (1959).

17. "Homosexuality," Committee on Public Health of the New York Academy of Medicine, July, 1964, Bulletin.

18. Robert Odenwald, *op. cit.* (Ch. 22, Note 12), p. 151.

19. Leontine Young, *Out of Wedlock* (New York: McGraw-Hill Paperbacks, 1954), pp. 40–41.

20. Harriet Holter, *op. cit.* (Ch. 20, Note 3).

21. Margaret Mead, *op. cit.* (Ch. 2, Note 1), p. 280; and Edna Rostow, *op. cit.* (Ch. 6, Note 7), p. 231.

CHAPTER 24

1. A. H. Maslow, "A Theory of Human Motivation," *The Psychological Review,* Vol. 50, 1943.

2. Alan W. Watts, *op. cit.* (Ch. 4, Note 4), pp. 145–206.

3. Michael Schofield, *op. cit.* (Ch 1, Note 4), pp. 65 and 90.

4. French Institute of Public Opinion, *op. cit.* (Ch. 14, Note 3), p. 112.

5. M. B. Loeb, "Social Role and Sexual Identity in Adolescent Males," *Case Work Papers,* National Association of Social Workers, New York, 1959.

6. Alfred Kinsey, *et al., op. cit.* (Ch. 2, Note 11), p. 760.

7. John Money, *op. cit.* (Ch. 21, Note 23), p. 58.

8. Alfred Kinsey, *et al., op. cit.* (Ch. 2, Note 11), pp. 755–761.

9. *Ibid.,* pp. 586–593.

10. *Ibid.,* p. 627.

11. John H. Gagnon and William Simon, "Pornography—Raging Menace or Paper Tiger?", *Trans-Action*, July-Aug., 1967.

12. Alfred Kinsey, *et al.*, *op. cit.* (Ch. 2, Note 11), p. 688.

13. Simone de Beauvoir, *The Second Sex* (New York: Alfred Knopf, Inc., 1953), p. 396.

14. John Money, *op. cit.* (Ch. 21, Note 23), p. 20.

15. Winston Ehrmann, *op. cit.* (Ch. 2, Note 11), p. 367.

16. Frank Shuttleworth, "A Biosocial and Developmental Theory of Male and Female Sexuality," *Marriage and Family Living*, May, 1959.

17. Jessie Bernard, "The Fourth Revolution," *Journal of Social Issues*, Apr., 1966.

18. Winston Ehrmann, *op. cit.* (Ch. 2, Note 11), p. 337.

19. Margaret Mead, *op. cit.* (Ch. 2, Note 1), p. 95.

20. Laurence Wylie, "Youth in France and the United States," *Daedalus*, "Youth: Change and Challenge," Winter, 1961–62.

21. Leonard Gross, "Sex Education Comes of Age," *Look*, Mar. 8, 1966.

22. Wayne Anderson and Sander Latts, *op. cit.* (Ch. 14, Note 16).

23. William Simon and John H. Gagnon, "The Pedagogy of Sex," *Saturday Review*, Nov. 18, 1967.

24. Michael Schofield, *op. cit.* (Ch. 1, Note 4), p. 225.

25. William Simon and John H. Gagnon, *op. cit.* (Note 23, above).

CHAPTER 25

1. William Stephens, *The Family in Cross-Cultural Perspective* (New York: Holt, Rinehart and Winston, 1963), p. 246; and G. P. Murdock, *Social Structure* (New York: The Macmillan Co., 1949), p. 265.

2. Margaret Mead, *op. cit.* (Ch. 2, Note 1), p. 92, and Margaret Mead, *Coming of Age in Samoa* (New York: William Morrow & Co., 1928. 1961 Apollo Editions cited here), pp. 98 and 155.

3. Albert Ellis, *Sex Without Guilt* (New York: Grove Press, Inc., 1958, revised edition, 1965, cited here), pp. 27–41.

4. John Cuber, "Adultery: Reality versus Stereotype." Paper at 1966 Groves Conference on the Family, Kansas City, Mo.

5. William Stephens, *op. cit.* (Note 1, above), p. 256 and pp. 338–339.

6. J. D. Unwin, *Sex and Culture* (London: Oxford University Press, 1934), p. 374.

7. *Ibid.*, p. 411.

8. *Ibid.*, p. 412.

9. Arnold J. Toynbee, "Why I Dislike Western Civilization," *The New York Times Magazine*, May 10, 1964.

10. Alfred C. Kinsey, *et al.*, *op. cit.* (Ch. 2, Note 11), pp. 685 and 686.

11. Pitirim Sorokin, *The American Sex Revolution* (Boston: Porter Sargent Publishers, 1956), p. 57.

12. David and Vera Mace, *op. cit.* (Ch. 4, Note 3), p. 102.

13. David Mace, *op. cit.* (Ch. 9, Note 4).

14. John Cuber, *op. cit.* (Ch. 16, Note 5), p. 180.

15. Oscar Sternbach, "Growing Toward Independence—Part I." Speech on Mar. 6, 1961, to the Child Study Association of America.

16. Arthur Schlesinger, Jr., "An Informal History of Love, USA," *The Saturday Evening Post*, Dec. 31, 1966.

17. Jessie Bernard, *op. cit.* (Ch. 24, Note 17).

18. Henry Fairlie, *op. cit.* (Ch. 10, Note 10).

19. Report of views of Ralph R. Greenson, Clinical Professor of Psychiatry, University of California, Los Angeles, School of Medicine, in *Today's Health*, Apr., 1967.

20. Cynthia Seton, "Little Lost Girls," *Redbook*, May, 1965.

21. Eugene Kanin and David Howard, "Postmarital Consequences of Premarital Sex Adjustments," *American Sociological Review*, Oct., 1958.

22. William Reevy, "Premarital Petting Behavior and Marital Happiness Prediction," *Marriage and Family Living*, Nov., 1959.

CHAPTER 26

1. David Truman, "The Morality of Today's Undergraduates," *Columbia College Today*, Winter, 1963–64.

2. Eustace Chesser, *op. cit.* (Ch. 4, Note 11), p. 34.

3. Ira L. Reiss, *op. cit.* (Ch. 4, Note 5), p. 236.

4. Lester Kirkendall, *Premarital Intercourse and Interpersonal Relationships* (New York: The Julian Press, Inc., 1961), pp. 6 and 10; and Lester Kirkendall, "College Youth and Sexual Confusion," *The Journal*, The National Association of Women Deans and Counselors, Jan., 1963.

5. Letter by Paul H. Landis, *Marriage and Family Living*, Feb., 1962.

6. Thomas Poffenberger, "The Control of Adolescent Premarital Coitus: An Attempt at Clarification of the Problem," *op. cit.* (Ch. 4, Note 11), p. 69.

7. Richard Hey, "Critique of Value Approaches." Paper presented to a Seminar at the 1966 Groves Conference on Marriage and the Family in Kansas City, Mo., April 18–20, 1966.

8. Erik H. Erikson, *Childhood and Society* (originally published by W. W. Norton Co., Inc., in 1950. Page citation here from Penguin Books edition, 1965), p. 255.

9. Winston Ehrmann, *op. cit.* (Ch. 2, Note 11), p. 338.

12. John Rule, "Must the Colleges Police Sex?" *Atlantic Monthly*, Apr., 1964.

13. Committee on the College Student, *op. cit.* (Note 11, above), p. 98.

14. *Ibid.*, p. 100.

15. In Rita Hoffman's, "Swept With Confused Alarms: Psychological Climate on Campus," *Mademoiselle*, Aug., 1964.

16. Dana L. Farnsworth, "Sexual Morality and the Dilemma of Colleges," *American Journal of Orthopsychiatry*, July, 1965.

17. David Truman, *op. cit.* (Note 1, above).

18. *Towards A Quaker View of Sex*, edited by Alastair Heron (England: Henry Burt & Son, Ltd., 1963).

19. "Situation Ethics: Between Law and Love," *Time*, Jan. 21, 1966.

20. William H. Genné, "The Churches and Sexuality," *SIECUS Newsletter*, Fall, 1966.

CHAPTER 27

1. "Unstructured Relations," *Newsweek*, July 4, 1966.

2. Phyllis and Eberhard Kronhausen, *The Sexually Responsive Woman* (New York: Grove Press, 1964), p. 236.

3. Margaret Mead, "The Life Cycle and Its Variants: The Division of Roles," *Daedalus*, Summer, 1967.

4. Ernest Burgess, *op. cit.* (Ch. 2, Note 4), p. 244.

5. "Trial By Marriage," *Time*, Apr. 14, 1967.

6. For a report on 2 such studies see Morton M. Hunt, "Help Wanted: Divorce Counselor," *The New York Times Magazine*, Jan. 1, 1967.

7. "The Divorced Woman, American Style," *Newsweek*, Feb. 13, 1967.

8. Alexander Eliot, "Let's Abolish Alimony," *The Saturday Evening Post*, Aug. 22, 1964.

CHAPTER 28

1. A. J. Prince and A. R. Baggaley, "Personality Variables and the Ideal Mate," *Family Life Coordinator*, July–Oct., 1963.

2. John Blazer, "Complementary Needs and Marital Happiness," *Marriage and Family Living,* Feb., 1963.

3. Marvin B. Sussman, "Parental Participation in Mate Selection," *Social Forces,* Vol. 32, 1954.

4. Eloise Snyder, "Attitudes: A Study of Homogamy and Marital Selectivity," *Journal of Marriage and the Family,* Aug., 1964.

5. Robert Coombs, "Value Consensus and Partner Satisfaction Among Dating Couples," *Journal of Marriage and the Family,* May, 1966.

6. Jan Trost, "Mate Selection, Marital Adjustment, and Symbolic Environment," *Acta Sociologica,* Vol. 8, 1964.

7. Robert F. Winch, *Mate Selection* (New York: Harper & Bros., 1958), and his article, "Another Look at the Theory of Complementary Needs in Mate Selection," *Journal of Marriage and the Family,* Nov., 1967.

8. Ernest Burgess, *op. cit.* (Ch. 2, Note 4), p. 100.

9. Peter Giovacchini, in *The Psychotherapies of Marital Disharmony,* edited by Bernard Greene (New York: The Free Press, 1965), p. 45.

10. See particularly James Schellenberg and Lawrence Bee, "A Re-examination of the Theory of Complementary Needs in Mate Selection," *Marriage and Family Living,* Aug., 1960; and John Blazer, *op. cit.* (Note 2, above); and Bernard I. Murstein's "Empirical Tests of Role, Complementary Needs, and Homogamy Theories of Marital Choice," *Journal of Marriage and the Family,* Nov., 1967.

11. J. Richard Udry, *op. cit.* (Ch. 21, Note 15).

12. Alan C. Kerckhoff and Keith E. Davis, "Value Consensus and Need Complementarity in Mate Selection," *American Sociological Review,* June, 1962.

13. Gunnar Boalt. For an English-language elaboration of his theory see *op. cit.* (Ch. 19, Note 8), Chapter 4.

14. D. D. Jackson, "Family Rules," *Archives of General Psychiatry,* #12, June, 1965.

15. Bernard I. Murstein, Progress Report, "Psychological Determinants of Marital Choice," June 1–Aug. 26, 1965 (mimeographed).

16. Emily Mudd, *et al., op. cit.* (Ch. 8, Note 1).

17. Gordon Shipman, "Speech Thresholds and Voice Tolerance in Marital Interaction," *Marriage and Family Living,* Aug., 1960.

18. Talcott Parsons and Robert Bales, *op. cit.* (Ch. 21, Note 16), pp. 123, 150, and 162–63.

19. A. H. Maslow, *op. cit.* (Ch. 23, Note 6), p. 153.

20. Emily Mudd, *et al., op cit.* (Ch. 8, Note 1), p. 38.

21. Helmut Thielicke, "Realization of the Sex Nature," *The Christian Century,* Jan. 15, 1964.

22. Robert O. Blood, Jr., and Donald M. Wolfe, *op. cit.* (Ch. 14, Note 4), p. 70.

23. Murray A. Straus, "Conjugal Power Structure and Adolescent Personality," *Marriage and Family Living,* Feb., 1962.

INDEX

INDEX

A

Abortions, 18, 247, 296, 424, 430-31
  estimated number of (1966), 453
Abrams, Charles, 185
Abu-lughod, Janet, 494
Adler, Alfred, 317
Advertising Age (magazine), 243
Ahlborg, Gunilla, 7
Ahlmark-Michanek, Kristina, 289
Aiken, Henry David, 27
Alcoholism, 59
Alfie (motion picture), 49
Alimony payments, 429-30
Allen, Gerald, 7
Allen, Lucile, 500
Amalgamated Clothing Workers Union, 102
American Academy of Political and Social Science, 123, 385
American Association for the Advancement of Science, 140
American Association of Marriage Counselors, 128
American Association of School Administrators, 322
American Federation of Labor-Congress of Industrial Organizations (AFL-CIO), 102

American Journal of Orthopsychiatry, The, 115
American Journal of Psychoanalysis, The, 117
American Medical Association, 12, 454
American Orthopsychiatric Association, 392
American Psychiatric Association, 30
American Psychological Association, 70
American Sociological Association, 131
American Sociological Review, 225, 438
Ames, Louise Bates, 6, 312, 316, 339, 501
Amherst College, 198
Amin, Lucy, 494
Anderson, Wayne, 496
Androgen hormones, 365
Apartment complexes, 188
Aristotle, 16
Arizona State College, 41, 104
Association of Existential Psychology and Psychiatry, 66, 250
Auken, Kirsten, 7, 290, 454, 460, 491, 499
Author's Guild, The, 100
Automobiles, 34, 64
  technological innovation produced by, 21
Avery, Emily, 264, 498
Avery, Paul, 264, 498